This is dedicated to the memory of our friend and colleague,

Liz Laycock (1939-2009)

Writing Under Control

Now in its third edition and reflecting changes in the Primary National Strategy, this best-selling textbook introduces primary teachers to key issues in the teaching of writing. Strongly rooted in classroom practice, the book includes:

- the history, theory and practice of teaching writing;
- children writing in and out of school;
- EAL and gender issues in writing;
- the development of writing across the years of the primary school;
- planning classroom routines and organising resources;
- balancing the composition and transcription elements in writing;
- monitoring and assessing writing;
- meeting individual needs;
- managing specific learning difficulties in writing, such as dyslexia.

With its companion, *Reading Under Control* (also in its third edition), this book provides undergraduate and postgraduate teachers with comprehensive guidance for the teaching of literacy.

Judith Graham recently retired as Principal Lecturer in Education at Roehampton University.

Alison Kelly is Subject Leader for English Education (primary) at Roehampton University, teaching on undergraduate and postgraduate courses.

Related titles

**READING UNDER CONTROL
(THIRD EDITION)**

Judith Graham and Alison Kelly
978-1-84312-461-0

**LANGUAGE KNOWLEDGE FOR PRIMARY TEACHERS
(THIRD EDITION)**

Angela Wilson
978-1-84312-207-4

THE PRIMARY ENGLISH ENCYCLOPAEDIA
THE HEART OF THE CURRICULUM **(THIRD EDITION)**

Margaret Mallet
978-0-415-45103-1

Writing Under Control

Third Edition

Edited by
Judith Graham and Alison Kelly

Routledge
Taylor & Francis Group

LONDON AND NEW YORK

First published 1998 by David Fulton Publishers
Second edition published 2003

This edition published 2010 by Routledge
2 Park Square, Milton Park, Abingdon, Oxon OX14 4RN

Simultaneously published in the USA and Canada by Routledge
711 Third Avenue, New York, NY 10017

Routledge is an imprint of the Taylor & Francis Group, an informa business

Typeset in ITC Garamond by FiSH Books, Enfield
Printed and bound in Great Britain by TJ International Ltd, Padstow, Cornwall

British Library Cataloguing-in-Publication Data
A catalogue record for this book is available from the British Library.

Library of Congress Cataloging-in-Publication Data
Writing Under Control / edited by Judith Graham and Alison Kelly. – 3rd edn.
  p. cm.
  1. English language–Composition and exercises–Study and teaching (Elementary)–
Great Britain. I. Graham, Judith, 1941– II. Kelly, Alison.
  LB1576.W77 2009
  372.62'3044–dc22

                          2009000387

ISBN 10: 0-415-48404-9 (pbk)
ISBN 10: 0-415-48405-7 (hbk)
ISBN 13: 978-0-415-48404-6 (pbk)
ISBN 13: 978-0-415-48405-3 (hbk)

Contents

Contributors   viii
Acknowledgements   x
Introduction   xi

1 From Copying to Creation: the teaching of writing before the 1980s   1
    Pat Pinsent

Teaching writing before 1960   1
Creative writing   2
Language and learning   3
Beginning writing   4
Children's writing development   6

2 Process, Genre, Strategy, Framework: three decades of development in the teaching of writing   7
    Rebecca Bunting

Understanding the process of writing   7
Understanding young children's writing   10
Understanding cultural and linguistic differences   11
Understanding the nature of written language   12
Text types and genres   14
Government intervention   16
Controversy in the teaching of writing   17
The role of the teacher   18

3 'This Is Different Writing': the world outside the classroom in children's texts   19
    Kimberly Safford

What is writing?   19
Writing in and out of school   20
Gendered play and practice at writing   22
The writing 'problem'   23
No single approach   28

Multimodal/digital contexts, audiences, purposes 29
Multilingual writers 36
Creating and shaping texts: thinking made visible 39

4 The Writing Journey 42
   Fiona Collins and Anne Washtell

Introduction 42
The Tea Party Lists (two girls 3 and 5 years) 44
Orville (Reception) 47
An Early Story (Reception) 49
Unaided Writing in Chinese Characters (Year 1) 50
When I was Naughty (Year 1) 52
I Love Papaya (Year 2) 54
Dear Mrs Wild (Year 4) 56
Quidditch (Year 4) 57
Escape from Ethiopia (Year 5) 59
The Monk and the Fish (Year 5) 61
The Writing Future 63

5 Routines and Resources 67
   Anne Washtell

Introduction 67
Planning for writing routines 68
Talk for writing 70
Shared writing 71
Guided writing 75
Independent writing 77
Unaided writing 78
Collaborative writing 85
Drafting 86
Writing workshops 90
Writing partnerships 90
Dictated writing 91
Copying and tracing 93
Writing on the screen 94
Bookmaking 96
Partnership with parents 97

6 Composition 100
   Fiona M. Collins

Composition and range 100
Narrative writing 106
Poetry writing 115
Non-fiction writing 120
Writing in role: narrative and non-fiction 126

7   **Transcription: spelling, punctuation and handwriting**   **131**
     Alison Kelly

     Introduction   131
     Spelling   131
     Punctuation   157
     Handwriting   170

8   **Monitoring and Assessing Writing**   **179**
     Liz Laycock

     Introduction   179
     Assessment for learning   179
     Target setting   193
     Assessment of learning   194
     Managing records of assessment   198
     Concluding points   200

9   **Meeting Individual Needs**   **201**
     Judith Graham

     Children who write willingly enough but with many errors   201
     Children who tend to write about the same topic again and again   204
     Children who write at length but with no commitment   205
     Children who claim that they hate writing and do the bare minimum or nothing at all   206
     Gifted and talented writers   208
     Children learning to write in English as an additional language   209
     Boys and girls   214
     Children whose work shows grammatical errors   218
     Formal arrangements for struggling writers   219
     A quick checklist if a child seems to be struggling   222
     Assessment   222
     Meeting individual needs in and out of the classroom   223
     Parental involvement   225

10   **Specific Learning Difficulties in Writing**   **228**
     Cathy Svensson

     A specific learning difficulty   228
     Defining dyslexia   228
     The inclusion context   229
     Assessing the written evidence   230
     A case study of Con   230
     Meet Sebastian in Year 6   237

References   **242**
Author index   **252**
Subject index   **255**

Contributors

Rebecca Bunting is Deputy Vice-Chancellor at the University of Portsmouth. She is a Director of the Board of the Society for Research in Higher Education and of the Higher Education Academy.

Fiona M. Collins is Principal Lecturer at Roehampton University and convenes the MA in English Education. She teaches on a range of modules linked to primary English teaching and children's literature at both undergraduate and postgraduate level. She has been involved in a variety of research projects linked to children, literature and reading. In recent years she has co-edited two books on children's literature, *Historical Fiction: Capturing the Past* and *Turning the Page: Children's Literature in Performance and the Media*.

Judith Graham taught in London schools, at the Institute of Education, at the University of Greenwich, at Roehampton University and at the University of Cambridge, where, in retirement, she still makes a small contribution. Her publications include *Pictures on the Page*, *Cracking Good Books* and *Cracking Good Picture Books* (all NATE). For David Fulton, she has edited and contributed to *Reading Under Control* and *Historical Fiction for Children*. She has also written several publications on authors and their books for Scholastic and PCET, and has written chapters – mainly on literacy, children's books and illustration – for many other edited books and journals.

Alison Kelly is Subject Leader for English Education (primary) at Roehampton University. She worked for many years as a primary school teacher in London. At Roehampton, she teaches on undergraduate and postgraduate courses and her current research interests include poetry. She is co-editor of *Reading Under Control* (David Fulton), has written several books of teaching materials for Scholastic and acts as an educational consultant for Usborne Publishing.

Liz Laycock is now retired after several decades' involvement in primary education – as a classroom teacher and an advisory teacher – in higher education and in ITE. She was Programme Convener for the Primary PGCE and Director of Programmes in the Faculty of Education at Roehampton University. She is a contributor to *Reading Under Control, The Literate Classroom, Historical Fiction for Children, Literacy Through*

Creativity and *Education in the United Kingdom* (all David Fulton). She has written several books for teachers on aspects of literacy teaching for Scholastic.

Pat Pinsent has worked at Roehampton University for many years, previously as Principal Lecturer in the English Department and currently as Senior Research Fellow in the National Centre for Research in Children's literature. She has been responsible for the production of distance learning materials for the MA in Children's Literature and has a tutorial responsibility for a number of PhD and MA students. Her 15 published books include *The Power of the Page: Children's Books and their Readers* (1993), *Children's Literature and the Politics of Equality* (1997) and a collection of studies of neglected twentieth-century children's authors (2006), together with many edited compilations of the proceedings of the annual conference of the International Board on Books for Young People (IBBY). She has had numerous articles published on both children's literature and her other main research interest, seventeenth-century poetry. Her main current preoccupations are the diverse ways in which children's literature is currently developing, and the relationship between it and spirituality/religion. She edits *The Journal of Children's Literature Studies*, together with *IBBYLink*, the journal of the British Section of IBBY, and *Network*, a journal for all women interested in spirituality, theology, ministry and liturgy.

Kimberly Safford is a lecturer at the Open University Faculty of Education and Language Studies, Department of Education. Previously, she was Senior Lecturer in Primary English Initial Teacher Education at Roehampton University. She was the research officer for CLPE (Centre for Literacy in Primary Education) where she published widely on school-based creative partnerships and how teacher–artist collaboration influences teacher practice and children's learning. She has worked with the Wandsworth Ethnic Minority Achievement Service and was a primary teacher in Wandsworth and Lambeth. She continues to work with the National Association for Language Development in the Curriculum (NALDIC) to promote inclusive and effective pedagogies for pupils learning English as an Additional Language. In an earlier career, Kimberly worked for 20 years as a radio and television journalist in San Francisco, New York and London.

Cathy Svensson is the Programme Convenor for Special and Inclusive Education in the School of Education, Roehampton University. She teaches on the undergraduate and postgraduate Special and Inclusive Education Programme in Roehampton, and both internationally and nationally. Cathy's research interests span communication related difficulties to include, particularly, specific learning difficulties and autistic spectrum disorders (ASD).

Anne Washtell is Senior Lecturer in English Education at Roehampton University. She was a primary school teacher in London and also worked as an advisory teacher for English. She now teaches on undergraduate and postgraduate courses as well as working with graduate trainees. She is particularly interested in the role of children's names in early literacy and student teachers' experiences of teaching synthetic phonics. She is a contributor to *Reading Under Control* (David Fulton) and has written teaching materials for Scholastic.

Acknowledgements

The contributors have been able to include accounts of teachers and children at work thanks to examples supplied by their students, their colleagues and classroom teachers with whom they have worked. In addition to those who contributed to the first and second editions of this book, for this, the third edition, the contributors would like to thank Kerenza Ghosh and Steph Laird for their careful reading and advice; Hilary Bower and Tanya Ying for their school's example of record keeping; Xiaoyu Yang, Associate Professor at the School of Foreign Languages at Southwest University, Chongqing, People's Republic of China, for her advice and interpretation of the piece of Chinese writing discussed in Chapter 4; and Fengling Tang, Lecturer in Early Childhood Studies at Roehampton University, for hand writing the Chinese characters for us.

The image on page 35 is reproduced with permission from Edmund Waller Primary School, Lewisham.

We would like to thank all those who have given us permission to use their work in this book.

We apologise for not attributing the dictation passage which occurs on page xi, we have been unable to locate its source.

Finally, our continued thanks to Conrad Guettler and Mark Pawley for patient support and unflagging interest.

Introduction

A teacher dictates this passage to his class of 80 nine-year-olds:

> While hewing yews, Hugh lost his ewe
> And put it in the hue and cry.
> You brought the ewe back by and by
> And only begged the hewer's ewer,
> Your hands to wash in water pure.

The children write carefully in their copybooks using copperplate handwriting. Older children – monitors – walk up and down the rows to check that the children are working hard and sitting up straight.

This is what a writing lesson might have looked like one hundred years ago when learning to write consisted of imitating adult models – copying or tracing letters, memorising spellings and transcribing passages from the Bible, Latin grammar or, for light relief, Aesop's fables. Younger children would write on slates; their efforts were no sooner accomplished than they had to be rubbed out in readiness for the next exercise. The nearest the children got to their own compositions is described by Sybil Marshall:

> The teacher showed the children an object of some sort, and from the entire class, ranged in their rows of desks before her, she elicited 'facts' about the object which could then be written down, e.g. 'We have a plum. The plum is red. It has a stone. The plum grew on a tree.' The sentences, composed by the teacher from the children's hesitant observations, were then written by her on the blackboard, from where the children copied them in whatever form of script they had been taught to write.
>
> (1974: 2)

Now, take a leap forward one hundred years. A Reception class has been visited by a storyteller. One of her stories is a native American creation tale about how the sun came into existence. Later, Matthew (age 5) dictates a story of his own to his teacher which she writes down for him:

> Once upon a time there was no such thing as a dog. There were just dogfish alive, until one day a dogfish came out of the sea and it started to live on land. While he was living on land some very peculiar things happened. He started to change. Instead of scales, it was fur.

Instead of no neck, it had one. Instead of flippers, it had a tail. Instead of fins, it had legs. Until one day he was a dog! This way life on earth has developed ever since.

Despite the role reversal, both the Victorian teacher dictating and the contemporary teacher taking dictation could be described as being 'in control' of the teaching of writing. Both based their practice on prevailing views of the writing process, of the nature of learning and of the relationship between child and adult. The Victorian teacher would have believed that 'We must not expect young people to invent matter, what they write should be infused into them' (John Walker, 1801, in a book for teachers, cited in Michael, 1987: 313), and his concern would have been to give children adult models to imitate with an emphasis on correct spelling, handwriting and grammar. The contemporary teacher is just as concerned that her children use these aspects correctly, but knows, too, that composing is important, and is giving her young writer the opportunity to compose with greater fluency than he would achieve if left to transcribe by himself. Early behaviourist thinking lies behind the often punitive Victorian regimes, where wrong spellings or poor handwriting could lead to the ultimate negative reinforcer – the cane. The contemporary teacher's interaction with a younger child suggests a more collaborative enterprise, where her adult model of expertise is still privileged but where it is exercised in a way that empowers the younger writer. The point is that we know much more now about the writing process and about the learner, and we bring this to bear on our teaching. Chapters 1 and 2 of this book chart the developing understanding about writing which has moulded the ways we teach writing.

We write this at a time when multiple changes have occurred in the teaching of literacy in primary schools. In 1988, the *National Literacy Strategy* prescribed exactly what we should teach and when. However, the renewed *Primary Framework for Language and Mathematics* (DfES, 2006a) represented a significant loosening up of this tight external control. In *Reading Under Control* (2008) we said that 'control in any area springs from a secure understanding of processes and enabling practices'. It is this belief that motivates the structure and content of *Writing Under Control* and we suggest that such a feeling of control is more important than ever today. After the historic update provided by Chapters 1 and 2, we move firmly into the early twenty-first century classroom with a new chapter for this third edition. Drawing from a rich range of examples, Kimberly Safford looks at what writing means to primary pupils today. Her discussion includes analysis of multimodal texts, emailing and blogging. In another new chapter, Fiona Collins and Anne Washtell take us on a writing journey (Chapter 4). The chapter starts with examples of very young children in the earliest stages of developing their understanding of what it is to be a writer. The journey through primary school unfolds through their presentation of samples from children of all ages. An account of the many different writing routines that are needed for the effective teaching of writing is offered in Chapter 5. In this chapter, Anne Washtell links these routines with the *Primary National Strategy (PNS)* and includes discussion of the resources teachers need. She also makes important points about the role of parents in children's writing lives. The next two chapters tackle the two distinct aspects of the writing process: composition and transcription. In Chapter 6, Fiona Collins looks at the demands of narrative, non-narrative and poetry writing and describes ways of supporting and scaffolding children's understanding of the complexities of composition.

In Chapter 7, Alison Kelly looks in detail at the three separate aspects of transcription: spelling, punctuation and handwriting. The impact of the *Rose Review's* recommendations about early reading is considered in relation to the teaching of spelling. Liz Laycock's chapter shows how crucial close observation, analysis and assessment are in shaping teaching, monitoring progress and setting targets. She adds an informative section on National Curriculum assessments and looks at recent developments in the assessment of writing, particularly in relation to marking and pupil self-evaluation. In Chapter 9, Judith Graham draws the threads of the book together through her analysis of the differences between the writing of children with literacy difficulties, gifted writers, boys and girls, and children with English as an additional language. The book concludes with Cathy Svensson's case studies of children with the specific learning difficulty dyslexia. The detail she offers illuminates areas including what is meant by an inclusive classroom and an Individual Education Plan.

This book offers another framework, then; one which is clearly linked with the *National Curriculum* and the *PNS*, but which is intended to offer you, the teacher or prospective teacher, a sense of control in all aspects of the teaching of writing. This sense of control is one which is achieved through clear understanding of all of the above; it is about knowing where we have come from in the teaching of writing and of how current views have shaped and changed practice. It should also arm you in readiness for any new initiatives that may be on their way!

There is another kind of knowledge that is important, too; personal control also comes about when we feel confident about the subject we are teaching. An important strand of this book deals with the subject knowledge teachers need, at their own level, to inform their planning and assessment. A confident grasp of the following will empower your teaching:

- the nature and role of standard English: Chapters 2, 8, 9;
- knowledge about word recognition: Chapters 7, 8, 9,10;
- knowledge about grammar: Chapters 2, 6, 7, 8, 9;
- knowledge about text types Chapters 2, 6, 8.

Chapter 7 also contains glossaries which will help you with technical terms.

Recent developments focus teachers' attention on individual components of the teaching of writing and there is a risk that more global considerations about writing become obscured. In our work with student teachers we often gather writing histories in which our students attribute their writing confidence and competence as writers to such experiences as: a teacher becoming excited or informed by a piece of their writing; a teacher setting up a dialogue in writing with them, enabling the work to be extended over a long period ('interactive writing'); the incentive of a diary or attractive notebook for private writing; the realisation that writing can, on some occasions, meet a creative need such as might equally be met by making a painting or a piece of music; the excitement of seeing ideas come forth as you write; the understanding that writing can, at difficult times, serve as a solace and an outlet for strong feelings; the satisfaction of seeing a piece through to a perfect end-product, and the reward of having others respond to and appreciate our work. These personal revelations about the role and power of writing are very relevant to your appreciation of the writing process and should frame and inform the reading of this book.

For children to be in control of writing a confident grasp of all aspects of the writing process is needed and this is why we are so insistent that an important strand of teaching writing is developing a healthy curiosity about language. Such curiosity should be fostered both with regard to the shapes and features of texts (narrative, non-narrative etc., Chapter 6), and with regard to the transcriptional aspect of writing (spelling, punctuation and handwriting, Chapter 7). We want children to delight in the curiosities and challenges of our spelling and punctuation systems rather than be fearful of or inhibited by them. A prevailing theme of the book is ensuring that our teaching leaves children free to attend to particular aspects of the writing, whether this is developing the structure of a story, character delineation, sentence construction or appropriate punctuation.

As in *Reading Under Control*, our preoccupation is with good teaching and with doing the very best possible work with children. Learning to write is an extraordinary feat and, as children become writers, we get glimpses of them at their most active, creative and imaginative. Children can surprise and delight us, as they learn that writing enables them to 'create worlds' (Smith, 1984: 152). *The Dogfish* story (p.xi) contains many different influences, ranging from the traditional story Matthew had heard in school to the final line, which he told his teacher he had heard on a video soundtrack. Yet its freshness both startles and engages the reader. When children discover that they can create such 'secondary worlds', then it is their turn to feel in control and empowered.

Chapter 1

From Copying to Creation: the teaching of writing before the 1980s

Pat Pinsent

TEACHING WRITING BEFORE 1960

Let us look at the experience of an imaginary English teacher – Mary Angell – who was born in the 1930s. Her early schooling, broken up by the Second World War, included such things as making many copies of 'headlines' in a copperplate hand. The intention of this (which seldom succeeded) was to inculcate handwriting skills, but the process also provided unwanted and decontextualised information, such as 'Linseed oil is derived from flax'. The whole process certainly conveyed the lesson that copying from adult models was the way to learn. This was supported by copying passages from books chosen by the teacher and reproducing from memory stories read to the class. Twenty years earlier there had been isolated, more imaginative initiatives such as that quoted by Shayer of a teacher who said, 'The best way, indeed the only way, to learn to write is to try to write' (1972: 81) He went on to provide interesting assignments like describing a sea-monster, but if Mary's teachers had heard about these they gave no indication of this in their lessons.

At grammar school, Mary's English education was extended by grammatical exercises and the requirement to write compositions about abstract topics such as 'Patriotism' or letters to non-existent recipients about holidays which did not take place. Comprehension, précis and accurate renditions of literary texts selected for examination rounded off the English curriculum. Mary therefore internalised the message that correct set pieces were what mattered.

When she went to college, in September 1953, to be trained as a teacher on a two-year course, Mary received conflicting messages. It was difficult to reconcile the narrow approach of 'Methods' (practical teaching approaches) courses with the kind of 'child-centred' approach which was beginning to appear in Educational Studies (educational theory). One of her assessed essays had been based on a quotation from Robert Browning:

> ...To know
> rather consists in opening out a way
> whence the imprisoned splendour may escape,
> than in effecting entry for a light
> supposed to be without...
>
> (*Paracelsus* 1835: I)

You may recognise this as a poetic 'empty vessels' type of argument!

Mary started work in a secondary modern school with many naive hopes about her career but little firm grasp of how to teach her subject, as what she had learnt at college tended to replicate the way she had been taught herself. The kind of English teaching expected from her gave little credence to her pupils' bringing with them to school any kind of inner light, or even any kind of knowledge about life or the writing process. The sole audience for writing in school was the teacher, and so little were the results valued that exercise books, once full, landed in the wastepaper basket. Mary felt that if she had been teaching younger children, there might have been more opportunity to liberate her pupils' 'imprisoned splendour'. In fact, there were very similar pressures in primary school (with the 11-plus examination) and no greater understanding of children's development as writers.

CREATIVE WRITING

In 1963, Mary, now Mrs Bright, returned to teaching after six years of bringing up her own children. She found herself readily welcomed, despite her secondary background, in the local primary school. Confessing herself out of touch, even in her own subject, she was heartened to read Sybil Marshall's *Experiment in Education* (1963), which had just been published. Marshall describes teaching in a village school during and after the Second World War. She discovered, while teaching in a cross-curricular way which combined music, art and writing, that the quality of the children's work in all these areas was greatly improved. Mary recognised how the ideals of educational theory which she had found exciting in her Educational Studies initial training, and which had been fortified by her experience with her own young children, could be brought to life in the classroom.

At this period, 'creative writing', under various names, was in full swing in primary schools. Over the next few years Mary read and implemented with enthusiasm the recommendations of Margaret Langdon (1961), Boris Ford (1963), Sheila Lane and Marion Kemp (1967) and many others. The title of Alec Clegg's book, *The Excitement of Writing* (1964), conveyed the enthusiasm these writers brought to their subject, and, as in the other books, it also included a collection of children's own work, showing the immense potential of child writers. David Holbrook's *English for the Rejected* (1964) gave an account of amazing results achieved with young people who had been written off by society. All the books abounded in ideas of how to foster similar qualities in other young writers. Basil Maybury's *Creative Writing for Juniors* (1967) advocated working through sense stimuli of touch, sight and taste to encourage writing. He suggested using, for instance, music as a stimulus, blowing bubbles or, more daringly, setting fire to paper.

Behind much of this creative writing was more general theory. Sybil Marshall, who later became Reader in Education at Sussex University, acknowledges in *Creative Writing* being influenced by Suzanne Langer, on whose work Marshall's definition of creative writing is based. She says creativity is 'the ability to create one's own symbols of experience: creative writing is the use of written language to conceptualise, explore and record experience in such a way as to create a unique symbolisation of it' (1974: 10).

Mary sometimes found it difficult to avoid the creative writing lesson falling into a limited pattern like, 'Listen to this music...what does it make you feel...now write a story . . . '. Nor did she feel comfortable criticising writing which clearly came out of the children's feelings. Sometimes the results were not very interesting and she wondered if she really was using the best way of drawing out the children's own experience, let alone building on it. It was difficult for someone not trained in psychoanalysis to be alert to the 'symbolic meaning', to how 'children's creative work symbolises...the quest for integration of the identity...' (Holbrook, 1967). She knew, too, that she should not neglect the tools of the trade like spelling and handwriting and had to admit that her pupils' strengths in writing stories and poems might not always help them much in the more subject-based curriculum of the secondary school, nor, indeed, with the practical written demands of life.

LANGUAGE AND LEARNING

It was partly because of feelings of inadequacy in this area, and partly to increase her professional standing, that Mary took advantage of the Open University's scheme to award credit rating for previous study, thus facilitating non-graduate teachers obtaining a degree. Teachers were particularly encouraged to select courses relevant to their professional interests, so Mary chose 'Language and Learning'. The course reader was entitled *Language in Education* (Cashdan and Grugeon, 1972) and among the papers included in it were several particularly relevant to the teaching of English. Mary read with interest James Britton's 'What's the use? A schematic account of language functions'. This article had a practical aim in mind, the classifying of 2000 pieces of writing from pupils aged 11 to 18, and it also was convincingly grounded in the earlier theoretical studies of Harding (1937), Langer (1951) and Moffett (1968). Although Britton's classroom-based research was initially concerned with secondary school pupils, it was not long before its results filtered into primary schools by way of the *Bullock Report, A Language for Life* (DES, 1975).

The *Bullock Report*, which appeared in the concluding year of Mary's degree studies, became sacred scripture to Mary and her colleagues. The language functions identified by Britton and his team in 1972 were described thus in Bullock:

> The three main categories . . . are Transactional, Expressive and Poetic. The Expressive is the central one. It is language 'close to the speaker', often the language used by intimates in a shared context . . . it provides the tentative stage through which a pupil's new thinking must pass on its way to the comparative certainty of knowledge.
>
> (p. 165)

The Transactional mode is defined as using language with the intention of getting things done, as in advertisements or regulations, while the Poetic mode, not confined to poetry only, stands back from the subject described. Elsewhere in the *Bullock Report*, attention is given to the kind of audience for which children are writing (themselves, the teacher or the wider world). The recommendation is also made that pupils should have the opportunity to draft their work before submitting the finished article.

Mary began to incorporate a variety of different forms of writing that were not simply based on the expressive and sometimes poetic functions which she had, up to now, generally been demanding from her pupils. Rules about how to behave in school, advertisements for imaginary or even real products and accounts of events the children had experienced all began to vie with story as outcomes of the English lesson. Her other lessons changed, too. Instead of insisting that her top primary pupils write up scientific work in dictated formulae, she let them use an expressive mode to note what they had actually observed. She created opportunities for her children to write for real audiences. Like other teachers throughout the country, she encouraged her pupils to write to children in other schools, to local newspapers, to suppliers of educational material, as well as recognising the fact that they might well write for themselves alone, in personal journals which she promised she would not even attempt to look at unless invited.

Mary soon discovered that Britton's work was probably the best known out of a body of writing emanating from a number of educationalists influential in both initial and in-service teacher education. An account of the genesis of this movement was to be found in John Dixon's *Growth through English*, first published in 1967 and reprinted many times. Based on a conference held for teachers of English in America and the UK at Dartmouth, New England, in 1966, it presents the various paradigms of English teaching, the 'skills' model and the 'cultural heritage' model, before expressing its own endorsement of the 'personal growth' model, in which writing should express something that the writer feels is worth saying:

> Language is learnt in operation, not by dummy runs. In English, pupils meet to share their encounters with life … in ordering and composing situations that in some way symbolise life as we know it, we bring order and composure to our inner selves.

(p. 13)

Mary and her colleagues were aware that some theorists such as Frank Whitehead (1978) did not welcome the approach of Britton and others to writing, but had she been asked her opinion she would have argued that the different functions had been very useful in extending the kinds of writing of her pupils, and their consciousness that they were writing for someone.

BEGINNING WRITING

Soon after completing her Open University degree in 1975, Mary found herself for the first time teaching a Reception class. At the same time, her taste for study had led her to start work on a master's degree, so it seemed a natural development to look into the writing of these very young children. As someone initially trained for secondary teaching, she had always dreaded having, as she saw it, to impart so much basic knowledge to children who had not even made a start on literacy, so it came as something of a surprise to learn from the researchers, and from her own observations, that children, in fact, brought much more knowledge about writing into school than she had ever given them credit for. Margaret Clark's influential study of 32 children who were literate before going to school, *Young Fluent Readers* (1976), while focused predominantly on reading abilities, showed that many of these children were interested in writing even before they were four.

Mary was particularly fascinated by Marie Clay's *What Did I Write?: Beginning Writing Behaviour* (1975), which charts the way in which children's earliest marks can be seen as representing discoveries of 'real' writing. These discoveries are only possible when the child sees people writing. Clay says:

The linear scribble that fills the lines of a writing pad has, for the child, all the mystery of an unfamiliar code. It stands for a myriad of [*sic*] possible things but does not convey a particular message. The child seems to say 'I hope I've said something important. You must be able to understand what I've said. What did I write?'

(p. 48)

Interpreting the 'linear scribble' of the five-year-olds in her class was both challenging and satisfying, but she wished she had known more about children's abilities when her own children had been young.

Mary also began to value the children's inventive attempts at spelling, and she learnt that as early as 1971, the research of Charles Read had explained how children use their awareness of the sounds of letters to enable them to write words without being explicitly taught by a teacher or parent. Carol Chomsky's 'Write now, read later' (1971), with its message that children could learn to read by creating their own spellings, was also congenial, particularly because it chimed with her own discovery that young children could be helped towards reading by means of their own writing. An approach that recognised this was the 'Language Experience' approach, which was published as *Breakthrough to Literacy* (McKay *et al.*, 1970). This material comprised plastic 'Sentence Makers' and little word cards which children could use to make their own line of writing, based on their own experience and what they said about it. Then they could transcribe it on to paper and draw a picture to go with it. She had seen it in use in other primary classrooms, but had some reservations about the repetitious sentence structures that emerged and the need to put all the little pieces back in the right places in their individual folders.

Mary's research and work with Reception class children had shown her that teaching writing and reading did not mean introducing them to something totally unfamiliar, but was a matter of helping them to build on what they already knew. She wanted her own small-scale research project to examine the nature of children's prior knowledge, so the kind of longitudinal study that Glenda Bissex had made of her own son in *GNYS AT WRK: a child learns to write and read* (1980), attracted her as a dissertation topic. The most important thing she had learned was never to underestimate young children.

Another revelation was the work of the Russian cognitive psychologist Vygotsky, whose writings had been translated and published from 1962 onwards. On the subject of writing, Vygotsky was both provoking and illuminating. His account of the difficulties which young children face in learning to write made the process of teaching them seem almost impossible. The high level of abstraction required in order to 'replace words by images of words', to address 'an absent or imaginary person' without any real motivation, and to be aware of the necessary alphabetical symbols to put all this down on paper (1962: 98–9), sounded as if it was well beyond her pupils, and certainly gave her an understanding of why some of them found learning to write problematic. Yet elsewhere Vygotsky's explanation of the 'zone of proximal development' gave her more encouragement as it showed how children might, in fact, learn this difficult process. He says, 'What a child can do with assistance today she will be able to do by herself tomorrow' (1978: 87). Mary realised that she had often found herself assisting pupils with the beginnings of writing and noticed that they were on the verge of achieving independence but needed just that little extra guidance towards it. The 'zone of proximal development defines those functions that have not yet matured but are in the process of maturation' (1978: 86).

CHILDREN'S WRITING DEVELOPMENT

Having worked with the youngest and the oldest pupils in the primary school, Mary Bright was naturally interested in the ways in which children's writing developed, and what might be expected from them at different ages. She found the Crediton research project (1980), directed by Andrew Wilkinson, gave her some information. The team had investigated the writing abilities of children aged 7, 10 and 13, using a framework for analysis based on stages of cognitive, affective, moral and stylistic development abstracted from the theoretical work of Moffett (1968) and Britton (1982). While the categories Wilkinson provides were far too complex for daily use in the classroom, Mary found that looking at a few pieces of children's writing in detail was quite illuminating. She felt that any research which makes the teacher more aware of some of the factors entering into child writers' perceptions about what they are doing, what they want to do and who they are writing for, provides a useful tool for the teacher. Wilkinson and his colleagues remark that the work of Britton has the limitation of perhaps over-stressing the cognitive aspect and ignoring the many others which enter into the child's writing development. Wilkinson also reminds us that, 'We need to make assessments of children's development in order to help them develop further. In other words, assessment is to be regarded rather as a teaching than as a measuring device' (pp. 223–4).

As Mary handed in her dissertation in 1980, she pondered many things. How she taught English now was a world away from the copying and conformity to adult models that had been part of her childhood. She knew much more of approaches which put the child at the heart of the process; she knew the pros and cons of creative writing; she found understanding of functions, forms and audiences enriched the range and quality of writing in her classroom; she looked at her very youngest children's writing with new eyes and understood her supportive role more clearly; she knew how valuable it was to analyse closely individual pupils' writing.

She reflected, too, that she had learnt most about the teaching of writing by engaging in her own writing. Many theorists she had read seemed to pay relatively little attention to the writing process as experienced by adults. Perhaps that was something for the future.

Further reading

Allen, D. (1980) *English Teaching since 1965: How Much Growth?* London: Heinemann.
Marshall, S. (1963) An Experiment in Education. Cambridge: Cambridge University Press.

Chapter 2

Process, Genre, Strategy, Framework: three decades of development in the teaching of writing

Rebecca Bunting

This chapter discusses approaches to the teaching of writing in primary schools from the early 1980s to the first decade of the twenty-first century. It provides an overview of significant development and is necessarily selective and general, since a detailed historical survey of the period, with an account of why certain approaches and trends prevailed, would be the subject of an entire book.

The last thirty or so years have seen radical changes in the pedagogy of writing and in resources for writing. In addition, rapid advances in technology have offered opportunities and challenges to the development of children's writing. Communication is changing, as social networking and the transitory nature of written communication become accepted norms, immensely influencing young people's lives. The impact of information technology on children's literacy is profound and is discussed in Chapter 3.

There has been a growing understanding about writing on the part of teachers and researchers, particularly in relation to the nature of the process of writing and the nature of writing itself. The period under review has also been the subject of controversy both about methodologies for teaching writing and about the very purposes of writing in school. Formerly, it was teachers who exercised their professional judgement in the teaching of writing; now, writing is a focus of public debate, driven by economic and social concerns and regulated by public policy.

UNDERSTANDING THE PROCESS OF WRITING

Process writing

Copying and behaviourist approaches to writing have been replaced in recent times by an emphasis on the process of the writing rather than the end-product. In a process approach, or process writing, as it is has also been described, teachers recognise that much more attention should be paid to the development of a piece of writing, as writing is more than the simple eliciting of a product by the teacher; it is a process that involves thinking and shaping meaning. There are various stages to be gone through in the production of the final piece of writing and young writers need support with these stages. A process approach views children as authors and treats their written work as creative and, most importantly, meaningful. Children's difficulties are treated as normal writers' difficulties, rather than failures of ability: so, for example, errors and misunderstandings need to be worked on, as a professional writer would, rather than punished by the teacher's correcting pen. A process approach encourages children to take more responsibility for their own writing, including decisions about revisions, corrections and presentation. Graves (1981) uses a property image in arguing for this approach: he says that 'owners' of their work are far more likely to take care of their 'property' than those who 'rent' their work from the teacher, to whom it really belongs. This image conveys the importance of children's interest and engagement with the writing process.

Very important in a process approach is the distinction between the composition involved in writing and the transcriptional aspects of writing such as spelling, punctuation and handwriting. Smith (1982) relates the composition aspect to the role of the author, and the transcription aspect to that of the secretary, a useful distinction for the developing writer. Fluent writers can attend to both these aspects concurrently, though with different degrees of attention, whereas young writers, Smith argues, need to attend to composition first and transcription later. Both are necessary and important but teachers should not try to develop the transcriptional skills at the expense of encouraging thinking and composing skills. This philosophy is in complete contrast to an approach which requires children to labour at spelling and punctuation exercises before being allowed to do some independent writing.

A process approach often involves children reflecting on their own writing. This reflection could be on the content of the written product, such as why certain decisions were made about what to include in the writing, or on the actual process of writing, such as how an effort was consciously made to vary sentence length. Such reflection develops children's metacognitive awareness, that is their conscious understanding of their learning and their metalinguistic awareness, in that their understanding of language is foregrounded. The reflection is often achieved through the use of writing journals or writing partners, where children conduct dialogues with the teacher or their partner about their writing (see Chapter 5).

A process approach also involves strategic and supportive intervention by the teacher during the process of the writing, rather than the teacher sitting in judgement when it is all finished. Smith (1982), rather ghoulishly but appositely, describes the traditional marking of an end-product as 'manicuring the corpse', trying to do something to improve the situation, make it look better, when it is too late. In this traditional model, children see writing as largely for assessment by the teacher, and they have only one attempt at the writing before handing it in, in what Richmond (1990) described as 'a fairground shooting game where you only have one shot'. These lessons about writing remain with us even much later in our lives, as Smith comments: 'Sitting on the shoulder of many writers is the wraith of a school teacher, waiting to jump on every fault of punctuation or spelling, on every infelicity of expression' (Smith 1982: 13).

One book, in particular, caught teachers' imaginations about the possibility of opening up the classroom as an environment to support writing development through a process approach. In *Writing: Teachers and Children at Work* (1983), Donald Graves advocates a workshop approach which focuses on the needs of the writer and uses the 'real' writer as a model. Graves carried out a longitudinal study of children learning to write in New Hampshire, USA, and his findings led him to advocate a model of writing which incorporates pre-writing activities (such as brainstorming ideas), drafting, editing, proofreading and publishing. In this model, children are permitted to choose their own topics for writing, helped to revise their work for publication and, most importantly, encouraged to reflect on their own development as writers, sharing and collaborating on their work with their peers and their teacher (Graves calls this 'conferencing').

Graves also argues that teachers should themselves write with and for their children because teachers cannot teach writing without understanding the processes the young writer is going through and without being able to demonstrate aspects of writing to the learner: 'We don't find many teachers of oil painting, piano, ceramics or drama who are not practitioners in their field' (1983: 6). Richard Andrews (2008), in his research report, *The Case for a National Writing Project,* indicates that projects which boost teachers' professional development and their personal creative talents make a big difference to their pupils' writing progress.

Graves' influential model for teaching writing clearly complements Smith's promotion of the distinctions between composition and transcription in teaching writing. Together they set an agenda which began to shape the teaching of writing in the 1980s and 1990s in the USA and beyond, with its emphasis on the writer's needs and the facilitating role of the teacher.

As the process approach gained momentum, so the centrality of the key concepts of audience and purpose for children's writing emerged. These concepts were not new; even in 1975, the *Bullock Report* (see Chapter 1) was arguing that children should be writing for audiences other than the teacher, because 'if a child knows that what he is writing is going to interest and entertain others, he will be more careful with its presentation' (DES, 1975: 166). However, it was *accuracy* that was the spur behind the Bullock advocacy of audience; more recently, a sense of audience is seen as central to the *development* of writing because it gives children experience of writing different kinds of texts for a variety of readers and of handling the complex relationship in their writing between writer and reader. This means that a writer has to make decisions about, for example, levels of formality and has to consider how explicit to be in the writing in relation to what the audience already knows. These are key skills in becoming a writer but it is only relatively recently that they have been considered seriously in the classroom.

Writers need a sense of audience because the intended audience influences the tone, nature and form of the writing. Writers also need to understand the purpose of their writing and that writing differs according to both audience and purpose. Without this understanding, children are writing in an abyss, with no sense of why they are writing, what their intentions are in writing, and for whom they are writing. This point is persuasively argued by Vygotsky who is critical of a Montessori nursery where the children's writing diet consisted of perfectly copied messages and greetings. Writing was taught as 'a motor skill and not as a complex cultural activity' (1978: 117). It follows, then, that children need experience of writing for a range of audiences and a range of purposes and that opportunities for these must be made in the classroom. When the purpose for writing extends beyond practising skills, the writing curriculum becomes reinvigorated and refocused.

Writers have to compose and order their thoughts, and many teachers have become more aware of the cognitive processes involved in writing: writing engages thinking and deepens reflective thought. For example, Scardamalia and Bereiter's research into composing processes (1985) addresses the question of how writing enhances knowledge and brings about different kinds of thinking. They argue that writing involves the creation of a synthesis between what the writer wants to say on the one hand, and textual constraints on the other. They explore the inevitable but valuable tension involved in simultaneously handling the content, the audience and the type of writing.

UNDERSTANDING YOUNG CHILDREN'S WRITING

A process approach is not restricted to relatively competent young writers. Children in the very early stages of learning to write can benefit from an approach which recognises that they have intentions as writers, that they are active in the process they are learning and that, through writing, they are learning about the world and how to represent it in written language. The practice of tracing, then copying the teacher's writing and then constructing simple sentences from key words became less acceptable as teachers became more aware of 'emergent literacy', the term coined by Teale and Sulzby (after Marie Clay, see Chapter 1). Teale and Sulzby (1986) argue that 'emergent' is a significant term because 'it connotes development rather than stasis' and that, as researchers have looked increasingly closely at literacy learning in very young children, they have come to the conclusion that 'it is not reasonable to point to a time in a child's life when literacy begins. Rather, at whatever point we look, we see children in the process of becoming literate, as the term implies' (Teale and Sulzby 1986: xxv).

Emergent writing (also known as 'developmental' writing, see Chapter 5) is an aspect of emergent literacy. An emergent writing approach recognises that children know a good deal about writing from a very early age. As we saw in Chapter 1, the marks children make represent meaning, and 'scribbles' are more often patiently and painstakingly constructed communications, as children learn both that language is a symbolic system for expressing meaning and that it has rules of usage. Perhaps the key point about emergent writing is that the writing is 'for real', not a rehearsal for proper writing later. Children are active 'meaning makers' (Wells 1987), a view of the learner that is very different from that of the passive child copying letters. In Chapter 4, 'The Writing Journey' you will find rich examples of such emergent writing.

An emergent writing approach encourages creativity and invention. It frees children from the fear and constraint of making mistakes and encourages them to experiment and to feel successful in what they have produced. The teacher can then respond to and monitor development as the children begin to learn about the writing system. For example, teachers can see that children's invented spellings are logical and can recognise the strategies the children use as they move through the developmental stages of spelling, from a stage where there is an imperfect match between sound and written symbol, to more or less fully accurate spelling. In an emergent writing approach, children are encouraged to hypothesise about spelling rather than relying on spellings supplied by the teacher. In working out how to represent sounds for themselves, phonemic awareness is developed, a key skill in learning to read (see Adams 1990 and Chapter 7 in this book). Teachers can also see how children handle the grammatical aspects of writing and can monitor children's development and support them in moving on to the next stage. Children are learning transcription skills through composition rather than focusing on the skills first.

An emergent writing approach accepts that writing does not start and end at the classroom door. As Kimberly Safford explains in the next chapter, teachers today are more aware than ever of the importance of children's cultural backgrounds and experiences and of the need to build on these educationally. In terms of writing, it means that teachers recognise that children already exhibit literate behaviours, that they are aware of some of the functions of writing and that they come from families and communities where writing is thought of and used in particular ways.

UNDERSTANDING CULTURAL AND LINGUISTIC DIFFERENCES

In school, particular kinds of writing are taught. Outside school, different social and cultural groups will have different attitudes to, and different ways of using, writing, some of which will accord with schooled practices and some of which may be in conflict with them. For example, Street (1995) describes Philadelphian adolescents with empty exercise books in school but notebooks and scrapbooks full of things like raps and messages out of school. These young people have resisted the kinds of writing the school values and have forged their own uses for writing and forms of writing outside school. This is a good example of Graves' idea of 'ownership' of writing with a more political edge.

Literacy is often viewed as a neutral technology, a set of skills you just learn to use, but many researchers and teachers argue that it is far from neutral, that literacy involves specific ways of representing knowledge and developing understanding. Some suggest that schooled literacy is too narrow in its conceptualisation of writing and that it inducts children into too limited a range of writing competences. Street, for example, draws a distinction between an autonomous model of literacy, defined as a single, dominant kind of literacy, and an ideological model, one which recognises a multiplicity of literacy practices specific to particular cultural contexts. A number of longitudinal ethnographic studies have examined the interface of these different literacy practices: for example, Heath (1983), in her study of three communities in the United States, examines the nature of these differing literacy events across the communities, demonstrating that the children in each community are inducted into very different literacy practices and learn differently about what writing is for and how it is used. More recently, and in an English context, Barton and Hamilton (1998) have studied the literacy practices of people in Lancaster, England, and there have been a number of studies of the literacy practices of children and families in minority ethnic communities which draw similar inferences. Hannon and Bird (2004) present an up-to-date picture of theory, policy and planning in the area of family literacy.

So for teachers to 'build' on children's backgrounds means more than asking them about their lives outside school: it means recognising that their literacy knowledge comes both from the school context and the home culture and that their experiences of writing will not be uniform. The teacher therefore needs to value and nurture the types of writing done at home, at the same time as introducing children to the kinds of writing done in school.

A recognition of home literacy practices is particularly important for children for whom English is an additional language (EAL). For these children, in the past, special provision separated them from contexts in which they could read, write and speak

English naturally. They were taught discrete skills before engaging with real writing. They were treated as though they were starting from scratch in their literacy development, yet many of the children were literate in a language other than English and such practices served only to hold back their development.

Teachers have become more aware that the needs of bilingual writers are very similar to those of first language writers. In addition, recent developments in understanding of EAL indicate the vital importance socially and cognitively of supporting the first language at the same time as enhancing the additional language, in reading, writing, speaking and listening. For example, Baker (1996: 136, 142) analyses research into bilingualism and thinking and concludes that 'the judgement of the clear majority of researchers tends to be that there are positive links between bilingualism and cognitive functioning' and that bilingual children may have an increased communicative sensitivity and increased metalinguistic awareness, an understanding of, and sensitivity to, language. You will find more detailed discussion of this in Chapter 3.

UNDERSTANDING THE NATURE OF WRITTEN LANGUAGE

Alongside developments in understanding the process of writing, there have been significant developments in teachers' and researchers' understanding of writing as a system, of the linguistic characteristics of written language. There are two main ways in which teachers' greater linguistic understanding of language is influencing practice in the teaching of writing.

Spoken and written language

The first area of increasing knowledge about the nature of writing is its relation to other modes of language, particularly to spoken language. Teachers need to understand something of the relation of spoken and written modes of language because, in learning to write, children have to learn to operate in a secondary discourse (speech is the first discourse they learn) and to put their language into written form.

Further, children have to move through a significant psychological stage of development in which they realise that written language represents speech which, in its turn, represents what they see, experience, feel, etc. Young children learn about representation or symbolism – making something stand for something else – initially through their play: 'a piece of wood begins to be a doll and a stick becomes a horse' (Vygotsky, 1978: 97).

Their early drawing efforts reveal their developing understanding of the ways that they can represent on paper the things they see in the world. This is what Vygotsky calls 'first order symbolism'. Writing involves a move to 'second order symbolism' because it is about understanding that the written word 'horse' stands for the spoken word, which stands for the horse itself; it is 'the creation of written signs for the spoken symbols of words' (1978: 115). The teacher's role is to help children through this transition. If teachers can understand how children are learning to operate in the secondary discourse of writing they may be better able to understand what the children are trying to convey and to discuss and explain differences in spoken and written language with them.

Speech and writing clearly differ in their processes: speech is more context dependent; usually takes place face to face, so is more interactive; can use all the resources of body language, intonation and volume; and is characterised by false starts, repetitions and hesitations. Written language must convey its meanings without face-to-face contact; must be more explicit; is usually non-interactive, more planned and less spontaneous; and relies on punctuation and other written features such as capitalisation or fonts to make its effects. Writers have to predict responses or misunderstandings and must be much more aware of the needs of the reader.

There is, however, a danger in thinking that speech and writing are totally different systems. Sometimes speech can be like writing, as in a formal lecture or public speech. Similarly, some writing is very like speech, such as personal correspondence or messages on notepads or emails. The important point here is that children need to understand that the purpose of the writing, and its intended audience, will determine the level of formality of the writing and that this in turn will determine the form of the writing.

There is a good deal of evidence to indicate that speech and writing also have different grammatical and syntactical organisation. Information units are bundled, or 'chunked', differently in speech and writing. In speech, the main linguistic unit is the clause. In writing, clauses are connected and related to each other into sentences, then sentences are linked into paragraphs, and so on. Basically, sentences are made from clauses and the task facing the writer is how to connect the ideas in the clauses. Writing, therefore, requires decisions about what the main ideas are, what is subsidiary, in which order to place things and which information is secondary to the main information units of the sentence. It also requires the handling of grammatical features common in writing but not in speech, such as certain subordinate clauses.

In relation to continuous prose, a reader can revisit what has been read to check any misunderstanding or to follow a line of thought, so the structure can be relatively complex. In speech, the communication is more linear and transient and a listener cannot keep checking what has been said, unless through repeated interruptions. So learning to write involves both developing control over the sentence and learning to be more explicit, and linguistic research can provide useful insights into these aspects of writing development. For example, Kress (1982) charts the development of control of the sentence in children's writing and argues that apparent irregularities or mistakes can be viewed differently by teachers once they understand how the child is moving from a spoken to a written mode of thought. Perera's research (1989) into whether children write as they speak, as is often suggested, found that this was not actually the case. Children increasingly edit out typical speech forms from their writing as they become more familiar with written language, demonstrating the importance of reading to writing development.

For many children, learning to write means adding standard written English to their repertoire. Writing is almost always conducted in standard English, though the style, register and genre will differ, whereas spoken language could be in the standard or another dialect. Teachers need to understand that as well as moving from spoken to written mode, children may be having to adapt to and use standard written English forms and that such forms may be quite different from those with which children are familiar.

The books children read provide models for writing, not just at the level of the content, or the genre, but also at the syntactic level, where children absorb linguistic structures. This is one of the reasons why it is important for children to hear written language read aloud, which is more challenging than they could read alone. The written language which children hear, then, provides a resource for their own grammatical and syntactical composing.

TEXT TYPES AND GENRES

The second area of linguistic knowledge which is having an impact on practice is that of a genre-based approach to teaching writing. This involves identifying the language features and structures characteristic of certain common written genres and teaching children explicitly about them.

Essentially, different types of writing have recognisable patterns of structural organisation and linguistic features. Genres are socially recognised text types (though precise definitions vary somewhat) and the argument is that in teaching writing, generic forms should be explicitly taught. Research in the 1970s carried out by Halliday on behalf of the Schools' Council, and continued in the 1980s and 1990s in Australia by Martin *et al.* (1987), among others, looked at the teaching of English in the context of developments in linguistics. In its later stages, and in relation to writing development, their research involved the extensive collection and analysis of writing done in school. They identified a small range of genres as predominant, yet found that little attention was given to the structure and linguistic content of these genres in the teaching context. In other words, the range of writing experiences the children were having was limited, and little attempt was made to explain to children how certain kinds of texts are structured and what their characteristics are. In a British context, similar concerns have been raised about the kinds of writing done in school. In the more distant past, the *Plowden Report* (DES, 1967) was very critical of the amount of story writing to the exclusion of other types of writing done in primary schools and similar concerns were raised in two further HMI reports (DES, 1978 and 1982), which found in the primary schools inspected a good deal of copying, much use of exercises in textbooks and, in terms of the range of types of writing carried out in school, a predominance of personal expressive writing and story writing. Later, in 1993, Ofsted found little had changed: inspection evidence indicated 'excessive copying and a lack of demand for sustained, independent and extended writing' (Ofsted, 1993: 8).

Linguistic research into the teaching of writing identified a number of principal genres, but in practice, many children were experiencing only a small number of these text types. The main genres are described as: recount (chronologically ordered retelling of events: 'last week I went to my nan's'); report (classificatory descriptions of processes and things: 'whales are mammals'); procedure (explanations about how something is done: 'the first player throws the dice'); explanations (of how something works or why something occurs: 'the sea causes the pebbles to move up the beach'); discussion (argument from a range of perspectives with conclusion: 'should fox-hunting be banned?'); persuasion (persuasive writing promoting one point of view: 'I think fox-hunting should be banned'); and narrative ('there was once a village where nobody grew old'). In early writing, other common genres are identified, such as labelling ('this is my teddy') and labelling/observation ('this is my teddy and I love him').

Whether this is a sufficiently inclusive list is an interesting question, but it does reflect the *National Curriculum (NC)* requirement for range in writing. The main question and contentious issue in genre-based approaches is to what extent the teaching should be explicit about specific linguistic features of texts and what the pedagogical implications are of direct teaching about linguistic forms. Most teachers feel reasonably comfortable talking about the audience for a piece of writing and how this will shape the language used, such as formal or informal, or the general form of the writing. However, beyond this, at the more detailed linguistic level, such as the type of verb used in a particular genre, or the implied question-and-answer structure of newspaper journalism, many teachers feel less secure and sometimes quite out of their depth. Lewis and Wray report from their research into teachers' practices in teaching writing that, when asked about writing:

> most teachers tended to concentrate their replies on the writing of narrative texts and that there was a general lack of knowledge of the range of texts, and at the least, a lack of a shared vocabulary with which to discuss text types. (The research) supports the hypothesis of Ofsted that teachers need to improve their own knowledge about the 'structures, functions and variations' of language.
>
> (1995: 11)

We might expect teachers to be more confident in the area of narrative, a common enough feature of primary writing, but even the writing of narrative receives little support in terms of the explicit teaching of generic features. In fact, the term 'story' is often used to refer to both narratives and recounts and for some children writing a story means writing a recount, rather than an actual narrative, with stages such as orientation and complication (see Chapter 6). Recounts are by far the most common genre in primary schools, which raises questions about whether children are experiencing the necessary range, particularly in relation to the requirements of the *NC*. Research into genre theory suggests that the narrow range of writing done in school should be extended to prepare children to write more socially relevant genres, so that writing is more meaningful in the 'real' world, though they also recognise that certain kinds of writing are expected in the curriculum and the formal examination system and must be taught. Teachers should be trying to achieve a better balance of genres but this is also problematic: for example, Barrs (1994) argues that the main problem with what the theory advocates is that it does not relate well to what we know of children's development as writers. Most writing by children, she says, mixes genres and does not reflect the kinds of genres identified by linguists. Such genres should not be deemed 'failed adult genres' but developmental genres in their own right. To expect children to write specific structures, and to expect teachers to adopt codified rules for writing, stifles writing development and is inappropriate in the primary classroom.

Genre theory purports to be a social theory of writing development because it identifies and teaches kinds of writing which are more significant in the world than the narrow diet of writing many children experience in school. What children learn to write, as well as how they learn, becomes an issue of entitlement and empowerment. How teachers move forward on this will depend on their view of the purposes of writing and their understanding of the linguistic issues involved.

GOVERNMENT INTERVENTION

The National Literacy Strategy

The *National Literacy Strategy (NLS)* (DfEE, 1998) arose from a concern about the variability of standards of achievement in literacy across schools nationally. The government felt that literacy was too significant an aspect of children's development and entitlement to be left to chance and that intervention was necessary to establish a model to control and shape how literacy should be taught in primary, and subsequently secondary, schools.

The introduction of the *NLS* marked a very significant change in the relationship between teachers and the government, in that for the first time, both the content of the curriculum and the methodology were prescribed. Its *Framework for Teaching* prescribed a syllabus for reading and writing for short- and long-term planning, and specified the orientation of a daily Literacy Hour of explicit literacy teaching, which required 'systematic, regular and frequent teaching of discrete aspects of language such as phonological awareness, phonics, spelling, grammar and punctuation'. Its linguistic premise was that language can be studied at three levels: word level, sentence level and text level. Learning objectives were organised in a managed framework which reflects this distinction.

In its more liberal interpretations, the *NLS* recognised that reading and writing are in a symbiotic relationship, rather than discrete processes, and encouraged a holistic approach to reading and writing development. This is well demonstrated in Barrs and Cork's (2001) study of the link between children's writing development in Key Stage 2 and the study of literature. They found that children in their study were able to find a voice in their writing and use new and challenging linguistic registers through deep engagement with literary texts, a powerful encounter of developing writer with professional writer. The *NLS* offered opportunities for such purposeful attention to written language and structured opportunities for its development, but there remained a view that it provided too few opportunities for sustained writing in schools and for writing across the curriculum and that it led to a reduction in the time available for the essential wider aspects of English teaching.

The Primary National Strategy (PNS)

However, in 2006, the publication of a renewed framework – the *Primary Framework for Literacy and Mathematics* (DfES, 2006a) – signalled a significant shift from the prescriptivism of the *NLS*. Moving away from the rigidity of the Literacy Hour and its allocated slots for text, sentence and word level, the *PNS* organises literacy outcomes (fewer than in the *NLS*) into 12 strands, including speaking and listening. With early years expectations integrated and those for Year 7 included, a much more flexible route through the objectives is possible. With a wealth of online resources, there are planning units of work based on text types that span several weeks. And yet, in one important respect, the prescriptivism not only remains but is also even more insistent. The *PNS* arrived on the back of the *Rose Review* (DfES, 2006e) of early reading. The findings of the review included a new 'simple' model of reading and recommended that all pupils be taught synthetic phonics. Importantly, it emphasised the need for a 'language-rich' curriculum and the centrality of speaking and listening (see Chapter 5). Clearly these recommendations held the most important implications for the teaching of reading but the emphasis on the reversible processes of blending (needed for decoding in reading) and segmenting (needed for encoding in writing) has had some impact on the teaching of spelling (see Chapter 7). Its insistence on a language-rich curriculum 'that generates purposeful discussion, interest, application, enjoyment (DfES, 2006e: 16) has clear implications for setting up classrooms as rich writing environments (see Chapter 5).

The Early Years Foundation Stage

In order to ensure continuity and progression, two government documents (*Curriculum Guidance for the Foundation Stage* (DfEE, 2000) and *Birth to Three Matters* (DfES, 2002) have been merged into the *Early Years Foundation Stage (EYFS)* (DCSF, 2008a) This covers care as well as learning and development for children from birth to age 5. Included in this document are Early Learning Goals for 'Communication, language and literacy'. (See Chapter 5 for more detail about this document.)

CONTROVERSY IN THE TEACHING OF WRITING

The *NLS* and *PNS* are only the latest manifestations of controversy in the teaching of literacy. Literacy has for a long time been a controversial aspect of education, because people have differing views about what counts as being literate. Lay and professional views often come into conflict and writing is regularly in the firing line because it is more tangible than reading: employers, for example, actually see and can comment on the writing of their employees, but reading ability is much less obvious and weaknesses less visible. Comments about standards of literacy focus almost exclusively on transcriptional aspects of writing and on the grammatical aspects of composition (and on narrow aspects of each), and public judgements of these are reported widely in the media. Most recently, in 2008, such is the concern about the outcomes of national testing of writing that the government plans to introduce a support scheme to help children in Key Stage 2 to reach expected levels: the cycle of crisis and intervention continues.

The question of whether standards are declining is a complex matter, not readily reducible to newspaper headlines. What is often lost in the debate is how children really engage with ideas and find their own voice in their writing. As Brian Cox, chair of the group which proposed the curriculum and assessment for the National Curriculum, remarks, 'the best writing is vigorous, committed, honest and interesting. We did not include these qualities in our statements of attainment because they cannot be mapped onto levels' (1991: 147). Grainger *et al.* (2005), in *Creativity and Writing: Developing Voice and Verve in the Classroom*, capture well Cox's point in the very title of their study: 'verve' is a wonderfully apt term for the commitment and vigour intrinsic to the best writing, but at risk, they argue, from the reductive accountability culture endemic in education.

In terms of pedagogy, writing is controversial because of debates about what children need to know about language: the question is whether they need to know about the forms of the English language in order to be able to write, or whether knowledge about forms emerges through writing; whether there should be separate, decontextualised language teaching characterised by drills and exercises or a more holistic and process approach to language development where children's knowledge about language is contextualised in their own reading and writing and they learn about the forms of the English language in meaningful contexts. Further controversy has arisen in relation to the question of how soon children should be introduced to structure and form in their writing. The *EYFS* has created debate about the appropriateness of explicit language teaching for very young children and whether literal interpretations of its requirements by teachers will mean that children will experience instrumental approaches to reading and writing, at great cost to their enjoyment and engagement with a wide variety of texts. Unpublished recent research from the Institute of Education, University of London (Curtis, 2008) indicated that the efforts to teach three-year-olds to write simple sentences with basic punctuation does not improve their success when they start school. Encouraging them to talk and communicate does.

THE ROLE OF THE TEACHER

This chapter has considered change in the teaching of writing. Some of this has arisen from research and publications which have influenced practice. Some has been regulated by government. All of the developments described bring to the fore the role of the teacher and questions about the most effective kinds of interventions teachers can make. 'Benign inertia', to use Michael Halliday's coinage, is no longer considered an acceptable practice. What is needed is informed facilitation involving judicious intervention to guide and model, a clear pedagogy which recognises and draws on the linguistic, literary, cultural and psychological processes involved in becoming a writer. All this should be taking place in a rich textual environment, which for the contemporary classroom includes the kinds of technological resources which Graves could only dream of. Writing remains under scrutiny and, more than ever, teachers need to feel that they have writing 'under control' and are secure in what they do to develop children as writers, so that the best of the past can combine with the new initiatives of today.

Further reading

DCSF (2008) *Getting Going: generating, shaping and developing ideas in writing.* London: DCSF.

Fitzsimmons, P., Harris, P., McKenzie, B., Turbill, J. (2003) *Writing in the Primary School Years.* London: Thornton Learning Nelson.

Chapter 3

'This Is Different Writing': the world outside the classroom in children's texts

Kimberly Safford

In this chapter you are invited to reflect on issues in literacy learning which intrigue, delight, puzzle and also sometimes frustrate us: How far should I encourage children to write about what really interests them? Why do boys tend to be reluctant writers? What are effective ways to use email or texting as a writing activity? Is it beneficial for a child who is learning English as an Additional Language to write in her first or home language in school? Whilst this chapter may sometimes raise more questions than it provides answers, we hope it helps you to develop confidence in responding to such situations as you encounter them in practice.

WHAT IS WRITING?

What constitutes 'writing' nowadays? More than ever before, it encompasses diverse methods to convey a range of messages. Electronic media have created new audiences and purposes for writing, as emailing, texting and online social networks and forums flourish alongside traditional channels of written communication. Today, the creation of a piece of writing can involve images and sounds which carry as much meaning as words, making messages distinctive and powerful.

The many modes in which children now read, online and visually, will make an impact on their knowledge and understanding of writing. Just as reading is more than decoding marks on a page, writing is much more than making marks. Strand 9 of the *Primary National Strategy (PNS)* (DfES, 2006a) acknowledges this when it refers to children 'creating and shaping texts' rather than 'writing'. Furthermore, we acknowledge the influences of family, language, community, culture and gender as well as digital worlds and multimedia on how children learn to read and the ways in which they read. Therefore, as teachers of literacy, we should be able to extend this same understanding to children's development as writers.

We often hear about the value and importance of children 'reading for pleasure' (Ofsted, 2004; Cremin *et al.*, 2008), but the same promotion of pleasure in writing has not always been made explicit in schools. In their survey of primary pupils (Grainger *et al.*, 2003), children were asked, 'What comes into your head when your teacher says, "Now we're going to do some writing"?' Reception pupils responded enthusiastically and considered themselves to be good writers; but by Year 6 many children responded with dread or boredom, and described themselves as poor writers. This study concluded that the reason for such a marked change in disposition was the result of decreasing autonomy and interaction: children in the Early Years Foundation Stage (EYFS) and Key Stage 1 (KS1) classrooms had frequent opportunities to play, talk, socialise, draw and decorate as they wrote, often in imaginary contexts such as role play and linked to familiar, pleasurable reading such as traditional tales; but children in Key Stage 2 (KS2) had few choices over content or genre as they were required to develop and sustain lengthy writing, independently and in silence, geared towards timed, end-of-key-stage National Currriculum Assessments.

You might reflect on the extent to which such findings are still relevant today, as many schools have developed a more creative approach to the teaching of writing where children draw upon their reading, carry out drafting, write collaboratively and use drama, discussion, art and ICT in the writing process. The *PNS* and the *National Curriculum (NC)* offer scope for teachers to decide on the most effective ways to enable children to meet the learning objectives for creating and shaping texts. Therefore, as you take account of overarching curriculum and literacy frameworks, you can also call upon the writing interests, knowledge and skills which each child brings to your classroom.

WRITING IN AND OUT OF SCHOOL

Writing is a normal, daily activity (Fitzsimmons *et al.,* 2003). We write in all kinds of places and at different times. Think about the writing you do over a week. You might create a table:

What I wrote	Where	When	For whom	Why

Now consider what a week of writing looks like for a child in a primary school classroom. Are there similar contexts, audiences and purposes? (see Chapter 6). You might discuss these questions:

- What counts as writing in school?
- What counts as writing outside school?
- Are there any overlaps?
- Are there similarities and differences in the forms of the writing?
- Are there similarities and differences in the content of the writing?
- How would these similarities and differences influence your planning for writing in the classroom?

As you thought about these points, you might have made comparisons to children's reading habits in and out of school. Whilst there has been a wealth of recent research into children's preferences as readers (e.g. Clark *et al.,* 2005 and 2008; Maynard *et al.,* 2007), there is correspondingly little on children's independent choices and actions as writers. Enquiries into home and family patterns of literacy have examined reading far more than writing. DeBaryshe *et al.* remarked on this gap in their observations of five- and six-year-old children writing letters with their mothers, a study which revealed how parents use a range of scaffolding techniques in composition and transcription:

...the nature of parent–child writing interactions has been largely ignored. This is unfortunate, as adult–child interaction during the joint performance of cognitive tasks is a crucial pathway for learning and socialisation...[Our] study shows parents to be skilled and sensitive writing tutors. Considerable attention has been paid to ways in which parents support literacy skills through joint book-reading interactions. Equal time should be devoted to studying joint writing activities.

(1996: 10)

If you were to take a survey of a primary school class today, what kinds of writing at home do you think children might describe? In 2008, Roehampton University trainee teachers, as part of an assignment on the teaching of writing, talked with children in their School Experience classrooms and asked, 'Who writes at home?' and 'Do you write at home?'

Year 1 girl: No, only in birthday cards, letters to Grandma. Sometimes Mummy asks me to help her write the shopping list...I see my Dad writing on the computer for work and sometimes my sisters write to their friends and Mum writes on the fridge.

Year 3 boy: Not really, I only write when I write stories for my parents. I make them mini storybooks for them to read...Mum writes the shopping list every week. Dad writes on his computer in his office. I see him writing letters too. My younger sister likes writing the alphabet on the fridge with the magnets.

Year 2 boy: I like writing in my comic book at home.

Year 2 girl: My Dad does writing for bills, but his handwriting is not very good...he doesn't even join the letters up!

Year 5 girl: My sister likes to write limericks, oh yeah, and my older sister, the one who is seventeen, is writing her CV and my other sister used to write when she was doing her law degree.

Year 6 girl: I write stories...I write in my diary...Dad writes text messages...Mum does office work and brings it home to finish.

It was fascinating to learn that children were often writing independently and with enjoyment at home, and that they observed adults and older siblings writing for a range of real-life purposes. It was also revealing to hear how children, responding to the question, 'Do you write at home?', would promptly answer, 'No' – but then go on to list several different types of writing (birthday cards, letters, lists, stories and writing within their reading such as comics), indicating that they did not classify these home texts as meriting the status of school writing.

As a teacher, you can begin to discover what children enjoy writing about out of school by inviting children to share their home texts in the classroom. A Year 2 teacher did this, and was surprised at the children's enthusiastic response:

The children brought in so much writing from home that I put up a bulletin board solely for this work. The home writing included stories, lists, drawings, diagrams, cartoons, letters and notes.

(Orange, 2005: 34)

Once this invitation was well-established, the Year 2 children also brought writing they had started at home to finish in class, and their teacher organised regular times for children to show their home writing or read it aloud. Through these sustained classroom routines, children were able to see writing as a pleasurable activity to share between home and school.

As you read on in this chapter, about gender differences around writing and digital/multimodal and multilingual texts, you can continue to consider issues raised briefly here, about how home and out-of-school experiences influence children's knowledge and understanding about writing.

GENDERED PLAY AND PRACTICE AT WRITING

> I was visiting a secondary school and I noticed two Year 11 girls were exchanging envelopes. I asked them what these were for, and they replied, 'They're letters.' 'What, to each other?' I asked. 'But you see each other every day and you sit right next to each other.' 'But still,' the girls said, 'we like to write to each other.'
>
> (Roehampton English Education tutor)

You may have observed that girls at very early ages will often play at writing and at being writers. In the classroom, or in your home or family experiences, you may see girls choosing to write letters, cards for birthdays and other occasions, notes, menus, invitations, postcards, lists, catalogues, poems, plays, stories, magazines, books complete with covers and blurbs – writing which is often detailed and decorated. Much of this play writing is communicative and social in nature, and also involves taking on roles: author, publisher, teacher, parent, world traveller, playwright, doctor, veterinarian, shopkeeper, designer, reporter, poet, chef or agony aunt. Girls are also known for keeping private writing journals and diaries which may involve working things out, friendship networks and space to develop fantasy narratives and roles.

> When I write I can be open … I can say anything: there are no good words or bad words. Writing can also cause trouble – like diary writing … I once wrote something nasty about my friend, she read it and now she doesn't talk to me.
>
> (Year 5 girl, in an interview with a Roehampton trainee teacher, 2008)

All of this play and practice at writing prepares girls for writing in school and and – in general, compared with boys – enables them to become confident writers in a range of genres, as Millard has observed:

> At Key Stage 2 many more girls than boys claimed to enjoy writing in school and chose to write for themselves at home. Half the boys questioned disliked most school writing…Girls were confident in a wider variety of genres, listing diaries, letters and poems as well as stories as things they liked doing at home. In contrast, boys mentioned drawing and work on computers more frequently than they mentioned story writing. They also preferred different subjects opting for action while more girls used detailed descriptions of person and place.
>
> (2001:1)

As a teacher, you value the wide range of writing abilities and interests which many girls demonstrate. Why might boys be less enthusiastic?

THE WRITING 'PROBLEM'

Research on improving boys' writing has grown over time into a huge educational territory, offering a multitude of strategies (Frater, 2000; Daley, 2002; Ofsted, 2003; Safford *et al.*, 2004). This focus has been driven by concerns over many years about boys' writing attainment which has lagged up to 15 percentage points behind that of girls in KS2 writing tests (DCSF, 2007a).

This gap has been persistent, and there is no single reason for it. Boys' fine motor skills are slower to develop, making writing more physically demanding than it may be for girls; family and societal patterns of literacy may present writing as a female activity (in spite of the presence of male role models in fiction, non-fiction and journalism); the writing curriculum may be too sedentary for active children; topics for writing may be uninspiring (see, for example, Barrs and Pidgeon, 2002).

In the classroom you may notice some boys who write as little as possible; this can be a strategy to limit producing errors and dealing with inevitable teacher feedback on spelling, handwriting and punctuation. You should be aware that these children are particularly at risk, as they are able to write but are not getting the practice needed to develop stamina and make progress as writers (see Chapter 9). In interviews with Roehampton trainee teachers in 2008, boys made these comments about writing:

Year 2:   It's boring, it takes ages. Every day we have to do it.
Year 3:   It hurts your hand.
Year 4:   I don't like writing when you [the teacher] tell me to write…I like to write about people beating each other up and stuff.

Think back to the earlier section about how girls play and practise at writing. If boys start school with less experience of such literacy play, what opportunities do they have in the classroom to catch up? Take a few moments to write down or discuss what you think play at writing would look like for boys at different ages in primary school.

As you did this you may have thought about what boys like to play at, and whether these interests are welcomed in school. Elements of boys' play may be considered offensive, violent or even deviant, such as guns and shooting, wrestling, kick-boxing, sword-fighting, car-racing, superheroes and online gaming. Whilst girls' play often seems to find a secure place in school, teacher attitudes and school policies may bar boys' play from the classroom.

> I was visiting a local authority nursery. A three-year-old boy had painted a picture – a big red blob – and the nursery teacher said, 'Tell me about your picture'. The boy said, excitedly, 'It's the Red Power Ranger!' and the nursery teacher immediately replied, 'You know we don't have Power Rangers here'. He went quiet. I wondered if he had said it was a Barbie or Bratz, would it have been OK?
>
> (Roehampton English Education tutor)

Holland (2003) has speculated that this kind of quashing of 'taboo play themes' in EYFS settings may cause boys to become disaffected with school literacy in later years. Although Marsh and Millard (2000) have usefully explored how children's outside school interests and popular 'crazes' can be used for classroom literacy activities, many practitioners may still feel uncomfortable with the nature of boys' play. Michael

Anderson (2003) is one of the few primary teachers who has attempted to engage fully with the violent media which seem to fascinate many boys. He looked at the writing of a boy in KS2 who infused his stories with battles and explosions. Anderson was able to see how the boy's experiences and the media he preferred powered his writing, and Anderson, in turn, reflected on his own experiences and preferred media, and saw how these influenced his attitudes to writing.

As a teacher, you will understand that boys and girls become skilled and confident readers by developing preferences in reading; likewise, you can acknowledge how personal interest (e.g. cars, sport, film, music, fashion, games) can stimulate a child to become an enthusiastic writer. Therefore planning for a range of writing interests, content and genres will underpin your inclusive practice and meaningful differentiation across the whole class. Consider the following examples taken from classrooms. You might discuss and evaluate the writing case studies and the children's responses.

Case study 1: Mr Gumpy meets the turtles

Reception children were asked to retell in writing the John Burningham picture-book story *Mr Gumpy's Outing*. Girls followed the original narrative faithfully. Here is Leanne's version:

Figure 3.1

Her story continues:

> They all did what they shouldn't have done.
> They tipped out the boat.
> They all went home.

She has played it very safe, following the original text and the teacher's brief; she could be encouraged to take more risks in her writing, perhaps incorporating her own play or fantasy interests. However, boys in the group took narrative matters into their own hands. Ted's story begins conventionally enough:

> 'Can I come?' said Cheza.
> 'Can I come?' said Ted.
> 'Can I come?' said Edwin.
> 'Yes,' said Mr Gumpy.

But this is where the narrative takes a dramatic twist:

Figure 3.2

And so the disruption continues:

Then Shredder
attacked them
and Raphael
and Leonardo
saved Mr Gumpy.

Figure 3.3

Loosely based on the original, this boy's story is vivid and engaging. But guns and shooting and cartoons (in this case the Teenage Mutant Hero Turtles) may feel risky as a topic in school. Schools will have different policies about this – and parents may also have views about violent content or popular culture in school writing. How comfortable would you be in using the boy's interests for literacy learning and teaching? Certainly as a teacher you would not make Teenage Mutant Ninja Heroes (or any of their contemporary equivalents) the sole resource for children's writing. Yet the boy's obvious enthusiasm offers an opening for his continuing writing development.

Case study 2: World Cup

During the 2006 World Cup, Year 6 children kept individual football journals which contained pages for writing and drawing. Most boys did little writing, however, and used their journals for cutting and sticking, covering the pages with images of brands (Nike, Adidas) and players, sometimes adding captions and headlines; they also drew and made lists of logos, players and teams. Teachers observed that boys valued the journals, often taking them between home and school during the matches. They enjoyed discussing the progress of the games and the different teams their families were supporting. Some boys had considerable expertise about football which they were able to share in class (Safford *et al.*, 2007).

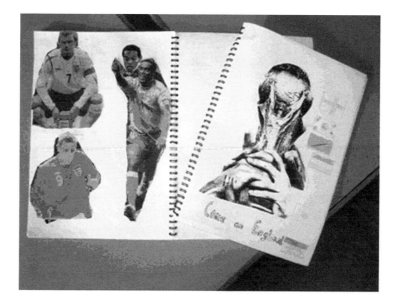

Figure 3.4

The journals offered a play-space for writing, drawing on boys' expertise and interests in a format which did not appear babyish. Cutting and sticking, list-making and drawing (all EYFS literacy activities) are appropriate in supporting writing development, and as a teacher you can plan opportunities throughout KS2 for children to continue to develop their fine motor skills, which, in turn, develop stamina for writing. What also motivated children in this activity was the event of the World Cup itself, a global occasion that dominated the media, gripped communities and which families and friends followed at home daily. As with any other topic, children can write in a range of genres about football: stories, poems, reports, profiles, instructions, discussions and persuasive arguments. Such activities need not exclude girls; in this World Cup project there were just as many girls who were enthusiastic about football as there were those who thought that the matches were 'boring as snoring'.

Case study 3: Writing about special objects

As an assessment task, Adam and Nicola in Year 4 were instructed to write about a special object. Nicola described a jewellery box:

> My special object is a jewellery box. My sister Catherine gave me it. It was her favourite object but I wanted it so she gave me it. It is special because she gave it up for me. I keep it in my bedroom on my bedside table. I keep necklaces and rings in it.

It is a cube shape with a silver lock that is broken. It is very dark blue with white and silver stars on the sides. The stars get smaller when they come up the side. There is a hook at the back which you wind and it makes a noise when you open it. It is made of plastic.

Inside there is a mirror. The inside is covered with dark blue velvet. There is quite a lot of room inside. There are 2 layers, one that you can take off the top and the other is fixed in the bottom.

I will keep it forever to remember my sister Catherine by.

(QCA, 1999a: 60)

Adam chose to describe his Playstation:

My special object is my Sony Playstation. It is very special to me and my brother because we spent so much time saving up for it. We bought it at Virgin Megastore in town. It cost £200, games included though. It is about 5cm tall, 30cm wide. It is grey. It has an open button, reset button and power button. You press the open button to open the lid, then you put the CD in. Turn on the telly and press the power button and your playstation is up and running.

The two games we've got are 'Final Fantasy VII' and 'Nagano Winter Olympics 98'. On Nagano you can have two players which means you need two hand controllers. We have got two. In FFVII [Final Fantasy VII] it is only one player so you only need one hand controller. We have also got a memory card, this means we can save our game.

(QCA, 1999a: 56)

Both of these writing samples were assessed at Level 4, but Nicola was rated slightly higher – at 'Secure' level 4 (4b) – than Adam, who was assessed as being 'Just' level 4 (4c). Review the two pieces of writing carefully. Do you think the children's choices of topics may have influenced the teacher-examiner's evaluation?

NO SINGLE APPROACH

Teachers who have undertaken classroom research into boys' underachievement found that it is not a monolithic problem that requires a single, one-size-fits-all strategy. Boys may experience a range of writing difficulties in transcription and composition and teachers have found that by focusing on the specific needs of individual children they are able to identify ways forward. The following approaches, which have been shown to support boys' engagement in the writing process, will support *all* children's writing development:

- extensive pre-writing time and flexible formats for planning: talk partners or groups, carrying out research in texts or online, collecting ideas and images, mind-mapping, making notes from drama or role play, drawing (see Chapters 5 and 6);
- active and visual approaches: drama, discussion, artwork, photographs or moving images to stimulate language for writing (see Chapters 5 and 6);
- collaborative writing: writing with a partner or contributing to a group effort supports less experienced writers who can see how a whole text develops and coheres without having to write it all themselves (see Chapter 5);
- writing-reading connections: reading powerful texts as models of written language in different genres (see Chapter 6);
- writing daily about what interests children: journals with the option to draw and decorate;

- digital options for writing: *PowerPoint* stories, emailing authors, word-processing letters, contributing to online discussion forums or class/school websites; and
- differentiating underachievement: knowing that children's performance in one-off, timed writing tests may not reflect what they can achieve in normal daily classroom routines (see Chapter 8).

We cannot hope to solve the problem of the gender gap in writing attainment here, but we hope this section has given you food for thought. In considering boys and writing, you may have identified a theme which forms part of a bigger pedagogical discussion: as teachers, how far should we acknowledge contemporary out-of-school literacy practices and popular culture in our classrooms? How can we use the world outside school in an imaginative, relevant way to promote children's writing development? In the following section you are invited to consider these factors in the teaching of writing.

MULTIMODAL/DIGITAL CONTEXTS, AUDIENCES, PURPOSES

> I don't like writing because it's boring . . . but it is important because you'll need to send letters and emails when you are older.
>
> (Paul, Year 3, to a Roehampton trainee teacher, 2008)

Children are experienced users of digital communication, and such communicative channels are often used in conjunction with multimedia (television programmes, websites, cinema, DVDs). Ofcom (2006) reported that 21 per cent of eight- to eleven-year-old children watch digital television and use the internet at home, and also have their own mobile phones. Significantly, out of the 92 per cent of children aged 8 to 15 who have either internet access, a mobile phone or digital television, nearly half (49 per cent) have interacted with this media through writing: responding to something they saw or read by sending a text message on a mobile phone or an email on the internet, or by posting a message on a website. This kind of writing may often include animation, symbols or icons, and abbreviated words or phrases. Somekh has observed seven- to eleven-year-old children learning to create such texts in an online 'GridClub':

Imogen: . . . if you manage to do it right, you can put pictures on or moving words that go through the screen, then disappear, and then they come back on again, and then they disappear, and then they come back on again. And I sent a note to [a moderator] asking how she done it and she replied something like, 'Hi Imogen! If you click on this icon (and it's got that underlined) then you can do what you want to do and you can put pictures and smiley words on,' and so I clicked on it and then you get all these instructions . . .

Evaluator: But why is it important to have an image and moving words?

Imogen: Because it makes it fun. Your friends think, 'Oh this is good, maybe I could try and copy it' and at the same time you're learning how to do things on the computer.

> (Somekh, 2003: 2)

Children are increasingly familiar with online and digital writing, and, daily, see adults writing in mobile contexts: texting, using laptops, wireless networks and PDAs (personal digital assistants). Children, such as seven-year old Imogen above, are also becoming experienced readers and writers of multimedia texts, but how do these worldly skills and knowledge fit into the writing curriculum? There are claims that the increasingly widespread use of 'textese' such as LOL ('laugh out loud') and CUL8R ('see you later'), on websites and mobile phones, is detrimental to children's writing development. As a teacher you will certainly see the influence of texting and abbreviated words and phrases on children's written language, and it is good practice to draw children's attention to the audiences and purposes of these forms: when, why, and to whom we might send or receive a text message or use abbreviated words or symbols such as 'emoticons' (e.g. ☺ or ☹) in writing. There are additional aspects to texting and literacy learning which are worth considering; professor of linguistics David Crystal has written about the medium's ludic and creative qualities:

> Children quickly learn that one of the most enjoyable things you can do with language is to play with its sounds, words, grammar – and spelling. The drive to be playful is there when we text, and it is hugely powerful…In short, it's fun.
>
> (Crystal, 2008)

Crystal goes on to say that 'texting does not erode children's ability to read and write' and that there are strong, positive links between children's manipulation of text language and their skills in using standard English:

> Children could not be good at texting if they had not already developed considerable literacy awareness. Before you can write and play with abbreviated forms, you need to have a sense of how the sounds of your language relate to the letters. You need to know that there are such things as alternative spellings…If you are using such abbreviations as lol and brb ('be right back'), you must have developed a sensitivity to the communicative needs of your textees.

The work of contemporary children's authors is a good starting point to explore non-standard digital forms. For example, from reading Jacqueline Wilson's novel *The Illustrated Mum*, you could invite children to text in role as the main character, Marigold, or write an exchange of texts between Marigold and her mother. As a different type of literacy activity, children could research how the English language has contained abbreviated words and phrases ever since it began to be written down. The use of 'IOU' for instance dates back to 1618. 'FYI' is used routinely in formal and business English. Words such as 'exam', 'fridge' and 'bus' are abbreviations which have become familiar as words on their own. And non-standard forms such as 'wot' and 'cos' are so much part of our literary traditions that they have entries in the Oxford English Dictionary ('cos' dates back to 1828 and 'wot' to 1829); these words can also be found in literary dialect by authors such as Mark Twain, D.H. Lawrence and Alan Bleasdale, as well as in the work of children's poets such as John Agard and Valerie Bloom. In the classroom, you can draw upon children's knowledge and enthusiasm for these playful, contemporary forms of communication, as the following examples from practice show.

Email

The following example is part of a wider project to promote boys' literacy achievement in KS2 (Safford *et al.*, 2004), where Year 5 classes read Louis Sacher's novel *There's a*

Boy in the Girls' Bathroom. The book's contemporary setting, language and characters were ideal for using email as a writing activity, and the project organisers opened an email account in the name of the main character, Bradley Chalkers, a disaffected boy who sits 'in the last seat in the last row' and whose worst subject is literacy. Teachers invited the class to email Bradley, and children immediately began to write, offering heartfelt advice and comparing their lives to his:

> Dear Bradley,
> … So you think you're cool. I think you are but I'm cooler. Trust me, you have trouble with girls, well you shouldn't. In my school I've got all the girls calling my name and no offense but I've never been beaten up by a girl. All of them are shy but in your school I'd probably have one purple and one black eye!…

This is only a fragment of Andrew's email, which he chose to write during his 'golden time'. Although children knew that Bradley was a fictional character, this did not stop them from entering the world of the novel to write with enthusiasm and interest. Other children emailed Bradley's sister in no uncertain terms:

> As soon as you get this email, tell your mum and dad you are picking on Bradley…tell Bradley to email me or you are going to get serious discipline.
>
> (Gus and Kwaku)

As the Year 5 classes continued to read the novel and write emails to Bradley, his school mentor and his sister, their class teachers, in role as Bradley, sent emails back to children responding to their comments; this created an ongoing, organic and spontaneous written communication. One of the teachers observed the thrill with which children exclaimed, 'Miss, we've got mail!' as real-life literacy practices flourished in the classroom. As two Year 5 girls were emailing Bradley, they had this exchange with their teacher:

Teacher:	What are you two doing?
T & G:	We're emailing Bradley. His worst subject is language. Our worst subject is literacy. We hate literacy.
Teacher:	But what you're doing is literacy!
T & G:	No it's not.
Teacher:	Yes it is – you're writing!
T & G:	This is different writing.

(Safford *et al.*, 2004: 80)

Comments such as these chime with children's perceptions about out-of-school writing as expressed earlier in this chapter. As teachers, we should consider why children may not classify email as 'writing' and how we can broaden their understanding of the diverse forms which writing can encompass in school as well as at home. You can easily set up a free email account in the name of a fictional character, drawing on traditional or contemporary poems or stories. Children could email their questions, thoughts and advice to the Big Bad Wolf, Tracey Beaker, the Lady of Shallot or the Gruffalo. Children can email individually or in pairs, or the email can be a whole-class shared writing activity (see Chapter 5). You can email back to the class in role as the character, posing questions and asking for further explanations. This kind of activity develops children's understanding of writing as an interactive, communicative experience; it draws upon children's knowledge of technology and their knowledge of texts, and it is a writing activity which motivates children to think about and respond to issues presented in their reading.

Blogging

This example is taken from a project exploring literacy and sport (Kelly and Safford, 2009). During the 2006 World Cup, in conjunction with the journals described earlier, teachers and researchers set up an online web-log ('blog') for two Year 6 classes for the duration of the games. In this secure online forum, which could be accessed from home as well as school, children wrote comments responding to the global sporting event. Children were enthusiastic about writing on the blog. They used 'in-the-moment' language of football commentary with enjoyment: the blog was enlivened with phrases such as 'the defence was sleeping', 'he skills up most of the team', 'cracking goal' and 'bicycle kick'. Teachers also observed that children felt they had permission to write in different registers on the blog. Some used the textese colloquialisms of a chatroom:

> Hey Katie, did u watch da football on Sat? – Yes England vs Paraguay, England won 1–0. I knew they were going to win. – but it was kinda borin' on Sat

Some children reflected speculatively or hypothesised:

> We are a little bit worried about England playing with Trinidad and Tobago because the way they played with Paraguay wasn't really a good performance. Even the goal wasn't their own goal, one of the players for Paraguay accidentally headed it in their own goal. We thought it was really embarrassing for their team.

> Wayne Rooney is a very talented young player. If I was as gifted as him I would consider myself lucky.

One of the most interesting aspects of the children's contributions to the football blog was the nature of their written sentence structures. The majority of sentences on the blog were complex sentences, and a significant number of these contained adverbial clauses of reason as children justified their observations and opinions:

- … because nothing much happened and the first goal was an own goal and in the second half we think the players were really hot and tired …
- … as he was the only forward on the pitch …
- … because he shot from far away from the goal and because they had better positions even though they missed …

Children's writing on the blog explained, hypothesised, predicted, speculated and evaluated. It is useful to consider how such opportunities for children advanced their ability to use sophisticated written language, and how the global sporting event, with its unpredictable outcomes, and the online forum created opportunities for expression within a community of writers.

I liked the web-log. You can write about how you felt about the game and how you think the match could have been better.

The blog is the best part, because you can put your own opinions into it.

There are many free or low-cost web-logs which you can set up and manage. Can you think of other national or local events which might grab children's interest and get them blogging?

The real-life, social nature of blogging, texting and emailing offers many opportunities to extend audiences, contexts and purposes for writing in the classroom; they are forms of written communication which invite (and sometimes demand!) a response from the reader. Nigel Hall explored interactive writing with children long before online writing was as commonplace as it is today. In this example, a six-year-old girl engages in a written conversation with her teacher. Although they are using pen and paper, you can easily imagine the same exchange online:

T: How are you? Do you like being in Year 2?
L: Yos I dow Mis KsateBec is nas tus (Yes, I do Miss Kate because there are nice toys)
T: I wonder which toys you like the best?
L: The sad is my best (Sand is my best)
T: I like playing with sand on the beach.
L: I dow as wall (I do as well)
T: Once I built a sandcastle right up to the sky.
L: Ut to the suln (Up to the sun?)
T: It was as tall as the sky and wide as the sea.
L: I will to the sea and I put the sad in the buct and wut
(I went to the sea and I put the sand in the bucket and water)
[...]
L: I will to atm tws I sad the tow in it I hd a nas toum and I win to the pup (I went to Alton Towers. I saw the tower in it. I had a nice time and I went to the pub)

(Hall, 1998)

This Year 2 girl may struggle with her spelling, but she is a real communicator: she asks questions, expresses feelings and describes experiences; she plays an active role in keeping the conversation going as she develops and practises written language. Keep these key qualities in mind as you plan to use ICT for writing in the classroom.

PowerPoint **and multimedia texts**

Children can use the *PowerPoint* program to write in a range of genres and also incorporate sounds, interviews, photographs or video into their writing. For example, Ben in Year 6 (below) created a *PowerPoint* presentation all about James Bond (the character, the movies, the actors, the cars, the gadgets, the villains, the Bond girls...). His use of sound effects (loud gunshots and screeching cars), moving images and animated text create a lively piece of writing driven by his obvious expertise and enthusiasm for his subject.

You can observe how Ben's play, media and narrative interests are fully expressed in his writing, and how he is gaining experience as a writer in this process. Ben created his *PowerPoint* presentation entirely at home, and brought it into school. His teacher,

Old Bond Cars

- This is the Aston Martin DB5
- Its an awesome car with the revolving number plates and the ejector seat
- Shall we move on?

Gadgets

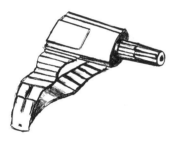

- Most Gadgets like the wrist dart gun save his life from those evil villains
- This is the wrist dart gun
- Lets go to the Bond Girls

Figure 3.5

however, was uneasy with some of the content of the text (guns and Bond girls) and was reluctant to share it with the class – an example of the tensions discussed earlier in this chapter which may exist between home and school cultures. If you felt Ben's text was inappropriate, how could you draw upon what he had created to promote his writing development? Are there similar topics or themes which might better fit the classroom context? (For a full discussion of the development of Ben's piece of writing, see the conclusion of Chapter 5.)

Digital texts such as Ben's can involve considerable research, and they can link to further fiction and non-fiction writing. If children are creating stories using *PowerPoint*, about bears for example, they could create hyperlinks to files of other writing about the habitats of bears, poems about bears, how hibernation works, or a discussion forum about the pros and cons of keeping wild animals in zoos; the whole class could contribute diverse written and visual elements to the overarching digital text, and this could be shared with parents on CD-ROMs, presented at an assembly or put on to the class or school website.

With programs such as *Photoshop*, children can digitally manipulate their own artwork and photographs and incorporate these into their writing. A Year 4 class created a series of images in paint, pastel and clay, and they also took photographs of themselves; all of these images were processed using *Photoshop* and then put into *PowerPoint*. Children then wrote stories describing adventures in the imaginary landscapes of their artwork, adding music and sound effects (King, 2005).

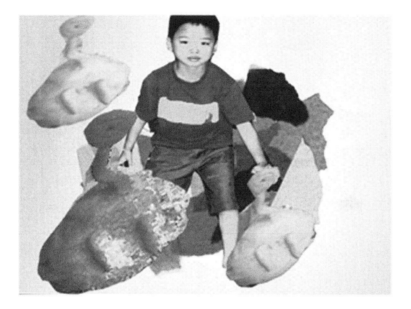

The statues stopped changing colour. They started to fly slowly up. One started spinning around the circle then the other followed and the other did as well. I was by the doorway I tiptoed into the circle. Now they are spinning around me.

Figure 3.6

The Year 4 teacher said writing with *Photoshop* inspired children to draw together a range of their communicative resources encompassing words and images to create a complete text, putting their considerable visual and digital literacy skills to work in their writing.

We have looked briefly here at ways in which you can plan creative approaches to the literacy curriculum using ICT. Writing which involves email, blogging, *PowerPoint* and *Photoshop* is fun and engaging for children, but as a practitioner, you would base the use of these resources on solid pedagogic ground by understanding how they contribute to children's language and literacy development.

MULTILINGUAL WRITERS

Wherever you work, you should expect to meet children who use English as an Additional Language (EAL) who now account for more than 14 per cent of primary pupils and whose numbers will continue to grow.

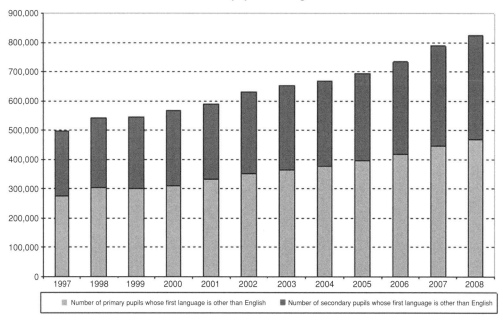

Number of pupils learning 1997–2007

Figure 3.7 (DCSF, 2007b)

Bilingual and multilingual children will be at various stages of English language learning: some may be new to English, whilst others may be UK-born and live in families where other languages are used. They may be familiar with a range of writing for traditional, cultural, community or religious purposes, such as wedding lyrics, Eid cards or email. You may encounter children who attend Saturday or supplementary schools to continue learning community languages and go on to take GCSEs or A levels in those languages. This learning may not always find expression in the mainstream classroom, however: for example, Gregory *et al.* (1996) found that teachers in east London were often unaware that their six-year-old pupils were becoming literate in Bengali; many of these children were receiving up to 11 hours of instruction a week in community language classes.

The cognitive benefits of multilingualism and how bilingual learners are able to make useful connections between languages and cultures is well researched (see CILT, 2006, for example). There are many practical steps you can take to draw upon the language knowledge of your pupils (see Safford and Collins, 2006). In her study of multilingual children in a nursery setting, Kenner (1999) documented how providing texts in community languages (such as video posters, calendars, recipes, letters, alphabet charts, newspapers, magazines and books) for writing activities encouraged young children to recognise and develop their literacy skills:

> Mohammed, who was being taught the Arabic alphabet at home in preparation for attending Qur'anic classes, showed a familiarity with the alphabet chart and flashcards which his mother used as teaching aids, when these were brought into the nursery. His mother made a large poster based on the chart, which the whole class could look at while they were learning a song based on the Arabic alphabet. Mohammed then wanted to make a similar poster. He was concerned with its overall appearance; his initial effort, a line of letters on a blank sheet of paper, left him dissatisfied because 'It doesn't look the same'. He was referring to the absence of the squared grid which characterised his mother's poster. When I drew this for him, he filled in each box in sequence, so that his poster bore a clear visual resemblance to his mother's...When his mother was shown the poster that afternoon, she reacted with surprise, saying 'He's never written Arabic before!' This highlighted the sustained attention Mohammed must have given to the script during his lessons at home.
>
> (Ibid., 1999:7)

Kenner found that bilingual nursery children showed a strong motivation to make use of community language texts to generate their own writing, and that they showed increasing understanding of the purposes and symbols (scripts) of these texts.

In KS1 and KS2, you can plan opportunities for children to write in their first or home languages, particularly for children whose receptive understanding may be ahead of their ability to produce oral and written English.

> When I was teaching Year 5, I read my class the novel *Bill's New Frock* by Anne Fine. After the first few chapters, children were instructed to write in role as Bill and how he felt waking up as a girl. I had a new arrival, a boy from Spain. He understood the story, but he asked if he could write about it in Spanish. As he had very little English, I agreed. But then other children began to ask, 'Can I write in MY language?' I had to be fair, so I agreed that they could. We had writing in Twi, Cantonese, Arabic, Tamil and Portuguese as well as Spanish and English. From then on I planned that once a week all the children could write in their languages. They really enjoyed doing it, and they enjoyed reading their writing aloud and comparing different scripts, words and sentences in different languages. They learned a lot from each other, and I learned a lot too.
>
> (Roehampton English Education tutor)

In planning routines where children discuss their writing, you can be alert to the ways in which children's first and home languages influence their written English. Nina Shah-Onwukwe, a newly-qualified Year 4 teacher, notices this in children's writing:

> Sometimes when I'm reading their work I can tell how they're thinking...making literal translations...'Do your brush' instead of 'Brush your teeth', and 'Close the light'.
>
> (in an interview with Roehampton English Education, 2008)

Roehampton University trainee teachers, in 2008, made similar observations about pupils learning EAL:

> [about a Year 2 girl, French speaker]...she wrote: 'he wrote it all <u>in</u> a quill' whereas it should actually be '<u>with</u> a quill'...

[about a Year 5 girl, Greek speaker]...her desire to include 'wow' words ('ecstatic', 'nervous', 'disheartened') has been dampened by the fact that although they are there, they have not always been used in the right context.

These kinds of observations will help you to identify patterns in the written English of children learning EAL so that you can support them more effectively. This is important even for advanced learners of English. Cameron and Besser (2004) analysed the texts of KS2 bilingual pupils who had high levels of English fluency and found that these children continued to demonstrate errors in written English. These included:

- formulaic phrases and collocations, e.g. 'They waited for long', 'For a lot of time', 'After some couple of weeks', 'She burst into happiness';
- 'small' words and prepositions, e.g. 'Help on reading', 'Regret of what they did';
- subject–Verb agreements, e.g. 'There are so much traffic', 'Everyone else are looking'.

Cameron and Besser advise that the moment to teach collocations and grammar explicitly is when you observe children attempting to use them orally and in writing. You can support multilingual pupils by correcting their errors sensitively and consistently, by modelling written English through texts and reading aloud, and in the focused teaching of elements of written genres (see Chapter 2), thematic phrases and idioms (McWilliam, 1998).

The sample of writing below is by Trevor (NALDIC *Pupil Portraits*). He is in Year 7 and arrived six months earlier from the Philippines with no prior experience of English. His first language is Tagalog.

> Mario have a expensive camera and she love taking photos
> christine: takes a photos of a little cat in a window
> Mario: what a little camera Mario's laugh
> christine: said don't laugh with may little camera
> crossties camera can shat with good photos
> christine: have a lot of money she take Mario into a summer holiday

You might find it useful to consider the following:

- What does Trevor already know and what can he already do in written English?
- How do Cameron and Besser's observations apply to his writing sample? Are there other kinds of errors which you notice?
- What kind of formative feedback would you give Trevor about his writing, in structure and in content?
- What kinds of texts could you provide as models to improve his written English?

Trevor knows how to tell a story in English, using his first-language knowledge of narrative, characters, dialogue and plots. He has demonstrated confidence and independence in producing coherent writing in a language he is just beginning to learn. As Cameron and Besser observed in the writing of KS2 bilingual children, Trevor makes errors with 'small' words ('a' instead of 'an', 'she' instead of 'he', 'into' instead of 'on') and with verb tenses. You might focus on his errors in tenses, prepositions or pronouns – although not all at once. Given the humorous, playscript nature of his writing, Trevor might benefit from reading books which feature dialogue and English collocations, and you could have a collection of these which would support the writing development of children at different stages of learning EAL.

You should also be aware that children learning English are developing a range of cultural as well as linguistic knowledge in order to participate in mainstream classroom writing activities, and that some published literacy schemes can make assumptions about children's language and cultural understanding, as Nina Shah-Onwukwe realised:

> I was teaching a lesson on the use of apostrophes. I had a book on sentence level work. There were phrases which you had to change into idioms. There was a clue and a word, and you had to guess the new word; for example OKRA would be LADIES' FINGERS. If you knew those idioms you would have got it straight away and you would have been working on your apostrophes. Children who may not have English as a first language were going to have problems with the idioms. Publishers haven't thought about things like that. I didn't use it. I made my own sentences.
>
> (Interview with Roehampton English Education, 2008)

You can take account of the specific needs of children learning EAL within your broad planning to support all children in developing skills for writing by:

- making adequate time for children to plan, review, and revise their writing;
- providing opportunities for children to read their writing aloud and explain what they mean orally as a way of re-drafting it;
- discussing how saying things orally is different to written expression;
- giving informal immediate feedback.

The specific needs of children learning to write in EAL are also addressed within planning for the wider interests and backgrounds of all children, taking account, for example, of your knowledge of gendered writing interests and children's digital/multimodal expertise.

Finally, you should be very cautious about conflating EAL with Special Educational Needs. The 1996 Education Act states that 'a child must not be regarded as having a learning difficulty solely because the language or form of language of the home is different from the language in which he or she is or will be taught' (DoE, 1996, s. 312).

> These children are at a very high cognitive level, perhaps in their own language...Yes, they do have problems with English, so you can't expect the same kinds of outcomes from them. But they do need to be thinking along their own level.
>
> (Sandra Davies, EAL specialist teacher, Cavendish Primary School, Hounslow, in an interview with NALDIC, 2008)

You would evaluate the writing development of children learning EAL in two areas: content and language structure. You would make assessments of these two areas of learning separately and holistically and decide how much to work on in each area, bearing in mind that such children are learning the curriculum and English language at the same time.

CREATING AND SHAPING TEXTS: THINKING MADE VISIBLE

In whatever language or mode, writing is a creative act which involves translating invisible and emergent ideas into visible texts that can be shared and changed. For children, creating and shaping texts involves active thinking, deploying and controlling cognitive and physical skills to make visible their knowledge and understanding on paper or on screen. 'Writing' can, at times, feel frustratingly inadequate to symbolise the diversity and richness of children's thoughts, internal narratives and mental images.

We can support children's literacy learning by planning routines for writing which foreground the thoughtful, communicative nature of creating and shaping texts, drawing upon the cultural, digital and linguistic resources which every child brings to the classroom. Inspiring contexts for writing will offer children opportunities to play at and practise writing as they think about fictional worlds and real-life situations, about what fascinates them and others and about new contexts and familiar patterns. They will be delighted to see their thinking made concrete on paper or screen.

In the following chapter you will learn about progression in children's writing development. As you consider children's writing journeys you can continue to reflect on the issues raised here, and how children's experiences of family, culture, technology, gender and language – are key influences on learning to write in school.

Further reading and websites

DCSF Standards site on gender and achievement

This site aims to help practitioners in raising the performance and aspirations of underachieving boys and girls by providing online resources, examples of good practice, analysis and practical guidance.
www.standards.dfes.gov.uk/genderandachievement

Multiverse

This is a website for teachers, teacher educators and student teachers addressing the educational achievement of pupils from diverse backgrounds.
www.multiverse.org.uk

NALDIC (National Association for Language Development in the Curriculum)

There is a section on this website (ITTSEAL) for trainee teachers on effective support for children learning EAL; current policy and relevant research are available as well as key readings and pupil portraits
www.naldic.org.uk

Teacher Training Resource Bank (TTRB)

This website provides access to research and resources informing teacher education in a wide range of areas including gender, ICT, EAL and cultural diversity.
www.ttrb.ac.uk

Further reading

Bearne, E. and Wolstencroft, H. (2007) *Visual Approaches to Teaching Writing*. London: Paul Chapman.

Bus, A. and Neuman, S. (eds) (2009) *Multimedia and Literacy Development: Improving Achievement in Young Learners.* London: Routledge.

Vincent, J. (2006) 'Children writing: multimodality and assessment in the writing classroom'. *Literacy*, 40(1), 51–7.

Chapter 4

The Writing Journey

Fiona Collins and Anne Washtell

INTRODUCTION

In this chapter we are going to take you on a writing journey. Our companions on this journey will be pieces of writing produced by 12 different children aged between three and eleven years. As we will discover, each piece of writing is a journey in its own right for its young author. We can also learn about some of the different, individual milestones which children pass as they gain more knowledge and experience of the writing process. It is not our intention here to offer a linear or hierarchical journey of development, yet the pieces do provide snapshots of the children's varied control over the different elements of composition and transcription. As you will remember from Chapter 2, composition involves the creating and shaping of a text, whilst transcription is concerned with the surface features, such as handwriting, spelling and punctuation.

All the pieces of writing that follow show commitment and a need to communicate to an audience. The pieces of writing were chosen to represent a range of forms, text types, ages, cultures, contexts and experience. They are as follows:

The Tea Party Lists (two girls aged 3 and 5)
Orville (Reception)
An Early Story (Reception)
Unaided Writing in Chinese Characters (Year 1)
When I Was Naughty (Year 1)
I Love Papaya (Year 2)
Dear Mrs Wild (Year 4)
Quidditch (Year 4)
Escape from Ethiopia (Year 5)
The Monk and the Fish (Year 5)
Le Lac d'Annecy (Year 6)

Most of the above pieces were written in school and these samples provide a flavour of the kinds of writing that children are engaged in on a day-to-day basis. For example, the range covers: name writing, narrative, letter writing and writing for information. In the only piece of writing that originated from home (*The Tea Party Lists*), the youngest child of three years of age is inspired by her older sister and her mark-making probably emulates the list her sister is making. In *Orville*, we see a child whose drawing and writing celebrate his conception of himself. *An Early Story* shows how the child's compositional skills are in advance of her transcriptional skills. We see a more defined start to the journey of conventional writing as the child grapples with letters as well as composing the recount orally.

Within many classes today, there are children who speak English as an additional language (EAL), and Ming, who wrote *Unaided Writing in Chinese Characters*, is such a child. His wish to communicate is shown in the piece as well as the influence of popular culture and television. By the time we reach *When I Was Naughty*, we see a sophisticated multimodal story where the child is making meaning through both text and images. Poetry also provides plenty of opportunities for children to express themselves. This is exemplified in *I Love Papaya*. The writing journey moves on to persuasive writing in the form of a letter, *Dear Mrs Wild*. The *Quidditch* description reflects a child's out-of-school interests in the form of popular fiction. Here the writer steps into Harry Potter's mind-set and shows his inner feelings as he prepares for a quidditch match. In the next piece, *Escape from Ethiopia*, we return to a child who speaks EAL, reminding us of the range of writers in our classrooms. This moving piece of cathartic, autobiographical writing shows the potential that writing may have for alleviating traumatic events. Another example of multimodal writing is to be found in *The Monk and the Fish*. This is influenced by an animated film, and again the child draws on out-of-classroom knowledge of the cartoon form. The chapter concludes with a remarkable story written by a gifted and talented Year 6 child.

Taken as a whole, the pieces of writing show how orchestrating composition and transcription is a constant issue for children. This holds good whatever the ages of the writers, their abilities or the genre in which they are writing. As will become evident, some of our writers have few problems about what they wish to say, whilst others are constrained by the efforts of controlling the transcription elements. For the bilingual child who wrote *Escape from Ethiopia*, transcription skills are the challenge. Scribing for this child sustains her sense of authorship whilst she learns about the grammatical and spelling conventions of the English language. The Year 4 child who wrote the *Quidditch* piece shows confidence and imagination, yet, as he expresses some of his ideas, challenges arise in relation to aspects of his spelling. As children begin to use a wider range of sentence types or manage ideas in lengthier pieces, new errors may creep in for a while. In *An Early Story* we can see that five-year-old Katrina's fine motor skills are still developing, which has a clear impact on her ability to control her pencil as she tries to commit her ideas to paper.

Gordon Wells (1987) has shown us that even from the earliest age, children are active meaning makers. As will be seen with some of the pieces from our youngest writers, the adult must work hard to make sense of and interpret the children's efforts. Indeed, we would argue that when reading any child's writing, we must try to consider the thought, intentions and actions that have gone into creating the piece and hold this in our minds as we analyse the writing itself. In the Year 1 piece (*Unaided Writing in Chinese Characters*) the monolingual teacher is faced with a huge challenge. Indeed, as we explored this piece with a colleague from China, we discovered that she based much of her interpretation of it on the likely cultural experiences of the child, including his possible viewing habits and the likelihood that he might be receiving instruction within his community in writing in his own language. Without her input it is unlikely that we would have reached that interpretation for ourselves.

To enable us to navigate the writing journey we have organised the pieces chronologically by age (youngest to oldest). As far as possible, we have managed the discussion of each piece of writing by following the same structure: context, composition, transcription and next steps. This framework enables us to give some initial orientation for each piece, followed by a discussion of the child's developing authorial skills and management of the surface features (spelling, punctuation and handwriting). It is not our intention to formally assess or level the pieces, but by concluding each piece with 'next steps' we make suggestions as to how the teacher can help the individual child move forward. (To read more about assessment see Chapter 8.) A wider range of writing samples would need to be gathered for each child in order to undertake a full assessment of their achievements. In the meantime, enjoy the writing journey.

THE TEA PARTY LISTS

Figures 4.1 Betty (age 5)

Figures 4.2 Lily (age 3)

Context

A family friend, Alison, was visiting the two sisters and their family. During the visit the three had a discussion about when the young sisters would visit Alison for tea. During this discussion the younger girl, Lily, sat on Alison's lap and Betty wrote a list of items they would need for the tea party. As the writing progressed, Alison and Betty engaged in a rich discussion about the tea party. The discussion was punctuated by Betty asking Alison to help with spellings. At the same time Lily started to quietly make her own 'list' for the tea party, unnoticed by Alison (Figures 4.1 and 4.2).

Betty: composition and transcription

Five-year-old Betty's list reads: 'tea, cookies, milk, pens, strawberries, paper'. Clearly there is an expectation that there will be more to this tea party than eating! Organisationally, the list follows the conventions one would expect to see, with items placed beneath each other. Lists are a very important way of helping young writers to understand that words are separate entities. Betty feels the need to organise the writing within unseen boundaries. Most of the words are aligned carefully, with the writing going from left to right. 'Milk' is the least distinct of the words. Written at an angle, it collides with the word above so she had to place the letter 'k' below. There is even logic to the placing of the 'k', which could have been under the 'm' but, in fact, is placed towards the end of the word. The gap between 'pen' and the letter 's' is not as easily explained. The word 'strawberries' is broken down into three sections, one underneath the other ('strav'(w) – 'wber' – 'ries'). The last two syllables of the three repeat the final letter of the preceding syllable. As a result, we can almost hear Betty pronouncing the word to herself as she wrote. This kind of experience shows us that she is beginning to consider the structure of polysyllabic words. She writes in clearly formed capital letters with only the letters 'N' and 'L' wrongly oriented. In the main, it is very easy for us to read.

Lily: composition and transcription

Lily was taking part in the discussions about tea and we can only assume that her list represented the items she wanted. However, you would need to talk with the child to be sure of this.

In terms of transcription, at a first glance Lily's mark-making could be dismissed as random scribble. However, we can see two arcs and six main zigzag lines arranged one beneath another with five smaller zigzags. It would seem that Lily is exploring how to control the writing tool by making both long, smooth lines and jagged ones. In the top right-hand corner there is an animal or insect of some sort. Here we see Betty making circular movements for the top of the head and an oval shape for what might be the body. To learn more about early mark-making and drawing see John Matthews' case studies of Ben and Joel (2003).

Next steps: Betty

This spontaneous writing experience happened in the home in an informal and playful setting. Betty had started school and it is likely that her Early Years Foundation Stage

(EYFS) teacher had many opportunities to talk with her parents. Through regular communication, teachers can learn about home literacy experiences and establish continuity in order to foster burgeoning skills. Here we give some ideas of how Betty's teacher might develop her writing further.

It will be important for Betty to sustain her list writing through her play. Her teacher might set up a meaningful context such as a restaurant where orders could be taken by waiters or waitresses from their customers. Through writing in role, Betty will further develop her understanding that writing is purposeful and is centred on communication. She will also learn that her list is of practical use to her. Through learning to compose simple instructional texts, such as a recipe for cookies, she can apply her knowledge further by listing the necessary equipment and ingredients. Embedding such activity within the practical experience of preparing and baking the cookies would offer Betty a further demonstration of the purposeful nature of written language. In addition, her teacher will want to expand her writing into other genres.

The evidence suggests that she is already curious about learning how to spell individual words. It would be interesting for her teacher to find out how many words she can write independently. We get some indication with the word 'strawberries' that she might be trying to vocalise words as she spells them. This suggests that she is ready for direct instruction in segmenting, which is likely to occur during the daily phonics sessions. Experience of rhyme and rhythm will further support her growing phonological awareness. She will benefit from being taught lower case letter formation.

Finally, her teacher might want to consider celebrating the writing that children do at home by actively encouraging them to bring pieces in. A 'Home Writing' board could be set up to display their work.

Next steps: Lily

Lily was not yet at school but she attended a nursery in which close communication with parents was a regular occurrence and there was plenty of provision for her to continue to explore and extend her mark-making skills. It will be important for her to have the opportunity to use a range of tools including paint brushes of different sizes, thick wax crayons, chalks, pencils and felt tips. Her hands themselves will also be important tools for mark-making and painting. She needs a variety of surfaces to work on and these should be of varying sizes. It is important for a child of this age to have the chance to make big sweeps and movements in order to explore the potential of their arm and hand actions. All of this lays firm foundations for her fine motor skills to develop. To develop her compositional skills, Lily will no doubt enjoy the opportunity to retell familiar stories which she can dictate for an adult to scribe for her. She will almost certainly be gaining experience and knowledge about the letters that spell her name.

ORVILLE

Figure 4.3 Orville (Reception)

Context

This piece of writing was undertaken independently by five-year-old Orville in an inner London school. In his classroom he had access to a writing resource area where he could freely select paper and a range of writing implements.

Composition

This is an exuberant and confident piece of early writing, dominated by Orville's extensive artwork. Two items in his pictures are instantly recognisable: the sun and a human figure who, presumably, is Orville himself. The sun has radials and appears to have some features of a face, possibly eyes and teeth. It is positioned at the top left of the sheet of paper in what we might expect to be the sky, part of which might be represented by the wavy line to the right of the sun (or clouds perhaps). The tilted figure of Orville himself is active and portrays movement through the positioning of the legs, one of which just touches the boundary line of his drawing whilst the other is stepping boldly through his name. He seems to be walking towards his reader with a warm and happy smile. As well as a mouth, the head also has hair, and two, carefully aligned, rounded eyes with the same shaded shape used for the nose. The figure is dressed with a tie, with darker shading used to infill the arms, legs and feet. At the end of the arms, radials have been used to represent hands or fingers. Interestingly, Orville has sketched in a frame or boundary around the complete picture as well as the text. This seems to provide an enclosure for his work. In addition, further shaded, overlapping, horizontal arcs sweep across the page in order to separate his name-writing from the other letters arranged beneath. There is a real sense of Orville exploring the terrain of the piece of paper in terms of how pictures and text might be best organised and placed in order to communicate with clarity. Perhaps he has established some conventions for this by drawing on his knowledge of how text and pictures are set out on the pages of picture books. What we have here, in effect, is a carefully composed page.

His actual written composition is brief and to the point. By writing his name he is stamping his identity on the piece. In the drawing of himself, Orville is utilising first-order symbolism (Vygotsky, 1978), yet in writing his name he has made the move to second, order symbolism. In the act of representing himself in both drawing and writing, he is presenting two different and fascinating ways of looking back at himself. The opportunity is thus opened up for him to realise that others (including those who are unknown to him) can recognise and name him without needing to engage in face-to-face contact. This is an important step in the journey of attributing meaning to print, understanding its permanence and the empowerment that comes with seeing oneself as a writer.

Transcription

Orville demonstrates through the accurate spelling of his name that he has developed a concept of what a word is. He has understood that every time he writes his name, he must select specific letters to represent it and that these are organised in an unchanging order. In other words, he is learning about the constancy and stability of print. Name-writing marks a major developmental milestone for young children as they start to learn how to spell. It provides a useful point of reference as they compare and hypothesise about other words which may or may not bear similarities to their own name. Their name is usually the first word that children learn to spell independently and with accuracy and is heavily imbued with personal meaning, which is why the written form is highly memorable for them. Underneath his name, Orville has written six more letters, most of which are recognisable. However, no meaning was attributed to them by him. Some of the letters of his name are utilised, as well as introducing what might be a capital 'R' and a 'y', which looks as though it has evolved from his mastery of the letter 'v'. He demonstrates that he can capitalise 'E' as well as use the lower case form in his name-writing. His handwriting is clear, with each letter given adequate space, and has been laid out from left to right.

Next steps

Orville has made bold inroads in his understanding of the writing process. He is ready now to expand his compositional skills, possibly by dictating texts for adults to scribe, which he can then illustrate. With his apparent confidence, he could, with the provision of appropriate contexts and purposes for writing, extend his independent writing. This could be done, for example, through the planned provision for writing within the role play area. His existing knowledge of the alphabet should be assessed and gaps addressed. This would need to be done both in terms of being able to recite and recognise the letters, but also in his ability to write and name them. Participating in phonic sessions will also help Orville to develop his phonemic knowledge and enhance his spelling of simple VC, CV or CVC words. Formal handwriting practice using appropriately spaced lined paper is another step that he appears ready to take.

AN EARLY STORY

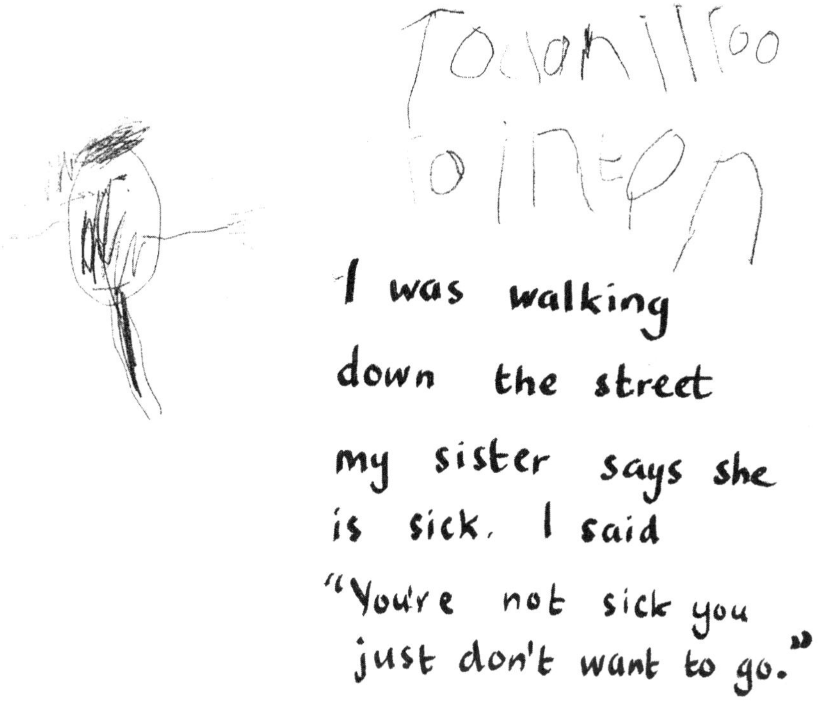

Figure 4.4 Katrina (Reception)

Context

This piece of independent, unaided writing followed by the teacher's transcription was created by a Reception child within a few weeks of starting school. The classroom in which the child was working had a well-stocked writing area which included home-made notepads and blank books to encourage children to play and explore writing and mark-making as a means of communication. This piece was written in one of these books. The writing was self-initiated and was one of her earliest attempts at independent writing, which was shared directly with an adult who then wrote down Katrina's words exactly as she said them.

Composition

Starting with the figure, we can see that she has drawn two arms outstretched with fingers, two legs without feet and a head which has two eyes, a mouth and some hair, but no ears. We cannot determine the gender of the person. The figure seems to be floating or flying on the page. The writing is a short, first-person narrative in chronological order. Within a few words, Katrina sets the scene – 'I was walking down the street' – and introduces a problem through reported speech in which her sister says that she is sick. The narrator responds directly in a crisp, no-nonsense tone through the use of direct speech. She employs past and present tense but has yet to sustain tense consistently. The drawing prompts questions which could be used to develop the composition: Who is this single figure? What is the figure doing? Why has the writer not drawn herself and her sister?

Transcription

The transcription bears little obvious relation to the spoken text written for the child by the teacher. However, we can see that she has written two lines of writing with letters that are clearly demarcated. We can recognise ten different letters within the two lines, nine of which occur immediately in the first line. She shows the ability to write upper and lower case letters. The child's name is Katrina and there is clear evidence of some of the letters of her name being used to generate her written text. We could surmise that she knows how to spell the word 'to' and 'in' and 'clan', although these words may have been arrived at randomly.

Next steps

The provision and ready availability of writing materials stimulated this child into composing this personal narrative. To move her on she should be encouraged to dictate texts to adults. However, the questions above could be used to help her extend and develop her ideas. By re-reading her dictated text with her, it is possible to make a powerful link between spoken and written language. This example helps to remind us how entwined talk, reading and writing are, especially for the young and inexperienced writer. This child was in the early stages of learning to read and had not yet secured one-to-one correspondence. At this point she also could not yet write her name independently. From this we can deduce that she does not yet have a fully developed concept of a word in its written form. Careful attention will need to be given when teaching her handwriting in order to ensure the correct formation of her letters.

UNAIDED WRITING IN CHINESE CHARACTERS

Context

This child was a new arrival in the country and in his class. The class was undertaking a writing task and the child independently chose to carry out this piece of writing.

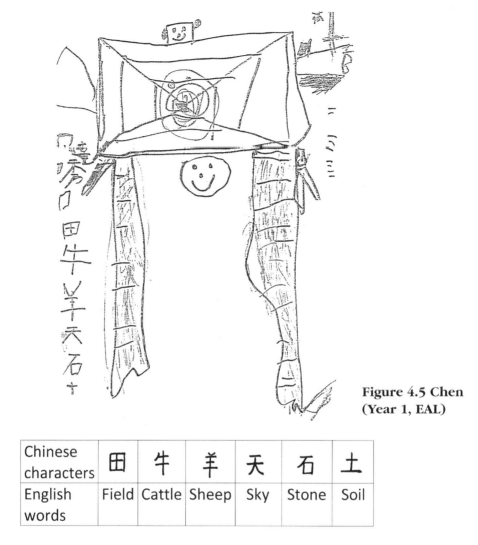

Figure 4.5 Chen (Year 1, EAL)

Chinese characters	田	牛	羊	天	石	土
English words	Field	Cattle	Sheep	Sky	Stone	Soil

Figure 4.6 Chen (Year 1, EAL)

Composition

The text is made up of two elements: a picture and Chinese characters, both confidently drawn. The large and dominating image could be a robot. However, a Chinese colleague, Xiaoyu Yang, suggested that it could represent a television set, showing a particular television programme, possibly some kind of talk show. If it is a television, there appears to be action going on in the form of concentric lines in the centre of the screen. The faces above and below the screen are smiling and friendly. Therefore we might presume that one is a viewer and one is a presenter. Down the side of the image are meaningful Chinese characters that are well-enough formed to be deciphered. They are individual words concerned with animals and nature (see Figure 4.6). Despite the language barrier for the monolingual teacher, we can say without a doubt that this child has a clear understanding that writing is a form of communication. Through carrying out this piece of writing he has made his mark within the writing community of his classroom.

Transcription

Two things strike us immediately about the appearance of the text: the first being the Chinese characters themselves and the way in which they are arranged down the page. Even though most of us cannot read the text we cannot fail to be struck by the precision and fine motor control that this child shows in the formation of these intricate characters.

Next steps

The ethos of the classroom was secure enough for this child to feel that his writing would be accepted and valued by the teacher. Xiaoyu Yang, our translator, has enabled us to understand that in his first language the child has already embarked on becoming literate. This has implications for sustaining his mother tongue alongside his development in English. Working at establishing links with his home or community will teach us much about his learning experiences outside school, which may include attending Chinese Saturday school. Although it is a challenge for the teacher to access every language spoken by the children within the school, there are support networks and materials that can help with this. The child's spoken English was in a very early stage, but providing him with context-embedded (Cummins, 2003) activities that are meaningful for all children will begin to open up opportunities for writing in English. The provision of dual-text picture books and enlisting the support of an adult to aid in the translation of his written texts into English will also be supportive for this child.

WHEN I WAS NAUGHTY

Context

Little is known about the context for this independent, unaided piece of illustrated writing. It originally appeared in an early National Curriculum document (DES, 1988). We are using it because it is difficult now to access this document and yet the writing itself deserves to be better known as it is full of interest.

Composition

The title of this narrative – *When I Was Naughty* – immediately gives a clear signal of the content to the reader. The reader then notices that half the page is an illustrated storyboard while the other half tells the story in words. This multimodal text aids the story telling through the use of the powerful images. The delightful story immediately invites the reader to engage in the narrative through the use of the first-person narrator. The story is one of theft, lying and punishment. It begins with a reference to the narrator's birthday and then leads directly on to the 'crime' of stealing crisps from a cupboard. The story has a clear chronological structure. The three characters in the

Figure 4.7 Child X (Year 1) (DES, 1988: 77)

story are distinctly crafted: the storyteller, the co-conspirator and the powerful figure of the father. We, as readers, can extract the strong moral message from the story: that you may be punished if you steal and lie.

The child's drawings and writing complement each other. The second picture shows the narrator leaning into the cupboard with her sister, Clare, watching. When the dark, sinister figure of Dad appears suddenly in the fourth picture, he challenges the girls directly: 'Have you tuck sumthing from the cupboard?' The girls deny this and the tension mounts as Dad reiterates his question, this time elliptically: 'Have you?'. The reader can imagine his tone. Caught in the act, the denouement shows the sisters disappearing off the page upstairs – 'sent to bed with owt eny supa'. The story ends with the narrator being blamed by Clare, although, as the reader knows only too well from the words and illustrations in the second frame, both sisters went to the cupboard.

Transcription

At a first glance, there appears to be little conventional punctuation in the story as it is written as one continuous sentence with a capital letter at the beginning, one comma and a full stop at the end. Despite accurate use of dialogue, this is not marked by speech marks. However, a closer look reveals that the writer uses the 'boxes' (except in one case) as her full stops and paragraph markers. The writer's adventurous use of a range of vocabulary linked to the morality ('blamed', 'lied', 'truth', 'naughty') poses some challenges for her spelling. With 'lied' and 'truth' ('lid', 'trooth') the writer has been 'tricked' by the complexity of the English language as there are alternative ways of spelling the medial sounds of these words. With 'blamed' and 'opened' ('blamd'/'opnd') she is depending on her knowledge of sounds and has not learnt about the common 'ed' ending of the past tense of verbs. The handwriting is clearly printed. There is some confusion with capitalisation with the word 'Dad'. In the main, the ascenders and descenders are correct.

Next steps

The writer succeeds in enticing the reader in through the drama and tension of her story. This demonstrates a strong sense of purpose and audience which should be nurtured. She has been adventurous in her language choices and has crafted a gripping story. To sustain and build on this quality of writing, the child would benefit from further use of multimodal texts and should be encouraged to develop her written description without losing the impact of the narrative. She is using dialogue to good effect and is ready to learn the conventions. Although she is clearly writing in clauses, she is not yet demarcating them with the expected range of punctuation. She is successfully using compound sentences and could be encouraged to notice and use a wider range of connectives. In relation to handwriting, the teacher may decide that she is ready to move on to using cursive script. Classroom work on vowel digraphs will help her standardise her spelling. She is ready to be taught the unchanging '-ed' inflection for the past tense of common verbs.

I LOVE PAPAYA

Context

This piece of writing was composed during a class topic on poetry writing. The children had been taught about rhyming couplets and the conventions for the line layout of poetry writing.

Composition

The subject of the poem, a papaya fruit, is carefully drawn below the text. In the original, this was coloured yellow in order to echo the first line of her poem. This descriptive poem uses two similes to good effect – 'as yellow as the sun' and 'it's as sweeter as my mum' (where we see a running together of two sentence structures: 'as sweet as my mum' and 'sweeter than my mum'). The rhyming couplets are sustained throughout: 'sun' and 'mum', 'juicy and fruity', 'sweet' and 'treat'. Through her

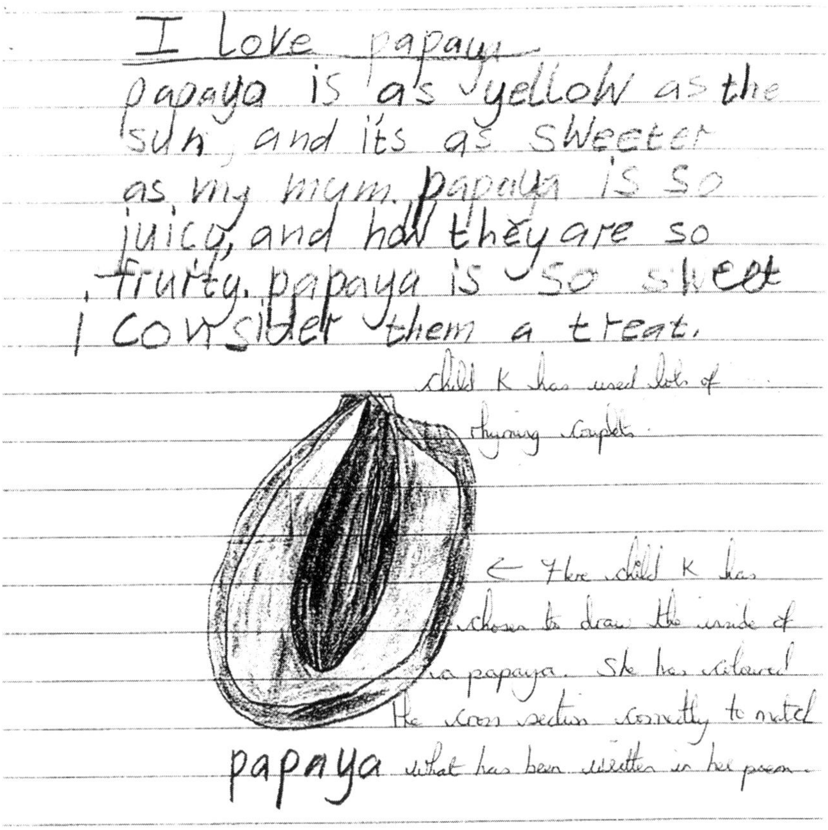

> I love papaya
> papaya is as yellow as the
> sun, and its as sweeter
> as my mum. papaya is so
> juicy, and how they are so
> fruity. papaya is so sweet
> i consider them a treat.

child K has used lots of rhyming couplets

← The child K has chosen to draw the inside of a papaya. She has coloured the cross section correctly to match what has been written in her poem.

> papaya

Figure 4.8 Girl K (Year 2)

description, she tells the reader about the papaya's colour, its sweetness, its juiciness and how special this particular fruit is to her. There is a slight awkwardness of expression in the phrase 'and how they are so fruity', but this may have come about in her efforts to make the lines scan and rhyme. Although she has been taught about line layout, the rhyming couplets do not come at the end of the lines. This may be because she has not started at the margin and has thus run out of line space. Another explanation might be that she has not fully understood that the rhymes need to come at the end of each line, which is a convention of this kind of rhyme scheme.

Transcription

The spelling is accurate throughout. Her handwriting is formed in clear, legible print. The 'ascenders' on her 'w's are slightly over-extended, which could be to do with the child experimenting with her handwriting style. Discussing punctuation in children's own poetry writing is tricky as poets themselves often exercise poetic licence and make creative and unconventional punctuation choices. Whilst these can be a profitable site for discussion with children, you may decide just to pick up on very clear misconceptions ('it's' for 'its', for example) rather than look at sentence punctuation.

Next steps

The teacher could ask the child to share her poem with a response partner in order to refine some of the issues discussed above. The child's partner may point out strengths that she notices and may comment on how she could formally alter the layout. The writer should be encouraged to re-draft it on the computer, scan in her illustration and use a desktop publishing package in order to present it for display purposes. With her good letter formation, this child may be ready to be taught cursive handwriting so that she can write more speedily.

DEAR MRS WILD

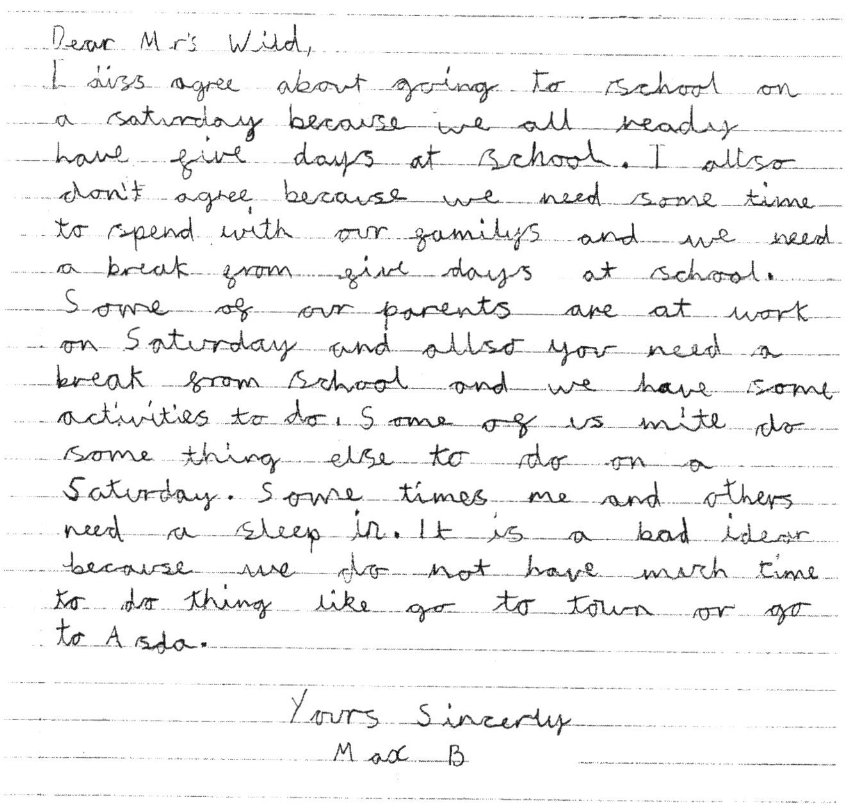

Dear Mrs Wild,
I diss agree about going to school on a saturday because we all ready have five days at school. I allso don't agree because we need some time to spend with our familys and we need a break from five days at school. Some of our parents are at work on Saturday and allso you need a break from school and we have some activities to do. Some of us mite do some thing else to do on a Saturday. Some times me and others need a sleep in. It is a bad idea because we do not have much time to do thing like go to town or go to Asda.

Yours Sincerly
Max B

Figure 4.9 Max (Year 4)

Context

The children had been working on a unit of work on the persuasive genre. Here, Max is trying to dissuade a head teacher from instituting school on Saturday.

Composition

This persuasive piece of writing opens strongly with an initial sentence which argues clearly that the children already spend five days at school. Some justification is given: for example, spending time with family. The child then reiterates his original point. As the piece unfolds, Max cites several further good reasons why Saturday school is such a bad idea. In attempting to shape a persuasive argument, he does encounter some problems. For instance, the sentence 'Some of us might do something else to do on a Saturday' is awkwardly worded. The repeated sentence opener of 'some . . .' suggests that he has partially understood the technique required for marshalling an argument but because of this repetition the impact is reduced. He does make the case for family time, free time, leisure time, shopping and time for sleeping, but what is lacking here is variety in his sentence openers (textual markers) which move the argument on coherently from one point to another. Towards the end, spoken language intrudes on the written form – 'Sometimes me and others need a sleep in' – shifting the piece from its formal tenor to something more informal. Sustaining the voice of a piece of persuasive writing is difficult when children first meet this genre.

Transcription

The writer has shown a readiness to spell some polysyllabic words correctly – 'activities', 'parents' and 'because'. However, some interesting patterns emerge when we look at his spelling more closely. He has not yet fully understood the use of prefixes ('diss agree', 'allso', 'all ready') and there is some lack of clarity about compound words ('some times', 'some thing'). He is inconsistent in his capitalisation of 'Saturday'. His punctuation is accurate and it is pleasing to see such well-formed cursive handwriting.

Next steps

The writer has understood the purpose of the persuasive genre and, in his pre-planning and research, he has listed many points. He now needs some support in shaping these persuasively. Re-reading the text with a response partner would be beneficial to Max as by listening carefully for repetition, words and phrases could be highlighted and then the piece revised. The writer spells the word 'activities' correctly; he could thus be asked to reflect on pluralising words that end in 'y' into 'ies'. He could then be asked to spell 'familys' and other similar words correctly.

QUIDDITCH

Context

The class was asked to write a descriptive passage based on their current reading. They were told to choose a favourite event in the book and to provide an elaborated snapshot of the main character's feelings.

Composition

This child clearly knows *Harry Potter* very well and he is working within the comfort zone of those books that he enjoys. His description shows that he understands Harry's

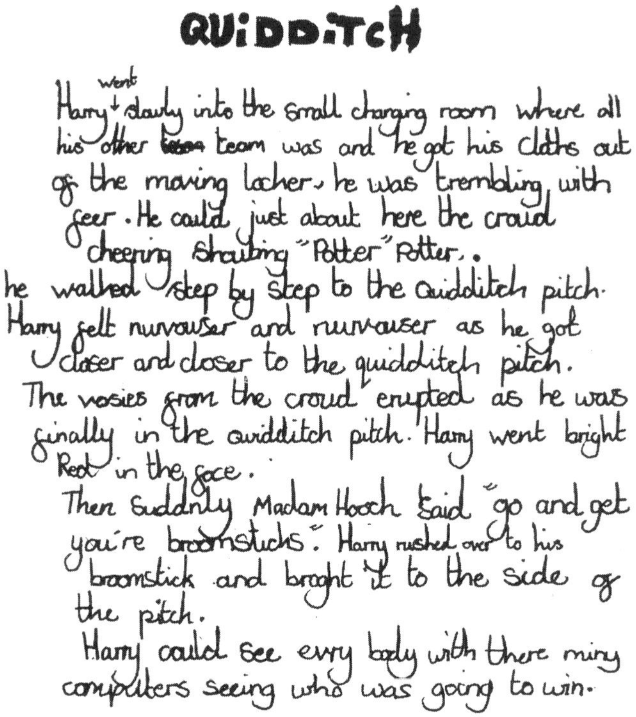

QUIDDITCH

Harry ⁺went slowly into the small changing room where all
his other ~~team~~ team was and he got his cloths out
of the moving locher, he was trembling with
feer. He could just about here the croud
cheering shouting "Potter" Potter..
he walked step by step to the quidditch pitch.
Harry felt nurvouser and nurvouser as he got
closer and closer to the quidditch pitch.
The nosies from the croud erupted as he was
finally in the quidditch pitch. Harry went bright
Red in the face.
Then suddnly Madam Hooch said "go and get
you're broomsticks." Harry rushed over to his
broomstick and broght it to the side of
the pitch.
Harry could see evvry body with there miny
computers seeing who was going to win.

Figure 4.10 Boy Y (Year 4)

feelings about going out to play Quidditch with all the responsibility that is resting on his shoulders. Tension is built up through providing minute details about Harry's pre-game preparations and the deliberate pace at which he operates. We are told that he was 'trembling with fear' whilst he could hear his name being chanted by the crowd outside. To reinforce this, the writer repeats particular words: 'step by step', 'nurvouser and nurvouser' and 'closer and closer'. This literary technique of the deliberate use of repetition is a sophisticated means of helping the reader empathise with Harry. However, he has overused this device with the words 'the Quidditch pitch'. The intensity of Harry's feelings is physically conveyed as we are told that 'Harry went bright red in the face' as he entered the Quidditch pitch and 'the crowd erupted'. The pace abruptly changes with the use of the words, 'Then suddenly' and, 'Harry rushed over to his broomstick'. The juxtaposition of the slow motion in the changing room, compared to the action on the pitch, is very sophisticated in its effect on the reader's response. In the final sentence we reflect again on Harry and share in his isolation and the pressure of having to live up to others' expectations.

The writer uses a range of sentence types appropriately. He also uses simple sentences to make points succinctly, which develop tension and pace. The one example of direct speech is used as a dramatic turning point in his writing.

Transcription

This piece has been clearly written in cursive handwriting although there are some issues about the alignment of the text along the left-hand margin. He can spell some polysyllabic words successfully: 'trembling', 'locker', 'erupted' and 'pitch'. However, it is interesting to consider his errors. In some cases he is not marking the vowel in the unstressed syllable of words, as in 'suddnly' and 'evry body'. In the words 'nurvouser' and 'vosies' we can see the logic behind his attempts. Lastly, he has problems with homophones: 'there', 'hear' and 'you're'. When punctuating, the child makes confident use of capitals and full stops. In the main, he can use speech marks and apostrophes successfully. However, he has made the very common comma splice error in line 3.

Next steps

There is so much potential in this short narrative that, at the end, the reader is left wanting to know more. In the future, the child could be encouraged to develop his authorial voice and thus write more sustained narratives. This could involve pre-composition activities such as drama, story mapping, visualising scenes and discussion.

In terms of transcription, the child will be helped by collecting different homophones. He may be helped with his spelling by chunking polysyllabic words and then ensuring that each syllable has a vowel (e.g. 'sudd-en-ly'). Tackling the comma splice error is more challenging as it involves understanding that when sentences are made up of main clauses, they have to be separated by conjunctions. Otherwise one needs to begin again with a new sentence. Talking about different sentence types and looking at examples in reading will help.

ESCAPE FROM ETHIOPIA

I am Daniel Muluneh's sister. I am two years older than Daniel and I remember what happened to us, so I am going to tell you.

My mummy and uncle decided to go to England because in Ethiopia there was a war. That is why I came to England, but I did not know where I was going.

We were trying to hide from the soldiers. First we walked. Then we saw Moslims with camels and they lent us their camels and they came with us. We travelled to a desert and there were mountains. One of them had a big hole, a cave and we slept there till morning. We stayed there for two days or three days and a girl came and she saw us. We had to pay money to the soldiers so that they would not take my uncle to be a soldier. We went to a different country and we met a lady in a village and she gave us some tea. The Moslims were still with us because they wanted to take their camel back.

A friend of my Dad came to meet us. We had our passports and I was happy that we were going. I thought we were going back to Ethiopia, but we were going to England. The reason I didn't want to go to England is that I didn't want to leave my Grandmother and my aunty and my family.

I couldn't speak English when we came. We spoke Tegrina. I found life hard in England. A lady here could speak Tegrina and English and she helped explain things to my dad. My Dad was already in England when we came. He can also speak Italian. There are Italians in Asmara. In the World War the Italians fought my country and ruled it.

When I came to Kentish Park School, I started to go to the language centre to learn English. Now you can see I can speak English quite well, but it would take me a very long time to write this whole story, so I wrote some of it and I told some of it to my teacher.

Figure 4.11 Selam (Year 5, EAL)

Context

Selam came from a family seeking asylum and had been in England for a year. Although her spoken English had been developing she needed help in writing her story. Her teacher decided to act as scribe for her.

Composition

This autobiographical piece of writing takes its power from the dramatic events that this writer has recently endured. It has a clear sense of audience: 'I remember what happened to us, so I am going to tell you'. This establishes an expectation in the reader that we are going to be trusted with some confidential and very sensitive information. Selam is writing a recount which explains why she and her family left Ethiopia. Her uncertainty about their destination helps the reader empathise with the scale of her predicament. The dramatic third paragraph gets to the heart of her ordeal. Through its tight chronology, she takes us on her perilous journey through war-torn terrain. In a few short sentences we learn about the people that she meets, the terrors and threats, the hardship and the kindness of strangers. In the midst of all this turmoil, note the detail about the camel and the way that this is tidied up at the end of the paragraph. In the fourth paragraph, when she is safe, her bewilderment and internal conflict are brought to the fore. As a child who has little understanding of the political situation, this brings into sharp relief her desire for a return to normality and the ordered world that she has known in the past. In the fifth paragraph, she tells us about the fresh challenges which she faced in relation to learning a new language. The bald statement, 'I found life hard in England' sums up the situation in no uncertain terms. In the final paragraph she declares how empowered she feels as the author of the piece.

Looking at the piece in its entirety, it has a clear chronology and provides the reader with all the relevant details. The pared-back style (short, simple sentences and much use of the conjunction 'and') probably reflects the child's current development in English. There is also evidence of her using compound and complex sentences.

The role of the adult

As this was a dictated autobiographical account, we can learn nothing about the writer's own transcription skills. There is no evidence of interference from her mother tongue in this piece and the adult has been faithful in recording the content as intended by the child.

Next steps

We need to remember that Selam's schooling may have been interrupted as a result of her plight but that her abilities to read and write in her mother tongue may be well in advance of her English skills. Dictating this story was obviously highly successful for this child in terms of developing self-confidence and in developing an end-product which she can share with others. Most importantly, it sustains her as an author whilst her transcription skills in English continue to develop. As readers, we may be curious about the opening of the piece and questioning might encourage her to elaborate on why she has chosen to identify herself as Daniel Muluneh's sister (especially as he does not feature in the recount).

Using the computer to transcribe her writing for her will give her the freedom to add and develop, for example, vocabulary and sentence structure. Nowadays, there are also many voice-activated ICT packages which provide much more support for our EAL learners.

THE MONK AND THE FISH

Context

This is a piece of writing from a Year 5 boy in a rural town in south-west England. The class had been watching *The Monk and the Fish*, a short, animated film which only has music to accompany the images. After watching the film, the class was asked to write their own version of the story and change the ending. The child's version took the form of a multimodal narrative storyboard that was retyped for this publication, retaining the transcription errors.

Composition

In order to alter the original happy ending, the child has created a shoal of fish with 'razor sharp teeth' who effectively finish the monk off. Although the accompanying images (whose style is influenced by the film) are spare, showing only such action and emotion as are strictly necessary, they nevertheless are dynamic and add considerably to the impact of the narrative.

The story has a clear narrative structure, focusing on the monk and his exploits. Because the child has been told to write an alternative ending, he needs a denouement. This is provided as we learn that the monk has decided to fish 'in the dense of night', and the ending unfolds from here. Note the telling facial expressions of the monk as his fortunes falter. Note, too, the detail provided by the moon and the sun: the chase has gone on for so long that the sun has come up in the fourth picture and is shining brightly as the monk meets his terrible end. The last picture shows the skeleton, all that is left of the monk. The writer has concluded the story very cleverly and with a sense of irony; that instead of the monk eating a fish, he has been eaten by a shoal of fish himself.

Meaning in a story such as this is enhanced by careful choice of vocabulary. This young writer uses such verbs as 'grabbed', 'exhausted', 'drenched', 'tear', 'screamed' and 'sped'; figures of speech such as 'in the dense of night', 'fishes flesh', 'speedy sardines', 'felt like ice'; even his single-word expressions such as 'Splash!' and 'Help!' aid the drama of the piece.

Transcription

The writer has not been afraid to use words that he cannot spell. He has made two attempts at 'hook' – 'hock' and 'hok'. Although he managed to spell 'dropped' correctly he did not double the consonant in 'grabbed' ('grabed'). He used 'hole' instead of 'whole', thus confusing these homophones. 'Sardine' ('sardean'), 'aqueduct' ('aquaduct') and 'stomaches' are also incorrect. However, these are difficult words to remember, especially if they are not used regularly.

In relation to punctuation, the possessive apostrophe in 'fishes stomaches' is omitted, but in fairness to the writer, this is a difficult apostrophe to deal with as the word is

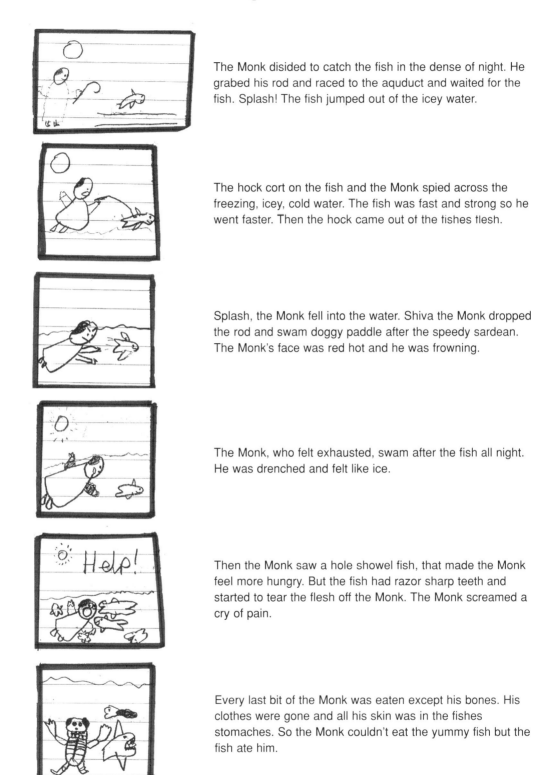

The Monk disided to catch the fish in the dense of night. He grabed his rod and raced to the aquduct and waited for the fish. Splash! The fish jumped out of the icey water.

The hock cort on the fish and the Monk spied across the freezing, icey, cold water. The fish was fast and strong so he went faster. Then the hock came out of the fishes flesh.

Splash, the Monk fell into the water. Shiva the Monk dropped the rod and swam doggy paddle after the speedy sardean. The Monk's face was red hot and he was frowning.

The Monk, who felt exhausted, swam after the fish all night. He was drenched and felt like ice.

Then the Monk saw a hole showel fish, that made the Monk feel more hungry. But the fish had razor sharp teeth and started to tear the flesh off the Monk. The Monk screamed a cry of pain.

Every last bit of the Monk was eaten except his bones. His clothes were gone and all his skin was in the fishes stomaches. So the Monk couldn't eat the yummy fish but the fish ate him.

Figure 4.12 Child Z (Year 5)

plural. However, he does use the apostrophe correctly in the third box when he describes the 'monk's face'. He also manages a contraction successfully in 'couldn't' and he uses commas correctly to demarcate a list of adjectives: 'freezing, icy, cold'.

The story was originally handwritten and there are some issues with the child's handwriting. At times the words do not sit directly on the line as can be seen below:

He also has problems with the formation of some of his letters. In relation to the words 'waited' and 'frowning', the 'w' has merged with the next letters making it difficult to read. Also in the word 'hungry', seen below, the letter 'h' looks like an 'n' because the ascender is not formed correctly.

Next steps

The use of an animated film and multimodal writing has obviously inspired this young writer to produce a most engaging story. It would be beneficial to continue with this type of work with him. Moving on to using computer software for storyboard writing would extend the writer and might encourage his creativity even further. He does need, however, to develop techniques in order to spell more consistently. Identifying specific words from his writing for him to commit to memory would be one approach to take as well as learning specific homophones, the plurals of certain words and the doubling up of consonants when verbs are in the past tense. He also needs to make his handwriting clearer and it would be beneficial to work on specific aspects of his letter formation as identified above.

THE WRITING FUTURE

To conclude the writing journey, here is a piece of writing that was inspired by a great work of art: Paul Cezanne's *Le Lac d'Annecy* (1986). The writer is a Year 6 boy who was identified by his teacher as gifted and talented, and because of this he worked in a group with a specialist teacher.

Before writing, the teacher and group looked closely at the picture and talked about their first impressions. Then the children started to plan and this child's plan included an introduction, moving into the picture, the plot and the ending. Following this, he drafted his story, which was read and commented on by the teacher: 'I must congratulate you, Michael on your outstanding achievement – you are a real author, aren't you? I wonder what Cezanne would have made of this?'

The version that you see here was typed up by the child for publication. To get the best out of this piece, we recommend that you read it aloud, ideally with the picture in front of you (www.courtauldimages.com).

Cezanne – Le Lac d'Annecy

There is a strange building hidden by a row of bushes, its reflection shimmering in the murky river. A dark brown tree hides in the shadows of the branches and the mountains in the darkness seem to block out the light of the evening sky.

I open the door of the bedroom and stare at the picture on the dusty wall on the old house. I gasp as the branches of the tree in the picture start to wave. I see an image coming towards me, then feel myself floating towards the picture. I start to choke and splutter as if I could taste the paint, my body falls forever then finally hits the ground and everything goes black.

I open my eyes, my hand immediately hovers over my head and I wince as my hand hits the large bump on my forehead. A young man is weaving something out of stripped bamboo sticks. He seems to be about twenty years old and has short brown hair. My eyes wander to the large scar on his forehead. He has dirty jeans, ragged from continuous wear, his shirt seems not so ragged but just as dirty. My eyes look above and I gasp as I see the tree from the picture, my eyes study the scenery, all of it seems to come from the old watercolour.

I snap out of my trance as my hand is grabbed and I am pulled to my feet, for the first time the man looks me in the eye. I lean on his shoulder as we walk along the river bank. I cry out as his big body trips on a root. His body plunges into the water with a splash, I am saved by that same root that sent him into the river. My trousers are caught and I clamber up to safety, I lay on the ground for a few seconds until the thought of the man makes me sit bolt upright. I breathe a sigh of relief as I see him up on his feet looking rather shocked. I decide to try and make conversation,

'Are you okay?' I ask, the man just grunts in reply. We walk along until we come to a boat. The journey across the river is uneventful until we are nearly across and I see the house from the picture.

'That house is….' I start.

'Yes,' replies the man 'I came through the picture too,'

'Oh,' I say not sure of what else to say. We get to the bank and I climb out.

'Here,' he says tossing me an apple.

'What's your name?' I ask,

'Peter' he replies. I wait for him to ask what mine is, he doesn't ask so I say,

'I'm Michael.' He doesn't reply to that either, I am really annoyed now. He takes me in and shows me a room, I go in and slump down on the bed, he shuts the door. I am so frustrated I hurl the apple across the room, it breaks into a hundred pieces that scatter across the dull room. At least I have a bed, I think.

I lie down and realise it isn't a bed but a bench. I try to get comfortable and finally doze off.

The next day I am woken by noise from outside my door, I expect to see sunlight flooding in from the small window, but instead there is nothing by darkness.

'Strange' I mutter. The young man walks in and I gasp as I see him, he is the same man but about ten years older.

'Come,' he says, 'I need to show you something.' He takes me to a safe, I try to see the combination but fail miserably. He hands me a picture which makes me feel sick. It is Peter, young then older and older. He hands me another, it is a picture of a funeral with my family there.

'They think I'm dead!' I say in shock, he slowly nods his head.

'Uhggg' I let out a groan as I vomit. I don't have breakfast and decide to stay in bed. I have a cup of water on my bedside table. As I lean forward to get it the bench starts to tilt, I jump back violently sending the water to the floor, I am shocked as I see the water disappear into many swirling colours on the floor. I find myself being sucked into the pool and cry out.

'HELP!!...Peter, ' the now middle aged man comes running in and throws a sheet over the hole.

'Look out for that,' he says. I smile nervously.

The rest of the week is fairly uneventful, the only thing that happens is the man gets older.

'Help' he says, he is so old I am scared of him. I can't take it any more I sprint out, running along the bank I spot a bush I dive into it quickly. I watch in horror as a frail man starts to walk towards me.

'Help' he croaks, I close my eyes but hear an ear-piercing scream and a thump as his thin body hits the ground. I ask myself 'Did the river do this to him?' I open my eyes and feel sick as I see a limp lifeless skeleton crumble into dust. I walk along the river bank, trip, hit my head and everything goes black.

I find myself in my real bed in my real house, I look down and gasp as I see my water-covered hand grow crinkles by the second....

Figure 4.13 Boy (Year 6)

When presented with a skilful piece of writing such as this, it is tempting to respond with congratulation such as his teacher offered, and the writer would certainly be encouraged by her comments. However, our role as teachers is always to seek out ways of moving writers on. Traditionally, teachers point out errors but it is more helpful to point out strengths, as then the writer is inclined to build on them. 'What are the strengths of this piece of writing?' is a question we should ask of all children's writing. If, on reading the piece (and reading aloud reveals much), you then reflect on the impact it has made on you, you are in a position to work out how the writing has achieved its effects.

In this piece you may want to comment on how subtly the writer reveals that the story is about the projected span of the narrator's own life and the possible manner of his death. The bump on his head is echoed in the scar on Michael's head. The photograph of his family at his funeral hints at his eventual demise. The supernatural details, especially perhaps the swirling, multi-coloured pool which threatens to engulf the narrator, hint at a watery end. This young writer overstates nothing but offers us a sophisticated reading of events thus creating a sci-fi or horror story of a classic 'doppelgänger' nature. To this end, his use of short sentences and of the present tense is wonderfully effective.

It would certainly be worth talking with this writer about those stories, such as Lewis Carroll's *Through the Looking Glass* or C.S. Lewis' *The Lion, the Witch and the Wardrobe*, where a character moves through an object into another world. He will probably be able to tell you about Terry Pratchett's novels where the characters enter and exit from the world created on screen. The children's picture-book, *The Picture* (Catherine Brighton) should fascinate him as the girl journeys into and returns through a picture on the wall, just as the narrator does in his story. Whether or not he is ready to read Oscar Wilde's novel, *The Picture of Dorian Gray*, he would certainly find that the story of the ageing portrait in the attic chimes with his own interest in contemplating change and decay in his other self.

It is worth asking a writer such as this to identify any aspect of the story that he may wish to improve. He may want to revisit the opening paragraph and clarify where his character is at this point. Most stories of this type begin and end in the same place; in which case the picture might need to be on the boy's bedroom wall. He may also decide to do some re-jigging in terms of chronology; it might be more effective for the photograph to be shown at the end as the old man starts to crumble to dust. If the writer reads it aloud, he will pick up repetition of 'gasp', which he may want to replace with substitutes as he shows he can do with 'say in shock' and 'let out a groan'. He may also decide that he could change the anti-climactic 'The rest of the week is fairly uneventful; the only thing that happens is the man gets older', to something more like, 'As the days pass, the man grows, steadily and horrifyingly, older and older'. None of these points is critical or negative; a writer as talented as this should appreciate the evidence that you have read carefully and responded fully to his piece. It is what a professional writer would expect of his editor or publisher.

On that note, we end this journey. All the pieces of writing we have used in this chapter have been a pleasure to read. *When I Was Naughty* and *The Monk and the Fish* have an immediate appeal in the way that they entertain us as readers through the skilful interplay of text and pictures. But all the pieces have intrigued us, some have puzzled us and one or two have opened the door into the child's personal world. We have seen the very earliest attempts that children make in the form of mark-making and we emphasise that, even here, children are communicating. We have looked at conventional writing, text dictated to a scribe, as well as drawings and diagrams. Through analysing this range of writing we have had the opportunity to acknowledge some of the styles, forms and genres that children are beginning to master. On the journey we have been able to appreciate various challenges (both compositional and transcriptional) that our writers have faced, as well as acknowledging the different influences on the children. Clearly identified audiences and purposes for writing, which make such difference to the writing task, have been stressed throughout. We have shown how all writing reveals strengths and weaknesses and we have kept our eye on those pointers that help children make progress. We have drawn on our experience as teachers to provide suggestions as to where we might go next with these children. However, we are sure that you will think of many more in relation to supporting their future writing development.

Further reading

Armstrong, M. (1991) 'Another way of looking'. *Language Matters*, 1, 23–8.
Armstrong, M. (2006) *Children Writing Stories*. London: Open University Press.
Grainger, T., Goouch, K. and Lambirth, A. (2005) *Creativity and Writing*, London: Routledge.
Matthews, J. (2003) *Drawing and Painting: Children and Visual Representation*. London: Paul Chapman Publishing.

Chapter 5

Routines and Resources

Anne Washtell

'Miss, you hold my hand and show me how to write.'

(Katrina, 5 yrs)

INTRODUCTION

These words, spoken in frustration by an inexperienced young writer, indicate the crucial and central role of the teacher in enabling children to succeed as they begin to take control of writing. In order to provide effective intervention and support, teachers must establish a set of regular, well-understood, purposeful classroom writing routines which will permit the understanding of all elements of the writing process to develop.

In this chapter, we look at a selection of commonly used writing routines, some or all of which you are likely to find in use in your classroom. As each writing routine is discussed, it will be linked, where appropriate, to the *National Curriculum (NC)* (DfEE, 1999a) the Primary National Strategy *Primary Framework for literacy and mathematics (PNS)* (DfES, 2006a) and The Early Years Foundation Stage (EYFS) (DCSF, 2008a).

What are writing routines and why do we need them? Writing routines offer regular opportunities for children to develop the strategies and skills that underpin the writing process. We need to provide these opportunities and we need to utilise them regularly so that no important element of writing is neglected and so that each child's needs are met. Key routines that we discuss in this chapter include shared and guided writing, drafting and writing partnerships.

Some writing routines may function at the level of regular practice with an emphasis placed on the learner, while others – for example, shared and guided writing – are used by the teacher to make aspects of the process explicit to the children prior to independent activity. We need, therefore, to provide children with a well-balanced range of writing routines in order that they do not become over-reliant on a narrow field of strategies and skills at the expense of others. Limited provision of routines by the teacher could lead to serious weaknesses and, ultimately, difficulties in the children's development and growing independence as writers. Therefore, building a selection of writing routines into medium and short-term planning is essential. If we do not think carefully about writing routines at the point of planning, we cannot guarantee balance and variety in terms of the strategies and skills that we want to encourage children to use.

PLANNING FOR WRITING ROUTINES

The Early Years Foundation Stage (EYFS)

Young children learn actively. Through their talk and their play, they manipulate, they experiment, they hypothesise and they practise. Sound planning for this age range recognises this and, as one would expect, the Early Years Foundation Stage document (DCSF, 2008a) offers a planning framework underpinned by clear principles about early years education. The EYFS principles are grouped into four distinct themes: a unique child; positive relationships; enabling environments; and learning and development. When considering the suitability of using writing routines with this age group it will be important to reflect upon their value in relation to these themes. The 'Communication, language and literacy' area of learning and development in the EYFS is comprised of strongly interdependent strands. So, when working with the writing strand, provision will be firmly embedded within children's play as well as making clear linkage with their language for communication (speaking and listening), language for thinking, reading, and growing awareness and knowledge of sounds and letters. The layout of the non-statutory guidance document (Practice Guidance for the Early Years EYFS) is very accessible when linking planning for writing with the other five areas of learning and development.

Key Stage 1 and Key Stage 2

Since the introduction of the Literacy Hour in the *NLS* (DfEE, 1998), concerns were voiced by practitioners about its structural rigidity as well as the effects of 'bite-size' planning on teaching and learning. Over the years, practice has moved on and this is reflected in the *PNS* documentation which acknowledges that 'undue rigidity' can act as a 'constraint' both organisationally and in terms of fostering children's learning. The emphasis now is firmly on flexibility when planning, organising and delivering literacy sessions. The framework provides increased guidance on planning for progression through longer sequences of lessons (DfES, 2006a: 8) in order to meet children's needs more effectively. The framework in its electronic form provides plenty of planning material (long- and medium-term) in blocks (which subdivide into units) ranging between two and five weeks' duration. Teachers can utilise these as well as online resources to develop appropriate teaching sequences for their children. Judgments about the time to be spent in any one phase are down to the effective use of Assessment for Learning (see Chapter 8) and the security of the children's learning within the phase.

The role of writing routines

The key teaching routines of shared, guided and independent writing that were core teaching strategies in the *NLS* continue to play an important part in the effective teaching of writing. However, as has already been indicated, the rigidity of the original Literacy Hour structure has been superseded in the *PNS* by more flexible ways of working and this has had an impact on the way that teachers now plan for and embed these routines in their teaching.

The teaching sequence for writing: PNS phases of planning

In the *PNS* planning framework, each unit of work is underpinned by 'phases'. These phases are described diagrammatically below in the form of overlapping circles

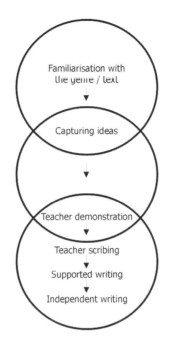

Figure 5.1 The teaching sequence for writing: *PNS* phases of planning (DCSF, 2007b)

(Crown copyright material is reproduced with the permission of the Controller of HMSO and the Queen's Printer for Scotland)

The model initially builds, via prior assessment on what the children already know and their current learning needs. As the teacher plans the teaching sequence she decides on appropriate learning objectives and success criteria for the class in relation to the writing that will be produced. The phases are characterised by regular ongoing assessment and evaluations of pupils' progress which may lead to adjustment of the planning in order to meet the learning needs of the children.

During the first phase – 'familiarisation with text type' – the children encounter the text to be studied through a wide range of experiences, many of which are embedded in speaking and listening or talk activities. For example, if working with a narrative text, the teacher might utilise techniques such as whole-class discussion, paired retellings, drama strategies and story mapping to explore and open up aspects of the text. Shared reading may also help the children begin to attune themselves to the structural and linguistic features of the text. In other words, the children are having the text opened up for them in such a way that they are reading as if they were the writer of the given text.

With the class, the teacher then moves on to 'capturing ideas' (but note that this phase overlaps with the previous one and also with the one that follows). Working in this phase could be described as 'pre-composition' which is the point in the writing process where the teacher deepens the children's knowledge of the text type. Staying with the narrative example, this might be done through role play, to develop empathy with characters, or using multimedia or visual texts as another route into the text or as starting points for the children's own writing. It could be said that the children are using 'talk for writing' (DCSF, 2007b) to help them as they take the linguistic features, nuances and structures of the written text into their own language repertoire. The teacher gathers the children's thoughts, filters them, shapes and clarifies them. This can be achieved in a variety of ways: through discussion, drama and perhaps drawing, as well as through the use of planning models (for example maps, diagrams or flow charts) to be used as points of reference later on. Shared writing (teacher demonstration – see below) may be used by the teacher at this point so that she can look at examples of the text type with the children and draw attention to key features that they may need to consider when they write independently. She might model a short stretch of text for the children accompanied by speaking aloud her thought processes and decision-making to help make specific aspects of the process of composition explicit. Teacher scribing and supported writing (see below) will precede independent attempts by the children themselves. Working within these phases, attention can be given to the different aspects of composition and transcription as well as revising, editing and presentation.

As the planning model clearly demonstrates, in order to try to meet every child's needs, a balance should be achieved between writing which is 'modelled' (where the teacher takes responsibility through, for example, demonstration) and independent writing (where the child takes responsibility for his/her writing). Learning to write is a journey from dependence to independence and the phased model clearly acknowledges this in its underlying structure. By using a range of teaching strategies at whole-class, guided group, and independent levels, we should be able to provide tailored support for children as they develop as writers.

TALK FOR WRITING

As has been indicated in the above discussion, it is important also to bear in mind the key role of talk as a vital tool in enhancing and supporting children's thinking and understanding in all stages of the writing process as well as in the successful creation of their own independent pieces of writing. The four strands of speaking, listening and responding, group discussion and interaction, and drama are core to the *PNS* and are integral to the teaching and learning of writing in any area of the curriculum.

It might be helpful at this point to consider the role of talk in moving learning forward. Douglas Barnes reminds us about the complexity of learning and the importance of acknowledging to ourselves that learning is not simply about adding new knowledge to that which already exists. He takes a 'constructivist' position, arguing that 'each of us can only learn by making sense of what happens to us, through actively constructing a world for ourselves' (1992: 123). He goes further by stating:

> Most of our important learning, in school or out, is a matter of constructing models of the world, finding how far they work by using them, and then reshaping them in the light of what happens.

> (1992: 124)

For this to happen, the teacher needs to help the child to work actively with and reflect upon his/her own prior understanding as new knowledge is encountered and experienced. Through testing out fresh ideas through a range of experiences, the child is able to adjust or reshape his/her mental 'model of the world'. To borrow Barnes' phrase, this is about the learner 'working on understanding' in order to reorganise past knowledge 'in the light of new ways of seeing things' (1992: 125). Planning for talk for writing needs to take account of this view of the child as a learner. Planning in a range of questions, or setting up talk activities, such as hot seating or conscience alley, will certainly ensure that talk takes place but will not in itself do the whole job for us. It is the type of talk and the social nature of the learning that is going on within these planned experiences that are the crucial elements in helping children clarify and develop their thinking. Barnes explains that 'exploratory' talk is particularly powerful in '[providing] an important means of working on understanding' (1992: 126). By engaging in this kind of talk children can work collaboratively on a problem and adjust their thinking. Through exploratory talk, they can bounce ideas off others, speak their ideas for writing aloud and listen to the effect of their words on the potential reader. Exploratory talk is very much about 'work in progress' rather than the polished variety of talk which Barnes terms 'presentational'.

'Social constructivism', influenced by the work of Vygotsky, amongst others, emphasises that talking is of its essence social and that we learn best through interaction and collaboration. By providing children with opportunities to use 'exploratory' talk and by engaging in 'dialogic' interactions with children, teachers can help children to challenge, extend and deepen their knowledge about how writing works. Alexander sees talk for learning as a reciprocal process where ideas are batted to and fro between the children themselves, as well as the teacher, as a powerful means of advancing learning. He puts it like this:

> So it is the qualities of extension and cumulation which transform classroom talk from the familiar closed question/answer/feedback routine into purposeful and productive dialogue where questions, answers and feedback progressively build into coherent and expanding chains of enquiry and understanding.
>
> (2008: 26)

The kind of dialogue described here requires time if it is to be of value. The long overdue inclusion of the speaking and listening strands in the *PNS* signals that talk must be at the heart of all learning for children and, as we shall see, talk is embedded within many of the writing routines discussed below. So talk in itself is not enough. It is the way in which talk is generated and sustained, through what Wells (1999) describes as 'dialogic inquiry', which makes the difference.

SHARED WRITING

The term 'shared writing' was coined in the mid-1980s. It was used by teachers and staff attending courses in London at the Centre for Literacy in Primary Education (CLPE). Shared writing was the natural development from another literacy routine known as 'shared reading'. Shared reading's roots can be traced to New Zealand and the work of Don Holdaway (1979) whose ideas were based on what he described as 'the bed-time story cycle', where certain characteristic routines (including returning to familiar texts and engaging in highly interactive dialogue) regularly took place between parents and children as they shared books. He felt that this experience was so enriching for children that it could be replicated in the classroom by means of enlarged texts. Through the use of big books, A1-size posters and, increasingly, the interactive whiteboard, the whole class or groups of children can learn collaboratively about any aspect of the reading or writing process that the teacher chooses to focus on. The teacher takes the lead and 'scaffolds' (to borrow Jerome Bruner's term) the children's learning by modelling skills and strategies that she wishes the children to experience and learn for later independent use. Through explicit and highly interactive teaching the children are introduced to new areas of learning but they also revisit and consolidate previous experiences. Most importantly, through the collaborative nature of shared reading and writing, the teacher can set high expectations by placing the children in what Vygotsky calls 'the zone of proximal development' (see Chapter 1). In so doing, the children are led towards new areas of knowledge and skills which they would not have found independently.

Shared writing can be undertaken with any age range and, importantly, with the whole class; it can be used for short tasks or more extended pieces of work. The teacher acts as scribe (taking the transcriptional strain) thus freeing the children up to participate in the creation of the text and to learn about the writing process, at the point of writing, from an experienced writer. This practice was a key feature of Graves' process approach (see Chapter 2) and it is something that the *NLS* endorsed as it shows how writers make choices and decisions 'at the point of writing rather than by correction' (DfEE, 2001: 13). In order for this to be effective, the teacher needs to be clear about her teaching objective(s) and prior assessment of the children as well as making sure that she provides a spoken, explanatory commentary as she writes. By using 'writerly' language and involving the class, the teacher can rehearse sentences orally, re-read text and make revisions as well as invite the children to identify errors that require correction.

The importance of spoken language and high-quality interactions cannot be underestimated when working with this writing routine. When we engage in shared writing we need to balance our own explicit, direct teaching about the writing process with asking the children searching questions that relate to our teaching objective(s) and which encourage good quality, focused teacher–child interactions. By listening to children's responses we can attune ourselves to their current conceptual understanding or misconceptions about the text type or aspects of the writing process and differentiate further questions accordingly. For example, in response to the question, 'Where should I start writing this text?', a child might point to the bottom of the piece of paper. Noting the child's misconception, the teacher might then ask the same child a more closed question such as, 'Can you point to the top of the page and show me where to start writing?'. We can also encourage the children to take on specific, previously introduced technical terminology, such as 'verb', 'paragraph' or 'speech marks'. We can develop children's use of metalanguage (a language with which to talk about language) by framing questions in such a way that they are required to try to use the terminology in their answers and explanations.

By talking about writing, we can help young writers make the move from dependence to independence as they begin to learn how to make explicit their implicit knowledge about how written language works. These collaborative opportunities to reflect on the writing process will be especially supportive to those children who have learning difficulties, those for whom English is an additional language and, indeed, for very able pupils as well. Children will be listening to their teacher and peers, absorbing knowledge and, understandably, it may take time before all children feel confident enough to share their ideas with the whole class.

In their publications *Grammar for Writing* (*GFW*) (DfEE, 2000a) and *Developing Early Writing* (*DEW*) (DfEE, 2001) the *NLS* identified three different teaching strategies within shared writing for teachers to work with in order to make this routine more versatile and fit for purpose within a teaching sequence. The three strategies are: teacher demonstration; teacher scribing; and supported composition. Although there is a clear rationale underpinning them, moving from dependence (teacher demonstration) through to increasing independence (supported composition), it would certainly not be necessary to use all of the three types at any one time or in a rigid sequence.

Teacher demonstration is, as its name suggests, teacher led. As she scribes in front of the whole class, the teacher (as expert) models how to write a text and will speak her thought processes aloud so that the children can hear exactly how she goes about composing a stretch of written text. While thinking aloud, the teacher will maintain a clear focus on the stated objectives for the session and in so doing make aspects of the writing process explicit for the children. In other words, the children are able to see for themselves how writers make choices as they go about the business of creating and shaping a text. For example, in a session focusing on conventions of direct speech in story writing, the teacher says, 'I must start a new line here because I've got a new person speaking'. Contributions from the children are not sought at this stage but the expectation is that they should be active listeners whose questions, comments and opinions will be sought later on.

Teacher scribing enables children to make contributions that build on or refine the teacher's initial demonstration. Using the above example, when the teacher reaches the point in her script when speech on a new line has been sufficiently demonstrated, she will ask the children what it is that she needs to remember as a new character starts to talk. Paired talk could be used here ('Tell the person next to you what you think it is I have to remember to do'). Then, through inviting the children to share their suggestions, the teacher can explore and refine these with the children in order to help her scribe the next piece of text and to clarify their understanding.

Supported composition (supported writing) shifts the focus on to the children's composition and is usually undertaken in pairs. It is a particularly helpful strategy to use for consolidation purposes. Picking up on our earlier example, the teacher may ask the children to write down a short conversation, for instance, between parent and child at the supermarket where the child is demanding sweets. Preceding their actual attempts at writing, the teacher may use paired talk partners to improvise the conversation first. Typically, the pace during this session will be brisk and the children will work individually or, more usually, in pairs, writing in their notebooks or on dry-wipe boards. As soon as the writing is completed the children's examples may be held up so that the teacher can make an on-the-spot assessment. The facility of on-the-spot assessment makes this a powerful tool for the teacher. Some successful examples may be reviewed with the class and misconceptions, via other examples, addressed sensitively. The teacher can then decide whether further practice is needed before the children work independently, and can readjust her planning accordingly. The intention here is that supported composition should form a bridge between shared writing and guided or independent writing. Having said that, this routine also provides a versatile way of quickly reactivating and revising prior knowledge.

The time spent on a shared writing session will vary. The age, experience and needs of the children should be given careful consideration. In a Year 4 class undertaking extended writing, supported composition was used as a strategy at several points in the lesson to help progress the children's learning. In a Reception class, teacher demonstration followed by a brief teacher-scribing session, lasted ten minutes.

The following examples show how these different types of shared writing can be orchestrated in work with younger children. A Reception class took a favourite book with a repetitive, predictable text, *The Monsters' Party* (Story Chest 1980), and rewrote it as *The Nice Monsters' Party*. The pattern of the story was simple: 'What can this nice monster do? He can dance, that's what he can do'. This patterning of the story was first modelled for the children through teacher demonstration. By composing the first sentence of the new version for the class it was possible to move easily into teacher scribing. At this stage they substituted new action words, such as 'leap' for 'dance', and invented a surprise ending for the story which went as follows: 'What can I do? I can jump in the cake like a kangaroo'. The draft was reproduced as a big book, illustrated by the children and re-read many times. The children also reenacted the book in role play. In terms of learning about shaping a text, the activity provided a model of a simple narrative structure. At the level of the sentence, it drew attention to the idea of questions and how we punctuate them. In addition, by focusing on a specific word class, the children discussed how some of the alternative verbs might be spelt. Some children used their graphic knowledge to draw attention to 'long' words and 'short' words.

Opportunities for providing a real context and purpose for shared writing with young children can readily arise from everyday events. In a Reception class, a child suddenly left the school midway through the term. The children wanted to send her a message in the form of a big poster. Through shared writing the teacher scribed the short and simple message, 'We love you so much Katrina'. Having re-read the message together through shared reading, the children spontaneously began to play at spotting the letters of their names in the text. This proved an exciting and intense activity which lasted for approximately ten minutes with many children participating at increasing levels of complexity. This example serves to remind us that children are as capable as teachers at initiating purposeful learning experiences. In this very young age group, the skill of playing with and manipulating language must be nurtured and encouraged.

As has already been suggested, shared writing is a flexible teaching tool to use with children. It can support any aspect of composition and transcription. In KS2, for example, it can be used to model the linguistic and structural features of more challenging writing genres, such as arguments or reports (see Chapter 6 on writing frames). Shared writing can also be very effective in teaching children skills which we as adults may take for granted. One such skill is that of note-taking. Through the shared reading of an enlarged extract from an information text on the interactive whiteboard, the teacher can demonstrate how to use the skills of skimming and scanning to extract information, listing key words and points. Helpful strategies and techniques can be demonstrated, such as using simple abbreviations which can speed up the note-taking process. For example, when writing notes about the Gunpowder Plot, a teacher used demonstration to show the class how to use the initials of the conspirators rather than writing their names out in full. So, Guy Fawkes became 'G.F.' and Robert Catesby 'R.C.' (A similar example is given in Chapter 7 but this time in the first draft of a child's independent writing.) To read more about teaching note-taking see Chapter 6.

When resourcing shared writing, teachers may prefer to use a whiteboard or work with a flip chart and felt pens. An interactive whiteboard is particularly effective for shared writing as text can be composed, stored, returned to, altered, manipulated and revised on subsequent occasions. The size of the teacher's handwriting is a further consideration, especially if children are seated at some distance. For supported composition the children need access to either easy-to-handle notebooks or dry-wipe boards and pens.

It is important that a proportion of shared writing drafts are reproduced as finished products. The type of product will be determined by the kind of text being produced. For example, a narrative text could be reproduced into a hand-made big book which the children go on to illustrate and re-read. Other texts will become posters, captions, sentences, letters to be posted or word lists to go on the wall. Some material will be word-processed and others turned into multimedia texts.

The following is offered as a checklist for what can be modelled through shared writing:

- A sense of purpose and audience: voice (formal or informal); planning; drafting; revising; proofreading; presentation (publication).
- Content and features of different types of texts: linguistic features; structural features (such as paragraphing); vocabulary choices for specific genres; words, phrases; grammatical features; use of connectives to sequence and structure text.
- Transcription skills: punctuation; spelling; handwriting; editing; proofreading; layout; organisation; presentation.
- Self-help strategies: correcting mistakes; re-reading; discussing; peer conferencing; collaborating; improving; redrafting; using resources.

GUIDED WRITING

Typically, guided writing follows on from shared writing with children being grouped according to ability and need. This routine has had a chequered history. When it was originally introduced as a key teaching routine by the *NLS*, the way in which guided writing was to be used was tightly prescribed (ability groups working with the teacher for set amounts of time each week). The guided group would be the teacher's focus group within the literacy session. Typically, guided writing would follow up, and take further, work undertaken in shared writing sessions.

Originally, this proved to be a challenging teaching routine to manage at several levels. However, as time has passed, teachers have gained ownership of it and there have been significant modifications. The modifications have helped with the rigidity of ability grouping and organisation of time for guided writing sessions as well as promoting sustainable strategies for independence for the rest of the class. In relation to this last point, a common solution has been to designate teaching assistants (TAs) to help support the independent groups or, indeed, to teach another guided group.

Some significant rethinking and adjustments were clearly signalled with the publication of *DEW* and *GFW* which are worth noting at this point. *DEW* dealt very briefly with guided writing and did not see it as a necessity in leading into independent writing. Instead, the document implied that supported composition, the third element of shared writing, is a much stronger conduit to independence. A similar message can be found in *GFW* with shared writing being acknowledged as 'the most significant and influential teaching strategy in the Literacy Hour' (DfEE, 2000a: 17). The document does go on to accept the obvious advantages of working with a group – these may be psychological or social – but states that much of the guidance provided for shared writing is equally applicable to guided writing. Guided writing is seen as providing more independence, 'where the onus is on the children to make decisions, compose and revise their own texts' (p.17). In 2002, Ofsted also expressed reservations that guided sessions were not as efficient as supported composition.

However, in 2007 guided writing was placed firmly back on the agenda with the publication by the *PNS* of *Improving Writing with a Focus on Guided Writing* (DCSF, 2007b). Guided writing is described as 'an essential component of a balanced writing curriculum, providing an additional supported step towards independent writing' (p. 6). The document indicates that the benefits of guided writing are clearly anchored in meeting the needs of the individual, albeit within a small group setting. In keeping with the *PNS* emphasis on flexibility, the grouping of children for guided writing is described in a much more subtle way in that children are grouped on the basis of need. This implies that the grouping of children for guided writing sessions will be driven by the teacher's ongoing assessment for learning (see Chapter 8). Groupings may vary according to individual needs in relation to the different *PNS* strands for writing, rather than children being placed in unchanging ability groups. For example, a child might be placed in a high-achieving group in order to create a first draft of a story but might be regrouped with other children who are at a similar level in terms of managing spelling and punctuation. In this way, the teacher is able to respond much more effectively and specifically to the child's individual needs. During guided writing sessions, children will produce pieces of writing more or less independently. However, the teacher will manage the session by working with current targets set for the group, discussing, analysing and responding to the pieces of writing produced by the children. Emphasis is placed on discussions about writing; such discussions provide the children with immediate feedback on strengths and areas for improvement. The children will be actively involved in the assessment process through self and peer assessment and should emerge from guided sessions clear about 'what next'?

Finally, guided writing can support any stage in the development of a piece of writing. The routine can be used before writing to look back at and build on previous shared sessions. This might be done, for example, by helping children gather their ideas; for oral rehearsal (children with literacy or language difficulties); for the teacher to remodel elements from the shared session and to review objectives and targets. These kinds of activities will help children as they plan and prepare to draft their work. Guided writing 'at the point of writing' (DCSF, 2007b: 13) supports children as they begin to write independently or later as they are revising their work. Activities such as re-reading for coherence; considering alternative vocabulary; reviewing the choice of sentence type; and tense consistency might be considered. Again, the group's targets and the teacher's objectives will pinpoint elements to be addressed in this kind of session. A third option suggested by the *PNS* is to use a guided writing session after writing in order to help children review and assess pieces of work that they have produced independently against success criteria and targets that have been set. It should not be forgotten, though, that at some point the piece of writing should be celebrated in its own right, read aloud, published, perhaps, and enjoyed by the other children in the group.

INDEPENDENT WRITING

To create independent, confident writers is our ultimate goal for all children. Wherever and whenever possible, there should be opportunities and provision made for children to write independently.

In relation to the teaching sequence for writing (see Figure 5.1), independent writing marks the end of the journey from dependence to independence for the child within a planned unit of work. An important point to consider here is that independent writing should be seen as a carefully scaffolded move from a task that has been worked through via shared and guided writing. *DEW* warns that, for the inexperienced writer, independent writing cannot be viewed as a disconnected, separate entity because the odds against success are too heavily stacked against younger and less experienced writers. All the work that will have gone on earlier in the teaching sequence, in order to familiarise the child with the text type, gather ideas, talk, plan and teach through shared and guided writing, is necessary preparation and work in progress for eventual success in independent writing. Independent writing gives children the opportunity to build on this experience by expressing their ideas for themselves as well as applying and consolidating their knowledge of all aspects of the writing process. In this way of working, children need not feel frustrated or defeated by the challenges of moving into independence. Ensuring a secure sense of purpose and audience and establishing engaging contexts for independent writing will add to the child's commitment and enjoyment. Planning for the involvement of response partners to test out ideas and provide ongoing feedback will also be highly supportive.

The adult also plays a crucial role in the success of this routine. It is worth remembering that conferences with children about their writing can be very short and snappy; it can take very little time to clarify minor difficulties or provide timely reminders such as how to manage unfamiliar spellings.

The major cause of difficulty with independent writing occurs when teachers ask pupils to work on tasks which have not been demonstrated or explained clearly enough. Not surprisingly, this can result in children being unsure about what they should be doing and, at worst, failing to engage with the task.

Finally, classroom organisation for independent writing needs to be thought through. Children will need to be briefed so that they can work independently, thus freeing up the teacher who can give her attention to guided writing groups that might be taking place at the same time.

UNAIDED WRITING

Unaided writing is a routine in which children work completely on their own. It involves the child marshalling all of his or her existing knowledge of the writing process in order to produce pieces of writing. In its purest form, as the word implies, the child is expected to write without turning to the teacher for support or referring to resources such as dictionaries. It is this kind of writing that is assessed in the *NC* Assessments for English (SATs).

With the youngest and least experienced writers, unaided writing is sometimes referred to as 'emergent' or 'early' writing. You may also hear this kind of writing described as 'early mark-making' or 'pre-alphabetic'. This can be a puzzling and yet intriguing experience for adults as they watch the boundaries between writing and other representational systems, such as drawing and numbers, apparently overlapping at the point of writing (see Chapters 2 and 4). Confusingly, children's own perceptions of the meaning of what they have written may shift; they may attribute no meaning at all to their writing or, on subsequent 're-readings', they may provide different meanings every time. For a more extended discussion of this, see also the section on 'Responding to unaided writing', later in this chapter.

Research evidence does suggest that from a very early age children are more than able to write (or communicate meaningfully on paper) for real purposes and audiences. Shirley Payton (1994), in a case study of her daughter Cecelia, provides evidence of the child's early attempts at compiling shopping lists and writing letters to friends. James Britton (1982) describes the 'pretend writing' of a young writer explaining how she gradually makes the crucial move from what Vygotsky calls 'drawing objects' to 'drawing speech'. Both Payton and Britton show us that very young children want to communicate meaningfully in their writing and will do so initially using non-alphabetic systems of representation. Figure 5.2 provides an example of a very young Reception child's sandwich list compiled in just the same way as her teacher daily compiles a class dinner list.

The list reads, 'Egg sandwich, cheese sandwich, cheese sandwich, cheese sandwich, salad'. A close look at the three central lines reveals that she has represented the words 'cheese sandwich' in a consistent way. Despite its non-alphabetic appearance, the writing is not random but systematic. Such opportunities for self-generated practice are most important in the EYFS, where children will spontaneously play with the writing system in the way that Marie Clay (1975) describes. Indeed, the EYFS provides a rationale for early writing, stating that it 'is about how children build an understanding of the relationship between the spoken and written word and how through making marks, drawing and personal writing children ascribe meaning to text and attempt to write for various purposes (DCSF, 2008a).

Whatever their age, when children engage in unaided writing, the text that they produce may well appear unconventional in some respect. Whether it be its appearance, layout or spelling, the unaided writing will provide valuable information about the child's current stage of development and understanding of the transcriptional aspects of the writing process. Sometimes, the intended message of the text may be difficult to decipher, particularly when children are in the early stages of development in spelling and handwriting or experiencing significant difficulties. In practice, the

Figure 5.2

teacher will make judgements about interventions and the level of support the child needs in order to succeed but the writing produced will largely be the result of the child's own efforts. The success of unaided writing as a routine rests on the degree of confidence and independence that the young writer has. All children, whatever their age, should have the opportunity and materials to engage in unaided writing and need to be supported in their endeavours.

From the assessment point of view, unaided writing is essential as it is only through the child's own written products that we can gain an accurate understanding of his or her current development and thus measure the effectiveness of our teaching. This point is demonstrated by the two pieces of writing by five-year-old Tommy. The two pieces were written on the same day. Tommy's previous experience had largely come from copying adult models and he had only recently begun to make the move into the unaided writing routine.

The first example (a copied sentence) reveals information about his ability in relation to handwriting and copying skills while the second is written completely unaided and reveals a wider range of information about his understanding of the writing process. The second one reads: 'Danny Farley and I play out'. It is immediately noticeable that Tommy's handwriting seems much less controlled. It is bigger, and the letter formation is a mix of upper and lower case. However, he does show an awareness of directionality, an understanding that words must have spaces between them, an

Figure 5.3

Figure 5.4

appreciation that sentences must end with full stops and a confidence in trying to spell all the words for himself. Both these pieces provide evidence about Tommy's transcription skills but it would be necessary to offer other writing routines, such as dictated writing, to form a better impression of his compositional abilities.

Resourcing unaided writing

Children are not going to be drawn into unaided writing unless they have access to resources. Available space varies in classrooms but some kind of central and accessible collection of resources is always possible. A writing or representation area provides an incentive and might include some or all of the following resources, depending on the age of the children.

- rough paper
- card and paper (various qualities, colours, sizes, shapes)
- loose-leaf folders
- envelopes and headed notepaper
- blank greetings cards, postcards
- blank official forms to fill in (e.g. travel agent, paying-in slips)
- ready-made address books, diaries, birthday books
- material for book covers
- ready-made blank books (variety of qualities)
- book-making material
- boards for book covers, ready-cut blank pages
- clipboards, bulldog clips, paper clips, staplers
- pens, pencils, felt pens, crayons, highlighter pens
- handwriting books, cards, sheets, line guides
- erasers, sharpeners, sellotape, glues, scissors and trimmer
- calligraphy materials, stencils
- brushes, paints

Additional items might include:

- post box
- notice board and messages board
- easel, large sheets of paper, thick felt pens
- board and chalks
- computer with access to a range of suitable packages, e.g. Clicker 5
- ABC books, dictionaries, thesaurus
- The computer (desk top publishing).

Displays might include:

- alphabet frieze; punctuation poster
- 'published' books of children's writing
- examples of different kinds of writing
- suggestions for starting points for writing
- key words
- ideas for drafting
- ideas for finding spellings and lists of current high-usage spellings
- class rules about maintaining the writing area.

A selective trawl of the above list of ideas should provide materials that are suited to the needs of different age groups. Calligraphy materials, for example, would be aimed at KS2. Health and safety considerations (scissors, trimmers, staplers etc.) would also need to be addressed before resourcing a writing area. Ground rules for use of the resources can avoid stock being improperly used.

Contexts for unaided writing

It is essential that we provide contexts for purposeful writing activities. It is not uncommon in the EYFS or KS1 to see a writing area or an office set up for the children, or for the role play areas, both indoor and outdoor, to be resourced as contexts for role play and writing. A typical example might be a café, where the waiters and waitresses write in role as they take their customers' orders. Older children will also find that role play, or writing in role, provides a valuable context for writing, and you will find examples of this in Chapter 6.

It is very important that we actively encourage boys to see unaided writing as a worthwhile activity for them. Evidence from QCA (1998) found that some boys tended to use dedicated writing areas less often than girls but did respond to role play areas where the writing was purposeful, for example, using a notepad in the large construction area. The clear implication of this is that we should try to provide writing materials and create purposes for writing in the areas that boys might prefer to play in. Setting up a 'B & Q', 'Wickes' or 'Homebase' store might hold more appeal for boys. Play in these contexts may give rise to large posters for writing out prices, safety rules and order pads to be used with customers. This is not to say, of course, that boys should not be encouraged to write in the usual writing areas as well.

Responding to unaided writing: early writers

You may hear some very young or less experienced writers providing a running commentary as they represent their ideas on paper. It is interesting to try to observe them as they talk to themselves and notice how their language accompanies or appears to make direct links to their mark-making or writing. When children bring us their writing, it helps to raise their awareness about writing as a mode of communication if we can encourage them to try to tell us what they intended their writing to say. In the early stages, their versions may vary from one reading to another, which reflects the lack of stability of children's early concepts about print. You may feel that it is appropriate to make a conventional transcription of what children say so that you can refer back to it in future re-readings or for assessment purposes. A tricky challenge for the inexperienced teacher occurs when the child brings a piece of 'pre-communicative' (see Chapter 7) writing and says, 'You tell me what my writing says'. Such a request is characteristic of some early writers and the teacher can always find positive responses such as: comment on and name all the different letters that have been used; talk about the use of letters from the child's name in the writing; discuss spaces between words; discuss the length of words; point out repetitions and consistencies. If the child has accompanied the piece of writing with a drawing or diagram, this may well provide a valuable starting point for talking about the piece as it will reveal helpful clues and cues for discussing the intended content. Later, working with a different writing routine such as shared writing or dictated writing, the teacher can continue to help the child to make the important connection that print holds meaning.

The empowerment of unaided writing

Unaided writing is also supportive to children who wish to write on topics that are of particular interest or importance to them, such as a lengthy story in chapters, or an ongoing diary or journal. The *NC* Programme of Study in KS1 acknowledges this need. Figure 5.5 is a piece of extended writing undertaken independently by a Year 2 writer which clearly indicates the positive benefits of spending a concentrated, uninterrupted period of time drafting a piece of writing.

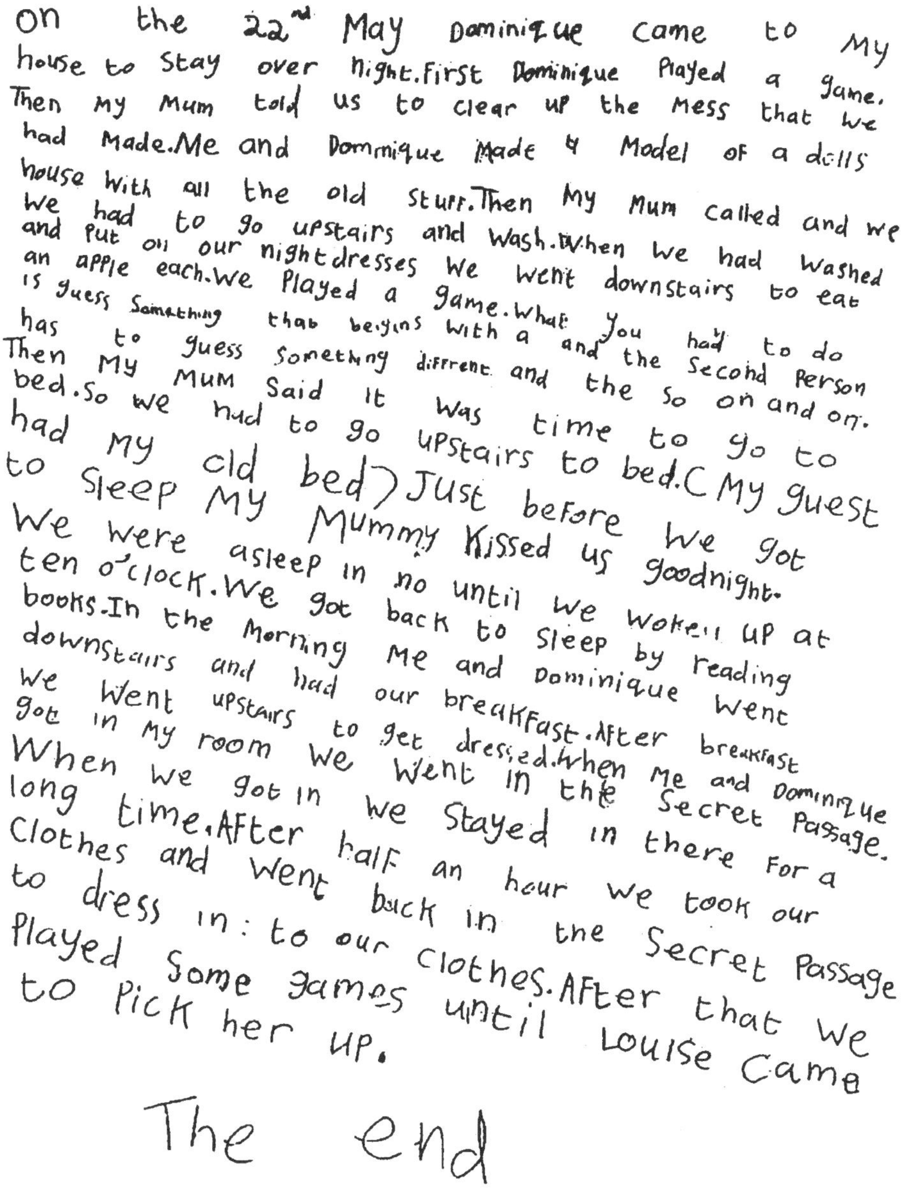

On the 22nd May Dominique came to my house to stay over night. First Dominique played a game. Then my Mum told us to clear up the mess that we had Made. Me and Dommique Made 4 Model of a dolls house with all the old stuff. Then my Mum called and we had to go upstairs and wash. When we had washed and put on our nightdresses we went downstairs to eat an apple each. We played a game. What you had to do is guess something that beginns with a and the Second Person has to guess something diffrent and the so on and on. Then my Mum said it was time to go to bed. So we had to go upstairs to bed. C My guest had my old bed) Just before we got to sleep my Mummy Kissed us goodnight. We were asleep in no until we woke up at ten o'clock. We got back to sleep by reading books. In the Morning Me and Dominique went downstairs and had our breakfast. After breakfast we went upstairs to get dressed. When Me and Dominique got in my room we went in the Secret Passage. When we got in we stayed in there for a long time. After half an hour we took our Clothes and went back in the Secret Passage to dress in: to our clothes. After that we Played Some games until Louise Came to pick her up.

The end

Figure 5.5

The child's piece exudes her determination to recount her adventures and she does this in an entertaining style, for example, with the use of parenthesis. She had not been directly taught about brackets but she seizes her opportunity in this piece of writing, using them appropriately, to make a direct address to her reader. For a first draft, this example reveals few surface errors but unaided writing can also be a very effective way of helping children to learn how to go on to re-draft, revise, edit and proofread their writing (skills which they are required to master in KS2).

Most importantly, unaided writing is empowering for all children who love to write and feel the need to write, no matter what their level of skill. For these children, working and playing with words or shaping and polishing an idea, is as satisfying and absorbing as the mixing of colours is to an artist. It is these children who may go on to write, whether it be for a personal or public audience, throughout the entirety of their lives.

Confidence and self-help strategies

Children will require a wide range of self-help and self-monitoring strategies in order to sustain their independence and avoid frustration and loss of confidence. Donald Graves (1983) characterises children of seven or eight as moving into a phase where they become very self-conscious as to whether their writing looks right or wrong. Some children by this age are only too aware of their shortcomings, especially in relation to their spelling power. Some children are very fearful of unaided writing because it requires them to take risks, thereby making mistakes, and some simply dislike the thought of their writing looking 'messy'. (See discussion on learning styles and strategies for independence in spelling in Chapter 7.) Other children will be struggling with several aspects of learning to write – for example – the getting of ideas and will need very achievable short-term goals set to help them (see Chapter 9). Setting an achievable target to be regularly reviewed is one way of helping such writers move forward. Involving children themselves in the target-setting process will also help raise their self-esteem and self-awareness. For example, a Year 3 child, Tom, who needed to remember to use full stops in his unaided writing agreed a three-step plan with his teacher: 'When I finish a piece of writing I will remember to read it aloud, to put in the full stops and then show my teacher'.

It will already have become clear in this chapter that writing routines are underpinned by a careful balance of direct teaching and collaborative and independent activity. Our observations of children while engaged in teacher-led and independent writing activities will inform us of areas of strength and elements that require further teaching from us (see Chapter 8). In literacy sessions, the ability to utilise self-help strategies is crucially important during the period when the teacher is targeting groups for guided reading or guided writing. The groups engaged in independent work need a wide range of strategies to enable them to maintain their independence and avoid disturbing the groups working with the teacher.

These strategies for independence are not learnt overnight. They will require repeated demonstrations from the teacher, especially in the early stages. McCormick Calkins (1983) describes these as 'mini-lessons'. In the early days with a new class, it may help to monitor carefully what makes the different routines operate smoothly. By identifying strategies that promote independence within each routine, it will then be possible to convey this information clearly to the children. Periodically, it is worth checking how successfully the children cope with the self-help strategies that have been put in place and make amendments as necessary. One of the best ways to work on self-help strategies is to involve the children themselves by discussing the problem with them and asking them to offer solutions. One class solved their spelling queue problem by devising their own self-help poster which children had to follow before asking for help from an adult. In this way, we are helping children to reflect on the problem for themselves and encouraging them to take control of possible ways of managing it. (See also Chapter 7 under Independence and risk-taking.).

The following will have an impact on sustaining independence and are worth reviewing if organisational and management challenges arise:

- availability of resources for writing: range, quantity and easy access for children;
- agreed ground rules for use of resources: care and use of resources, e.g. sharpeners/rubbers; sharing; returning materials once finished;
- accessibility and use of support materials, e.g alphabet strips, word banks, word walls, word books, dictionaries, ICT, etc. understanding how to use these resources; reminder posters for finding spellings;
- getting stuck: demonstrations and discussions about common problems; peer support; reminder cards; what to do whilst waiting for help.

COLLABORATIVE WRITING

Unlike supported composition, in this routine children work together, independently of the teacher, to produce a shared written text. The text could be written on a dry-wipe board, large piece of paper or composed on screen. As it requires a high level of co-operation, collaborative writing is probably best suited to the top end of KS1 and to KS2. For children to succeed in this writing routine, the groups should be small (preferably even numbers) and carefully constructed to ensure compatibility. The ground rules for participation should also be clearly explained and, ideally, everyone in the group should take a turn to write with the mutual support of the other group members. Collaborative writing can have a place in literacy sessions but also works well in other areas of the curriculum such as science. In a Year 3 class, the children were working in groups testing out a range of materials for absorbency. Each group first discussed the materials and, in pairs, noted down their initial predictions on mini-whiteboards. Each pair then took turns to discuss these with the rest of the children in their group, adjusted the predictions and listed these on an A1-size chart. Comparisons were then shared with the whole class. At this point, the teacher used the interactive whiteboard to collate the agreed predictions for all the groups, so that these could be referred to later on in the session. Collaborative writing was used at several points during the science lesson to record their findings.

A Year 2 class had been working with their teacher on traditional tales. They were asked to listen carefully to their teacher's re-reading of a familiar tale that they had shared several times before. They were then asked to quickly retell the story orally in pairs and, again in small groups, to think carefully about the sequence of events. Using a story board, the teacher then modelled the writing of the opening sequences of the story for the children. Then, in groups, the children were asked to rewrite the main sequence of events to accompany a set of pictures. The pictures had already been sequenced and stuck on to a large piece of paper in the previous session and the children's main task was to compose and write their sentence to accompany each illustration. A group working independently of the teacher supported one another, taking turns to suggest possible sentences, agreeing on the best one and then working in pairs to write the sentences down. Children who were waiting for their turn to write, either helped with suggestions for spellings or wrote a rough draft of their sentence on smaller pieces of paper. In the plenary session, the group read their story aloud to the rest of the class.

Safford *et al.* (2004) write about the writing opportunities offered by the traditional tale of *The Seal Wife*. Here are Lizzie and Younis (Year 4) orally drafting their own version of the story. You will appreciate the power of the collaboration if you read the dialogue out loud. Observe how closely they attend to each other, building on and enriching the ideas.

Lizzie	It was a sunny morning and a fisherman...
Younis	an old
Lizzie	an old fisherman decided to go for a walk on the beach. He was looking around when he saw a group of people
Younis	normal
Lizzie	normal people dancing
Younis	He looked very surprised and
Lizzie	speedily
Younis	walked over to them. When they saw him they dived towards a pile of seal skins
Lizzie	one of them did not take their skin. They stopped and looked at the fisherman.
Younis	The fisherman grabbed her skin
Lizzie	immediately
Younis	The woman begged 'Please, please, my skin, give it to me'.
Lizzie	The fisherman did not care one bit.
Younis	He pulled the sea woman by the wrist and took the lady to his house.
Lizzie	As the years went by they got married and had children.
Younis	The children were not sea people but they had a little web between their fingers...

(2004: 94–5*)

*Please note that this publication shows the final written story, but observation notes from the research project documented the in-the-moment collaborative writing process as the two children talked and wrote together

The children's final stories were powerful and vivid. The teacher's comments remarked on the quality of the writing but also posed the question: 'What is good about writing in a team?' thus drawing their attention to the potential of the collaborative process.

DRAFTING

For many years in schools, it was usual for re-drafting to be in the form of a 'fair copy'. *The Bullock Report* (DES, 1975) made brief reference to the place of drafting in the classroom but it is through the work of Frank Smith (1982) and Donald Graves (1983) on the writing process that we have come to a better understanding of what drafting is and its role in the writing process for primary-age children. As has already been indicated in Chapter 2, Smith and Graves were concerned that all too often children were being asked to write 'one-off' pieces of writing which tended to lead to an over-emphasis on the presentational aspects of writing at the expense of the content. Through his classroom-based writing workshops, Graves began to help teachers to see the value of asking children to re-draft their work. Central to Graves' approach was to make the whole writing process explicit to children (from pre-composition to publication) and to promote independence in their approach to writing. By the mid-1980s, teachers in this country were encouraging drafting as a routine. For many children this proved to be a liberating experience, although others found it challenging to be asked to re-draft their work. In confident hands, the approach worked successfully but it soon became clear that a sense of balance was needed. Questions were raised, such as: Did every piece of writing need to be redrafted? If so, how many times? Wasn't there still a place also for 'one-offs'? Was re-drafting necessarily appropriate for all children? Did re-drafting entail copying out the complete text again or using editing techniques such as 'cut and paste'? Did children understand that the purpose of re-drafting was to improve their writing? How much support was given to children in re-drafting techniques? The *NC* helped, to some extent, to clarify the way forward, placing drafting carefully within a clear sequence that required children to 'plan', 'draft', 'revise', 'proofread', 'present' and 'discuss' their work. Drafting sits comfortably within the *PNS* teaching sequence (Figure 5.1) as it can be planned for and modelled within shared writing and targeted within guided writing sessions.

It is now commonplace for teachers to introduce the idea of drafting with younger children through oral re-drafting. This can be demonstrated by reading aloud from a short passage during shared writing and, through teacher scribing, by involving the children in decisions about improving small sections of the text. Alternatively, an individual child's own writing can be discussed and suggestions made about how it could be improved. This requires sensitive handling and the teacher will need to have modelled examples of good questions to ask. In order to introduce this technique to children, some teachers use a short piece of their own writing and ask children to comment on it and make suggestions as to how it might be improved (see also Writing Partnerships below). Shared writing can also be used to model, through teacher demonstration, drafting techniques, including planning, moving paragraphs, marking omissions, changing vocabulary and refining sentence structure. If the children are paired up as 'writing partners' they can support each other with all aspects of drafting, including proofreading. It is also worth teaching the children some basic marks for editing and encouraging them to use them as they draft. Suggested marks include:

- ∧ the omission mark;
- circling spelling or alternatively using a wavy or straight line (under a word);
- 'sp' in the margin to mark spelling errors;
- // to indicate a new paragraph is needed.

The word processor is an essential tool, which children should use as part of their learning about drafting. Editing functions such as clicking on 'cut' and 'paste' or dragging across sections of text can assist in the easy movement of paragraphs and sentences while the range of fonts and print sizes provides plenty of scope for the final presentation of pieces of work. Many children are already very familiar with these editing functions but they can be easily demonstrated and discussed with the whole class using the interactive whiteboard. One potential drawback when using the word processor for drafts is that it can conceal the different drafts that are produced or earlier drafts can be lost. It is useful, occasionally, for assessment purposes, to keep a sample of the complete life history of children's pieces of writing, which shows the progress from initial plan through to the final copy.

Finally, some children want to re-draft their work because they can see the value of improving it. Figures 5.6 and 5.7 are from a Year 2 child who speaks English as an additional language and show marked developments from first to second draft.

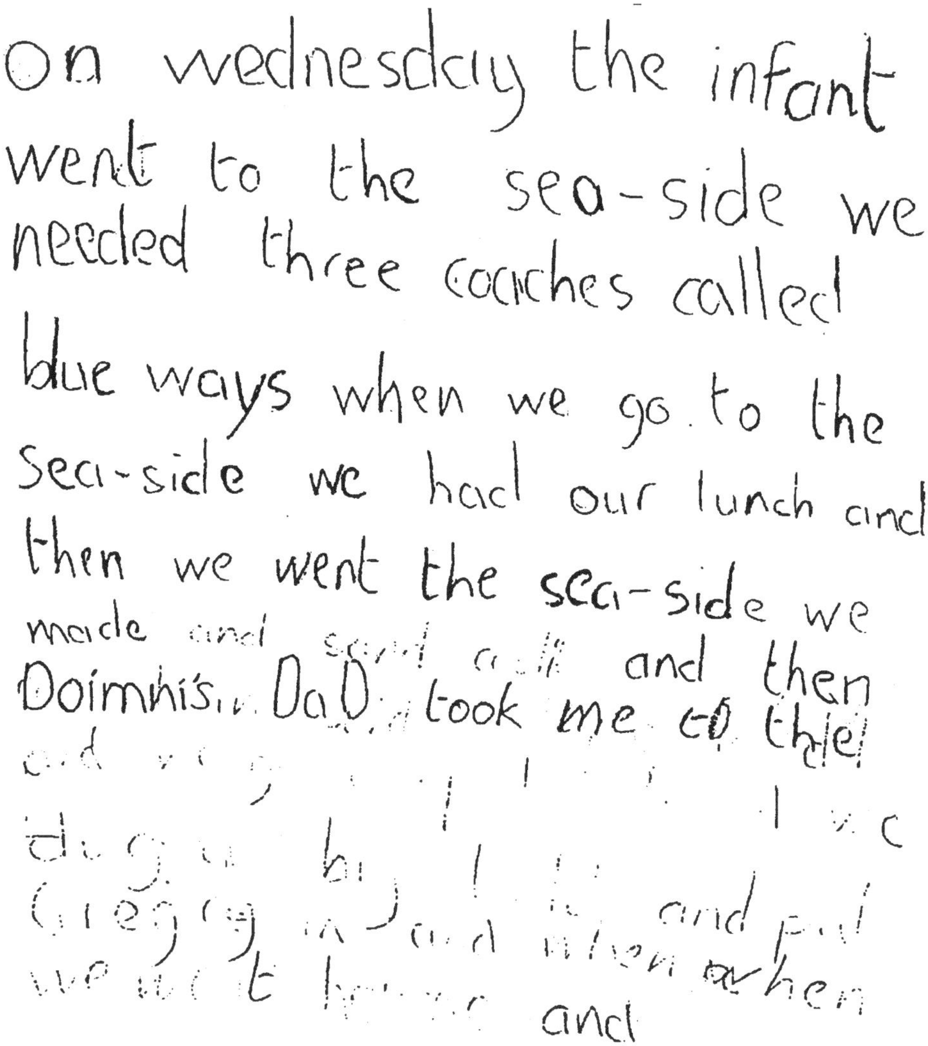

Figure 5.6

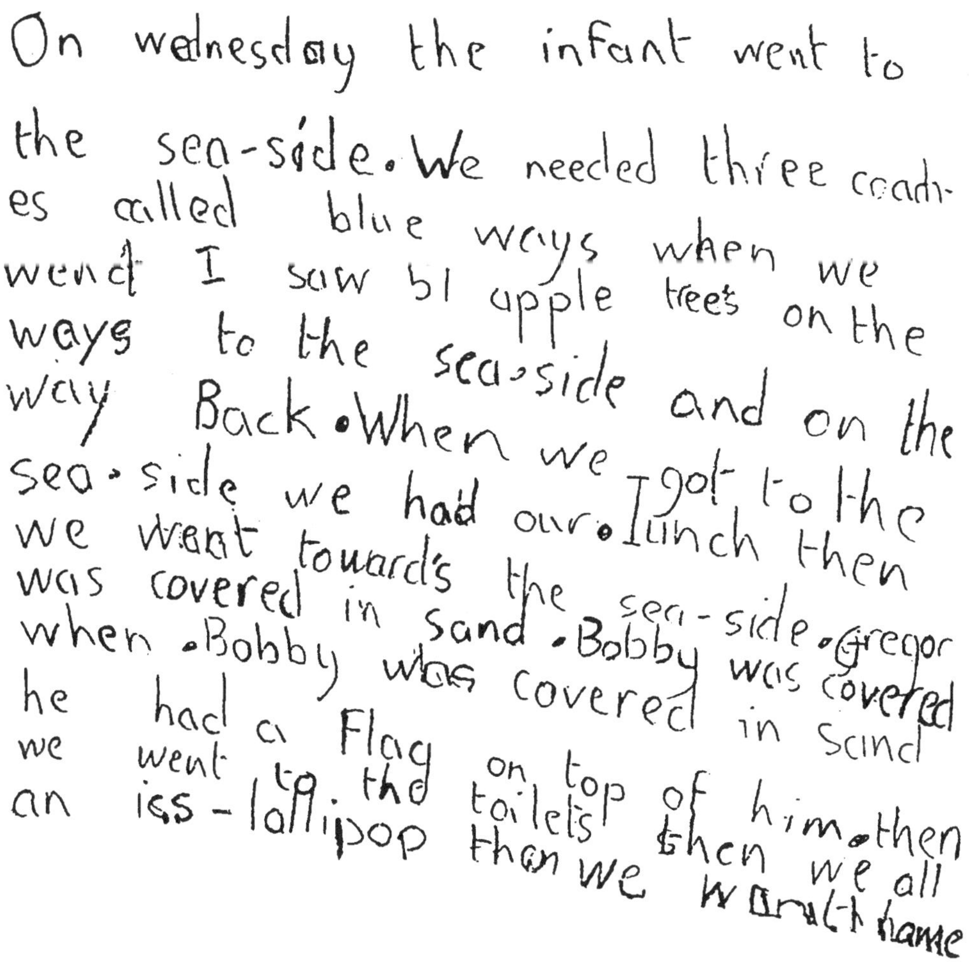

On wednesday the infant went to
the sea-side. We needed three coach-
es called blue ways when we
wend I saw bl apple trees on the
ways to the seaside and on the
way Back. When we got to the
sea·side we had our·lunch then
we went towards the sea-side·Gregor
was covered in sand·Bobby was covered
when ·Bobby was covered in sand
he had a Flag on top of him·then
we went to the toilets then we all
an iss-lollipop then we wraut hame

Figure 5.7

Figure 5.6 is a recount of a school trip to the seaside. The child became dissatisfied
with his work, tried to rub sections out (which accounts for the apparently poor quality
of the figure) and finally asked if he could start again on a fresh piece of paper. Before
doing so, there was a brief discussion on the areas that were causing him difficulty and
he was given some ideas on improving the content and the sentence structure. This
resulted in a second draft, Figure 5.7, which proved a much more satisfying piece of
writing. Not only does he add more detail about his trip but he has also tried to
regularise his sentence structure and punctuate the piece. There are, of course, still
some errors, including confusions over the use of the apostrophe, but the child was
much happier with the second draft. For assessment purposes, both drafts (which could
have usefully been dated) provide a wealth of information about the child's growing
ability to take control of the writing process and to monitor his own work.

WRITING WORKSHOPS

The idea of the writing workshop comes from Donald Graves (1983) and his research associate Lucy McCormick Calkins (1983). As the name suggests, writing workshops involve the whole class writing together (although not necessarily at the same stage in the writing process). The aim of writing workshops is to make the different stages of the writing process explicit to children and to enable them to work independently by taking their pieces of writing through from 'pre-composition' to 'publication'. It was intended that children would learn how real writers work by drafting, re-drafting, revising, editing and proofreading their pieces prior to publication. As you will remember from Chapter 2, the emphasis of Graves' work was on ownership and children taking an active rather than passive role in their writing.

Teachers who have implemented Graves' model have been impressed by the degree of independence and confidence his approach gives children. They have managed to reduce some of the pressures caused by the mechanics of writing and they have helped children focus more closely on content. While it is less common to see writing workshops operating in quite these ways today, there have been many spin-off practices which we almost take for granted. These include: 'everyone writing together'; demonstrations or modelling by the teacher (recognisable now in shared writing as teacher demonstration); writing response partnerships; talking about the different stages of the process with children; mini-lessons; and bookmaking.

WRITING PARTNERSHIPS

In school, the child's first and most significant writing partner is the teacher. It is the teacher who usually provides the first audience and initial response to a piece of writing. The teacher's feedback may also include constructive criticism and guidance on improving the piece of writing. However, as a context for responding, writing partnerships between children can also be very effective and this writing routine is well suited to the KS2 age range. The Programme of Study states that children should be given the opportunity 'to discuss and evaluate their own and others' writing' (DfEE, 1999a). Donald Graves sowed the seeds of writing partnerships through what he termed 'conferencing'. He recommends that conferencing should be a routine part of the drafting process and that, initially, the teacher should demonstrate to the class how to respond in a positive and constructive way to a piece of writing. He suggests that the teacher starts by using one of her own first drafts in order to help the children learn how to respond.

For this routine to work, children need to learn how to ask purposeful and worthwhile questions and how to offer comments in such a way that they do not undermine their partner's confidence. Graves offers two powerful prompts to help children to begin to do this effectively. The first is, 'Tell me something you like about your writing', to be used when the piece is first read aloud. This gives the writer confidence and helps him or her to begin to evaluate the quality of the work. The second prompt, 'Tell me something you want to know more about', is asked by the writer to his or her partner, after the piece has been read aloud. The intention here is to help the children develop their sense of audience by identifying gaps in the writing where more detail or information is required. Ways of operating writing partnerships do vary. Some children are asked to swap their writing, while others read their drafts aloud to one another before their partner responds. The idea here is to get the first responses directed towards the content. This could include suggestions for clarifying points, expression of ideas or choice of vocabulary. Suggestions might also be made in relation to the cohesion of the piece and sequencing of ideas. At the proofreading stage, the response partner might focus on the presentational aspects including spelling and punctuation. Although face-to-face discussion between writing partners is the norm, it is possible for them to use ICT to share their responses. If the original draft has been typed on the word processor, tools such as 'track changes' or 'comments', can provide a forum for making editorial suggestions (with the option for the writer to take or leave the advice).

McCormick Calkins provides some detailed examples of how children were inducted into responding to each other's writing. She lists a series of questions which the children found helpful, including:

- What is the most important thing you are saying?
- Which is the most important part of your story? Why?
- Are there places where you could describe more?
- Is there any other way you could order this?

(1983: 129–30)

With careful induction into being sensitive support partners, children can be helped to reflect on their writing and evaluate it. Partners need to be paired thoughtfully and flexibly. Friendship and compatibility might be one basis for struggling writers, while for the most able children in the class, pairing by ability might provide more challenge, leading to improvements in the revised drafts. However, partnerships between the least and most experienced in the class can also be fruitful. For all children it can be the site where they help each other in the setting of achievable targets and the supportive evaluation of existing ones. Some of McCormick Calkins' ideas outlined above could be adapted for use in supported composition sessions and in guided writing groups.

DICTATED WRITING

A five-year-old told me a wonderful 'chapter' story which was full of vivid description and interesting twists of plot. When she had finished, I asked her to write her story down. Slowly and laboriously she managed to write one sentence, 'I love my dog.' She stopped in dismay, saying, 'I've done my best' and I, as her teacher, was also left feeling disappointed. Between the two of us, we had lost that wonderful story. This example will probably sound familiar to many teachers of young children and I include it here to illustrate the gap between the child's potential competence as an author and her performance as a writer. As a result of years of being told and read stories at home, this child was a skilled 'author' but she was also a very inexperienced writer in terms of her secretarial skills (see Chapter 2). For this child and many others like her, dictated writing is an important routine as it maintains, sustains and develops the child's skills as an author while the child begins to come to grips with the physical aspects of the writing process. Dictated writing, as its name suggests, involves the teacher (or other adult) working on a one-to-one basis with a child in order to scribe for the child. It is distinctively different from shared writing, not only because it is on an individual basis, but also because the teacher transcribes exactly what the child dictates. It is a labour-intensive routine, but adults are surprised and delighted not only by the extended pieces of writing that can result, but also by the complexity of the language structures used and the richness of vocabulary. You may at this stage want to look back at the 'Dogfish' example we gave in the introduction to this book. The EYFS endorses the adult acting as a scribe for children and suggests that, 'After they say a sentence, repeat the first part of it, say each word as you write, and include some punctuation' (DCSF, 2008a: 60)

Liz Laycock (1996) provides an important account of several young children and their dictated stories. She reminds us that to create and tell stories is a very human activity: 'In telling our stories, putting our fears, doubts, excitements, joys or sorrows into words, we are shaping them in order to make sense of them, both for ourselves and for the listeners' (p. 54). This may in part explain why this writing routine is so popular with many young children. She analyses the narrative structure of stories dictated by children in a Reception class, showing that such young children already know a great deal about how narratives work.

Although dictated writing is usually thought of as an EYFS routine, it is acknowledged in the KS1 Programme of Study for writing that pupils should 'write extended texts, with support (for example, using the teacher as writer)' (DfEE, 1999a: 48). This routine also has considerable potential for children who are in difficulties with writing or who are disaffected by writing. For this reason, children may be asked to tape stories in KS2 for the teacher to transcribe later on (see Chapter 9). Alternatively, a suitable voice-activated word processing computer package could be used. Whatever the age range, dictated writing can be turned into valuable reading material for the children.

Teacher dictating to the class

'Dictation' has a rather old-fashioned tone, but one Year 5 teacher has a successful routine called 'You are my secretaries'. On one occasion the class had been writing letters of complaint and the teacher decided to read them a letter she had composed to provide a further model of the linguistic features of the genre. She then asked them to 'take a letter' and dictated a short passage to the children. This was followed by pair or group work where the children compared the versions that they had written down and then they extended these to produce a final version. The plenary session was then used to read out and defend their versions. Ruth Wajnryb (1990) has developed a method of dictation to young children which is also suitable for children for whom English is an additional language, where she reads a passage to her listeners several times with the children noting down as many words each time as possible. In pairs, the children then attempt to reconstruct the whole text.

Although dictation is not mentioned in the Programme of Study, many teachers find it a useful routine to use occasionally and briefly, especially when they are trying to gain direct feedback on a particular aspect of the child's knowledge of the writing process. Dictation, in its traditional form, places heavy, simultaneous demands on the child's working knowledge of the writing system. These days, teachers may choose to use the technique rather more flexibly than the nineteenth-century teacher you read about in the introduction to this book. For instance, the teacher might use it to consolidate a specific teaching point on spelling, which would take the form of dictating a short, specially tailored piece of writing rather than a lengthy stretch of text which tested everything. In this way, teachers could reinforce teaching objectives about genre, sentence structure, punctuation, paragraphing, layout, spelling and handwriting. The dictation of short stretches of text could be used sparingly for diagnostic purposes within guided writing sessions to help confirm children's consolidation of a particular target or objective.

COPYING AND TRACING

As with the previous routine, copying and tracing have had a long and at times controversial history (see Introduction and Chapter 1), especially in terms of their overuse at the expense of those other routines which place more emphasis on the active participation and hypothesising of the child. However, copying and tracing routines are still in evidence in EYFS classrooms, and with some children in KS1 who might still benefit from them. They are important routines for several reasons: they help in the child's physical development by improving hand–eye co-ordination and by providing opportunities to refine the child's fine motor skills; they play their part in developing the child's growing awareness of print by drawing his or her attention to key concepts about print; children seem to benefit from the time that these routines give them to reflect on their writing – and they love the neat end-product!

Go into any children's bookshop and you will see plenty of attractively produced, graded, exercise books that focus on copying and tracing. The tracing activities teach children about directionality and familiarise them with the key movements that underpin handwriting and letter formation. The task is made achievable for the child by virtue of tracing on top of a 'good model' of the particular pattern to be practised. It could then be argued that through tracing the child gets a 'feel' for handwriting.

In EYFS classrooms, teachers may plan, at a continuous level, a variety of tracing-related activities to help children practise the necessary skills involved in learning how to hold and control a writing implement. The child may trace over a wide range of pre-drawn outlines of everyday objects and shapes. Literacy-related tracing activities will include tracing over handwriting patterns, tracing over individual letters of the alphabet to develop knowledge of shape and orientation, and, most significantly, tracing over the child's name. Kinaesthetic provision will also be made for independent experiences arising from tracing, such as writing in wet sand, tracing the finger over raised letters or finger painting. Some of the routines described here are also used with older children with serious literacy and fine motor difficulties (see also Chapter 9).

For many children, copying marks the first stage towards independent handwriting. The first word that most children copy, with some degree of accuracy, is their name. Through name-writing they will begin to develop an awareness that letters can be written in both upper and lower case. In the Early Learning Goals for writing, children are expected to be able to write their names, and for handwriting to 'use a pencil and hold it effectively to form recognisable letters, most of which are correctly formed' (DCSF, 2008a: 62). By participating in a range of the experiences discussed above, young children can begin to develop this knowledge. A wealth of information can be provided through talking with children when they undertake these tasks especially in terms of the impact that they are having on children's learning and to find out what they find easy and difficult. Copying and tracing without teacher intervention tend to be very passive activities and, therefore, less useful.

Another common practice in EYFS classrooms is to ask the child to compose a sentence which the teacher writes down. Then the child copies underneath. It is important to offer a good model of handwriting and to remind children who are new to copying where to start writing. This could be done by marking the appropriate starting point on their page with a dot. You may find that some children try to write over your writing or copy words, or indeed letters, out of sequence. A Reception class teacher who observed this decided to introduce a midway step which she called 'overwriting'. In this procedure, instead of copying underneath, the child overwrites the teacher's handwriting. This forms a bridge between tracing and copying. The quotation from Katrina at the beginning of this chapter underlines the value of this kind of support.

In KS1, the demands on copying rapidly widen as children will be beginning to copy words from books, including dictionaries or class word banks. They may also be copying work from the board which, in KS2, becomes an increasingly important routine. To make this workable for children, children need to be seated so that they can see the board properly and are comfortable. As with shared writing, your handwriting must be large and clear and, where necessary, cursive (joined up). If the children are copying a list such as spellings, where accuracy is vital, make sure that no errors have occurred during the copying. Remember, it is a long distance from the board to the child's book and consider the act of memory involved in maintaining and holding on to the correct letter order. Try to discourage children from copying spellings one letter at a time (see Chapter 7 on developing visual spelling strategies). As accuracy is so important, it may well mean that you need to check the children's books after they have copied the list down. For some children, who have limited short-term memory spans, this kind of copying may prove too demanding. You may need to make other provision – for example, photocopying the list for them. The time may not be far off when you write on an interactive whiteboard and the children are able instantly to download your writing directly on to their personal laptops.

In both KS1 and KS2, making fair copies of drafted writing marks the final stage in the writing process. The KS2 Programme of Study for writing states that children should 'prepare a neat, correct and clear final copy' (DfEE, 1999a: 56). Children may well be working from drafts that have been revised and edited and may need motivating to put in the final bit of effort. An awareness of the ultimate destination of the final copy will provide an incentive for the children, as will the provision of good-quality paper and writing implements with which to execute the task. However, we need to balance the skill of being able to write neatly for publishing purposes against the obvious advantages of using a good-quality desk top publishing package.

WRITING ON THE SCREEN

The use of ICT to support the writing process is now commonplace in classrooms. The interactive whiteboard has become a key tool for teaching and learning, and most schools now have networked ICT suites. The range of 'easy-use' word processing packages is steadily increasing and improving: they can combine word processing with multimedia and access options such as speech.

In the EYFS the children will need time to explore and play with the computer. 'Talking' programmes are especially useful as they give the child immediate feedback. With adult guidance, children can successfully compose collaborative pieces of writing directly on to the computer. Multiple copies can be printed so that the children have something immediate that looks good and can be taken home. Further copies can be produced for display and record-keeping purposes in the classroom. Planning for the provision and use of the computer within role play scenarios, such as the vet's or doctor's reception area, is another way of providing very young children with purposeful experiences. It is possible to download customised role play software from reputable sites in order to facilitate such opportunities for writing.

ICT has already featured earlier on in this chapter as an increasingly significant and versatile tool within key writing routines. For example, it can facilitate shared writing through teacher demonstration and teacher scribing. The teacher is able to model clearly for the children how writing can be revised, altered and even deleted.

As they get more experienced, children will use the word processor to enhance the drafting stage of their writing. By being introduced to tools such as 'cut' and 'paste', grammar checkers, spellcheckers and the thesaurus, they can undertake revising and editing tasks systematically. On the positive side, the physical effort is greatly reduced, but, on the other hand, there is a risk of passivity in terms of understanding these automatic corrections. There is a potential tension here, for example with spelling, in terms of balancing the use of these facilities with a wider range of self-help strategies. Indeed, concerns have been voiced about spellcheckers 'masking' potential difficulties in some children's management of spelling and the monitoring of their spelling development. Other writing routines, such as guided and independent writing, should avoid these potential pitfalls.

Many packages now offer a wide array of fonts, tools and layouts, which will have immediate appeal to children. These tools can be particularly supportive to KS2 children, who are expected to make decisions about layout and presentation and who are also required to produce different finished products such as guidebooks and pamphlets. Multimedia applications including *Microsoft's PowerPoint* and *Publisher*, animation, the use of digital video and software which can manipulate photos can all add to the quality and impact of the finished text.

ICT can also raise the self-esteem of struggling writers, especially those with handwriting and spelling difficulties. One example is *Clicker 5* (www.rm.com) which is equipped with numerous special functions, including speech, to support inexperienced or struggling writers. For example, through the use of 'Clicker grids' teachers can customise material which can be tailored in order to try to meet children's individual needs. When being used, the actual Clicker grids sit across the bottom half or third of the screen. The grids contain demarcated cells in which the teacher can assemble a selection of pictures (for instance, about the seaside) and associated words or phrases that the child will need in order to fulfil a specific writing task. As the child composes, he or she simply clicks the mouse on a particular cell and the picture, word, or phrase which is in the cell will appear on the blank part of the screen above the grid. In effect, clicking on a cell is equivalent to using the keyboard.

It is becoming more common to see children with specific learning difficulties using their own laptops for a wide range of class work and many programs have been designed specifically with the struggling writer in mind (see examples in Chapter 7 for spelling and Chapters 9).

Finally, it can be useful to find out about children's use of ICT for writing beyond the school setting. By encouraging children to bring in some of their writing done on the computer at home, we may be pleasantly surprised and even have cause to rethink how we perceive the child as a writer (see the account of Ben at the end of this chapter).

BOOKMAKING

Bookmaking is about the final stage of the writing process: publication. Bookmaking sends out powerful signals to children that their writing will have an active future life and a real purpose. If we make books, we assume that we have a readership who will respond to and be interested in our efforts. Books made by children can form part of the class or school library collection and be read aloud for enjoyment as well as revisited. Books made with a previous class may be used by the teacher to inspire a fresh cohort of children as they undertake a similar writing task. Despite the obvious presentational and time-saving advantages of ICT bookmaking packages, children should still, at points in their primary schooling, be encouraged to make their own books, an activity which can easily be linked with Design and Technology. There is an intrinsic pleasure and appeal in the craftsmanship that hands-on bookmaking gives. As adults we often treasure and enjoy handling these early efforts at authorship because we can still see and, perhaps, even marvel at, the unique 'stamp' that our own handwriting brings. However, increasingly, time is of the essence, and for this reason hand-made books can be constructed with varying levels of sophistication from quickly made simple folded ones, such as concertina books, to the hardback, fully bound variety. For practical suggestions consult the many books by Paul Johnson, two of which are listed at the end of this chapter. Some teachers include bookmaking resources within or alongside their writing area. Health and safety requirements need to be considered but provision could include:

- variety of staplers (including long-arm);
- small-size trimmer;
- comb binder;
- needles, thread, scissors;
- paper;
- boards for covers;
- bookbinding tape;
- glue sticks;
- off-cuts of wrapping paper/wallpaper (for covers);
- instructions and ready-made examples.

There is a financial implication here, and bookmaking materials can be expensive to provide. However, the 'Blue Peter' spirit can prevail and alternative materials can be improvised quite easily. There are, of course, numerous ICT packages available (e.g.

EasyBooks Deluxe) that can take the strain out of bookmaking for those seeking a more professional finish.

PARTNERSHIP WITH PARENTS

Although contact with parents is a routine of a different order from others discussed in this chapter, it is nevertheless of such importance that working with parents needs to be part of your daily practice if children are to make progress in writing, as in all other areas.

It was research into literacy before schooling such as that of Gordon Wells (1987), Glenda Bissex (1980) and Shirley Brice Heath (1983) which drew attention to the key role of parents in introducing their children to reading and writing. Parents have always helped their children with reading and writing but for many years teachers were either unaware of this or did not actively encourage such involvement. As recently as the 1980s, it was understandable and not uncommon to hear parents saying such things as, 'We don't want to go against school', and showing some wariness about becoming actively involved in their children's reading and writing. However, home–school reading partnerships (or PACT schemes, as some were known) began to flourish at about that time and marked the clearest sign of a shift in attitudes. Schools quickly realised that a two-way dialogue with parents was positively advantageous and supportive to children's development. Some schools took parental involvement a step further by using the 'parent conference' from *The Primary Language Record* (Barrs *et al.*, 1988) as a method of providing two-way information about the child's development in reading and writing. Another appreciable advance has been the increased role of parents inside school, supporting reading and writing in the classroom. One of the most positive benefits has been that parents and teachers are able to communicate on a much more regular basis and share their expertise and understanding.

Many schools who have children who speak English as an additional language have been able to tap into the languages spoken and written at home. Parents have been approached to help with the translation of reading and writing material and to put stories and rhymes on to tape. Where writing is concerned, teachers have sometimes been surprised to discover that children whom they may have perceived to be struggling as writers of English are, in fact, writing confidently in their home and community languages. *The Primary Language Record* and Hilary Minns (1990) provide further details on the importance of maintaining the child's first language in the service of learning a second. They also point out the value of teachers having an awareness of the home-based literacy experiences of EAL learners.

Parents can be involved at many levels in their child's writing development, both formally and informally. With the youngest children, at an informal level, a 'Home Writing' board or 'Our Messages' board in the classroom can encourage children to bring in pieces of writing they have done at home. Such pieces will come in all shapes or forms. They might be handwriting practice on the back of an envelope, a list of family names on a scrap of paper or a computer-written story. In one class, a child brought in a copy of the alphabet written in Arabic script. Another brought in a story that he had written, which his parents had translated into Spanish. The resulting excitement and pleasure that the sharing of this writing has for both pupils and teachers indicates that it is a very positive and worthwhile activity to encourage.

Schools will have a whole-school policy on partnership with parents which will indicate the level of commitment expected on each side. Some schools have established formal contracts with parents in order to guarantee support for children's reading and writing development at home. It is not uncommon now to see short booklets or brochures being given to parents, explaining the school's approach to reading and writing. These booklets may give detailed information about the ways in which handwriting and spelling are to be taught. In addition, information might also be provided about the school's marking policy for writing so that parents are not dismayed or puzzled by the teachers' response to the children's use of invented spellings. In KS2, parents may also be asked to participate in the school's homework policy, which is likely to include the regular learning of spellings and writing assignments to be completed at home and brought into school. It is not uncommon now for schools to run workshops for parents to show them how aspects of the English curriculum are taught.

Occasionally, both school and parents are unaware of the writing that children choose to undertake at home. There have been examples of children who have written 'chapter books' or have written their own collections of poetry or maintained diaries over lengthy periods of time. An example involves a Year 6 pupil called Ben. Ben has worked hard with his writing at school and does what is required, but writing is not one of his preferred activities. Outside school, Ben is a big fan of James Bond. Every other week, when his James Bond 'fanzine' arrives, Ben eagerly seeks out the pack of collector's cards (which he trades with other young collectors). For the uninitiated, there are five types of cards: allies, villains, vehicles, gadgets and locations. Ben also enjoys spending time using the family's computer. With close supervision and monitoring from his mother and older brother, Ben has been allowed to download and copy suitable images from one of the James Bond websites. Not surprisingly, he is especially interested in downloading pictures of gadgets and vehicles. Unknown to Ben's mother, he taught himself how to use *PowerPoint*. He wanted to learn how to use *PowerPoint* because he wanted to devise a presentation about James Bond to entertain his family and friends. Completely unaided, Ben created a series of slides that were illustrated with a selection from the downloaded images he had, by now, taught himself to animate. Each slide was accompanied by text. As a *PowerPoint* slide has a limited amount of space for text, it worked like a sort of frame which kept the text-based side of the enterprise containable for Ben. In order to view the show, Ben first makes his reader decode a secret message. Once into the main presentation the reader is immediately engaged as images appear on the screen from different directions and in different forms. To support the images and text, Ben has used sound effects. He is particularly fond of ricocheting bullets and the sound of breaking glass. When Ben's father eventually caught up with him, he helped him to burn a DVD of his presentation and create a distinctive label. To do all this work took Ben a considerable amount of time, but what was noticeable to his parents was his high level of commitment and staying power as well as the huge enjoyment that he was gaining from his enterprise. Ben's father was so impressed with his son's creativity that he took the DVD to work and presented the slide show to his colleagues with the wry comment, 'If my ten-year-old son can do this, we as a company should as well!' The recognition of his efforts by his friends and family has done much to boost Ben's self-esteem and enthusiasm for writing. Having published his DVD, he also now sees himself as a successful and established author. When last heard of, Ben was busy planning his next publishing venture!

Further reading and websites

Alexander, R. (2008) *Towards Dialogic Teaching: Rethinking Classroom Talk.* York: Dialogos.

CLPE (1990) *Shared Reading, Shared Writing.* London: Centre for Literacy in Primary Education.

DCSF (2007b) *Primary National Strategy: Improving Writing with a Focus on Guided Writing.* London: DCSF.

Hall, N. and Robinson, A. (1995) *Exploring Writing and Play in the Early Years.* London: David Fulton Publishers.

Johnson. P. (2000) *Making Books.* London: A & C Black.

Johnson, P. (2005) *Get Writing: Creative Book-making Projects for Children.* London: A & C Black.

Wilson, R. (2003) *Strategies for Immediate Impact on Writing Standards.* Wakefield: Andrell Education.

Family Reading Matters: www.literacytrust.org.uk/familyreading/index.html

National Literacy Trust: www.literacytrust.org.uk/index.html

Primary National Strategy: www.standards.dfes.gov.uk/primaryframework/ literacy

Chapter 6

Composition

Fiona M. Collins

COMPOSITION AND RANGE

> Composition is what powers the writing. It is vital that the focus, in relation to children's writing, is first and foremost on composition, and that children perceive that this is so.
>
> (Barrs 1987: 2)

What is composition?

Composition is about creating ideas, structuring a piece logically, developing individual voice and being able to write in different forms for a range of purposes and audiences. This chapter looks at what we understand by composition, its place in the writing process and how children can be encouraged to extend and develop their range of narrative, non-fiction and poetry writing.

As we saw in Chapter 2, there is a useful distinction to be made between 'composition' and 'transcription' in the writing process. Smith (1982: 20) shows it in this way:

Composition	*Transcription*
(author)	(secretary)
getting ideas	physical effort of writing
selecting words	spelling
grammar	capitalisation
	punctuation
	paragraphs
	legibility

Composition, like any imaginative or creative process, involves a willingness to take risks and impose order on one's thoughts. It is important that children do not feel constrained when writing by difficulties in controlling the secretarial aspects; as Barrs says, 'the focus . . . is first and foremost on composition'.

The *National Curriculum (NC)* Programme of Study for writing recognises this distinction with separate headings for Composition and then for transcriptional skills (Punctuation, Spelling, Handwriting and Presentation). For Composition, the emphasis in Key Stage 1 (KS1) is on vocabulary, sequencing, full sentences, awareness of purpose and audience, and the role and influence of the literature children read. In Key Stage 2 (KS2) the emphasis is on purposes and forms; widening vocabulary; linguistic and stylistic choices; and organising text; again drawing on books read. Both the *NC* Programme of Study and renewed *Primary National Strategy Framework* (DfES, 2006a) cover a range of forms for both key stages. The *PNS* groups these forms into three main themes: narrative, non-fiction and poetry, and focuses on encouraging young writers 'to make informed choices about form, audience and purpose' (2006a: 15).

Writing is explicitly taught within the framework of English, whether it is in a dedicated literacy lesson or in other English sessions. However, children are also asked to write in other curriculum areas, such as history, geography or science. Thus progress and development can be fostered and monitored in writing across the curriculum.

Audience, purpose and context

Audience, purpose and context help the young writer to develop a voice and gradually to control the written word to make meaning. Children often write with a particular audience in mind such as other members of the class, younger children, their parents, the local community or a specific organisation. These audiences may be known or unknown. For young children, it is important that audience is identified from the outset because it helps with decisions about tone, choice of language and structure. The *NC* requires that KS1 children write for 'teachers, other adults, children and (the writers) themselves', and at KS2 this range widens to include 'the wider community and imagined readers'. Sometimes such real and varied audiences are difficult to contrive, and writing in role, discussed later, can be used as a context to provide imaginary audiences.

The *PNS* gives detailed suggestions for KS2 children that take into account the reader of the text. For instance, in Strand 9 (Creating and Shaping Texts) for Year 4, the learning objective states writers should: 'Use settings and characterisation to engage readers' interest', and for Year 6, 'Use different narrative techniques to engage and entertain the reader'. However, from the very earliest stages of writing, children need to be aware of who will be reading their writing so that they can ensure that it makes sense to the reader, whether it is narrative or non-fiction. Thus, although these *PNS* learning objectives are identified at KS2, discussion about the reader who will eventually read the writing is also important with younger children.

The purpose of the writing, whether it is to entertain, persuade or explain, also affects composition. Purpose influences the linguistic structure of the piece and helps the child consider the language choices to be made. The purpose of the writing also links with the form that the writing will take, maybe a letter, diary or pamphlet. It should not be forgotten that one form of writing can be used for different purposes and different audiences; just think of all the different types of pamphlets you see in a week, some informing, some persuading and some warning.

The context for the writing provides purpose and gives the writer direction and involvement in the piece. A purposeful context can also be motivating and encouraging. By 'context' we mean the stimulus – where the writing springs from. For example, writing arising from a class story or poem can stimulate children to write imaginatively, in the role of authors creating imaginary worlds and characters. The provision of role play contexts for writing is most important for children.

As well as teacher-provided contexts, children are often motivated to write from their own interests, reading and life experiences. Television and video stories, characters and events are important influences and frequently appear in children's writing, sometimes in the same story as favourite book characters. Such influences can affect the plot of the story, the pace, the style and the use of dialogue. The influence of popular culture is often short-lived as one fashion replaces another. However, although the particular programme may disappear, the impact of popular culture on children's writing will always be apparent.

The links between reading and writing are strong and widely recognised. The more children read, the more their work reflects wider horizons; they employ book language to create feelings, thoughts and questions; they experiment with plots, themes and ideas. The *PNS* in its Guidance on Literacy Planning clearly states that, 'Success in writing is partly determined by the experience of reading. The child who is familiar with the conventions of different types of texts holds valuable information for composing their own texts.' (DfES, 2006a).

CLPE investigated this link further in their year-long research project *The Reader in the Writer* (Barrs and Cork, 2001). The project explored the influences that quality literature – along with specific activities such as drama, reading texts aloud and discussion – had on the writing of Year 5 children. As stated by Barrs and Cork:

> we (also) wanted to track the influence on children's writing of the literature that they read and studied. In doing this, we wanted to look not only at how challenging literary texts influenced their writing stylistically, but also at how they affected their deeper understanding of the way in which meanings can be explored, developed and communicated through writing.
>
> (p. 26)

The evidence was clear that children's writing had been marked by the exposure to quality texts in terms of the quality of the language used, the complexity of their sentence structures and their ability to sustain narrative voice and perspective. Some children gained more from the project than others but the work reflected clearly that by bringing the text alive through expressive reading aloud, regular discussion of the narrative and exploring the themes and issues within the stories through drama, all the children made progress in their writing.

As well as experiencing quality literature, first-hand experiences and interests also colour much of children's writing and, indeed, are at the heart of all talented composition. Many small boys will turn all their stories into football accounts as you can see in this five-year-old's story:

> A Match at Wembley
> Once there were eleven tigers and eleven lions. All the lions and tigers fans came to Wembley stadium. They were going to play a football match. Everyone in the whole nation came to watch...

It is, however, sometimes difficult to persuade older children that their experiences merit written exploration and attention, but writing about what you know intimately nearly always results in better writing.

In this discussion on audience, purpose and context, we should remember that writing is not always in the public domain. It is also for thinking and learning. It is important that children are encouraged to write down their feelings or to use writing to reflect on what they have actually learnt, for instance, in a science lesson. Myra Barrs argues that activities that link writing and learning are just as important as those driven by audience and purpose, and she quotes Katherine Perera: 'Writing is not merely a way of recording speech, but a different form of language in its own right which can lead to different forms of thinking' (Barrs, 1991: 1).

Types of writing

Writing can be divided into two broad categories: narrative and non-fiction (or fiction and non-narrative). Although these are loose categories and there is some overlap, they are helpful as the separate characteristics of each can be identified and deliberately used by new writers. Note that poetry can fall into either category: many poems tell stories (narrative) but many are the expression of strong feeling and opinions and have no narrative element.

The characteristics of narrative writing are: characters, settings, problems, solutions and resolutions. Narratives may be set in the present, in another time, in this country or another place. They may be realistic or fantastic. The main purpose of narrative writing is to entertain the reader. In children's literature, there are many different types of narrative writing such as traditional tales, adventure stories, historical stories and personal narratives. The *PNS* requires children to write from personal experience, to compose traditional tales, myths and legends, fables, playscripts and poems (which will not necessarily be narratives). By Year 6, the children are expected to be reading and writing, at least in modest ways, a range of fiction genres such as mystery, humour, sci-fi, historical and fantasy.

Non-fiction writing, unlike narrative writing, is not just to entertain (although it often does), but is written for different purposes and for different audiences. It is not about specific characters and their problems; it is about general matters, processes and arguments. It comes in different forms and aims, amongst other things, to inform, persuade and instruct. These different purposes and aims give rise to the many different text types, or 'genres', that are characteristic of non-fiction writing. You will remember from Chapter 2 that genres, or different text types, are socially recognised and are 'different kinds of writing that have different functions in written discourse and in society' (Barrs, 1991: 9). The genre influences the overall structure of the text and language choices made. The EXEL project was established to look at ways of improving children's writing in different genres. Writing up this project, Lewis and Wray (1995) identified six non-fiction genres used regularly within our society (recount, report, procedural, explanation, persuasion and discussion) and they argue that children need to understand the structural and linguistic characteristics of the genres.

Katherine Perera (1984), among others, classifies writing in a rather different way. Rather than using narrative and non-fiction she employs the terms 'chronological' or 'non-chronological'. In other words, writing can either be organised with reference to time, or not. Examples of chronological writing are: directions to a particular place; a recount of a day visit; a recipe or a mystery story. You will see that this list includes both narrative and non-fiction writing. All of this is not intended to confuse; the fact is that chronological writing, narrative or non-fiction, is easier for young writers to manage than non-chronological writing, and thus there are implications for your teaching. For those of you working with older children, you will need to pay careful attention to the planning of non-chronological writing which becomes more of a challenge once you lose time and sequence as an organiser. You will see this if you consider the organisation of these examples of non-chronological writing: reports written in science or geography; a discussion about hunting; or an argument for the banning of whale killing in the world.

The *Early Years Foundation Stage* document (DCSF, 2008a), the *NC* and the *PNS* all provide lists as to which types of non-fiction writing should be taught. For instance, children in the EYFS will typically be writing lists and instructions. KS1 children will be experimenting with instructions, recounts and non-chronological reports, and by the end of KS2 they will have added explanations, persuasive writing, and biographical and autobiographical writing to their writing repertoire. There is also guidance, particularly in the *PNS* planning units, about poetry writing and its different forms, from shape poems to linked haiku poems.

Children as writers

From a young age most children feel the need to communicate. As they see adults responding to print in and out of the home they will start to understand the different purposes for written communication. Wanting to communicate in writing themselves arises when they see writing actually happening; children who play at taking an order in a café have been fortunate to see this use of writing in their own lives. The adult purposes and forms of writing become ever clearer and children start to copy these. They write letters, especially to Father Christmas, prescriptions whilst role playing doctors and nurses, lists of friends to invite to their party and notices banning siblings from their bedrooms. These non-fiction forms of writing, which have their counterpart in the adult world, often occur within the realm of narrative play, so long before children arrive at school they know a great deal about imaginary worlds and the roles that writing can play in such worlds. As we saw in Chapters 4 and 5, they will also be able to compose narratives even if they do not have the transcriptional skills with which to record these.

So when children arrive at school, they know a great deal about writing – about stories and non-fiction forms of writing. As children grow older, we see – and research confirms – that some boys lose interest in narrative and do not want to write stories, so it is most important that their natural inclination to write about facts is recognised through balanced teaching of a range of text types. (This does not mean that story becomes marginalised; it may mean we have to think carefully about the stories we are sharing in our classrooms.) Perhaps the revised (in 2003) KS2 tests recognised this as the tests do not always require the children to write a piece of narrative.

Some children are able to compose in different languages and, as you will remember from Chapter 3, this biliteracy is cognitively healthy and needs to be actively encouraged. Composing involves thinking, and if you are thinking in one language and being asked to write in another it may not be very easy to be fluent. If this is recognised by the teacher, opportunities can be provided to discuss, plan and compose in first languages in the early stages of writing. At a later stage the move can be made into English. You may find that children are more comfortable writing straightaway in English when the writing is in school curriculum areas (science, geography, etc.), whereas stories, which may spring from early experience in the mother tongue, may be more readily composed in that first language. At an early age some children will experiment with both languages together and there may be evidence of such code-switching in their writing. (See Figure 7.6 and Figure 9.3 later in the book for examples of this.)

Where linguistic diversity is valued and the children's use of different languages and dialects is actively promoted, there are exciting possibilities for joint composition. Two nine-year-old girls worked intently together to produce a dual-language text in English and Turkish. What you will notice in Figure 6.1 is their delight in offering this 'new' translated version which lures the reader in with the promise of 'jokes all the way along'.

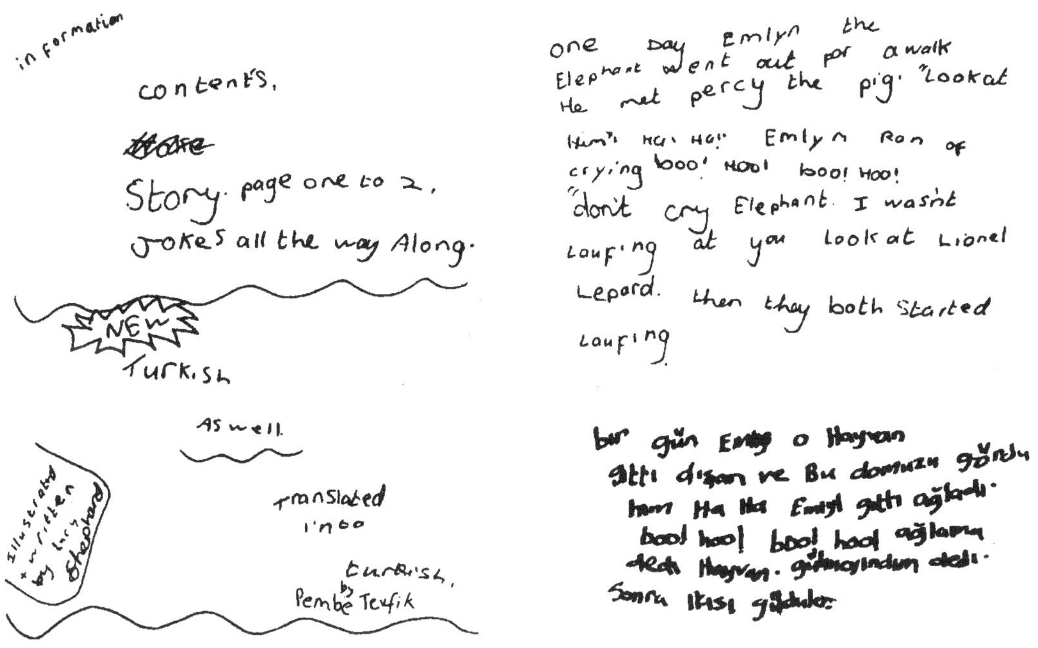

Figure 6.1

Teaching new text types

Whether teaching narrative, non-fiction or poetry, the same sequence of teaching can be followed.

Reading aloud

The teacher needs to read aloud the new text type in order that children can compose in the same genre. Hearing a piece of prose or poetry read aloud helps the child listener to hear the language and 'voice' of the poet or author.

Non-fiction writing also needs to be read and discussed so that children can tune in to the rather different structures and rhythms that belong to non-fiction genres.

Analysis

After such immersion the class need to be supported in analysing some of the different linguistic and structural features of the text. For instance, if you want to teach the children about the procedural genre you might offer them a recipe with all the verbs deleted in order to draw their attention to the use of the imperative.

Teacher modelling

Now the teacher builds on her children's emerging understanding and models the writing through sharing her thought processes as she writes in teacher demonstration. She may make use of a writing frame if she intends the children to use one in follow-up work.

Supported writing

Then children need to be supported in their independent writing efforts. This can be achieved through teacher scribing and supported composition within shared writing or by using an appropriate writing frame in guided group work.

Writing independently

Writing independently is always the goal of any teaching about writing and thus children should ideally be given the opportunity to compose their own text, whether for a known or unknown audience, and then be encouraged to reflect on the effectiveness of this writing.

NARRATIVE WRITING

> The promotion of children's understanding of narrative texts, and opportunities to create them, are core aspects of children's literacy development.
>
> (DfES, 2006a, see 'Planning', Year 2)

Stories have a basic structure: a beginning, a middle and an end. Children quickly realise this from hearing stories read and reading themselves. They also learn about this basic narrative structure from watching cartoons and dramas on children's television. Narratologists have analysed the structures of stories in order to show common patterns or story grammars and such descriptions can help our work with children. For instance Hoey (1983) gives us the following labels which could be easily understood and used by children: 'Situation', 'Problem', 'Solution' and 'Evaluation' (by which Hoey means how everything turns out and what has been learned).

At KS1, children may write stories that include familiar characters, settings similar to where they live, and personal experiences. They may also write about characters taken from fiction, exotic settings and fantasy experiences. Such stories may be simply structured with a beginning, perhaps taken from a traditional story ('Once upon a time . . .'), an event, and an ending with a resolution ('. . . and we all went home for tea'). Some young children may also write stories that are a series of linked events rather than including a problem or an inciting moment which is significant in narrative structure. The *PNS*, in acknowledgement of this, has placed emphasis on the link between reading and writing stories as well as teaching different aspects of story writing, which build on children's natural interest in narrative and books. It states that pupils should 'Use key features of narrative in their own writing' (Year 1, Strand 9) and 'Sustain form in narrative, including purpose and tense' (Year 2, Strand 9). The *PNS* also acknowledges that story writing is not just a set of learnt skills, 'but an essential means for them [the children] to express themselves in creative and imaginative ways' (DfES, 2006a); this is a key understanding for all who are involved in teaching writing in the primary classroom.

The question of how children develop their narrative writing is complex. Some young children's narratives will display surprising complexities of plot with narrative twists, chained episodes and the introduction of minor characters. (This is especially true when they are given the opportunity to dictate their stories, see Chapters 4 and 5.) This ability to handle complexity may have been acquired through wide reading rather than through being explicitly taught within the primary classroom. However, we cannot depend on this. As some children get older, they may experience problems with narrative writing such as: poor structure, lack of focus, too many linked incidents, poor endings or unwarranted shifts in narrative voice. The *PNS* suggests explicit teaching at KS2 of the component parts of narrative writing including character descriptions, narrative viewpoint and story structure in order to aid young writers in the craft of writing narrative.

Teaching narrative writing at KS1

This section provides a case study on fable writing carried out with a Year 1 class.

In planning this scheme of work the teacher had to think about the particular features of a fable, how to help children understand the structure of a fable and how to give them support in writing a fable for themselves. She started by reading a selection of Aesop's fables (including *The Fox and the Grapes*, *The Frog and the Stork*, and *The Boy who Cried Wolf*) and she discussed the differences and similarities between them.

The following sequence of activities was intended to encourage the children to think about narrative structure, choice of language and how the plot is linked to the moral. She wanted the children to see that each of the fables has a moral, a structure in common, and uses animal characters.

After the initial readings children retold a fable to one another, showing how important oral storytelling can be for such work as it brings about real personal engagement with the story. (It is particularly appropriate for stories like these that have been told for generations by word of mouth.) After this, the children carried out two written activities: a cloze procedure where they had to replace certain words in the story thus focusing their attention on the meanings of words in context, and a story board activity to help them reflect on the sequence of main events in a fable.

The children were then asked to write their own fable using animal characters and including a moral. Before the actual writing started, the children brainstormed relevant opening lines such as: 'In a far away land...', 'There was once...' and 'Long, long ago...'. After this the children discussed how such stories could end and two possibilities were decided on: either the characters learn a lesson or they meet a sticky end.

Finally, the teacher wanted to extend the children's use of vocabulary so she discussed words that the children might use in their writing. Together they compiled a list of useful adjectives which might suit the different characters ('curious', 'greedy', 'vain', 'massive', etc.). These were written on the board as a reference point for the children.

To help their thinking about structure the children were given a storyboard planner on which to plot the basic events of their fable. Michael's completed planner is shown in Figure 6.2.

Figure 6.2

After the planners were completed, the children discussed them with the teacher allowing her to respond to their attempts. This discussion is all-important, as it provides a context for the children to develop their thinking and creativity and also to be shown any problems in their story structure. Then, with their planners beside them, the children started their own independent story writing. The teacher continued to discuss their writing with them and enabled the kind of development below by Rebecca. This is the first draft of her writing:

The Cow and the Mirror
Once upon a time in a far away land lived a cow. The cow was very vain. The cow kept looking at herself in the mirror. One day the mirror smashed.

At this point Rebecca thought she had finished, but after discussion with the teacher she continued:

> ...into tiny pieces. She found a river and she went closer and saw her reflection. She got so close that she fell in the water. She was very sorry for herself and learned her lesson not to be so vain.

The completed story is more sophisticated in structure, with the moral linking quite clearly with the events of the story. Finally, here is Michael's completed fable:

> The Tiger and the Zebra
> In a hot country called Africa there lived a bright orange tiger who was so proud of his stripes. The tiger really couldn't think of another animal that had them. Every day he went to show off to the other animals. Then he went to sleep feeling very very proud of himself. When he woke up and went to show off to the other animals he saw a zebra and that zebra had stripes just like him. He was very upset with himself. He was so upset he couldn't sleep or speak to other animals because he was so upset. The moral of the story is don't show off.

In this we see Michael's grasp of story structure. He provides an opening 'situation', a tiger living in Africa. The 'problem' is that the tiger believes he is the only animal with stripes and thus becomes very vain; the 'solution' is that he sees the zebra and realises other animals have stripes; and the 'evaluation' is that he learns a lesson which is not to show off. Such well-organised, lively and coherent writing is a direct result of the teacher's well-thought-through approach to the teaching of narrative structure in fables.

Traditional stories are not, of course, the only narratives to be worked on at KS1; children will want to write in many other ways and it is important to support and respond to their interests and efforts.

Teaching narrative writing at KS2

In this section, the teaching of more complex narrative aspects – such as characterisation, more varied beginnings and endings, settings and descriptions, and narrator's point of view – are considered.

Tantalising beginnings and satisfying endings

A good beginning will engage readers and encourage them to want to read on. They will want to go on to discover the story, answer questions that have been posed and fill gaps that have been left by the author. Many an author hints at secrets that will be revealed later in the book (as in the opening of *Gulf* in the example below). Reading a range of literature allows children to experience different beginnings and consider the ways that authors engage the reader's attention. Some use arresting dialogue: "Where's Papa going with that axe?" said Fern', from *Charlotte's Web* (E. B. White); some involve us immediately with the character's dilemmas: 'I loved my brother. Right from the start. But did I love him enough? You shouldn't use people you love. Maybe what happened to him was all my fault...', from *Gulf* (Robert Westall); and some shock us with the drama of the opening statement. 'When Bill Simpson woke up on Monday morning, he found he was a girl', from *Bill's New Frock* (Anne Fine).

As children develop their reading and writing, so their personal beginnings start to diversify. Below is a selection of KS2 beginnings that mirror the different categories discussed above:

And what do you think you are doing in my garden? snapped Mary.

(Year 6)

Suddenly everything went dark, I panicked.

(Year 5)

It was on a Sunday evening when I went to church to say my prayers, when all of a sudden a beam of light shone down on me.

(Year 6)

However, it is not only the first few lines that make an impact on the reader; it is also the first page. Comparing interesting and dull first pages will help children think about their own writing. Try looking at the first page of *Cold Shoulder Road* (Joan Aiken). What is it that makes us want to read on?

Every night, around nine o'clock in Cold Shoulder Road, the screaming began. It came from the end house in the row. It was not very loud. The sound was like the cries of the gulls who flew and whirled along the shingle-bank on the seaward side of the road. People who lived in the road (there were not many of them) took no notice of the screaming. It's the gull, they thought, or the wind: or, whatever it is, it's no business of ours. Only one person felt differently, and she lived next door to the house from which the screaming came. Night after night she clenched her hands and stood trembling by the window. Something has got to be done, she thought. Something must be done. At last she did it.

The impact of repeated words ('gull', 'screaming'), a short paragraph and the closing focus on the girl with her clenched hands who is going to take action all contribute to the power and tension of this opening.

Completing a story may be difficult for the young writer, especially if the organisation of the story does not support a conclusion. Often children's stories conclude weakly with, 'I woke up and it was all a dream', or, 'I went home to have my tea'. To move children on from this stage it is important to discuss endings of favourite novels with the class, to find out if they were satisfying and left a feeling of 'Yes, I agree with this'. As with beginnings, different endings do different things: some answer questions, some leave questions unanswered and some raise new questions. Endings can entail physical movement – for instance a person walking out of sight along a road, a character travelling to a new country or getting into a car and looking back. All these leave the reader with the impression that the story is moving on, and that the narrative continues even though the book has finished. These and other techniques discussed here leave the reader with a sense of fulfilment in the narrative and it is worth spending time with children looking at interesting endings such as this one in Michael Rosen's *The Bakerloo Flea*:

She told me I was the first person she'd ever told the story to, and told me never to tell anyone. The scandal would be terrible. I don't know whether to believe her or not.

Such work will help children reflect on their own writing, just as Ricky (Year 5) did: 'It was a really exciting story. Only I knew who the burglar was till the end when I revealed ALL – like on the telly!'

The key to a good ending lies in the planning and structure of the story, although this will not always come when you start the planning. Once the writer has established the basic structure of the plot and started writing, then the ending or resolution will fit more easily into place. To conclude with a satisfying ending, here is Rachel's (Year 6) 'epilogue' to her World War 2 family saga, *Father at War* (see p. 113):

> I never saw Mrs Whitby again, but I will never forget her. Some memories cannot be forgotten. Like the war, not that a war is an easy thing to forget, with all its deaths, bombs, battles. I want to forget the war, like waking up from a bad dream, but as much as I try I know I will never forget it.

Planning and structuring plots

Young writers often find the structure of a story difficult to manage and, as a result, their stories may become a lengthy string of events which do not have much relevance to the outcome of the story. As Jamil, a Year 6 writer, commented, 'You have to work your way down and when you get to the middle and end you have to decide. You've been writing the first paragraph and then you have to jump into something else. Description is okay but what happens is difficult.' Jamie hesitates after the first paragraph because he knows that he cannot just launch into an irrelevant event. If he does, he will have 'lost the plot'. QCA focuses on endings which are satisfying only if they spring from all that has gone before: 'A lack of structure is evident in the frequency of ineffective endings of narrative. Stories often begin well, but endings do not link back to openings or offer satisfying solutions' (QCA, 2001: 3). One of the reasons that traditional tales are so pleasing and offer such powerful models for children's own writing is that no element of the story is superfluous. Goldilocks eats little bear's porridge; she breaks his chair; she sleeps in his bed. All these events are significant; the bears go over the same territory and find Goldilocks asleep. She leaps up and leaves the house which she entered so heedlessly at the start of the story.

The *PNS* attempts to help young writers structure their narrative writing and understand the significance of relevant events to a plot. However, unless a child is allowed the time to write a complete story she will not be able to put into practice what has been learnt during the dedicated literacy lesson. Many schools arrange for at least one slot of extended writing each week so that longer pieces of writing can be shaped and completed.

A young writer needs time to think and create as story writing seldom happens instantaneously. Ideally, time should be taken to think about and internalise the task. Some children will draw during this time, others will discuss their ideas with their writing partners (see Chapter 5), and others will search for inspiration in earlier pieces of writing and in books. Preliminary work on plot, characters and setting could be carried out during the dedicated literacy lesson while the extended writing itself could be done outside this period when the children have the time needed to work on longer pieces.

Story planners or prompts help structure narrative, as well as prompting ideas. Some children will need more structure than others and it is advisable to differentiate according to need. Below is an example of some planning prompts that can be adjusted to meet the different needs of children. These could be organised in clearly delineated sections.

Story planner
- Who are you writing the story for (audience)?
- What is the story about?
- What type of story is it (adventure, horror, fantasy, historical or other)?
- Who are the main characters?
- Where and when is the story set?
- Who is telling the story and how much do they know (narrator's voice)?
- What is the first sentence? Have you interested the reader?
- How are you going to develop the plot?
- Ideas for the ending? (These can be added to as you are writing the story.)

Sharing a clearly structured story with children supports creativity in their writing as the following example, from a Year 3 child, shows. The story imitates Jill Murphy's book *On the Way Home*, but the young writer has added her own reasons for the accident:

> Rosie was going home to tell her Mum she had a bad knee. On the way home she met her friend Harry.
> 'Look at my bad knee!' exclaimed Rosie.
> 'How did you do it?' gasped Harry.
> 'Well,' said Rosie. 'There was a wild horny bull over in the calm countryside but luckily I managed to close the gate and he banged his head and the gate banged my knee and that's how I got my bad knee.'
> 'Oh my!' gasped Harry.
> Then she met her friend Lucy.
> 'Look at my bad knee!' gasped Rosie.
> 'How did you do it?' asked Lucy.
> 'Well' said Rosie. 'There was an angry aqua dolphin and it tried to drown me! But luckily I got out of the water so I couldn't drown but when I got out I tripped over and that's how I got my bad knee.'
> 'Oh my!' screamed Lucy.

And so the story continues with Rosie making up a different reason for her bad knee every time she meets a friend. This tight framework gave support to the young writer and in doing so allowed for the child's imagination to create different situations in a most successful manner.

Characterisation

For children to develop characters in stories, they need to consider the techniques writers use to depict character. An obvious technique is to give character details through the narrator's description of what the character looks like, their past, their thoughts and their actions. A second device is to allow characters to reveal themselves through direct speech. An author can also show us the character through the thoughts of other people in the story. To draw on all these techniques it is useful to give children a checklist of questions:

- What does the character look like?
- What do other people think of them?
- What are the typical things this character would say?
- What are they seen doing?

The most common of these techniques, narrative description, is explored below and concludes with a piece of writing by a Year 6 girl, Rachel, which demonstrates all the above techniques in her competent characterisation.

Young writers need to be reassured that they can draw from the people they know – their friends and family – as well as people they read about. Many teachers ask children to compose descriptions for their classmates to identify. They can be reminded of memorable characters they have met in their own reading (Harry Potter or maybe Dahl's Big Friendly Giant) and help them to see how the author uses the above techniques. Consider a passage such as this initial paragraph from a short story by Bill Naughton where he introduces us, through a narrator's description, to the main character:

> Spit Nolan was a pal of mine. He was a thin lad with a bony face that was always pale, except for rosy spots on his cheekbones. He had quick brown eyes, rather stooped shoulders, and we all knew that he had only one lung. He had had a disease which in those days couldn't be cured, unless you went away to Switzerland, which Spit certainly couldn't afford. He wasn't sorry for himself in any way, and in fact we envied him, because he never had to go to school.
>
> (1970: 20)

Using such a passage, you might ask the children to highlight the things they learn about Spit in one short paragraph: his appearance, his disability, his poverty and his positive outlook. From this activity, the children could then carry out a 'search' for similar objective descriptions in their reading.

To conclude this section, here is the beginning of the third chapter of Rachel's World War 2 saga:

> Father At War
> A few days after the scene in the dining room there were hasty goodbyes at the railway station, my mother talked on about eating well and not getting to sleep too late until my father gave her a brief hug, a quick peck on the cheek and disappeared into the crowds of uniformed men. 'Well that's your father off,' she said briskly to us and tickled me on the tummy, I stared back at her with big eyes. 'Well come on' she snapped as if cross at me for not laughing as my tummy was very ticklish. When we got home mother busied herself in the kitchen making tea. Mary, George and I scrambled up the stairs and into Mary's room where we all sat on the bed and talked. We talked about the war and all the changes that would come into our lives. We talked about father and what he would be doing now. Mary was scared and she and I cried, me clinging onto Mary like a rag doll. George was brave and stern now that he was the man of the house but I often saw a flicker of fear pass through his eyes.

In shared text work, the teacher could show the class how Rachel has portrayed the mother's character through the narrator's description ('she snapped'); through an account of actions (she 'tickled me', she 'busied herself in the kitchen'); through direct speech ('Well, that's your father off!') and through other characters' thoughts (she 'talked on about eating well'). The class could then go on to look at how she has characterised Mary, George and the narrator and how skillfully suggestive the writing is of trials that are to come.

Point of view

A story can be written in the first or third person, although most narrative writing for children is in the third person. Narrators may, in 'omniscient' mode, tell us everything a character or characters are doing, thinking and feeling. Alternatively, narrators may only 'report' on their characters' actions and leave readers to infer how they must feel and think. Just as in first person narratives, a single character is usually the focus of the narrator's attention. We as readers usually have no problem in knowing who is the character to watch. Writing in the first person is something children will be doing readily in their recounts: 'We were in Lanzarote and we went to the lagoon. I said to my Mum, "Can't I go scuba diving with Emma my new friend I met at the swings?"' (Year 4). However, making the kind of shift to first person narrative writing that Rachel, in the above examples, does so successfully usually requires teacher support. Children need to understand that the first person narrator does not have to be them, but may be a fictitious person telling the story from his or her point of view, as the wolf does in *The True Story of the Three Little Pigs* (Jon Scieszka):

> Everyone knows the story of the *Three Little Pigs*. Or at least they think they do. But I'll let you into a little secret. Nobody knows the real story, because nobody has ever heard my side of the story.

Considering another person's perspective can be difficult but placing children in imaginary situations allows them to write successfully as a particular character, as this Year 5 writer has done, taking the role of the dormouse in her revisiting of the Mad Hatter's tea-party:

> The Mad Hatter and the March Hare were having their tea. I was asleep. Alice had just sat down after the Mad Hatter had said, 'No room!'. Alice started telling us her story when all of a sudden she brought Dina into it. Dina is her cat! 'Cat!' I yelled. I jumped up and ran into the Mad Hatter's arms. The Mad Hatter asked the March Hare to give him some treacle to put on my nose. I love treacle. After that I was put back in the teapot and I went back to sleep.

Talking whilst writing

Alongside planning, an important aspect of any young writer's work is the continuing discussion and feedback that usefully takes place during the process of writing. Guided writing is the ideal place for this to occur. One of the most significant teaching points is when a teacher intervenes or supports a young writer while they are actually in the process of writing. Teacher intervention can occur at any point in the writing process, whether the group is just beginning a story or is in the middle of a draft. A supportive and sensitive comment or suggestion can help the young writer's understanding of structure, perspective and voice. Even when the work is complete, sharing with an audience will also give children opportunities to sharpen their writing.

Narrative writing engages children's imaginations. It allows them to explore the literary world for themselves and become real authors. In order to do this children need careful support and structure offered through interactions with both books and teachers.

Further reading and websites

Armstrong, M. (2006) *Children Writing Stories*. Milton Keynes: Open University Press.

Barrs, M. (2004) 'The reader in the writer', in Grainger, T. (ed.) *The RoutledgeFalmer Reader in Language and Literacy*. London: RoutledgeFalmer.

Corbett, P. (2001) *How to Teach Fiction Writing at Key Stage 2*. London: David Fulton Publishers.

DfES (2006b) *Progression in Narrative*. London: DfES. www.standards.dfes.gov.uk/ primaryframework/downloads/PDF/Prognarrative.pdf (accessed 21 September 2008).

Goodwin, P. (2005) *The Literate Classroom* (Chapter 11). London: David Fulton Publishers (first published 1999).

Lewis, M. (2005) 'Developing children's narrative writing using story structures', in Goodwin, P. (ed.) *The Literate Classroom*. London: David Fulton Publishers (first published 1999).

Sedgwick, F. (2001) *Teaching Literacy* (Chapters 1–3). London: Continuum.

Thomas, H. (1998) *Reading and Responding to Fiction: Classroom Strategies for Developing Literature* (Chapter 1). Leamington Spa: Scholastic.

Everybody Writes www.everybodywrites.org.uk (accessed 21 September 2008).

See also:
Read and Respond series: Scholastic
Writing Guides (for fiction): Scholastic
50 Shared Texts series: Scholastic

POETRY WRITING

> Reading and writing poetry helps me understand myself, clarify my thoughts and see things in a new way. It keeps the mind alert and also satisfies that basic urge we have to create something unique.
>
> (Brownjohn, 1994: 15)

The *PNS* argues that, 'Exposure to, and opportunities to engage with, poetry are core aspects of children's literacy development'. As a result poetry units are included in each of the seven years. In the EYFS, children are encouraged to build on their knowledge of poetry by playing with sounds and words, making up rhymes and singing songs. This chimes with what we know about young children's early interest in playing with rhyme and rhythm. Songs, advertisements, TV jingles, nursery rhymes, rhyming stories and finger and action rhymes foster and exploit this early delight in language. As they get older they find that poetry comes in different forms, not always rhyming, and is to be found on the page as well as in the ear. They learn that words in poetry have been memorably ordered to represent feeling. They learn that Walter de la Mare can evoke moonlight perfectly, just as Michael Rosen can sum up how they feel about a younger sibling.

Children will find out about these joys when enthusiastic adults surround them with the work of many poets. We need to read a great deal to them and let the poems and poets do the work for us. We can be sure that poets like John Agard, Charles Causley and Christina Rossetti will work their magic. Sandy Brownjohn reminds us that, 'The teacher should be interested in and enthusiastic about poetry; otherwise the children themselves will be indifferent towards it' (1994: 85). Many schools have found that a visit from a poet who shares his or her working approaches results in increased confidence and interest in writing poetry. By sharing and enjoying poetry, children will realise that they, too, can represent images and feelings through words which they choose and work on with care. Six-year-old Claire did just that with her first poem:

> Out in the playground
> Mark stands at the top of the slide
> Afraid to come down.

In the above example, Claire has not only worked from her own observations and understanding of feeling, but she has also benefited from her teacher's help in looking at form, in this case the three-line haiku. Such inspection of form is an important part of teaching children to compose poetry.

Sandy Brownjohn advocates that teaching different techniques to children will develop their skills as composers of poetry, encourage them to play with language, give them the freedom to manipulate words and allow them to control what they say. She separates 'all the individual details which go to make the whole. Every part is understood as it is conquered' (ibid.: 7). She suggests that a great deal of this type of work can be carried out through games and puzzles. Her 'Furniture Game' (ibid.: 19) helps children with description and develops their use of metaphor and simile. It is a guessing game with one child thinking of a person that the rest of the children know and describing this person as a piece of furniture, a plant, a type of food and a time of day. The following example comes from a Year 4 child. Look at the way in which the exercise has enabled her to follow her three similes with a metaphor:

> She is like a cushion
> She is like a sweet smelling rose
> She is like a cheesy pizza
> This person is an afternoon person.

This child and her classmates were being encouraged to appreciate the effects you can create through manipulating language. Just four lines of this sort of work can be put on the page and begin to look like a poem.

At this stage children need to know that there are formal ways of crafting poetry, and they will enjoy experimenting with these. However, the *PNS* paper *Progression in Poetry* argues that: 'mastery of many forms is highly skilled and young children may find themselves constrained by attempting demanding structures' (DfES, 2006c: 1). Such structures can be seen as a support for young poets that 'should not interfere but should liberate creatively'. Unlike the *NLS*, which included a comprehensive coverage of the forms, the *PNS* identifies a more modest range of simple forms that children should draw on in their own writing:

- collage or list poem
- free verse
- shape poems (free verse in a shape)
- short patterned poems, for example, haiku, cinquain, kennings
- borrow or invent own pattern, for example, pairs of lines
- simple rhyming form, for example, rap.

(DfES, 2006c: 1)

Whenever a new or revised form is taught the teacher can model these in shared writing. The success with which children use such forms will be determined by maturity, experience and ability, and by the appropriateness of the form; if you want to lament your cat's death you are more likely to choose the form of an elegy rather than a limerick.

One such form that all poets enjoy is shape (or concrete) poetry, where the poem is written in the shape of the object that is being written about. A very young child might enjoy making a shape poem to represent a snail. George Herbert, the seventeenth-century poet, made a sophisticated shape poem in the shape of angel's wings. Figure 6.3 is written by a Year 4 child in the shape of a rose.

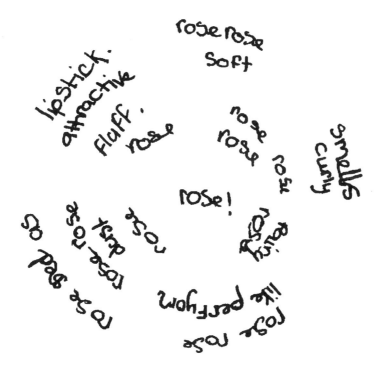

Figure 6.3

As well as being given support with technique and form, children need to be aware that poetry springs from many different starting points but particularly from 'personal or imagined experience'. As the *PNS* states: 'Children write most effectively about subjects that they have experienced and that matter. It is the desire to capture and communicate to a reader or listener real experience and genuine feeling, or to play with language, that leads to the most powerful writing' (DfES, 2006c: 2). Michael Rosen, a poet who has inspired many children in recent decades, believes that better poetry is written if children value their own experiences ('I broke my mum's vase yesterday'), using the actual words that people speak ('That's my favourite vase you've broken') and their own responses and feelings ('Why does she keep going on at me? She shouldn't have left it in the sink anyway'). All of this can be the stuff of their poetry. 'My point in asking children to write down what people say and what they think, is that this is knowledge they already possess. It isn't something they have to concoct or translate' (1989: 43). Jill Pirrie (1987), a teacher who has worked with many children, believes that the close observation that she encourages in her children, whether it be of ants in the grass outside the school or of how they feel about a promise being broken, is what lies behind an effective poem.

Such work can be particularly empowering for children who are regarded as 'low achievers'. If these children work with familiar content, with a prescribed and supportive framework, and with no expectation that they have to write at length, then they have a real opportunity to compose successfully in ways that they may not be able to do in prose. Sandy Brownjohn states:

> Teachers should be prepared to be surprised by the good quality of writing that may soon be in evidence from children who were hitherto low achievers. In fact, it is not always the most able children who write the best poetry in schools.
>
> (1994: 5)

In the writing of poetry the points that are made throughout this book about process (issues such as drafting) and product (issues such as presentation and publishing) are particularly significant. When children are working on what are often quite short stretches of text, then the motivation to shape and work on writing is enhanced. Children's poetry should not only be published, decorated and displayed but also performed to other children and parents. Many teachers make anthologies and tape collections of children's poetry which are highly motivating. All of this will contribute to the sense of audience and purpose with which they can approach the composing.

Teaching poetry writing involves experiencing poems, exploring words and language, looking at different forms and believing in the validity of one's own experience. 'The pursuit of form, coupled with the encouragement to revise and refine first impressions, leads writers back to their experiences and makes them respond more deeply to them' (Tunnicliffe, 1984: 151).

Finally, Figure 6.4 is a lullaby, a song written to lull babies to sleep, but in this case written for the sleepy dormouse in *Alice in Wonderland*. Influenced by Clare and Helen's reading and their knowledge of the form, this poem still contains their voices in its final cautionary advice. Notice also how they have enjoyed presenting their poem.

Dormouse's Lullaby

Rock-a-bye Dormouse,
In the teapot.
Sucking your treacle,
And sleeping a lot.
When nightfall comes,
You will climb up the spout.
But do watch out,
'Cause Queenie's about!

by Clare and Helen

Figure 6.4

Further reading and websites

DfES (2006c) *Progression in Poetry*. London: DfES. www.standards.dcsf.gov.uk/primaryframework/downloads/PDF/Progpoetry.pdf (accessed 21 September 2008).

Lockwood, M. (2008) 'Poetry for children', in Goodwin, P. (ed.) *Understanding Children's Books*. London: SAGE.

Morgan, M. (2003) *How to Teach Poetry Writing at Key Stage 1*. London: David Fulton Publishers.

Morgan, M. (2003) *How to Teach Poetry Writing at Key Stage 2*. London: David Fulton Publishers.

Poetry Library Children's Zone www.poetrylibrary.org.uk/education/children/ (accessed 21 September 2008).

PoetryZone www.poetryzone.ndirect.co.uk/content.htm (accessed 21 September 2008).

Children's Poetry Archive www.poetryarchive.org/childrensarchive/home.do (accessed 21 September 2008).

See also:

Scholastic *Writing Guides* for Poetry and PCET posters (and teachers' notes) for Michael Rosen and Roger McGough.

NON-FICTION WRITING

Non-fiction writing in primary schools covers a range of purposes and forms and children need to be given opportunities to write in these, in meaningful contexts, for clearly defined purposes and for specific audiences. In this book there are examples of very young children writing lists, captions and labels. At Key Stages 1 and 2, non-fiction writing occurs across the curriculum as, for example, children label diagrams in science, write diary accounts in history, captions in geography and instructions in design and technology.

Cross-curricular links

Most of the examples of writing discussed in this section come from different curriculum areas. However, the language and structural features of these different types of writing will be taught explicitly in the dedicated literacy lesson. For instance, in Year 2, instructional, explanation and non-chronological report writing are all taught. Non-chronological report writing is returned to throughout KS2, an indication of how much there is to learn about this text type and of how the teaching can be and needs to be planned in a coherent way that builds on previous understanding. An important point to remember about the link between the *PNS* and other curriculum areas is the need for children to apply their understanding of the text type they are learning about. For instance, when children are learning about non-chronological report writing in a literacy lesson, they need to apply this understanding by using this type of writing in either science or geography, subjects which frequently demand report writing. Here is an example of a Year 5 child's writing in geography:

> Igneous Rocks
> Rocks are sometimes formed from a red-hot liquid that has cooled down and slowly hardened. This type of rock is called igneous. Here are some examples of igneous rock: granite, basalt, diorite, obsian and andesite. Another example of igneous is pumice. It is cooled lava that comes to the surface of the ground. People sometimes use it to clean dry skin off their feet. Granite is a quite a common rock. It is hard, tough cooled molten lava. The speckles are really compact crystals mixed into the lava, which can't be seen to the naked eye. It can be pink, white or grey and sparkly. The whole of Dartmoor is really one big block of granite. But one thing the stones look completely different and I think I know why. It is because the pumice is made on the surface and so it gets more air and that's why it looks bubbly and smooth but granite on the other hand is made under the surface and does not get so much air and that's why it is so solid.

This is a competent piece of writing that demonstrates the way in which a report is structured and all its characteristics. It includes an opening general statement, use of technical vocabulary, generalisations and the use throughout of the present tense. As a class teacher you could use such a well structured piece to show the class, perhaps on an interactive whiteboard in shared text work, how to organise this genre. (As a teacher you would note that the personal tone of the hypothesis at the end is not strictly a feature of reports, but you would nevertheless be pleased to see how writing, thinking and learning unite at this point.)

Within many of the foundation and core subjects writing is used to help children think and learn, to remember what they have learnt and to give the teacher some

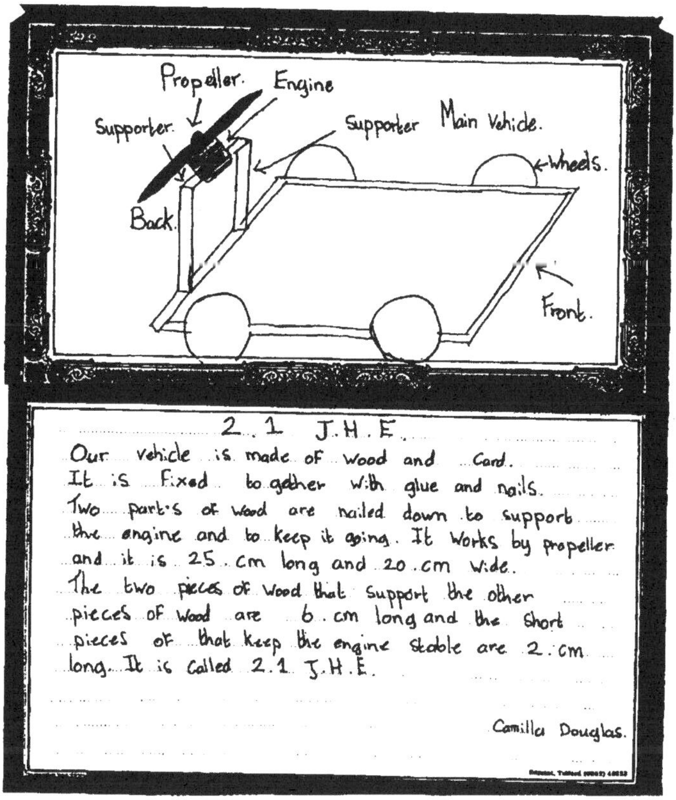

Figure 6.5

evidence to assess their learning. One example of this is seen in Figure 6.5, an explanation of a vehicle designed and made in a Design and Technology lesson.

The diagram gives the reader a clear idea of what the vehicle looks like. It is labelled, with arrows to show the different parts of the vehicle. The text does not have an opening paragraph as most explanations do, but the diagram may act as such.

A subject such as history gives children opportunities to write in a range of genres for different audiences and in different contexts. A topic such as The Victorians will allow older children to write explanations of the growth of the Empire, newspaper reports that argue for the abolition of child labour or discussion papers on whether to have the Great Exhibition or not. The *PNS* confirms this: 'Application across the curriculum gives children opportunities to make informed choices and decisions about form and purpose when writing' (DfES, 2006d: 1). By linking other curriculum areas to literacy teaching, the children's learning becomes much more effective than in one-off lessons. Cross-curricular links need to cover not only non-fiction writing but also narrative and poetry. An example of this would be to write a poem or story about living in the past.

Teaching about genres (text types)

Generally, as children move through the key stages, non-fiction writing features more strongly across the curriculum. To help children learn about different text types – recount; explanation; report; procedural; argument; and discussion – it is important for the class teacher to model these for the children. This can be achieved through shared writing, with the whole class or in a guided writing group, which allows children to investigate the structure, language and purpose of the genre. It is important to have examples of such writing displayed in the classroom for the children to read and explore themselves. Reading and discussing information books will also help children hear and understand the different language patterns and features of texts, as will exposure to information books in group and guided reading sessions. Lewis and Wray (1995) argue that the careful support that children need in writing different text types can be provided by 'writing frames' – a series of prompts specific to a genre. In the worked example below, a procedural genre (recipe writing) is being taught. The example demonstrates how a writing frame can be used. In the following section we are going to focus on the teaching of one specific genre – procedural – in order to illustrate both the teaching strategies and also progression.

Procedural writing

The procedural genre is one of the easier genres to understand because it records a sequence of events in time (chronologically), and aspects of it can be taught to children of all ages. It can cover any set of instructions which use a series of sequenced steps: instructions for playing a game, using a DVD recorder or building a model. The *PNS* recommends that in Year 2 procedural writing is modelled for pupils – for instance, instructions for playing a game or planting a seed for a science activity. Children can then write their own simple instructions independently for getting to school, for example, or playing a different game. In Year 5, pupils are expected to write 'a set of instructions which deviate from the norm in terms of structure and language features (e.g. recipes)' and then test these out with another pupil (DfES, 2006a; see 'Planning' Year 2).

As discussed in the introduction to this chapter, when introducing a new text type to children it is important to read and analyse the text. A selection of recipes, for instance, is shared with the children and used to explore features of this type of writing. The use of imperative verbs such as 'stir', 'shake', 'fold' or 'beat', the layout and organisation of the text and the use of adverbs in describing how to carry out the actions are all features of this genre which the teacher would focus on. The following is a selection of investigative activities that the children could attempt before beginning their own instructional writing:

- Find the (imperative) verbs in the recipe, e.g. 'mix', 'stir', 'beat'.
- Add some adverbs to a recipe, e.g. 'Mix the batter *thoroughly*'.
- Find the temporal connectives, e.g. 'next', 'then'.
- Reassemble a cut-up recipe.

From investigating published recipes children can then move on to being supported in writing their own, initially as a shared writing exercise. At this point an enlarged writing frame can be used as a model. A writing frame gives a series of prompts specific to the genre so a writing frame for a recipe might look like this:

- How to make . . .
- Ingredients . . .
- Equipment . . .
- Method . . .
    First
    Next
    Next
    Finally

With this support, the children could either go on to individual work with frames or they could write their own recipes independently. For a child who needs more support additional information can be inserted into the writing frame (e.g. some of the ingredients with quantities); for the more experienced child you could delete prompts under 'Method' shown here. (Full examples of a variety of frames are outlined more fully in the books by Lewis and Wray.) When the child is using the frame with confidence, recipes can be written independently. Such scaffolded teaching is powered by and is a clear demonstration of Vygotsky's (1978) theory of the zone of proximal development (see Chapter 1).

Many teachers in KS1 also teach the procedural genre through the use of recipes after children have been cooking. At this age the work might focus on broader aspects of layout, particularly how the ingredients appear as a list (*NC*, p. 9). Preliminary activities to 'warm' the genre could include reading and sharing recipes, and sequencing cut-up recipes. With an enlarged version of a favourite recipe a shared text session could be used to identify and label the different 'sections' in the recipe. After shared work on an enlarged frame the children could proceed to individual work, this time with a modified version of the one above. For instance, the stages in the method could be numbered.

In summary, we have seen children in the examples above:

- clarifying the audience and purpose;
- exploring and discussing different texts in an interesting and structured way;
- writing the genre alongside the teacher;
- using a frame to support their own writing, either alone or with a partner;
- writing the genre independently.

In the next example a group of Year 5 children use the procedural genre to write an instruction book for a school camera, which used film. The handbook had been lost and the class was asked to write new handbooks for different people in the school. This gave the children real audiences and a purpose for doing the writing. One group wrote a handbook for the nursery children and staff, another group for children of their own age, and another wrote for the staff of the school. The teachers had instructed them to make the text simple, straightforward and understandable! As it was Christmas, the children included 'Snappy the Reindeer' to act as guide for the book – an ingenious play on words. The manual was word processed.

Preparations
To take a photo takes a lot of preparation.
First of all you have to buy the film.
To load it you pull a catch on the bottom of the camera on the right side. That will open the back.
Pull up the little switch (called the rewind button) on the top right of the camera. With the little knob on the bottom of the film, slot it into the channel on the left hand side inside the camera. Push the rewind button home again and pull about four inches of film across from the reel and put the holes of the film on the sprockets which are on the two cogs. Slot the bit of the film that gets narrower into the take up spool on the right side of the camera and turn it slowly clockwise until the film catches. Close the back of the camera and wind on the film until the numbers on the top of the camera reach O. You are now ready to position your aspect, ready for the photo.

The text makes some use of imperatives, such as 'pull', 'slot' and 'push'. Although unconventionally laid out in one block, it takes the reader clearly through the sequence of steps required to take a photograph. It might have been more appropriate for the instructions to be laid out in numbered or lettered bullet points which would help the reader follow the instructions. Such support could have been introduced through the use of a writing frame.

The last example shows how an equally purposeful context, this time personal understanding of her pet guinea pig, motivates the Year 5 writer to take on board the features, including layout, competently.

How to Look after a Guinea-Pig
You will need:

- A guinea-pig
- Some straw
- A hutch
- Water
- An old tooth-brush
- A run
- Some grass
- Guinea pig food

1 Gently pick up your guinea-pig.
2 Get an adult to set up the run on a patch of grass.
  Now gently put the guinea-pig inside the run. DO NOT drop the guinea-pig. If it starts kicking gently put it down inside the run.
3 Get inside the run. Get your old tooth-brush and gently pick up your guinea-pig and place it on your lap.
4 Gently brush your guinea-pig's fur like this.
5 Put some straw in your Guinea-pig hutch, some food and water. (Ask an adult to help.)
6 DO NOT leave your guinea-pig alone, because a cat could kill it or it could escape.
7 Pick up your guinea-pig and put it in the hutch.

Taking notes

In many non-fiction writing activities, both across the curriculum and within the dedicated literacy lesson, children need to research specific pieces of information. Such pre-writing activity and research may involve reading information books, searching CD-ROMs, or exploring the Internet. In such research children need to make notes and this is something they need support with, particularly in overcoming the problem of verbatim copying of facts. In Year 5 the *PNS* states that children need to 'Make notes on and use evidence from across a text to explain events or ideas' (Strand 7). Wray and Lewis (1997: 37) remind us that 'to neglect the link between purpose and recording is to risk leaving children feeling that they have to note down all the information they read, even if it is only slightly relevant'.

As with other forms of writing the teacher can model note-taking in shared writing with the class or guided writing with a group. Such modelling could use the interactive whiteboard, a CD-ROM or a DVD as well as written text and could be reinforced in guided reading and writing sessions. Another way of helping children is through the use of a frame or grid which will help them consider what they already know and what they want to find out. Here is one example of a 'Know, Want, Learn' (KWL) grid with the third column allowing for note-taking:

What do I know? What do I want to find out? What did I learn?

(Wray and Lewis 1997: 47)

When reading information texts, children can be shown how to identify words and phrases that are significant. Teacher modelling can illustrate how this can be achieved, using an interactive whiteboard. After this, children can work on their own photocopy, highlighting key words and writing notes in the margin. A further suggestion might be for children to read a piece of information writing and then retell it to a partner in their own words. This oral rehearsal allows children to articulate what they want to write down and thus gives clarity to their thoughts. The important thing in all of this is to keep the link between purpose and recording very clear for the children.

Layout

Children know quite a lot about how texts are laid out from their experiences of writing outside school. Rules for playing games, instructions for assembling Lego models, catalogue pages and video packaging are all very much part of their reading lives. We can build on this implicit knowledge to help children explicitly reflect on the role of organisation and layout in non-fiction writing.

Different types of writing require different layouts and, even though writers may not attend to this aspect in the early stages, knowing about layouts and, ultimately, using them can aid the organisation of the composition. In your discussions and modelling of layout with children you will, of course, look at the layout of some narrative texts such as play scripts and poetry where layout plays such an important part; there are also some layouts, such as those used for letters, which relate to both narrative and non-fiction texts. Some are specific to non-fiction: lists, rules, instructions and so on. Some layouts are very familiar in our society and children will use them with ease; others are not so visible and children will need more inducting into their conventions.

As we saw in the examples above, layout is an important aspect of some genres, governing, as it does, the reader's expectations. For instance, look back at 'Preparations' and consider how much the use of headings and sub-headings and the use of bullet points would have helped the reader. Writing on screen enables layout aspects to be worked on easily.

WRITING IN ROLE: NARRATIVE AND NON-FICTION

One further area to explore in this chapter is writing in role. This allows children to explore imaginary situations and can give them encouragement and support in writing in a range of text types, which links clearly with the *PNS* drama strand (4). Writing in role allows young writers to feel a real need and purpose for writing; it gives them a strong context for writing and empowers them to write for a real (albeit imaginary) audience. Taking on writing in another role is a possible follow-up from reading or drama as the two examples below demonstrate.

Writing after reading

One of the most productive contexts for working on non-fiction is, paradoxically, the context of a story. A text such as *Mrs Plug the Plumber* (Allan Ahlberg and Joe Wright) could stimulate writing activities such as:

- a catalogue of a plumber's equipment, labelled and in alphabetical order;
- safety notices for certain pieces of equipment, e.g. the blowlamp;
- a leaflet to advertise Mrs Plug's services;
- tickets for the world cruise and luggage labels;
- a note to cancel the milk;
- a postcard home from the Plugs.

Figure 6.6 is an example of the postcard which Elloa has written using the information that she gained from the story. (The address was clearly scribed on the reverse of the card.) She is writing in role as Mrs Plug although she does not completely sustain it as we see when she switches into her own name as she signs off.

The story has enabled Elloa to write in a generic form, in this case a recount which is quite a comfortable genre for children as it is often personal and about people and events familiar to them. She uses 'I' and 'we' and the past tense, all generic features of recount, and not difficult to manage because of the clear links with writing in the first person narrative.

All stories can give opportunities for genuinely contextualised writing in non-fiction genres. At KS2, a novel such as *The Runaways* (Ruth Thomas) could give rise to writing a missing person's poster, a newspaper article about the missing children and a police report on progress in the investigation so far. A historical novel such as *The Wreck of the Zanzibar* (Michael Morpurgo) gives opportunities for persuasive writing, promoting the grandmother's and Laura's view that the turtle should not be eaten, and procedural writing in the form of instructions on how to reach the Scilly Isles. Within this context children not only have a real purpose for writing but also develop and extend their understanding of the narrative. This has clearly been outlined in the research by Barrs and Cork (2001) described in *The Reader in the Writer* in which Year 5 children learnt, and developed their writing through the opportunities given to compose in role.

TO ELLOa FroM MRs PLug

We saw some fying
Fish and some ice Bergs
on the sea. the Flying
Fish were Jumping
UP and DowN in the
sea LoveNFRoM ELLoa

Figure 6.6

Under some circumstances children do seem able to write in the kinds of genres that genre theorists regard as socially important. It is observable, for instance, that children writing in role, either as part of a drama or in what might be termed 'drama on paper' can take on voices that they never usually use, and write as politicians, scientists or news reporters (Barrs, 1994: 255–6).

The Volcano: Learning through Drama (ILEA, 1985) is a drama resource pack that places children on an island with an active volcano. Although this pack was devised many years ago the ideas are still relevant in the primary classrooms of the twenty-first century. Through the drama each child takes on the persona of a character who lives on an isolated volcanic island. A crisis occurs as the volcano starts to erupt; the islanders all decide to leave except for one who stays to look after the animals. Usually the class teacher or drama teacher will take on this character and carry out a hot-seating activity with the class in order to identify who this person is and why they have decided to stay on the island. After carrying out the initial drama, a class of Year 5 children, with

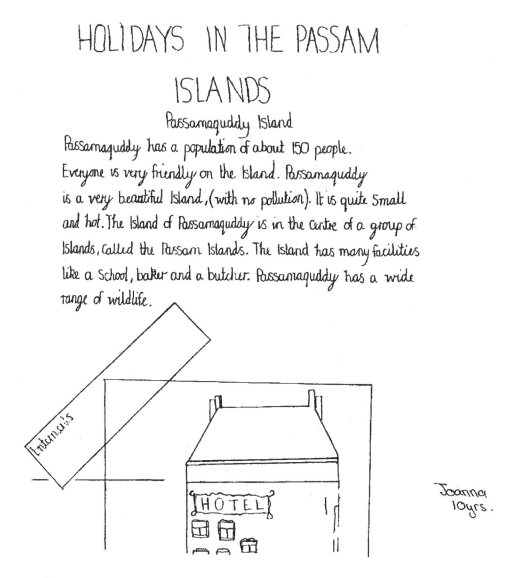

HOLIDAYS IN THE PASSAM ISLANDS

Passamaquddy Island

Passamaquddy has a population of about 150 people. Everyone is very friendly on the Island. Passamaquddy is a very beautiful Island, (with no pollution). It is quite small and hot. The Island of Passamaquddy is in the centre of a group of Islands, called the Passam Islands. The Island has many facilities like a school, baker and a butcher. Passamaquddy has a wide range of wildlife.

Interiors

HOTEL

Joanna
10yrs.

Figure 6.7

total involvement and commitment to the drama, wrote in a variety of styles and forms. The first example, a flier from the tourist office, is a piece of writing that had been written before the eruption, intended to encourage eco-tourists to visit the island.

This is another example of the persuasion genre, here organised in the form of an advertisement. The piece is written for tourists who want a quiet, environmentally friendly place to visit and the flier suggests the island has 'no pollution' and 'a wide range of wild life'. Such a piece could have been developed further by reading travel brochures to understand the language and structure that are often used to encourage tourists.

The next example is a word processed newspaper report from *The Daily Scoop*:

The islanders of Passamquddy fled in terror from the volcano, Mississippi. The Mississippi last erupted in 1928, over 60 years ago. The Mayor held a meeting on the subject last Monday. It was decided that the island should be evacuated but a 16 year old girl named Geraldine Harris said she would not be forced to leave Passamquddy. Geraldine is now living on Passamquddy alone. On leaving Passamquddy a boat went down off the coast of South America. Geraldine is quite sure that Mississippi will not erupt so she will be quite safe.

Finally, a child in role as Bert Robinson, the butcher, wrote to the only islander who remained on the island. His letter is a mixture of persuasion and recount genres.

24 Mathale
Flamingo
Brazil
28 March 1990

Dear Geraldine
        You can't imagine how concerned I feel about you. Are you sure you won't change your mind and leave because we could still send out a boat?.
I am now living in Brazil with Judy and little baby Tom. The other people that were on the Island have gone to England and Canada.
I do hope that the volcano won't explode and we hope to see you soon.
        love from
          Mr Bert Robinson
            the butcher

Figure 6.8

There were many more examples written after just one morning's drama. The children were stimulated and eager to write as the project allowed them to explore writing within an imaginative framework that gives them a real purpose and audience. Although such lengthy drama work cannot be attempted within the structure of the dedicated literacy lesson, the follow-up writing can be. Other such drama contexts can be developed in order to encourage a range of writing such as: a proposed development of a piece of land in order to build an office block, the closing of a youth club or the banning of all ball games in the playground.

It is important that young writers of non-fiction understand the links between reading and writing, and from this they will begin to understand the structure and form of different types of writing. With appropriate support, children will move on to writing the genres independently for themselves. When children come to understand the purpose of the task, they will appreciate and enjoy the craft of non-fiction writing.

Many of the ideas in this chapter intended to aid children's composition in narrative, poetry and non-fiction writing are explored because young writers need encouragement to produce and shape writing, especially in new forms and especially when the transcription elements in the writing process have not yet become automatic. The role of the teacher is clear: she keeps the composition process going from 'warm-ups', through discussion, sharing of information and key words; she helps with clarifying form, purpose and audience; she provides prompts and interest during the writing; she helps with revision; she shows respect and pleasure when the work is finished. As Margaret Meek explains in the introduction to *The Reader in the Writer* 'When young writers believe that their teacher is interested, really interested, in what they want to communicate, they will do their best to get their meaning across' (2001). Composition is at the heart of writing and the creative process is at the root of many of the most important activities that humans engage in. We need to nurture these impulses and ensure our writers leave the primary school as eager to compose in writing in every sphere as they normally are in their speaking.

Further reading and websites

Andrews, R., Torgerson, C., Lowe, G., McGuinn, N. and Robinson, A. (2006) *Teaching and Learning Argumentative Non-fiction Writing for 7–14 year olds: A Systematic Review of the Evidence of Successful Practice*. London: EPPI-Centre Social Sciences Research Unit, Institute of Education. www.standards.dfes.gov.uk/research/themes/English/non-fictionwriting/ (accessed 21 September 2008).

Goodwin, P. (2005) *The Literate Classroom*, Chapter 12. London: David Fulton Publishers (first published 1999).

Palmer, S. (2001) *How to Teach Writing Across the Curriculum at KS2*. London: David Fulton Publishers.

See also:

PNS Progression papers for different non-fiction text types
   www.standards.dfes.gov.uk/primaryframework/literacy/Papers/progression

Scholastic *Writing Guides* for Non-Fiction

Scholastic *50 Shared Texts*: Non Fiction

Chapter 7

Transcription: spelling, punctuation and handwriting

Alison Kelly

INTRODUCTION

> My earliest memories of writing, and the only thoughts that still remain from my primary
> school days, are of continually repeating letters and words in set spaces, making sure that all
> the letters were the same size...
>
> (Year 1 undergraduate on BA [Primary Education] course)

This is the experience of many children – that 'writing' means the physical aspects of spelling, handwriting and punctuation. You will remember that Chapter 2 introduced the distinction between 'composition' and 'transcription' and the children's work presented in Chapter 4 was analysed in relation to the children's understandings of both these aspects. In Chapter 6 we took a careful look at supporting composition. These earlier chapters discussed the importance of ensuring that children have a balanced view of the writing process and are aware of the importance of the content of their writing as well as its 'presentation' as the National Curriculum (NC) describes it. But now we turn to the secretarial aspects of writing: spelling, handwriting and punctuation, which are, of course, very important.

SPELLING

In order to teach spelling effectively, teachers need to have a clear personal grasp of some of the principles and difficulties of the English spelling system; these are the focus of the first section. With this underpinning, we go on to examine effective spelling strategies, concerns about the teaching of spelling and what is known about how children learn to spell. The final section provides practical suggestions for effective teaching.

What do teachers need to know about spelling?

In this section we look at the spelling lessons we have to give ourselves in order to teach children effectively.

The English Language

> I take it you already know
> Of tough and bough and cough and dough?
> Others may stumble but not you,
> On hiccough, thorough, laugh and through.
>
> (in Rosen, 1995: 36)

English has an alphabet of 26 letters but a spoken language which uses at least 44 single sounds (phonemes). So, as the anonymous extract above shows, the 26 letters have to work hard to represent such a multitude of sounds!

One difficulty lies with the alphabet used for English, which is not one that was intended to fit English sounds. Its history can be traced back over thousands of years and thousands of miles to 1700 BC in the Middle East, where a north Semitic language, very similar to Hebrew, was spoken. This alphabet was passed from the Phoenicians to the Greeks, whose model influenced the Etruscans, who, in turn, influenced the Romans. Christian missionaries arrived in this country in the sixth century and brought the Roman alphabet with them (Crystal, 1995).

In addition, as you will see in the section below on etymology, our language has also been profoundly influenced by the many different groups of people who have settled here over the centuries, all bringing with them their own languages. So an alphabet ill-matched to the sounds of the English language, and a history of repeated invasion, have both contributed to a rich and sometimes bewildering linguistic hotchpotch.

Etymology

Etymology, the history of words, is full of stories about language. It is a fascinating and rich area that can engage children's interest and stimulate their curiosity. It is an area of study that demands we know a little about the history of the English language itself. This history is about the many different groups of people who arrived and settled here across the centuries. They brought their own languages and we can find traces of these in English today. The chart in Table 7.1 provides an overview of these influences.

Etymology explains connections between words: for instance, 'telephone', 'television', 'telepathy' and 'telegraph' all share the same prefix, 'tele-', which comes from Greek, meaning 'at a distance'; 'centigrade', 'per cent' and 'centipede' come from the Latin root 'cent', meaning 'one hundred'. Etymology accounts for oddities such as silent 'k' (as in 'know'), which used to be sounded: in Saxon times, the Old English word for 'knife' was 'kanif', and it was only when the word became shortened to 'knif' that sounding the 'k' was dropped. The study of etymology also reveals how word meanings have changed over time. For example, David Crystal (1995) shows how the word 'silly' started life in Old English some 1300 years ago as meaning 'happy' or 'blessed' and moved through several shades of meaning, such as 'innocent' (Middle English), to its current meaning, 'foolish'.

Morphology

Morphology, the structure of words, provides one way of overcoming some of the difficulties created by the nature of the English language.

It is an area that teachers need to know about explicitly because it enables them to help children see unchanging patterns in spelling. Take the word 'teach', which is the root (or stem) of '*teach*er', '*teach*ing' and 'un*teach*able'. The bits that come before and after word roots are called affixes. There are two sorts of affix: prefixes which come before the root and suffixes which come after the root. So in the word 'unteachable', 'un-' is a prefix and '-able' is a suffix. (It helps to know that 'pre' comes from Latin and means 'before' and the 'su' in suffix comes from the Latin 'sub' meaning 'under'.)

Table 7.1

Date	Influences	Words still in use
500 BC	Celtic tribes speaking different languages	crag, torr
43 AD–410 AD	Romans invade and settle. Latin becomes official language of government. Celtic languages persist.	discus, campus
350–600	Angles, Saxons and Jutes invade. Old English (OE) develops from their Germanic dialects.	under, in, skirt, mother, farm, love
597	Arrival of first Christian missionaries (Roman). Latin becomes more influential.	altar, wine, candle
500–800	OE written down using Latin alphabet which did not have symbols for some sounds, e.g. 'th'. OE spoken in different dialects. Celtic and Latin also spoken.	
Late 700s	Viking invasions (from Scandinavia) and settlements begin bringing Old Norse with them.	sky, egg, Thursday, sister
871–899	Alfred defends Wessex against the Vikings. Develops use of English to promote national identity. Records, literature written in English. Some Latin works translated.	
1066	Norman invasion: French becomes the language of the court, ruling classes, government; Latin still used in church; OE still spoken. Norman scribes import French conventions, e.g 'qu' for 'cw'.	beef, court, castle, prison, tax
1100–1450s	'Middle' English develops from French influence.	
1362	King's speech at opening of Parliament made in English.	
1387	Chaucer's *Canterbury Tales* written in English.	
1300–1600	Standard English develops out of east Midlands dialect (used by universities, court, government). First grammar books written.	
1476	Caxton's printing press contributes to standardisation.	Introduction of 'gh' for hard 'g' sound, e.g. 'ghost'.
Renaissance	Renewed importation of Greek and Latin words with revival of interest in classical languages.	'dette' becomes 'debt' (to show its Latin source: 'debitum').
1755	Samuel Johnson's dictionary stabilises spelling conventions still further.	

Affixes work in two ways: inflectionally and derivationally. Inflectional suffixes (and they are always suffixes) show changes in meaning and mark grammatical contrasts. The main inflectional endings in English are as follows:

- plural: e.g. dog*s*;
- to mark possession: e.g. the dog'*s* collar, the dogs' collars;
- regular verbs: the past tense: e.g. I walk*ed*; past participle: e.g. I have walk*ed*; present tense, 3rd person singular: e.g. she walk*s*; present participle: e.g. walk*ing*;
- comparatives and superlatives: e.g. bright, bright*er*, bright*est*.

There are exceptions to all of these and you will find that children's errors frequently demonstrate their over-generalisation of such endings; for instance, they may write 'mouses' instead of the irregular plural 'mice'. Another difficulty that children may encounter with inflectional endings is the fact that they sound different; try saying 'ripped', 'pinned' and 'plodded' and you will hear the same '-ed' ending sounding as '-t', '-d' and '-id' respectively. Plurals can be heard differently, too, as you can see in a child's spelling of 'dogz'. There is more consistency in the look of words than there is in their sounds. The '-ed' remains constant in writing despite changes in pronunciation. The important thing for children to know is that it is the meaning that is privileged over and above the sound of the word.

'Derivational affixes' are used to create new words; they both add and change meaning. Adding the prefix 'un-' and the suffix '-able' to 'teach' makes for a total change of meaning! It is interesting for you (and older children) to note that a derivational suffix changes the word class of the root it is added to, but a derivational prefix does not. So the addition of the suffix '-er' to 'teach' changes the verb 'teach' into the noun 'teacher'. On the other hand, while the prefix 'un-' changes the meaning of 'happy', it has not changed the word class: 'happy' and 'unhappy' are both adjectives.

Affixes and roots are morphemes – 'the elements out of which words can be constructed' (Crystal, 1995: 198). These are the smallest chunks of words that make meaning and cannot be broken down further. There are two types: 'free morphemes', which are just that, free to stand on their own ('teach', 'dog', 'talk'), and 'bound morphemes', which have to be bound or tied to another morpheme to make sense. Inflectional suffixes, such as the 's' in 'dogs' and the 'ed' in 'talked', are bound morphemes, as are the prefix and suffix in '*un*teach*able*'.

Two free morphemes may be combined to form a compound word such as 'earthquake', 'seaside', 'goosebump' and 'goldfish'. These are usually nouns and the spelling of the two morphemes remains the same in the compound as it did when they stood alone. Sometimes, though, the morphemes are blended together as in 'channel' and 'tunnel', which come together as 'chunnel'.

Language change

As this last example shows, one of the most interesting aspects of any kind of word study is what it reveals about the dynamic nature of language: it never sits still, as the addition in the 1990s of 'Teletubbies' to the stock of 'tele-' words demonstrated.

Prefixes move in and out of fashion, too. The prefix 'mega' (from Greek meaning 'big' as in 'megaphone') was reborn in the late twentieth century and is used to kick off any number of phrases ('mega-hungry/sad'). Melvyn Bragg (*Roots of English*, BBC) provided a wonderful example of the merging of old and new when he reported on the use of the word 'megashant' by youths in one Cumbrian village. Here the prefix 'mega' is combined with 'shant', an old Cumbrian dialect word meaning 'shamed'. Changing technologies play their part, too. If you type 'cool' as predictive text into your mobile phone the first option that appears is 'book' so, for a while, 'book' became the new synonym for 'cool'.

Our language is rich in borrowed (loan) words like 'café' (French), 'bungalow' (Hindi) and 'tycoon' (Japanese). We add new words (neologisms) such as 'internet' and 'website'; the Oxford English Dictionary has an 'Addenda' section for these. After a while, of course, these either become so commonplace that they are no longer neologisms or they slip out of usage completely. Crystal (1995) cites the examples of 'blurb' (coined in 1907), which has stayed with us, whereas 'gubble' (to indulge in meaningless conversation) did not find a niche for itself! Then there are acronyms like AIDS (Acquired Immune Deficiency Syndrome), INSET (In-service Training) and SCUBA (Self-Contained Underwater Breathing Apparatus).

Spelling rules

Morphology, informed by etymology, provides a rather more reliable way of understanding the regularities and constants in our complex spelling system than looking at what were traditionally known as the 'rules' of spelling. Following such rules is not straightforward, partly because of the inconsistencies in our language and partly because the rules are sometimes just very hard to understand. This one seems simple enough: 'there will be a double 'l', 'f' or 's' after a single vowel at the end of a short word (e.g. tell, sniff, fuss)', but then there are the exceptions – 'pal', 'if', 'of', 'us', 'bus', 'gas', 'this', 'yes' – to name a few. Other rules are more extended and, therefore, harder for young children to get their heads round: 'Words ending in both a single vowel and a single consonant always double the last consonant before adding an ending beginning with a vowel (e.g. stop, stopped, stopping)' (rules taken from Bannatyne and Cotterell, 1966).

Rules are only useful when they apply to a large number of words, when there are few exceptions and when they are easily understood. Mike Torbe (1995) suggests that the following might be helpful; he calls them 'descriptions' rather than rules:

1. 'q' is always followed by 'u' and another vowel always follows the 'u'.
2. 'i' (pronounced 'eye') at the end of words is spelled 'y' or (less often) 'igh'.
3. Words that sound as if they have an 'o' in them generally spell it with 'oa' in the middle of the word and 'ow' at the end.
4. Words that sound as if they have an 'a' in them generally spell it 'ai' in the middle and 'ay' at the end.
5. English words do not end with 'i', 'o', 'u', 'j' or 'v'. Instead they follow these patterns: i = ie or y; o = ow; u = ue; j = ge or dge; v = ve.
6. The 'er' sound at the end of words is generally spelled 'er'.
7. When you add 'full' to the end of a word, it drops one 'l' and becomes 'ful'.

(ibid., pp. 77–8).

Spelling strategies

So how are spellers to contend with the complexities of the English language? This classroom snapshot demonstrates the range of strategies that we call on as we spell.

I am watching five-year-old Billy writing a story. His first sentence reads: 'the likl dog hd a spotid tale' (*the little dog had a spotted tail*).

He starts with 'the', which is, of course, spelt correctly – it is part of his repertoire of known words, his 'sight vocabulary'.

We can imagine the effort that has gone into his encoding of 'little': he has segmented (separated out) each phoneme and made a valiant attempt to represent each one as he hears it. And it is a very good approximation: 'little' splits into four phonemes – /l/ /i/ /tt/ /le/ – and Billy has tried to represent these – /l/ /i/ /k/ /l/. The American researcher Treiman (1993) has shown just how complex the cognitive processes are when a child engages in such an apparently simple task. First the child has to segment the word into its spoken elements, then remember the order of these and then choose the appropriate graphological fit for each unit. It is only on the third stage that Billy has stumbled as he assigns inappropriate graphemes for the phonemes /tt/ and /le/. And it is a very logical assignation, for /k/ is the way Billy pronounces /tt/ in this word. A more mature speller who pronounced the word in the same way as Billy would know that this pronunciation is not echoed in the spelling.

Billy started with the opening consonant phoneme /d/ for 'dog', but then he hesitated before completing the word in one confident move with its rime '– og'. He has been reading about the adventures of Meg and Mog and it is highly likely that he has made a link (or analogy) between the rime that 'dog' and 'Mog' share. He is not so successful with 'hd' where, again, he picks up the dominant consonant phonemes but uses the 'd' to stand for the whole of the rime, omitting the vowel completely.

Billy goes about spelling 'spotted' just as he did 'little', by segmenting the phonemes and trying to represent them with graphemes. But 'spotted' holds an additional challenge: its two morphemes (spott/ed). If Billy had picked up the inflectional suffix 'ed', he might have had more success. Again, Treiman's insights are helpful here as she shows us that not only do children have to analyse a word into its spoken, phonemic units but they need to detect the morphemic units as well.

Billy's use of the homophone 'tale' for 'tail' shows him using graphic (visual) strategies. 'Tale' is part of his repertoire of sight words and is a perfect match in terms of sound, but not meaning.

Billy's efforts reveal what a complex and multi-faceted process spelling is. This young writer is already orchestrating different types of knowledge from different sources. What follows is a summary of these sources: we need to draw on all of these and there is no particular hierarchy or order in which these can be learnt. The point is that some words will yield more easily to being encoded by one strategy and others by another.

Phonemic strategies: segmenting

Segmenting is the process of picking out the separate phonemes and representing these graphically. It is the reverse of blending, the process in reading, whereby a child comes to a new word and blends its phonemes in order to decode it. In the case of segmenting (before writing), the child already holds in her head the whole word (e.g.

'duck') that is to be encoded (/d/u/ck), whereas in blending (when she is reading) she has to amalgamate the sounds to create a 'new' whole word (/d/u/ck/ – 'duck').

Phonemic strategies: onset and rime

Research offers another way of splitting words up: into their 'onsets' and 'rimes'. Many words, such as 'bread' and 'tread', can be broken down into an onset (the opening consonant or consonant cluster, i.e. 'br', 'tr') and rime (the vowel sound and any other consonants, the unit which rhymes, i.e. 'ead'). Several researchers (Bryant and Bradley 1985; Goswami and Bryant 1992; Goswami 1995) have investigated the importance of children's early phonemic awareness and the impact this has later on their ability to use phonic strategies. These researchers show that early experience of rhyme (through nursery rhymes, rhyming books etc.) lays important foundations for phonemic awareness. These foundations are established as children draw on their experience of rhyme to make rime analogies which draw their attention to phonemes. So a child may be able to link the words 'man', 'van', 'pan' and 'can' because she can hear the shared rime ('-an'). In Figure 7.1 a five-year-old enjoys the power of onset swapping!

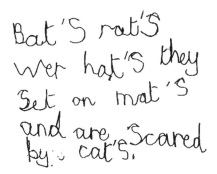

Figure 7.1

Onsets and rimes provide a way of seeing regularities between words that are more reliable than sound strategies. Goswami (1995) tells us that there are 90 words that share the 'ight' rime, while common rimes such as 'en' (in 'ten') and 'an' (in 'fan') have a staggering 904 and 750 respectively!

Morphemic strategies

As we saw above, in the section on 'Morphology', understanding the morphemic make-up of words provides stable information about spelling patterns. A more mature or experienced speller than Billy would have recognised the inflectional suffix '-ed' in 'spotted'. Morphemic understanding is enhanced by etymological knowledge. So the child who has learnt about the Latin prefix 'bi', meaning 'two', will avoid starting a spelling of 'bicycle' with either 'by' or 'buy'.

Graphic strategies

We also use visual, or graphic, strategies when we spell. This means we may remember whole words (as part of a sight vocabulary) or parts of words (significant letter strings maybe as in 'banana'). You will realise that none of these strategies operates independently or discretely of one another. A child may aurally split a word into its onset and rime but will also bring graphic strategies into play when making an analogy (as Billy did with 'dog').

High interest words

Even spelling has an affective dimension, and there are some words that are highly significant for children that they can spell with ease. Consider how effortlessly a dinosaur-obsessed child will spell 'tyrannosaurus', 'stegosaurus' and other challenging polysyllabic words.

In summary, we have to draw from a range of features when we spell. These are listed below with an indication of where they appear in the *NC* Programmes of Study for Writing:

- the look of the word (Key Stages 1 and 2);
- the phonemes in the word (KS1 and KS2);
- common letter strings (KS1) e.g. -ough...;
- knowing that groups of words are linked by meaning (KS2), e.g. fact, factual, finite, definite, infinite;
- inflectional endings (KS2), e.g. flapped, glided, soared;
- rime analogies, e.g. m*ight*, f*ight*, l*ight*, c*at*, b*at*, r*at*;
- etymology (KS2), e.g. *volvere* (Greek – to roll): *revolve*, *revolver* (pistol with a revolving mechanism), *Volvo*;
- prefixes and suffixes (KS1 and 2), e.g. im-, bi-, -ed, -ing.

Concerns about the teaching of spelling

As the Introduction and Chapter 1 in this book show, early approaches to writing focused exclusively on transcriptional aspects at the expense of composition. Rote learning and copying were the order of the day. By the 1960s, the pendulum had swung back with the 'creative writing' movement, where all the focus seemed to be on the production of imaginative writing. A teacher from that era was quoted as saying that 'spelling is learned naturally by the children and, from the reading, punctuation becomes increasingly familiar' (quoted in Clegg, 1964: 40). This idea that, for some children, spelling can be learned 'naturally' is one that recurs from time to time and Margaret Peters' research into spelling (first published in 1967, revised edition 1985) gave us a neat soundbite for this with the title of her book *Spelling: Caught or Taught?* Peters cites evidence of challenges (and counter-challenges) to the systematic teaching of spelling from the very beginnings of this century, and the more recent writing 'process' movement and 'developmental' or 'emergent' approaches to writing have been criticised for marginalising the teaching of the presentational skills of writing.

Writing process approaches

Let us start with the writing process movement (see Chapter 2) which drew teachers' attention to the composition/transcription distinction and suggested that it was necessary for children to be clear about that separation too. A teacher's prompting that children should, in the first instance, concentrate on getting the ideas down without worrying about the spellings is indeed a worrying one if that is all that is going on. But for many, such advice was seen only as the first step in the process of writing and the children would go on to 'edit' their work, paying proper attention to the spelling and other surface skills of writing. It could be that the separation of composition and transcription, with the apparent relegation of transcription to second place, led to some misunderstandings about the importance teachers were placing upon it. This may have been the case for some teachers, but many carefully attended to the teaching of spelling and handwriting.

'Developmental/emergent' approaches

The tension between composition and transcription is possibly most visible for a very young writer when the strain of forming letters and spelling words can seriously inhibit the fluency of writing. This is why routines such as dictated writing (see Chapter 5), which allow a focus on composition, are so important in the early years.

As we showed in Chapter 2, research into children's early moves into literacy revealed how they can make active and creative hypotheses about ways in which all of the writing system works. Chapter 4 offered several examples of such active engagement (see especially Figures 4.2 and 4.3). Now look at Figure 7.2 below, Madeleine's representation of her first day at play group.

Figure 7.2

As well as drawing the teacher and children, she has 'written' their names underneath. She knows that drawing and writing are different, that they look different and that they have different functions. Arriving alongside insights about composition and transcription, such findings had exciting potential for work in the early years. It became clear that encouraging children to make unaided spelling guesses not only showed teachers what the children knew and understood about writing but it also freed children from the transcriptional strain of 'getting it right' at the first attempt. They were enabled to focus on what it was they wanted to say. So the suggestion that children should 'have a go' at their spellings stems from a concern to free up composition.

At about the same time, interesting research was being published about the nature of the children's invented spellings. For instance, the work of Ferreiro and Teberosky (1979), two researchers who were influenced by Piaget's work, suggested that children pass through stages in their writing and that it is possible to describe a developmental progression. *The Beginnings of Writing* (Temple *et al.*, 1982) was read by many teachers and reinforced the idea of spelling stages. We will return to the idea of spelling stages below but the important point is that the idea of stages can be interpreted as suggesting that there is a natural progression and this can marginalise the teacher's role. The danger with labels like 'developmental' or 'emergent' is that they might suggest that the teacher can simply let it all happen and does not need to do any specific teaching. The notion of stages also suggests a rigidity and uniformity in children's learning and that all children will pass through the same stages in the same way. Teachers know that this is not the case!

How do children learn to spell?

What do we know about how children learn to spell? This is an area that has inspired some fascinating research over the last 30 years, which has had a significant impact on classroom practice.

Some children appear to learn to spell quite easily without any apparent spelling lessons and one source of anxiety for teachers about their role could rest with an implicit view that somehow we are born as 'good' or 'bad' spellers. Such a view can leave the teacher feeling uneasy about the effectiveness of her teaching so it is helpful to know what does contribute to the success of some children. This is what Margaret Peters (1985) looked at in her study of children who appeared to have 'caught' spelling. She found that verbal ability and interest in words, good visual perception and what she terms 'carefulness' in handwriting were important factors in the children's success (p. 21). Such research provides helpful classroom pointers and we shall look at practical activities which support the development of these factors in the sections below on teaching spelling and handwriting.

Spelling development

Another area we know much more about now concerns spelling development. New knowledge about spelling development has enabled teachers to identify what counts as spelling progress. Research into early literacy (e.g. Clay, 1975; Bissex, 1980; Goodman, 1984) has yielded fascinating insights into the very beginnings of spelling development, and knowing about these early stages can inform our teaching considerably. One commonly used model of spelling development comes from Richard Gentry (1982), who identifies five possible stages. His work is based on the case study of a single child (Bissex, 1980), which means that we do need to approach it with some caution. The labels he uses for the different stages describe what the child is doing, not the teacher. As we said above, the notion of stages can be a very beguiling one and it is most important that we use this understanding flexibly and do not treat the stages as neat milestones through which every child will pass in just the same way. Here is a brief summary of some of the features of Gentry's stages:

1. *Pre-communicative*
   - knows that symbols can be used to say something;
   - uses a range of symbols (invented, numbers, letters – upper and lower case);
   - does not make sound–symbol connections.
2. *Semi-phonetic*
   - is beginning to make sound–symbol connections;
   - knows about word boundaries, how writing is arranged on a page;
   - may shorten some words.
3. *Phonetic*
   - uses sound–symbol connections consistently;
   - uses known words (sight vocabulary).
4. *Transitional*
   - uses visual strategies;
   - uses most conventions of spelling system.
5. *Correct*
   - has basic knowledge of spelling system and rules;
   - knows about word structure (morphology);
   - has a large sight vocabulary.

Uta Frith (1985) offers another model of spelling development. This is a more fluid, flexible model with 'phases' rather than 'stages' but, like Gentry's model, Frith's analysis provides teachers with helpful ways of understanding children's spelling efforts and focusing teaching appropriately. She shows how children progress from reading whole words (the logographic phase) to a phase where they start analysing parts of words (through onset and rime or at the level of the phoneme). Finally, they move from this analytic phase to the orthographic one, where whole words are read and can then be spelt. The model is neatly summarised by O'Sullivan and Thomas (2000): 'what Frith describes is a movement from whole words to parts of words, and back to an attention to whole word structure' (p. 16).

Another strength of this model lies in the way Frith clarifies how spelling and reading connect. Essentially, what she shows is a shifting in the balance of power between reading and writing. At first, it is reading that powers the process as children recognise whole words in context. But the balance shifts to spelling as children's analytic skills develop through their early efforts to segment and analyse words into onsets and rimes. Reading takes over again as the primary site for the development of children's orthographic skills.

The two models are complementary as Figure 7.3 shows. What is important is that

FRITH   **GENTRY**

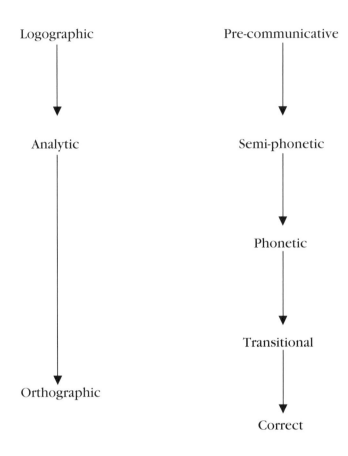

Figure 7.3

we use these models to inform our understanding and appreciation of the children's efforts.

The progress of one child across her first year in school illustrates aspects of these models. First, a word about the context of these pieces. They were written by Kelly when she was five-years-old and attending a primary school in south-east London. She was a confident and outgoing child, neither an over- nor an under-achiever. It was part of the school's assessment policy that samples of children's writing would be kept regularly and be passed from teacher to teacher in a portfolio (see Chapter 8). The samples were to be unaided (i.e. containing the children's own spelling attempts) so that both composition and presentation could be monitored. Such unaided writing was only one part of the writing curriculum in this Reception class. Shared writing, copying, dictated writing, spelling and handwriting were all regular classroom routines and it is important to remember this when looking at the examples below, as such development came about as part of well structured and carefully focused teaching. There is much to be said about the composition of Kelly's pieces but the focus of this chapter is spelling. The reminder about content is important, though, and in this classroom the teacher was most rigorous in responding to the content of the pieces as well as to the presentational aspects. Finally, the intention of presenting these pieces here is to illustrate spelling development; I will look at practical issues concerning the nature of our responses to such early attempts in a later section.

In her first week at school Kelly (age 5.3) wrote the story in Figure 7.4.

Figure 7.4

This is what she told her teacher the writing said:

> The fox in the wood. What can he see? Some ducks playing in the pond. A little boy called Sean came along. The little boy said, 'Get away you nasty fox'. The fox ran away and the boy said to the ducks, 'Don't be afraid, I am only a little boy'.

This is an example of Gentry's 'pre-communicative writing' in that there is no apparent evidence of sound–symbol correlation. The label 'pre-communicative' is slightly misleading as she clearly is communicating meaning, but remember that 'precommunicative' is a label for the spelling. (You might find 'pre-phonemic', as used by Temple *et al.*, 1982, a more useful label.) However, she already knows quite a lot about the presentational aspects of spelling: she knows writing runs from left to right and is arranged on the page in lines; she knows that writing consists of strings of letters (but not that these are divided up into units – words – yet) and that the same letters can be used in different combinations. In common with many young writers she draws heavily on the most familiar of all strings of letters at this point – her name.

As an important aside, compare Kelly's work with that of a bilingual child, Shirin, in the same class, as seen in Figure 7.5.

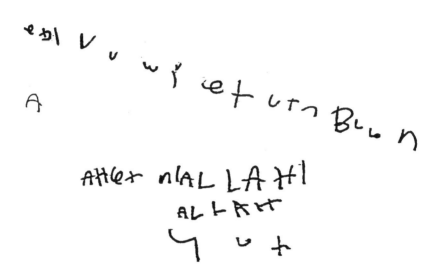

Figure 7.5

This was Shirin's response to her teacher's request to write something about her holiday. A fluent Urdu speaker, the writing shows what a remarkable amount Shirin has already grasped about two quite separate writing systems. She started with the top line which ran from right to left and includes distinctive characters influenced by the Urdu alphabet. When she went on to write 'Allah' on the next line she used the characters of the English alphabet written from left to right. Such early attempts need to be recognised, applauded and built upon. In this case, the teacher went on to make a book with Shirin who dictated what she wanted it to say to the teacher and then her father was enlisted to translate it into Urdu. These two versions allowed the teacher to build on the child's mother tongue while supporting her development in reading and writing English.

Back to Kelly who, a month later, wrote the caption in Figure 7.6 for a picture: 'I am in the garden and my friend is in the garden and we found a frog. The frog hopped away'.

Although this is still 'pre-communicative', you will see that Kelly has made considerable progress in her understanding. Most importantly, she seems to be moving towards the concept of words, as the underlining and the relished full stop after 'kien'

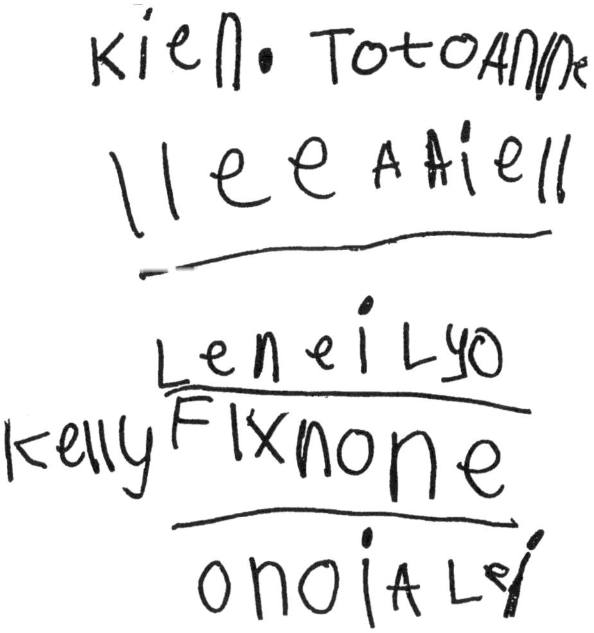

Kieɲ. TotoAnɲ̌

lleeAɲiell

Leneilyo

Kelly Fixnone

onojALeʏ́

Figure 7.6

suggest. There are words she can spell, 'To', 'to' and 'Anne' (her friend's name), and she is using a greater range of letters. Still in the early stages of reading, her identification of a few whole words and her recognition of words in the environment are typical features of Frith's logographic stage.

In December she makes a most significant leap with the reply in Figure 7.7 to her teacher's 'post-it' on a message board enquiring about Kelly's weekend plans. She replies: 'My friend's coming tomorrow and we are going to play with each other'.

me nonꜱ re nonon

To mono

a

We re

onTo noswenꬶ

Figure 7.7

We see here the beginnings of sound–symbol correspondence as Kelly starts to map her graphological knowledge on to her phonological knowledge. She has moved into Frith's 'analytic' phase, and what Gentry terms 'semi-phonetic' writing. Look, for instance, at her partially successful segmentation of the phonemes in 'tomorrow'. There are sight words in use, too: 'to' and 'we'. The use of 're' for 'are' is characteristic of this stage where the child draws on the name of the letter – 'R' (for that is what she hears). Importantly though, the 'e' at the end of 're' shows that she is not only making use of phonemic strategies but also using the look of the word; we cannot hear the 'e' on the end of 'are', we see it on the page. In Frith's model, this is where the balance of power between reading and writing has shifted to writing: as children begin to segment the phonemes in their writing with such intent concentration so their attention will be drawn to the phonemes in their early blending efforts in reading. Goswami (1995) shows how children's attempts at writing words help crystallise the concept of the phoneme, thus enhancing phonemic awareness, an important underpinning for effective use of phonic strategies in reading.

The next piece, written in February, is a caption for a drawing: 'I like this flower because it smells nice and it is lovely'. There is a real attempt here to spell each word relying mostly on the phonemes, especially initial ones. She is no longer using letter names. Apart from the omission of 'is' in the last line, there is one-to-one correspondence (i.e. matching of spoken and written units), there is more evidence of sight words and, in the brave attempt at 'because', evidence of sight strategies – she knows there is a 'u' in there somewhere! She is on the way to the 'phonetic' stage where there is an attempt to represent each sound.

Figure 7.8

The final sample from this year is the first page of a story (Figure 7.9) written in June, which shows Kelly continuing to progress: 'One day there was a little boy who wanted a little bear but his mummy wouldn't let him have one. 'Then I'll be upset', said the little boy.'

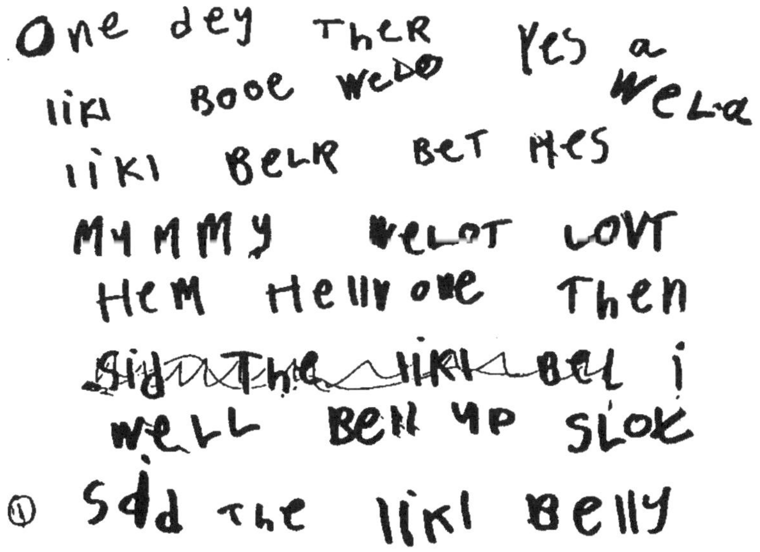

One dey ThcR Yes a
liki Booe wcbo Yes WeLa
iiki BeLR BeT Hes
MymmY veLoT LovT
HeM Hellrone Then
sid The liki Bel i
weLL Bel up slok
① sdd The liki Belly

Figure 7.9

She continues to use phonic strategies ('likl booe'), graphic strategies ('sid' for 'said') and known words. The fact that she resorts to the earlier strategy of using her name when really stuck – see her last attempt at 'boy' ('belly') – is a useful reminder of the fluidity of these early writing stages and the fact that children do move backwards as well as forwards! The important thing is to be able to recognise the strategies being used so that you can respond appropriately.

Gentry's final stages are 'transitional' and 'correct'. A transitional speller will be using vowels in each syllable and beginning to develop visual strategies. We have evidence of Kelly doing the latter but not the former. In Figure 7.10 a Year 2 child is showing a confident grasp of aspects of the transitional stage.

Note the spellings of polysyllabic words such as 'beautifulest', 'keeper' and 'expensive'. (Two other points of interest are the circled words being the ones that she has identified as needing help with and the use of the initials 'ct' for 'Christmas tree' which stems from class discussion about drafting techniques.)

Learning styles

It is clear from looking at the transcripts and tone of Kelly's work that she is a confident young writer; this is not the case for all children and we do need to take account of what we know about children's different learning styles when we plan our teaching. A longitudinal study by Bussis *et al.* (summarised in Barrs and Thomas, 1991) has illuminated our understanding about this. Focusing mainly on reading, it revealed that some children favoured the so-called 'big shapes' (the pattern and language of the texts) whereas others went for 'smaller units' (words and sounds). The former group

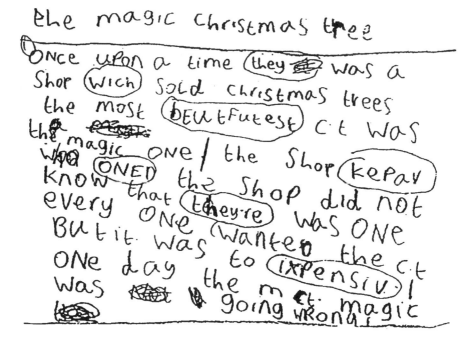

Figure 7.10

tended to be risk-takers as they went for the overall meaning and fluency of a text, sometimes at the expense of word-for-word accuracy. Those who went for the smaller units were not such confident risk-takers preferring a step-by-step approach as they tackled individual words and letters. Bussis' findings suggested that such learning styles were not restricted to reading and extended to other curriculum areas and it seems highly likely that the same findings will apply to the confidence with which children approach spelling tasks.

In the section on spelling strategies we look at ways of developing children's confidence. More recent research (Dombey and Moustafa, 1998) suggests that difference in learning styles also extends to whether the children initially draw from visual or aural data. The important issue here is to take on board these different learning styles and to be mindful of Bussis' finding that, provided the teacher was offering a balanced teaching 'mix' which addressed all aspects of reading, then the children were not disadvantaged by their learning style. So when we come to think about planning for spelling, it is most important that we structure it to include a balance of strategies.

Teaching spelling

When?

Pupils in the EYFS will be working with the rich experiences of speaking and listening laid out in Phase 1 of *Letters and Sounds* (DfES, 2007). The activities suggested here all fit well with the organisation and routine of early years settings. By the end of this stage, and certainly by KS1, the expectation is that pupils will be experiencing a daily discrete session of synthetic phonics teaching into which work about spelling (segmenting, for example) is built. At KS2 you may also be planning such discrete slots of teaching. For children throughout the two key stages, spelling lends itself well to short, sharp bursts of teaching; maybe a quick five minutes focusing on a word many children are finding hard – 'because' is always a good contender! Draw the class together to look closely at the word, identify its particular difficulties, highlight these, maybe make up a class mnemonic ('bears eat cakes and unpack suitcases early'), and draw analogies with another word – 'cause', amusing yourselves with the change in pronunciation. Regular slots like these, taken at a good pace, can tackle individual difficulties and generally raise the children's interest in words. However, it is vital that children have opportunities to apply the knowledge gained from such slots so you will need to plan opportunities for teaching spelling into your regular routines such as shared reading and writing (see Chapter 5). These routines provide ideal opportunities for consolidating and reinforcing previous work. Your ongoing assessments of pupils' progress (see Chapter 8) will inform the way you plan these routines (see Appendix 3 of *Letters and Sounds* for guidance and pro-formas on keeping useful records). Some of your teaching will arise more incidentally from ongoing pieces of writing as the children work on editing, and you may identify a number of common difficulties that you choose to tackle in a specially planned whole-class or group session.

How? Four more 'rules'

How do we go about teaching spelling? The first rule is – positively! Spelling is an area of enormous anxiety for many children so the quality and tone of our response to their attempts is important. Look back to Figure 7.10 and the child's guesses for 'which'/'wich', 'beautifulest'/'beutfutest' and 'expensive'/'ixpensiv'. In each case she has got more of the word right than wrong; children will be most encouraged when this is pointed out to them. As well as engendering a more positive attitude this also focuses the children's attention on the different parts of the word; having identified what they have got right, they are then encouraged to look with care at the part of the word that is wrong.

Closely tied to this comes the second rule: encourage the children's interest and curiosity in words. Enthusiastic teaching can offer the children a model of spelling as a topic that is fascinating, not fearful. Many of the activities below encourage the children to find out about words, their history and their make-up. Activities that focus on the regular features of language such as prefixes and suffixes (see teaching ideas on these below) will be most supportive in enabling children to see regularities and consistencies and increase their curiosity and confidence.

Thirdly, make sure the children can attend to spelling in a focused way. Previous chapters have emphasised the importance of ensuring that transcriptional strains do not stifle the children's compositional powers and it is, of course, just as important that children should be similarly free to attend to transcription. So, as described above, discrete sessions are needed, as is an emphasis on attending to spelling in the editing stage. Occasionally, a compositional context – rewriting a known story, for example – will be fairly undemanding, so a focus on spelling would be manageable and appropriate.

The fourth rule, and it is one that holds good for all aspects of presentation, is to do with context and the importance of reminding children that such work belongs to the realms of real-life reading and writing. A cautionary tale comes from my early years of teaching when I worked hard to teach my eight-year-olds how to do cursive (joined-up) writing. After a few weeks I realised that they were doing beautiful joined-up writing in their handwriting books but nowhere else! Try to ensure, as this Year 2 teacher does, that work on discrete aspects of spelling is grounded in shared texts work. The class were learning about the prefix 'un-'. After some shared writing about an unhappy caterpillar, the teacher goes on to make a shared list of words with the children that take the 'un-' prefix. Later in the week this is revisited with the whole class, whose attention is drawn to this page in an enlarged version of *Six Dinner Sid* by Inga Moore: 'Unlike Aristotle Street, the people who lived in Pythagoras Place talked with their neighbours'. In independent group work the children work as 'word detectives' hunting out their own examples from a range of carefully chosen picture books and pages from comics and newspapers.

What?

As very young children make early moves into writing, teachers can begin to alert their attention to letters and words. The child's own name is a significant first source of information as is the environmental print he or she sees all around on packets, signs and notices. You need to ensure that your classroom is print-rich and exploits these early understandings by providing many opportunities for children to write (e.g. shopping lists pads in the role play area, a noticeboard with examples of environmental print, children's names prominently displayed). Shared reading and shared writing provide ideal contexts for making links with letters that the children already know. As well as a rich range of literature and non-fiction you will need a selection of alphabet friezes and books, and lots of rhyming texts. As you know from an earlier section in this chapter, there is important work to be done with such texts in the early years in developing phonemic awareness. We cannot start work on individual sounds if children are unable to single them out, and plenty of reading aloud as well as sharing nursery rhymes and finger rhymes will all feed such awareness. It is this phonological awareness that forms the basis of Phase 1 of *Letters and Sounds*. This phase is divided into seven 'Aspects', each of which focuses on a different element of sound awareness (e.g. environmental sounds, instrumental sounds, body percussion etc.).

After Phase 1, *Letters and Sounds* offers four further phases which form the backbone of phonics and spelling work in KS1. For each phase the content to be taught is presented, a clear teaching sequence delineated and a timetable for teaching suggested. Teaching strategies, some exemplified on the accompanying DVD, are included for all activities. Phase 5, and, particularly, Phase 6 focus very specifically on spelling. For instance, Phase 5 suggests activities that teach alternative spellings for phonemes; at Phase 6 children are introduced to the past tense and then learn about adding suffixes for this tense. There are strategies here for teaching spelling of long words and for practising and applying spelling.

The *NC* provides a list of what should be covered in Key Stages 1 and 2, but *Letters and Sounds* and the *PNS* give detailed guidance and objectives. The *PNS* has two strands devoted to spelling: Strand 5, 'Word recognition: decoding and encoding', which runs through from EYFS to Year 2, and Strand 6, 'Word structure and spelling', which carries all the way through to Year 6. Many KS2 teachers will find that both Strand 5 and Phases 5 and 6 of *Letters and Sounds* offer useful support for pupils struggling with spelling. However, for the majority of KS2 teachers, *Spelling Bank* (DfEE, 1999b), is the prime teaching resource. *Spelling Bank* promotes an investigative approach to the teaching of spelling at KS2 and provides activities for all the spelling objectives.

The suggestions that follow are grouped around broad strands. Some are particularly appropriate for the EYFS or later KS2 work, but many can be differentiated according to the needs and abilities of the children you work with. They complement the activities offered by *Letters and Sounds* and *Spelling Bank*. There is not room in a book like this to include detailed activities so some books are recommended that have full details of useful activities. They are all included in the booklist at the end of the chapter. In addition, of course, there are many software packages that claim to teach spelling. As with any published resource, you will need to exercise your professional judgement as to their usefulness and relevance for your class. The *Teacher Resource Exchange* (http://tre.ngfl.gov.uk/server.php) is a database of resources and activities created by teachers and offers a useful starting point for you. And try NAACE (see references at the end of this chapter) for a wealth of reviews and articles about using ICT in the classroom.

Alphabetic knowledge
- Have a good range of books and friezes (on the wall and on the tables).
- Sing and chant the alphabet.
- Make alphabets for younger classes.
- Make address/phone books/registers.
- Encourage multi-sensory learning by providing different materials with which to form letters (paint, sand, magnetic letters, plasticine, play dough, alphabet cutters, felt tips, chalk, crayons).
- Play 'I spy...'.
- Use software such as *abc-CD: the talking animated alphabet* (Sherston).

Names
- Make name cards for the children.
- Make personalised (laminated!) placemats for use at lunchtime in the nursery.
- Spot letters and letter strings from names in other words (especially environmental print with young children).
- Make books featuring children's names and names of popular characters from children's TV (Bob the Builder, Finley Fire Engine, Little Robots to name but a few. Google 'cbeebies' and 'CBBC' if you need to brush up your knowledge!)
- Play with names, e.g. make up alliterative phrases.

Rhyme and word play
See *Letters and Sounds,* Phase 1

- Make regular use of songs and finger rhymes.
- Read nursery rhymes and rhyming texts aloud regularly.

- Collect jingles.
- Encourage children to participate in shared reading of rhyming texts.
- Make lists of words that rhyme from texts you have read together.
- Make up games, e.g. rhyming snap.
- Make up alliterative phrases and sentences. Spot examples of alliteration in poetry.
- Older children can look for rhyming patterns in poetry and try writing their own, e.g. limericks.
- Use a CD-ROM such as *Ridiculous Rhymes* (Sherston), which gives the children the opportunity to listen and/or sing along.

Homographs and homophones
- Build on word play ideas to look at words that are spelled the same but mean different things (homographs), as in 'Follow my lead, drop the lead, use unleaded petrol', and to look at words like 'bare' and 'bear' that sound the same but are spelled differently (homophones).
- Make books to illustrate these differences.

Onset and rime
- See 'Rhyme' above.
- Read books like *Mig the Pig* (Colin and Jacqui Hawkins) where the changing onsets are made very clear through the use of split pages; go on to make one like it using a different rime.
- Set up activities where children can physically change the onsets of words, e.g. with cards, magnetic letters.
- *Rhyme and Analogy Activity Software* (OUP) complements the *Oxford Reading Tree* but can be used independently of this.

Learning words
Children need to develop a sight vocabulary of known words and the *Letters and Sounds* (Appendix 1) includes Phase-linked lists of both 'decodable' and 'tricky' words, the latter of which will need to be learnt as whole words. Try to vary the ways in which you teach these:

- Point them out in shared reading and writing.
- Use 'look-cover-write-check'.
- Play games, e.g. snap.
- Focus on one a day ('word of the day').
- Include them in wordsearches and crossword puzzles.
- Group them, e.g. by initial sounds, meaning, letter strings…
- Have children keep personal lists ('my spelling targets for the week'). There are numerous software packages that include on-screen word banks (e.g. *Clicker 5*).
- Make a shared list with the children of ways of remembering spelling (see list under 'Spelling Strategies' above).
- Find out about software that allows children to practise spelling, e.g. *I Love Spelling* (Dorling Kindersley) for older children has an intergalactic setting in which children travel to different planets to meet spelling challenges. *Starspell* (Fisher-Marriott) uses

'Look-cover-write-check' strategies and speaks the words for the children (in an English accent).

- Use talking books software on the computer, e.g. Talking stories *Oxford Reading Tree* (OUP) is available in this form. You can highlight particular words by clicking on them.

See Hackman and Trickett (1996) for a useful selection of activities on 'How to Learn a Spelling'.

Developing graphic strategies

As well as learning whole words, children need to develop visual (or graphic) strategies to remember strings of letters. All of the suggestions above will help these, as will the following:

- Play 'Shannon's Game', which is like 'Hangman' but you have to guess the letters in order, which encourages the children to predict common letter strings.
- Teach and encourage the use of analogy, e.g. by collecting words that share the same rimes such as '-ight' or '-an'.

Work on phonemes, consonant clusters (also known as 'adjacent consonants') and digraphs to support segmenting and blending

This work forms the backbone of the *Letters and Sounds* activities and needs to carried out systematically and faithfully along the lines of the scheme that you are using. The ideas below would complement your daily discrete phonics teaching session.

- Find examples in shared reading and writing.
- Find examples in the children's names.
- Make up tongue twisters and alliterative sentences.
- Make word wheels.
- Make a *br*ick wall of words that start with the 'br' cluster, a *tr*ain of 'tr' words and so on!
- Make a display of objects and pictures starting with the phoneme/cluster/digraph.
- Make a shared list of words that children can add to during the week.
- Play 'I spy...'; children could make 'I spy...' quiz cards for a particular sound, e.g. '...something beginning with "ch"'.

Work on roots, prefixes and suffixes

See *Letters and Sounds*, Phase 6

- Look at roots of words and see how many different ways you can make them 'grow' using prefixes and suffixes, e.g. 'eat': 'uneatable', 'eating', 'eater'.
- Use shared reading and shared writing to demonstrate fixed inflectional endings such as '-ed' and '-s'.
- Make shared lists of prefixes, find out where they come from (Latin or Greek) and what they mean, e.g. 'photo-' is from Greek and means 'light'; 'bi-' is from Latin and means 'two'. See Pratley (1988) for useful lists.
- Collect verbs that take the regular '-ed' suffix and sort them according to the different sounds these endings make, e.g. ripped, pinned, rushed, robbed, saved, plodded, laughed.

- Make collections of words that share prefixes, e.g. 'un-'. Take a theme such as 'giants' and use this as a starting point for drawing and/or writing about the unwell, unhappy, unwise, unreasonable, ... giant.
- Investigate the ways in which derivational suffixes change the word class, e.g. 'eat', a verb, becomes a noun with the addition of '-er': 'eater'.

Polysyllabic words
- Model drawing on the context of the word when tackling tricky polysyllabic words.
- *Letters and Sounds* suggests that children clap the syllables and then attend to segmenting the sounds of each syllable
- See Phase 6 of *Letters and Sounds* for many more ideas.

Compound words
- Collect examples.
- Make up new ones.
- Make a set of cards for Pelmanism consisting of different elements of compound words (e.g. wind/mill, white/board etc.).
- Enjoy the literal meanings of some compounds (babysitter, heartbroken); children could illustrate these.
- Allan Ahlberg's book *The Clothes Horse* is a whole exploration of compound words and the poet Roger McGough plays with compound words and collocating phrases in *On and On...* (in Patten, 1998)

Using dictionaries and word banks
- Have a good range of dictionaries in all classes.
- Use word-level slots or short class/group sessions to demonstrate dictionary skills.
- Turn class word banks into mini-dictionaries. A word bank for your work about Victorian England can become a Victorian dictionary.
- Make topic-related word banks (e.g. for Hogwarts School).
- Multimedia information sources now include dictionaries, e.g. *Concise Oxford Dictionary* (OUP on CD for WINPC) and see Hackman and Trickett (1996) for an excellent range of dictionary activities. There are many online dictionaries, too. Try 'Ask Oxford' for instance (www.askoxford.com/).

Finding out about words: etymology, loan words and word families
- Encourage curiosity in words.
- Show children how to use an etymological dictionary (which will always list the abbreviations used, e.g. 'L' for Latin).
- Look at lists of loan words and research their origins, e.g. judo (Japanese), zebra (Bantu), pyjamas (Persian), yacht (Dutch).
- Categorise words into families, e.g. centigrade, centurion, centipede.
- Make collections of acronyms (LASER etc.) and neologisms.
- Find out about the stories of words, e.g. the silent 'b' in 'debt' came about in the sixteenth century when scholars wanted to show off their knowledge of Latin, so changed 'dette' (Middle English word) to 'debt' to show they knew it came from the Latin 'debitum'. Look for other examples of these in Chapter 4 of Liz Laycock's book *Spelling and Vocabulary*.

- Introduce children to an online thesaurus such as: http://thesaurus.reference.com
- Enjoy Terry Deary's *Wicked Words* in the Horrible Histories series (Scholastic).

Independence and risk-taking

While some children will happily 'have a go' at spellings, others are much more reluctant. We have already talked about the importance of focusing on the bits of the word that the child has got right. Here are a few more ways to boost confidence:

- Give them 'have a go' books or encourage them to have a go on a separate piece of paper.
- Encourage them to write as much or as little of the word as they can, even if this is just the first letter.
- Suggest they draw a 'magic line' where the spelling should be if they are really stuck (but be careful about this one; some children latch on to this too readily and their writing becomes a mass of magic lines!).
- Make sure that you demonstrate that crossing out is acceptable when drafting; do this ostentatiously during shared writing.
- Encourage the child to work on a word processer right from the start (it is not just for the final product!) and to use the spellcheck function. Alert children to the aspects computers do not check, e.g. grammar, so that 'She gave them there dinner' would not be picked up because 'there' is correctly spelt.
- Use a spellcheck package like *Co-Writer* (www.donjohnston.com/) which allows you to type a few letters and then shows possible words which the child can click on to choose. *Write: Out Loud* includes a checker which interprets early spellings beyond the first two letters (which is all that conventional checkers respond to).
- Use a hand-held spellchecker where the child types in a word and it gives alternatives.
- Use speech support on the computer; most new PCs come with this option whereby each word is spoken as the child writes (or it can be set to read back after each sentence or as you prompt).
- Discuss spelling strategies with the whole class thus reminding them of the many different ways they can tackle spellings (see section above on spelling strategies).
- Make class lists of relevant spellings for a topic, e.g. on a word mobile.
- Make a class list of different ways the children can find out how to spell a word without asking you, e.g. from notices on the wall, from books, from a word bank, from a writing partner.

Glossary

ACRONYM	A word made up from the first letters of words, e.g. LASER (Light Amplification by the Stimulated Emission of Radiation)
ADJACENT CONSONANTS	See 'Cluster'.
AFFIX	Prefixes and suffixes joined to base words, e.g. 'un-' and '-ing'
ALLITERATION	Where words start with the same phoneme, e.g. 'six sizzling sausages'

BLEND	In its noun form, 'blend' is used to mean what is now called a 'cluster' (see below). Its more contemporary use is as a verb ('to blend'), referring to the process of sounding out (or putting together) phonemes in an unknown word when reading.
CLUSTER	Phonemes which run together e.g. 'br', 'slp'. Each separate phoneme can be distinguished. Note that *Letters and Sounds* refers to 'words containing adjacent consonants'.
BOUND MORPHEME	A morpheme (see below) that has to be attached to another morpheme in order to make sense, e.g. 's' on the end of 'dogs'.
COMPOUND WORD	The combination of two free morphemes, e.g. 'whiteboard'.
DERIVATIONAL AFFIX	This creates a new word, e.g. 'teach' changes meaning with the addition of the suffix '-er' to become 'teacher'.
DIGRAPH	Two letters combine together to make a single phoneme e.g. 'ch' (consonant digraph) and 'ee' (vowel digraph).
ETYMOLOGY	The history of words.
FREE MORPHEME	A morpheme (see below) which can stand on its own, e.g. 'dog'.
GRAPHEME	You may find different definitions of a grapheme. Its most common usage is as the smallest unit of sound represented as a written symbol (so it is the graphic equivalent of a phoneme). The twenty-six letters of the alphabet are graphemes and so are the groups of letters that make a single sound, e.g. 'ch', 'ee'. However, there are broader definitions such as this one from Crystal: 'the smallest unit in the writing system capable of causing a contrast in meaning (1995: 257). So, for Crystal, punctuation marks and symbols such as '&' would count as graphemes because they affect meaning.
HOMOGRAPH	A word that looks the same as another but means something different, e.g. 'font' (as in church and on the computer).
HOMOPHONE	A word that sounds the same as another but means something different, e.g. 'bear'/'bear'.
INFLECTIONAL AFFIX	A suffix which marks grammatical contrasts. In English these are used to mark plurals, possession, subject–verb agreement and comparatives and superlatives.
LOAN WORD	A word that has been 'borrowed' from another language, e.g. 'bungalow' from Hindi.
MORPHEME	A unit of meaning that cannot be broken down any more, e.g. 'dog'.
MORPHOLOGY	The study of the structure of words.
NEOLOGISM	A new word.
ORTHOGRAPHY	A language's writing system (i.e. letters, spelling and punctuation conventions).

ONSET AND RIME	An 'onset' is the consonant or cluster of consonants at the beginning of a word or syllable that precede the vowel, e.g. 'str(-ing). A 'rime' is the rest of the word or syllable, including the vowel, which enables the word to rhyme with other words, e.g. '(str-)ing'.
PHONEME	The smallest unit of sound that can be spoken or heard, such as 'b' in 'bat'. Meaning changes with the replacement of a phoneme, e.g. 'cat' or 'bag'. Over 44 vowel and consonant phonemes have been identified in English.
PHONEMIC AWARENESS	The ability to detect phonemic distinctions.
PHONOLOGICAL AWARENESS	The ability to hear and detect differences in the sound of a language.
PREFIX	An affix at the beginning of a word, e.g. '*dis*appear' or '*un*pleasant'.
ROOT	The 'base' or 'stem' of a word to which prefixes and suffixes can be added, e.g. 'teach'.
SEGMENT	Separating out the phonemes in a word for encoding. This is the reverse process of blending as the child already holds the word, ready for segmentation whilst spelling. In contrast, blending involves sounding out and reassembling the phonemes of an unknown word for reading.
SUFFIX	An affix at the end of a word, e.g. 'count*ed*', 'help*ful*'.
SYLLABLE	Segment of a word that always includes a vowel (with 'y' counting as a vowel in this case).

Further reading

Corbett, P. and Thomson, R. (2003) *Black's Rhyming and Spelling Dictionary*. London: A & C Black.

Crimmins-Crocker, J. (2007) *Practise with Puzzles: Phonics and Spelling Books 1–6*, London: Folens.

Huxford, L. (2006) 'Phonics in context: spelling links', in Lewis, M. and Ellis, S. (eds) *Phonics: Practice, Research and Policy*. London: PCP/UKLA.

Ramsden, M. (1993) *Rescuing Spelling*. Crediton: Southgate.

Useful websites

For crossword makers and word searches to download http://variety-games.com
NAACE (Advancing Education through ICT) www.naace.co.uk/newsletter
NAACE Primary http://primary.naace.co.uk

PUNCTUATION

'…it breaks it up; otherwise it would just make a lot of nonsense.'
'…annoying little things that make you stop writing.'

(Two six-year-olds talking about punctuation)

Despite the second child's misgivings in the above, punctuation is crucial to coherence, clarity and meaning in writing but it is a more elusive and low-profile aspect of presentation than spelling or handwriting. Why is this? At a glance it seems to be rather straightforward, with a relatively small number of punctuation 'marks' whose functions seem quite clear (see the glossary at the end of this section to check those functions). Its elusiveness is partly because there is relatively little research evidence about punctuation compared to the wealth that has been amassed about other areas of writing. It is also because understanding punctuation is part of a larger web of complex understanding that the child has to grapple with: namely the differences between spoken and written language and, in particular, the concept of a sentence.

The inclusion of punctuation in a chapter on transcription is itself questionable because of the central role it plays in determining meaning. Michael Rosen (1995: 40) gives us these examples – which Key Stage 2 children enjoy – and which make a telling point:

> The butler stood by the door and called the guests' names.
> The butler stood by the door and called the guests names.

Indeed, the first version of the English *NC* included punctuation in Attainment Target 1 (Composition) because 'it helps the reader to identify the units of structure and meaning that the writer has constructed' (Cox, 1991: 148). Interestingly, and maybe reinforcing the earlier point about scant research in this area, this is the only reference to punctuation in Cox's chapter on Writing. In this book we have chosen to discuss punctuation alongside spelling and handwriting as we believe it is more easily understood and tackled as part of the secretarial aspect of writing. As the well-crafted little story in Figure 7.11 by a six-year-old shows, an insistence on correct punctuation in the first draft of a piece of writing could be as stifling to the child's compositional confidence as could a similar insistence on correct spellings (as we discussed in the section on spelling).

In this section I will look at what punctuation does, at some of the problems it presents and at what is known about how children learn to punctuate. The final section provides teaching suggestions.

What is punctuation?

Martens and Goodman give us the following definition:

> Punctuation is the conventionalised means by which an author shares with a reader necessary information about meaning or language structure not contained in the words of the text. Grammatical divisions such as sentences, clauses, phrases and words, along with marks signifying meaning, such as exclamations, support, clarify and enhance written messages for the reader.
>
> (1996: 37)

In spoken language we use a range of linguistic and paralinguistic devices to make our meaning clear. These devices include intonation, stress, gestures and pauses. None of these is available to the writer who has to turn to the orthographic device of punctuation to do this work. If you think of the way your voice rises at the end of a

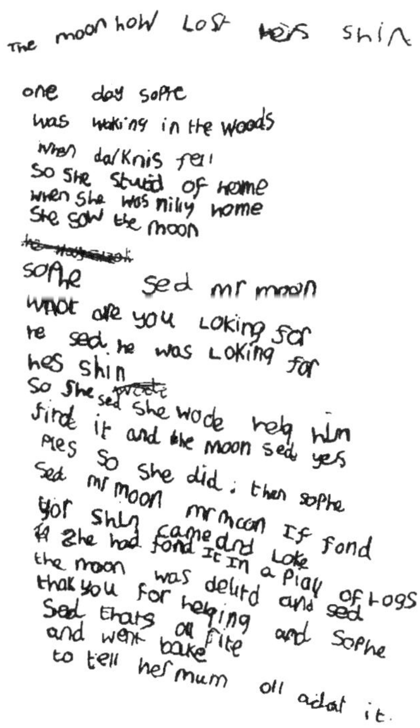

The moon how Lost his shin

one day sofie
was waking in the woods
when dalknis fell
So she stued of home
when she was nily home
She saw the moon

sofie sed mr moon
whot are you Loking sor
re sed. he was Loking for
hes shin
So She sed she wode helg him
find it and the moon sed yes
Ples So she did; then sofhe
sed mr moon mrmoon If fond
yor shin came drd Lok
it she had fond it in a Play of Logs
the moon was delitd and sed
thak you for helging and Sophe
Sed thats al rite
and wen bake
to tell her mum oll adat it.

The Moon Who Lost His Shine
One day Sophie
was walking in the woods
when darkness fell,
so she started off home.
When she was nearly home
she saw the moon.
Sophie said 'Mr Moon,
what are you looking for?'
He said he was looking for
his shine.
So she said she would help him
find it and the moon said 'Yes
please' so she did. Then Sophie
said 'Mr Moon, Mr Moon, I've found
your shine, come and look.'
She had found it in a pile of logs.
The moon was delighted and said
'Thank you for helping' and Sophie
said 'That's all right'
and went back
to tell her mum all about it.
(corrected version)

Figure 7.11

question you can see how a question mark provides a written equivalent. Now try the same with exclamation marks: 'Get me some honey or I'll hit you with my bommy knocker!' shouts the giant in *The Hungry Giant* (Story Chest, 1980). Take away the exclamation mark and see how much calmer his demand becomes. You could even try replacing the exclamation mark with a question mark (which may feel clumsy but bear with the activity) and see what a difference that makes to the way you read the piece. So question marks and exclamation marks contribute towards stress (or emphasis) and intonation.

Other punctuation marks act as boundary markers. They differentiate between different structural units: phrases, clauses, sentences and direct speech. Look at the sentence I have just written and note the colon between the main clause and the list (which is a phrase), the comma separating elements of the phrase, and the full stop marking the end of the sentence. If you feel unsure about these conventions the best way to reinforce understanding (and this works very well with children) is to seek out examples in literature.

Punctuation problems

So far so good, but it is not all quite so easy. For a start, the rules of punctuation are a convention and not very stable; they have been and continue to be subject to much change. Secondly, hearing and identifying the structural units mentioned above is not something children find easy. I will take each of these problems in turn.

Changing rules

Like spelling, the conventions surrounding punctuation have changed over time. Crystal (1995) tells us that the very earliest texts did not even have gaps between words, let alone any punctuation marks. It seems that punctuation was first introduced as a way of indicating how the text should be read aloud, as reading aloud – 'oratory' as it was called – used to be a high-status activity. In fact Parkes (in Hall and Robinson, 1996) found that, in Roman times, it was the *reader* who inserted the punctuation. In England, it was not until the seventeenth century that punctuation began to be used to mark grammatical distinctions. The notoriously problematic and misused apostrophe for possession (as in 'the dog's tail' or 'the dogs' tails') was not introduced until the second half of the seventeenth century and speech marks were not used for direct speech until the eighteenth. Commas and full stops are two of the oldest marks, whereas the question mark is a relative newcomer on the scene (Clark, 1996). Some marks are no longer used: for instance, Crystal describes an ivy leaf-shaped 'hedera' which was used in Anglo-Saxon writing to mark the end of a piece of writing. Maybe its descendant is the small, black square that some magazines use to indicate to readers that they really have reached the end of an article scattered over several pages.

Caxton's printing press (1476) was a major stabiliser for different aspects of language, particularly for the development of a standard English (the east Midlands dialect) and spelling. Spelling conventions were further consolidated in 1755 with Samuel Johnson's dictionary, which was not the first but was certainly a most significant early dictionary. Therefore, although the printing press did bring some stability to punctuation conventions, they have not been subject to the same degree of standardisation as spelling and remain quite flexible. As I write, there are renewed calls for the apostrophe that marks possession to be abolished.

Older children will enjoy knowing something of punctuation's evolution and it will help them think about the functions of contemporary punctuation marks. You will find ideas below which will encourage this.

Spoken and written language

We look now at punctuation's function as a boundary marker in writing. One major difference between speech and writing is that speech occurs in 'utterances' – chains of clauses which are rarely completely formed sentences. Typically these clauses will be joined by conjunctions such as 'and', and there will be many pauses, false starts and 'vague completers' (i.e. implied appeals to the listener such as 'isn't it/innit' and 'you know'). Look back at Chapter 2 for more detail about these differences.

Writing, on the other hand, uses the sentence as its basic unit, so a prerequisite for placing full stops, question marks and exclamation marks appropriately is an understanding of what a sentence is. As teachers you need to know that a sentence needs a subject and a finite verb but such a definition would be too abstract for pupils. Typically, children may be told that 'a sentence must make sense on its own' or even that it 'starts with a capital letter and ends with a full stop'.

Hall (Hall and Robinson, 1996) gives us a clear overview of some of the difficulties children can experience with grasping such definitions of a sentence. He suggests that the idea of a sentence 'making sense' is problematic: 'Does a word have complete sense? Does a sentence have complete sense if it is part of a paragraph, or a chapter or a book?' (Hall and Robinson, 1996: 15). The second definition presupposes that the children know where to place the capital letter and full stop: a chicken-and-egg situation. You will see children in school finding their own ways of tackling these difficulties, maybe by imposing physical boundaries and putting capital letters at the beginning of a line and full stops at the end, regardless of meaning. One such example is illustrated in Figure 7.12.

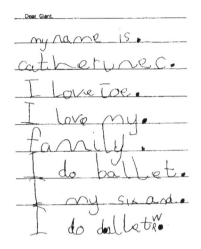

Figure 7.12

You need to be aware of these potential difficulties but not deterred from teaching about sentences. The *PNS* offer some useful guidelines:

Children need to understand the following:

- A sentence is a complete thought, for example *This is a toy*, not, *A toy*.
- A sentence is not the same as a line of writing, even though it might take up a complete line.
- A sentence needs a capital letter to start and a full stop to end. However, capitals and full stops only exist as signposts to show where a sentence starts and ends; putting capitals and full stops in a sequence of words doesn't make it a sentence.
- You can add extra information into a sentence, for example *This is a toy* can become *This is my favourite toy*.

(Source: *PNS*, Year 1 planning, Unit 1: Non-fiction)

There are practical ideas included in the final section which are informed by what we now go on to look at: the experiences and understanding that children do bring to learning about sentences and using punctuation.

How do children learn to punctuate?

Despite the lack of research in this area it is possible to draw on our understandings about children's moves into writing in order to illuminate some key aspects of learning about punctuation.

Learning about sentences

Unless children have experienced some kind of language delay, they generally come to school as competent speakers of their mother tongue. This means that they have a fund of implicit knowledge about how language works syntactically (such as the order in which words occur) in spoken language but they will not be so attuned to the concept of a sentence, which belongs to written language. In Chapter 2 Kress (1982) showed how children's difficulties in learning about sentences are best understood when seen as part of the child's moves from spoken to written mode.

However, many children will have made a start in securing understanding of written language, particularly if they have been read to from an early age. Studies of children's early reading behaviour (Holdaway, 1979) and of their dictated stories (Fox, 1993, and Chapter 5 of this book) show children using structures from written language in oral retellings. As a child retells a story or dictates one, he or she will pause or add appropriate emphasis in ways that suggest an understanding, again implicit, of the sentence as a unit. Here is a dictated story by a four-year-old; obviously you cannot hear him tell it but if you read it aloud you will see how sure his understanding is of sentence boundaries and other punctuation conventions such as exclamation marks. Included in Matthew's story is a favourite video character, Captain Planet, and two characters, Mr Wiggle and Mr Waggle, who featured in a story he was told at school:

> Captain Planet was flying about looking for his friend the Planeteer. He saw Mr Wiggle and Mr Waggle. He said, 'You can play in my spaceship but you don't touch any of the buttons.' But the naughty pair touched a big red button which sent them flying off to the moon in one hour. Captain Planet flew to the moon and told them not to press any more buttons. The next day they went exploring and Captain Planet got them some flying pizzas. Captain Planet said 'You can fly home now and tell your friend Matthew what happened.' When they woke up they thought it was a dream but then they heard 'Look out!' [child asked for this to be written 'big'] and Captain Planet swooped down from the ceiling and said 'Do you think it was a dream? No such thing as dreams.'

Now look back at Figure 7.11, the six-year-old's story called *How the Moon Lost His Shine*. If you read it through, you will find that it is syntactically accurate and that you can infer the punctuation quite easily even though she has only used a full stop twice. Take the opening: 'One day Sophie was walking in the woods when darkness fell so she hurried off home'. This complex sentence has three clauses and the child has organised the units on separate lines showing an awareness of them as different from each other. If you look at the rest of the story you will see that, although she does not make consistent use of such a device throughout, she does seem to be making some use of layout as a substitute for punctuation.

It is reassuring, then, to have evidence like this that shows children do develop implicit early understandings about sentences. The stronger these implicit understandings are, the more potential there is for making children's knowledge explicit, and it is for this reason that we include reading aloud, shared reading and shared writing in the section on teaching punctuation. The latter two routines can both provide opportunities to teach about specific aspects of punctuation, but joint readings and composition will also develop more explicit understanding about sentence structure. The practice of encouraging children to read their written work aloud works in the same way, encouraging them to draw on implicit knowledge about word order and the flow of language.

Learning about punctuation: the marks and the system

Environmental print is a rich source of information about writing, and it is not hard to find examples of question marks and exclamation marks scattered liberally around the supermarket and television screen. However, some aspects of punctuation are more visible and accessible than others. Exclamation marks and question marks are high profile and easily observed, so children can relish detecting and using them. The same cannot be said for apostrophes, especially as there are so many public misuses of them ('lunche's' being just one example spotted recently). There are implications here when considering the order in which punctuation marks should be taught; these are addressed in the teaching sections below.

Research mentioned in other parts of this book shows the discoveries very young children make about the form and functions of writing and examples of children's earliest writing attempts will often include punctuation-like marks. Figure 7.13 shows writing by a Reception-age child who told her teacher, 'It's the story of *Knock, knock, who's there?* The writing arose from a shared reading session where one focus was on question marks. She has gone on to incorporate them into her own writing but not with a clear understanding of the function of the symbols themselves. Her use of a range of different writing-like symbols is typical of the earliest stages of writing. Such symbols may include up and down lines (as in Figure 7.2), letters, numbers, letter-like shapes,

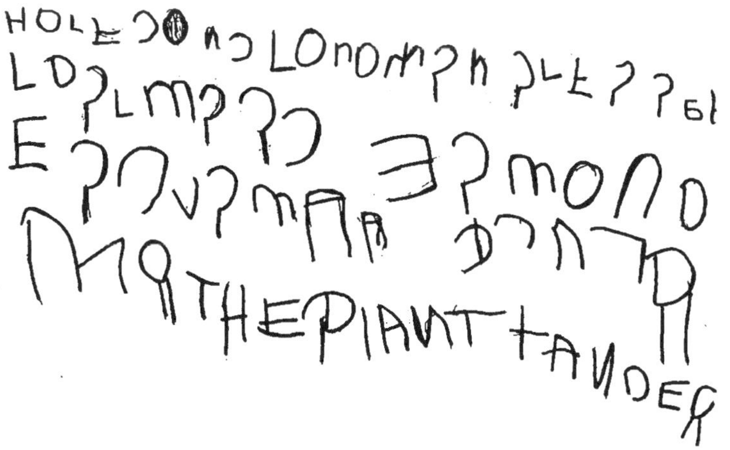

Figure 7.13

letters from different orthographies (see Figure 7.5), mathematical symbols and punctuation marks. A key element of early writing is the enjoyment children experience in playing with and organising these different symbols. There is something graphically satisfying about punctuation and you will all have favourite examples of children of all ages relishing the use (and often overuse) of a newly learned mark. Figure 7.14 shows a Year 2 child making accurate and enthusiastic use of the full stop.

Figure 7.14

There is, of course, an important difference between using a symbol and understanding its significance and as children's understanding develops, so their use of symbols becomes increasingly differentiated. Martens and Goodman (in Hall and Robinson 1996) looked at young children's use of punctuation and found examples of children working with punctuation in specific ways that reflect the nature of the system. Some examples show invented punctuation symbols which added meaning to writing and they give a wonderful example of an eight-year-old's invention of a 'sadlamation' mark:

> I've invented a new punctuation mark. A mark for something sad. It is used in a sentence like this. I had a dog. It died [*mark inserted – a v with a small circle attached to top of left side*]. It does look funny but it will get better looking soon, just like all of the others.

> (p. 38)

Nigel Hall's overview of research into children's learning about punctuation suggests that it is a complex process and not 'a passive process in which children simply learn a set of rules and can then punctuate accurately' (p. 33). What the studies did show is that, in common with other aspects of the writing process, children work actively in trying to build up an understanding of the system. Look back again at Ben's apostrophes (Figure 7.1): he knows they are used with the letter 's' when it occurs at the end of a word but has not yet grasped the possessive principle.

A sense of audience

A factor that contributes to children's understanding of the punctuation system is their developing sense of writing for an audience, which was discussed in the chapter on composition. The point here is that, as children write for a range of audiences and purposes, they become increasingly aware of the fact that we write with a reader in mind and that punctuation is there to help that reader (and this is included in the Programme of Study for KS1). This was Brian Cox's (1991) reason for including punctuation with composition, and you can see how vital it is that children keep in touch with the idea of an audience, a reader for their writing. So work on punctuation needs to be grounded in a rich writing environment in which authentic contexts, purposes and audiences are planned for. The stronger the sense of audience the greater the imperative to punctuate correctly.

Teaching punctuation

When?

As with spelling, you will need to plan opportunities to teach punctuation in shared writing sessions and in guided writing where specific personalised teaching can occur. As well as discrete teaching slots, opportunities to reinforce understanding can be taken in shared reading.

How?

Again, you need to look back to the 'How?' section in 'Teaching spelling'. Working positively with what the children already know and use continues to be important. As the section above on 'Changing rules' showed, punctuation, like spelling, is an area that can be a source of interest for children, so make sure you include activities (such as inventing new punctuation marks) that will foster their curiosity. Keep your work contextualised, and make sure that children really are free to focus on the particular aspect of punctuation you are trying to teach and are not trying to contend with too many different things at once. Be ready for some over-generalisation as children start to adopt new conventions in their writing; we have seen Ben's vigorous use of apostrophes (Figure 7.1) and Figure 7.15 shows an energetic overuse of exclamation marks. This nine-year-old is using exclamation marks to inject expression into a lively piece, which is quite close to spoken language. You could refine her use of them by looking at examples in books and demonstrating their use in shared reading and writing.

What?

The *NC* gives broad guidelines for what is to be covered and the *PNS* offers progression across the year groups in Strand 11 ('Sentence structure and punctuation'). This starts with using capitals in Reception right through to secure use of the semi-colon in Year 6. Given what we have said about the visibility and impact of some marks – especially question and exclamation marks – you might want to explore children's understandings of these a little earlier than the *PNS* suggests (Years 2 and 3). The *NLS* publication, *Grammar for Writing* (DfEE, 2000a), provides many activities for punctuation work at KS2.

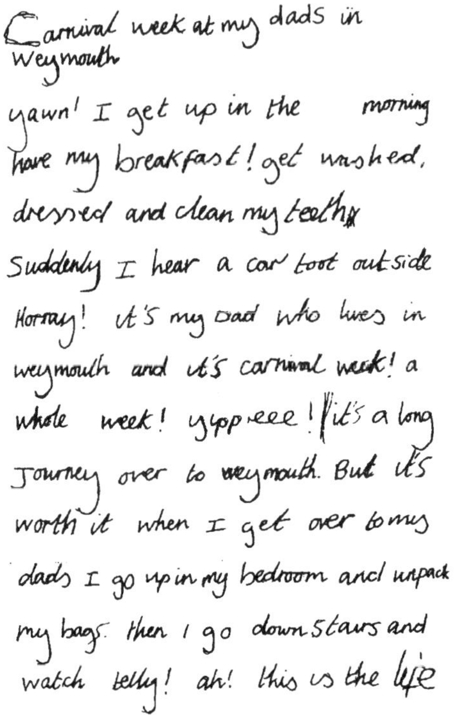

Carnival week at my dads in
Weymouth

yawn! I get up in the   morning
have my breakfast! get washed,
dressed and clean my teeth
Suddenly I hear a car toot outside
Hooray! it's my Dad who lives in
weymouth and it's carnival week! a
whole week! yippeee! it's a long
Journey over to weymouth. But it's
worth it when I get over to my
dads I go up in my bedroom and unpack
my bags then I go downstairs and
watch telly! ah! this is the *life*

Figure 7.15

We have looked at the use very young children may be making of marks in their early writing and those of you working in early years settings will need to observe such use and make sure that shared reading and writing opportunities include some reference to marks that children have picked up on. Your displays of environmental print should also include examples that you can draw on.

Developing a sense of audience
- Provide writing opportunities for a range of audiences, e.g. books for each other (see Chapter 5) and other classes, invitations to class assemblies, notices and so on.
- Support these opportunities through the provision of a range of writing contexts, e.g. class café, shop etc.
- Shared reading and writing sessions where you omit punctuation will help children understand and develop a sense of audience.
- Encourage children to read their work aloud, either to themselves or to a writing partner.

Developing an understanding of sentences
- Remember that a sentence has to have a subject and a finite verb.
- Children read their work aloud (as above).
- Read aloud to the children.

- Use the children's own writing corrections – 'How did you know it wasn't right?'
- Discuss with the children what they think a sentence is; discuss examples of non-sentences and sentences; encourage the children to generate definitions and rules.
- Focus on a particular type of sentence, e.g. interrogatives (questions); look for and make up examples.
- Focus on particular parts of speech, e.g. verbs, as another context for discussing sentences.
- Use shared reading and writing to talk about sentences. Give children an assortment of sentences split up into their subjects and predicates (e.g. The pirate/brandished his cutlass; The fairy/flapped her wings; The boy/wanted mum.) Let the children reassemble these, making the silliest sentences possible. Go on to give them strips of paper to make up their own examples for others to try out.

Teaching specific aspects of punctuation
- Model during shared reading/writing. Give the children punctuation fans (*Grammar for Writing* has templates for these: www.standards.dfes.gov.uk/primary/publications/literacy/63317/nls_gfw010702fans.pdf). Children can use these to indicate omitted or concealed marks in shared reading/writing. Alternatively, they can write their suggestions on whiteboards.
- Use the children's own work to target specific aspects.
- Punctuate text with the aspect you want to teach omitted.
- Use comic strips and speech bubbles to teach about speech marks.
- Get children to make up their own punctuation marks, e.g. different 'hedera' (Crystal, 1995 on p. 161) for different genres of writing, or tell them about the 'sadlamation' mark and make up marks for different emotions.
- Write style guides for younger children, e.g. how to use an exclamation mark!
- Find out about the history of the mark you are teaching (e.g. question mark: 'Q' is for 'quaere', Latin word for question. Originally the whole word 'quaere' was written after a question, then shortened to 'Q', before being replaced by the mark we now use (Jarman, 1979). You may have noticed that in Spanish the question mark is used upside down at the start of sentences as well as in its normal position at the end.
- Find examples from favourite classroom books, make lists and see if the children can start to make rules.
- Use a CD-ROM such as *The Punctuation Show* (Sherston). This provides four different sporting contexts (football, grand prix, etc.) in which children can practise and reinforce their knowledge of different punctuation marks.
- Older children could seek out examples of punctuation misuse in the environment. Start a 'Punctuation Howlers' board.

Play with punctuation and graphic effects
One way of helping children to understand the way punctuation functions is to 'play' with its effects.
- Exchange exclamation marks and question marks and see what the effect is on reading aloud.
- Collect examples of exaggerated and attention-grabbing uses of punctuation, e.g. from advertisements and cartoon characters ('Aargh!!!').

- Give children cards with ambiguous sentences that rely on punctuation for their meaning (such as the example on p. 158), or 'The man's computer knows its boss.'/ 'The man's computer knows it's boss.'). They should read these aloud in pairs considering the effect on meaning the different punctuation evokes.
- Use ideas from Michael Rosen's lively chapter in *Did I Hear You Write?* where he suggests ways that children can represent different effects in their writing, e.g. a word or phrase said loudly, or a single word said very slowly, as we do when we call out for mum (!) (1989: 41).

Glossary

APOSTROPHE ('):	Apostrophes have two uses. They can be used to show where a letter or letters have been omitted (contraction): *Don't you worry Harry. You'll learn fast enough.* (*Harry Potter and the Philosopher's Stone*, p. 66) An apostrophe placed at the end of a noun and before the 's' indicates possession (*wizard's hat*). Where the noun is plural, then the apostrophe goes after the final 's' (*wizards' hats*). Note that the possessive pronoun 'its' does not follow this rule: *it's* always indicates *it is* or *it has*.
BRACKETS ():	Brackets contain extra material within a sentence: *He could hear (though he had no idea what Black's voice might sound like) a low, excited mutter.* (*Harry Potter and the Prisoner of Azkaban*, p. 158)
CAPITAL LETTERS	Capital letters are used at the beginning of sentences, for 'I' and at the start of names, places, titles, days and months.
COLON (:)	A colon is used to precede a list or a quotation. It may also be used in a sentence where the second half of the sentence explains or unfolds from the first: *He was striking to look at: he was no taller than Lord Asriel's hand span, and as slender as a dragonfly.* (*The Amber Spyglass*, p. 60)
COMMA (,):	They may be used to separate units in a sentence which could be words, phrases or clauses: *Every time they passed the third-floor corridor, Harry, Ron and Hermione would press their ears to the door to check that Fluffy was still growling inside.* (*Harry Potter and the Philosopher's Stone*, p. 167) They may also be used to separate items in a list comprising single words (*She saw lions, tigers, penguins and cheetahs.*).
DASH (–):	A dash may be used like brackets or may precede a final comment.
ELLIPSIS (…):	Ellipsis denotes omission of words or an interruption.
EXCLAMATION MARK (!):	An exclamation mark is used at the end of a sentence to add force and emphasis. It is used for a range of emotions, e.g. anger, happiness, surprise.

FULL STOP (.):	A full stop is used to mark the end of a sentence.
HYPHEN (-):	A hyphen is used for a word break at the end of a line and for compounds such as *tail-ender*.
QUESTION MARK (?):	A question mark is used at the end of a question.
SEMI-COLON (;):	Semi-colons are used to separate items in a list that contains lengthy items:

The basket contained a strange array of foods: fresh, brown, enormous eggs; seven squashy, mouldy bananas; chocolates that had seen better days; and a pork pie.

They are also used to punctuate sentences with two main clauses that could stand as separate sentences but where the ideas are closely linked and benefit from closer linkage than a full stop allows:

Harry didn't speak at all as they walked down the road; he didn't even notice how much people were gawping at them on the Underground. (Harry Potter and the Philosopher's Stone, p. 66)

Note that a full stop or connective ('and' would work here) could be used in place of the semi-colon, but not a comma which is insufficiently strong. (Misuse of a comma between two main clauses is known as a 'comma splice' and is a very common error.)

SPEECH MARKS (" " or ' '): Speech marks (sometimes known as 'quotation marks') are used to demarcate direct speech. Punctuation that belongs with the direct speech is kept within the speech marks:

'Where are you going?' the child asked. 'I hope it's not far.'

Further reading

To strengthen your own subject knowledge:

Associated Press (2008) *The Associated Press Guide to Punctuation*. Cambridge, MA: Perseus Books Group.

King, G. (2004) *Collins Good Punctuation*. London: Collins.

Truss, L. (2003) *Eats, Shoots & Leaves*. London: Profile Books.

These books by Truss & Timmons are for children:

Truss, L. and Timmons, B. (2006) *Eats, Shoots and Leaves: Why Commas Really do Make a Difference*. London: Profile Books.

Truss, L. and Timmons, B. (2007) *The Girl's Like Spaghetti: Why You Can't Manage Without Apostrophes*. London: Profile Books.

Useful websites

www.bbc.co.uk/schools/revisewise
www.correctpunctuation.co.uk
www.collaborativelearning.org/punctuationgames.pdf
www.mape.org.uk/startower/starpunc/index.htm

HANDWRITING

> At Standard 1 children should be able to form on the blackboard or slate from dictation, letters capital and small manuscript.
>
> (1862 Standards for Writing [in Aldrich, 1982: 81])

> The ability to write easily, quickly and legibly affects the quality of a child's written output, for difficulty with handwriting can hamper his [sic] flow of thoughts and limit his fluency.
>
> (DES, 1975: 184)

The teaching of writing used to consist almost entirely of handwriting exercises. The logbook from an Oxfordshire village school records younger children copying letters on to slates while the older ones were still copying but had graduated on to 'moral' sentences to be written in copybooks (Wendlebury, Oxon – private copy). We have a richer and more balanced writing curriculum now, but as the quotation from *The Bullock Report* (DES, 1975) above reminds us, nearly one hundred years later, handwriting remains as a most important secretarial aspect of the writing process and so it does today despite the advent of word processing.

Aims of handwriting

The *NC* requires that we teach children a legible and fluent style, and Rosemary Sassoon (1983), author of many practical and useful books about handwriting, suggests that there are three aims we should have when teaching handwriting. These are: that it is legible; that it can be speedy; and that teaching allows for development of an individual style of writing.

You might find the following activity a useful way of illuminating these aims and helping you to reflect on what is involved in handwriting. Find someone to work with and copy a passage of prose at speed for five minutes. When the time is up, look at your two pieces of handwriting and discuss them using the following prompts:

- Who was able to write faster?
- Is the handwriting always legible?
- Were you both comfortable, i.e. could you have continued to write at speed for some time?
- Are there features which might interrupt the flow of the handwriting? Are any of these solely decorative?
- How do you both feel about your handwriting?
- Do you use different styles at times, e.g. in exams, for an important letter?
- Is either of you left-handed?
- Do you have any 'favourite' writing implements?

You might also like to compare the way you positioned yourselves, held the writing implement and placed the paper. You should have found that the process of observing closely was revealing and, of course, the same holds good for our work with children. We will return to the practical implications of these observations later in the section.

Issues in the teaching of handwriting

A motor skill

Handwriting is a physical activity that requires very specific teaching in order to develop the fine motor skills that it involves. Although watching a fluent writer as she writes is important, ample practice with writing implements and guidance is necessary for children to become skilful handwriters.

This is why providing the right equipment and seating arrangements (see Checklists 1 and 2 below) are so important. You will find suggested ways of developing very young children's manipulative skills in Checklist 3 (and see Chapter 5 on copying and tracing routines). You may also find some of these suggestions useful when supporting children with handwriting difficulties (see Checklist 5).

Speed and automaticity

In a fascinating review of research developments in the area of handwriting, Medwell and Wray (2007) draw our attention to two factors whose importance has been underestimated: speed of handwriting and 'automaticity' (that is, writing automatically without thinking about it). Drawing from a range of research data, they show that there is more to handwriting than the fine motor skills already discussed and that memory processes have a part to play as well. Further, there is persuasive evidence to suggest that once speed and automaticity have been achieved, memory is effectively freed up to engage with composition or, as they phrase it, 'higher-order composing processes' (p. 13). The implications of this are two-fold. Firstly, it seems that for all children an increased emphasis on handwriting and the development of a speedy style is crucial. However, as Medwell and Wray cite studies that suggest boys struggle more with handwriting than girls, we need to be particularly conscious of the impact that strong handwriting policies could have on boys' achievement.

A personal style

As well as developing the appropriate motor skills, we also have to foster each child's individual writing style. When I look back through examples of writing from children I taught over twenty years ago, their handwriting still evokes each individual child as vividly as ever. Perhaps you have childhood memories of experimenting with different styles, implements and ink colours. Handwriting is part of our identity, our own particular hallmark, and this could be why the tradition of collecting autographs persists. You might feel that the idea of a personal style is becoming less relevant with the ever-increasing use of word processors, but in word processing personal styles also develop. We realised, as we began to edit first drafts for this book, that our colleagues had distinctive word processing styles. They had preferred fonts, made different choices about spacing, layout and whether to print in 'draft' or not. I have childhood memories of trying to copy the handwriting style of a friend as I thought it would mean I would write with her fluency and ease. It is the notion of individuality in handwriting that brings us back to a strand that has been running through this chapter concerning the development of children's curiosity about different aspects of writing. Such curiosity can and should extend to handwriting and you will find some ideas for this in the section on teaching handwriting.

Audience and purpose: making presentational choices

Ellen and Nicola (Year 2) have been asked to make a notice for the book corner reminding the class to keep the books tidy. The notice has been planned and checked for correct spelling so now they have started on the final version. Halfway through I find Ellen standing at one end of the book corner holding the notice while Nicola is reading it from the other side of the classroom. 'We just want to make sure people can read it, miss,' they tell me.

While the notions of audience and purpose are not directly linked with the physical formation of writing, they do need reaffirming with regard to handwriting. One of the prompts in the opening activity concerned the choices we make about legibility, size, and, perhaps, style, which will depend on the audience and purpose of the piece of writing. You will find that the *PNS* specifies the need to 'adapt handwriting for specific purposes' (Strand 12, Year 5) and to 'Use different styles of handwriting for different purposes with a range of media' (Year 6). This ties in closely with points made in Chapter 6 regarding the different types of presentation that accompany different genres of writing. Secure understanding of both writing process and product will also enable children to make confident use of a more informal script for note-taking than they would for the scribing of a favourite poem for a class anthology in their 'best' handwriting.

Cursive writing

The handwriting exercises that the children at Wendlebury Village School carried out a hundred years ago would have been written in copperplate – a cursive hand. Jarman (1979) tells us that this joined-up handwriting style developed in the eighteenth century at a time when more handwriting was needed for commercial purposes and book-keeping than ever before. (Its name derives from the traditional use of a plate of copper on which a printing design would be engraved.)

This changed after 1913 when a scholar called Edward Johnston gave a lecture to London teachers in which he suggested that children's reading would be improved by the adoption of a print script, sometimes called the 'ball and stick' method.

Jarman (ibid.) points out that, while this did provide a clear model for reading, the 'system of building up letters from separate parts' was not conducive to a fluent and speedy hand.

There was a return to cursive writing for many children with the publication of Marian Richardson's copybooks in the 1930s. However, this return was not wholesale and different handwriting schemes have been published since then. Many of these offer a compromise between print and cursive, with letters given entry and exit strokes (ligatures) in readiness for joining up.

Recently, there has been a rather more persistent move to revive the idea of teaching children a cursive hand from the start. The argument is that it is better to start as you mean to continue, rather than learning one way and then having to re-learn (as I expected of my class in the example given in the Spelling section). Penni Cotton (1992) cites the French model where children are taught *l'ecriture anglaise* (cursive!) right from the start. In the nurseries, classroom labelling, letters that go home and early reading texts are in cursive script. This early exposure is reinforced outside school where many books (such as Brunhoff's *Babar*), comics and displays also use cursive. Most French teachers – now and in the past – use a very similar form, so children are also likely to meet this in their parents' handwriting. For more information about cursive writing, there are two Teachers' TV programmes referenced under 'Further reading' at the end of this chapter.

While there are issues here about the extent to which such an approach might suppress the development of an individual hand, there are also persuasive arguments about a joined-up script following on more naturally from children's first writing attempts (as in Figure 7.3). It is claimed that it is easier for the children to detect separate words because they do not get muddled by spaces between letters and between words. It allows for useful links to be made with spelling, as strings of letters can be seen as a whole unit and handwriting practice can be used to reinforce such strings. Charles Cripps, in a lecture (date unknown), argues that such an approach sets up a motor pattern for common letter strings (e.g. -ing, -tion) and that this acts as a back-up for the visual pattern.

Some schools report enthusiastically on the benefits of this approach; others remain more sceptical, arguing that very young children's cursive attempts are poorly controlled and do not offer the clear graphic information needed in spelling. The *PNS* recommends that handwriting joins should be taught from Year 2. Whatever the pros and cons, the outcome needs to be a system that allows the child to concentrate on composition so that letter formation does not 'hamper his flow of thoughts and limit his fluency' (DES, 1975).

Teaching handwriting

When?

The best time to show a child how to hold a pencil and form letters is when she or he first shows an interest in writing implements and writing. Young children are likely to hold pencils and other writing implements long before they know about letters, so helping to establish a good grip may come before demonstrating letter formation. In the nursery, this means ensuring the provision of a range of writing materials and implements as well as the kinds of enticing writing contexts we have discussed elsewhere in this book. In addition to this, young children need opportunities to develop the fine motor skills they will need for handwriting (see Checklist 3). So you will need not only to think about overall provision (see below) but also, through your observations, to be responsive to individual children's needs.

Handwriting should be taught discretely but, in common with other aspects of transcription, you will also want to plan other opportunities to demonstrate and reinforce work through regular routines. Shared writing is a good context to remind children about correct letter formation and, for younger children, copying and tracing activities provide valuable extra practice (see Chapter 5). There are some television programmes that provide well-contextualised opportunities for handwriting practice (e.g. *Words and Pictures*, which also has a well-designed website). Look back, too, at the ICT suggestions in the spelling section; many of the software packages there offer spelling and handwriting practice.

How?

Again, it is important to remember that your teaching should be positive and well-contextualised. Make the most of the links between spelling, phonics and handwriting and use handwriting sessions as an opportunity to reinforce and revisit spelling patterns or phonic work that you have taught earlier. On the whole, handwriting is best taught either as a whole-class session or during teacher-focused group work, as it is most important that you are able to observe the children so that you can check an uncomfortable grip, awkward posture or inaccurate letter formation. There will be times, however, when children are working independently (as in the earlier example of writing out a favourite poem for a class anthology).

Your own handwriting is important: you should adopt the school's style as far as possible and use it when you write on the board, in children's books, on worksheets and in shared writing.

What?

Most schools will have a policy for handwriting with regard to letter formation – not every school will want to teach entry strokes as well as exit strokes – and when to start joining. This may be backed up by a published scheme, such as *New Nelson Handwriting* (Smith and Inglis, 1984) or the *Jarman Handwriting Scheme* (Jarman, 1982), which provide graded exercises and copybooks. If you should find yourself without such support, then you will find Rosemary Sassoon's (1990) book, *Handwriting: The Way to Teach It*, provides useful guidance on possible models. The DfEE publication *Developing Early Writing* offers clear guidance on letter formation. Strand 12 of the *PNS* offers a broad progression through from Foundation Stage to Year 7 but you may find it useful to look back at the word level requirements in the *NLS* as well, as these are much more specific (e.g. Year 2, diagonal joins to letters without ascenders: 'ai', 'ar', 'un').

You will also need to find out if there is a school policy with regard to the use of lined or unlined paper and the types of writing implements that are available (and whether these are specific to particular age groups). See the section on Provision below for more ideas on this. As the opening activity of this section demonstrated, teaching handwriting is about more than just forming letters; the way we sit and the way we hold our pens are just two other aspects we have to think about. Checklist 1 gives some guidance on these preliminaries. The rest of this section has been organised as a series of checklists, mostly for you, but there is also one for children. You will find much more detail in the books listed at the end.

CHECKLIST 1: Preliminaries

- Are the children sitting comfortably, looking ahead and leaning forward a bit?
- Are the tables or desks at a suitable height?
- Is the lighting sufficient? Left-handers will need it directed over their left shoulder.
- Is the child holding the writing implement with a comfortable and usable grip?*
- Is the paper positioned well (i.e. to the right of the body for right-handers and left for left-handers, top of page slanted to the left for right-handers, other way and at a greater angle for left-handers)?

- Can the children all see the board/copybook they are using?
- Have the children all the appropriate equipment (good-quality paper and implements; you cannot form letters with care using coarse paper or soft unsharpened pencils)? Are the paper and implements the right size? Rosemary Sassoon (1983) says small children need small bits of paper so that their writing arms are neither stretched nor cramped.
- Can you observe all the children?

* The question of grip is problematic. Traditionally children were taught to use the so-called 'triangular grip' but this is not comfortable for everyone. You will need to observe the child's grip 'in use' in order to ascertain whether it is allowing for fluency and legibility. The older the child the harder it is to undo an unwieldy grip. Left-handers might find it easier if they hold the implement further up than right-handers so that they can see what they are writing.

CHECKLIST 2: Provision

Early Years Foundation Stage:

- Material to encourage experimentation and early mark-making, e.g. range of colours, sizes and types of paper, pencils, crayon, felt tips, paint, sand, plasticine.
- Examples of environmental print, frequent use of children's names (which will probably be the first word they try to write and your first opportunity to show them how to hold the implement and form the letters).

As children get older set up a handwriting area.

- Include many different writing implements. Talk about using different ones for different purposes; discuss children's favourites; try Rosemary Sassoon's idea of getting the children to try out different implements and record their findings, e.g. 'the pen because it's comfortable to hold...and I can grip it better' (Sassoon, 1990: 41).
- Include lined and unlined paper, line guides, rough and best paper. Again, talk with the children about the most appropriate uses for these, e.g. rough for notes, unlined with line guide for writing for classroom wall.
- Include examples of different types of printing and writing, e.g. James Berry and Louise Brierley's (1994) beautifully presented picture book *Celebration Song*, which has a cursively written text.
- Include different alphabet posters (English and in other scripts, too, e.g. Urdu, Bengali, Turkish).
- Include examples of illuminated letters which children can use to enhance presentation of special pieces of work, e.g. postcards from the *Book of Kells* and from manuscripts in the British Museum, Jan Pienkowski's (1984) *Christmas*.
- Encourage children to present work using a package such as *Microsoft Office Publisher* which offers a wealth of presentational opportunities.
- Include examples of books with striking borders, e.g. Antonia Barber and Nicola Bayley's (1990) *The Mousehole Cat*, Selina Hastings and Juan Wijngaard's (1985) *Sir Gawain and the Loathly Lady*.

Establishing an area like this is best done with the children, so that you can discuss the different materials and involve them in decisions about what type of implement or paper might be best suited for a particular purpose. Sassoon (1990) suggests the children could survey all the different material and draw up 'dos and don'ts for handwriting lists'. She includes some lovely drawings by children showing good and bad positioning for writing (p. 41).

CHECKLIST 3: Developing fine motor skills

- Give children practice in copying and tracing shapes before progressing on to patterns (see any of the publications under 'What' above, for guidance on these).
- Provide activities that develop children's manipulative skills, e.g. jigsaws, bead-threading, cutting and model-making.
- Ensure there are ample opportunities to develop children's graphic skills through painting and chalking as well as drawing, colouring and mark-making.
- Let the children manipulate letter shapes in sand with playdough and with wooden and magnetic letters.

CHECKLIST 4: Promoting an interest in handwriting

As well as including the range of scripts, books and letters mentioned above there are other ways of fostering children's curiosity about handwriting. You could:

- find out about the work of graphologists: people who analyse handwriting and tell us about the psychological significance of the way we form letters. Did you know, for instance, that a 'd' written with loops suggests that you are vain? (Crystal, 1995: 269).
- collect pictures and photos of children writing; there are many images of Victorian schools to be found;
- collect examples of handwriting from famous people; discuss autographs;
- find out about calligraphy as a craft, e.g. writing implements through the ages – Jarman gives instructions as to how to make a quill pen (1979: 134–5).

CHECKLIST 5: Possible problems

- Are the letters being formed correctly, completely and consistently? (Watch out for the starting point, stroke direction, poor joins, closure of letters such as 'a', which if not closed looks like 'ci'). Look at the inconsistencies evident with the child's joins in Figure 7.15 and the trouble Kelly has with 'p' in Figure 7.7.
- Are children waiting – as they should – until they have completed words in cursive script before dotting the 'i' and the 'j' and crossing the 't'? In other words, check that they are not lifting their hands unnecessarily from the page.
- Is spacing between letters and words accurate? Note the difficulties the child in Figure 7.14 has with spacing.
- Are ascenders and descenders (see below) the right height and length (i.e. no more than twice the length of lower case letters)? Look at the difficulties the child has with this in Figure 7.14.
- Are all the downstrokes parallel?

- Is the writing too big or too small?
- Is the writing sitting on the line? Note how lined paper would have supported the child's efforts in Figure 7.11.
- Are bits of letters being taken out or put in (and does it matter)?

And for left-handers:

- Is the paper to the left of the child's body?
- Is s/he too close to a right-hander? Rosemary Sassoon recounts this useful little rule devised by a child for when left- and right-handers are sitting next to each other: 'Don't knock funny bones' (1990: 33).
- Is the child holding the implement comfortably? (see Checklist 1 on grip).
- LDA (www.ldalearning.com/) have a really good selection of resources to support pupils' fine motor skills including useful guidance on left-handed writing skills
- For those of you who are right-handed: the best way to understand the difficulties left-handers have is to try writing left-handed yourself. One thing you will find is that left-handers will be pushing the writing implement rather than pulling it which makes for a less smooth action and has the effect of covering up (rather than revealing) the writing. Many left-handers come at their writing from above the line which keeps their script visible.

(Some of these ideas come from John Foggin's (1992) *Real Writing* and some from Jarman.)

Finally, here is a checklist that children could use. You would probably want to adapt it depending on the age and experience of the children you work with.

CHECKLIST 6: My handwriting checklist

- As you get organised to do some writing, ask yourself these questions:
- Are my pens and pencils in good condition?
- Have I cleared my table so that I've got room to write?
- Am I comfortable and do I have my writing paper in a good position?

Before you start writing, ask yourself these questions:

- Is there anything I need to think about to improve my handwriting?
  - the formation of letters that I find difficult to write;
  - joining my letters up;
  - making my writing sit on the line;
  - making my writing bigger or smaller;
- What sort of writing do I need to do?
  - drafting;
  - my neatest writing;
  - note-taking;
  - word processing.

When you finish writing ask these questions:

- Can I read my writing?
- Can other people read my writing?

- Is my writing tidy enough?
- Did I use the right kind of handwriting for the job I was doing?
- Next time, what could I improve on?

Glossary

ASCENDERS:	occur in b, d, f, h, k, l, t; the part of the letter above the midpoint
CURSIVE:	joined-up writing
DESCENDERS:	occur in g, j, p, q, y; the part of the letter below the line
DIAGONAL JOIN:	all letters in cursive script join to their next letter with a diagonal join except o, v, w and, in some cursives, b
ENTRY STROKE:	join or line going into the letter (ligature)
EXIT STROKE:	join or line leaving the letter (ligature)
HORIZONTAL JOIN:	o, v, w and, in some cursives, b join to their next letters with a horizontal join
LIGATURE:	joining strokes
LOWER CASE:	small letters a, b, c etc.
PRINT:	writing that is not joined up
UPPER CASE:	capital letters A, B, C etc.

Further reading

Medwell, J. and Wray, D. (2007) 'Handwriting: What do we know and what do we need to know?' *Literacy*, 41 (1), 10–15.

Montgomery, D. (2006) *Spelling, Handwriting and Dyslexia*. London: Routledge.

Taylor, J. (2001) *Handwriting. Multisensory Approaches to Assessing and Improving Handwriting Skills*. London: David Fulton Publishers.

Useful websites

Words and Pictures
    www.bbc.co.uk/schools/wordsandpictures

Teachers' TV

Two interesting programmes on using a cursive script from the start.
'Teaching Handwriting: How they do it in France'
    www.teachers.tv/video/5416
'Primary Special Needs – A Passion for Handwriting'
    www.teachers.tv/video/24021

Chapter 8

Monitoring and Assessing Writing

Liz Laycock

'I like it when my teacher ticks my work and writes 'good'. But I don't really know what 'good' means. I know it's better than 'good' when I get a gold star.' (Year 5 pupil in conversation with Roehampton tutor)

INTRODUCTION

The purpose of this chapter is to help you to get the assessment of writing under control and to offer guidance and procedures which allow teachers to monitor progress. We will consider what is involved in responding to, monitoring and assessing children's writing both formatively and summatively.

Assessment *for* learning (sometimes referred to as formative assessment) allows you to identify the aspects of writing the pupil needs to work on and thus informs the plans you make for further teaching about writing. But it is also about the children self-evaluating and reflecting on their progress. The teacher's cumulative record of formative assessments will provide the evidence needed for assessment *of* learning (summative assessment), which records what the child knows and is able to do at a particular stage. Both types of teacher assessments are needed to provide fuller information than will be gained from tests or National Curriculum assessment (previously known as SATs) scores alone. Such scores only provide a snapshot of how a child performs on one day, with one task, in one genre.

ASSESSMENT FOR LEARNING

In order to help children improve all aspects of their writing, teachers need to give explicit guidance based on careful observation of the child engaged in writing (the process), as well as the end-product. It is also important to remember that you should consider examples of writing from all curriculum areas. You will need both to observe writers at work (particularly during guided writing) and to look closely at samples of writing in order to analyse the children's writing strategies, their level of independence and confidence as writers and their current knowledge and understanding of writing. Planning for writing tasks should include opportunities for you to focus on specific children while they are writing and to keep these observations in mind as you assess the final product. The information you gather will enable you to provide feedback – often orally – which will make clear to the child what she needs to work on. If you plan to focus on a few children each time, you will be able to collect annotated samples of writing, gathering valuable information about a whole class over a term. In order to build up a balanced picture of the child's overall competence, the writing samples will need to reflect the whole range of different purposes and types of writing (see Chapter

6). It is this observation and sampling process which is at the heart of assessment for learning, enabling children to monitor their own progress and to understand for themselves what they need to focus on.

Observation and sampling in the Early Years Foundation Stage

However young the child, it is possible, through observation of the writer at work and through analysis of the product, to identify the child's current knowledge about the purposes for writing and the kind of writing, as well as his/her hypotheses about the conventions of writing in English.

Figure 8.1

In Figure 8.1, which is by a child in a Reception class, much is visible. The inspiration for this story was a toy mouse (Freddie) in the classroom, about whom the children had composed a story through shared writing. Many then wanted to write their own stories about the mouse. Hanife told her teacher that it said: 'Freddie the mouse came out of the cupboard. Freddie the mouse came out of the door to see if it was safe. Then Freddie had a terrible fright. It was Jade's cat.'

The telling of this short story shows that Hanife has a good sense of the characteristics of the narrative form: it has a series of events leading to a climax. She was also clear about the purpose for the writing – she wanted to contribute another story about Freddie, in booklet form. The child approached the writing task with absolute confidence; she knew she could write a story and that her efforts would receive a positive response from her teacher. The picture was drawn first, on the left-hand side of the page (following the convention of many picture-story books), and represents the startled mouse meeting the cat. The writing was then fitted into the space on the right-hand side. The first three lines were written from left to right but she then completed the page writing from right to left. The text is a mixture of real letter shapes, many of which are the letters in her name, 'Hanife', alongside letter-like shapes. There is some evidence that she is grouping letters together as in words, but there is no attempt to match the letters to the phonemes of the words she is writing nor of one-to-one correspondence. The writing has a mixture of upper and lower case letters and many of them were formed in an unconventional way. (See Gentry's 'pre-communicative' stage in Chapter 7.)

Much of this information was available because the teacher had observed the writing in progress and had heard Hanife's running commentary as she completed the task. For example, Hanife had told the teacher what was in the picture and the teacher had been able to observe the shift in directionality as the child wrote. She was also able to see the way in which she formed the letters. The teacher had not intervened because she wanted to observe the child's current knowledge and understanding about writing; this was not an occasion for teaching, but for assessing before teaching. As we saw in Chapter 7, the use of known letters, most commonly from a child's name, to generate new writing is typically observed in young children's early writing and indicates that the child understands that writing is made up of letters. It is important, when samples like this are being collected, to ensure that full annotations of the context, of the child's intentions and approach, confidence and independence, are recorded, so that the evidence in the sample can be drawn upon in planning further teaching.

This teacher now knows that she will need to work on directionality of writing in English and on handwriting, as well as alphabetic and phoneme–grapheme correspondence knowledge. She also knows that Hanife has a basic understanding of how stories are structured, which can be built on by encouraging her to write more and possibly by inviting her to dictate stories (see Chapter 5). She may also give her opportunities to experiment with other forms of writing (e.g. letters, lists).

Sampling in Key Stage 1

In Figures 8.2 to 8.4, three pieces of writing from a Year 2 child, Martin, have been selected, though more of his output would certainly be taken into consideration over the year by the child's teacher. The examples selected are three different genres.

The scientific investigation in Figure 8.2 approximates to what we would normally call a recount, as it is a retelling of the experiments Martin did. As we discussed in Chapter 6, the recount genre is one that young writers feel quite comfortable with. In fact, scientific writing such as this would typically be written as a report or a piece of procedural writing. However, unless the teacher has specified and supported the type

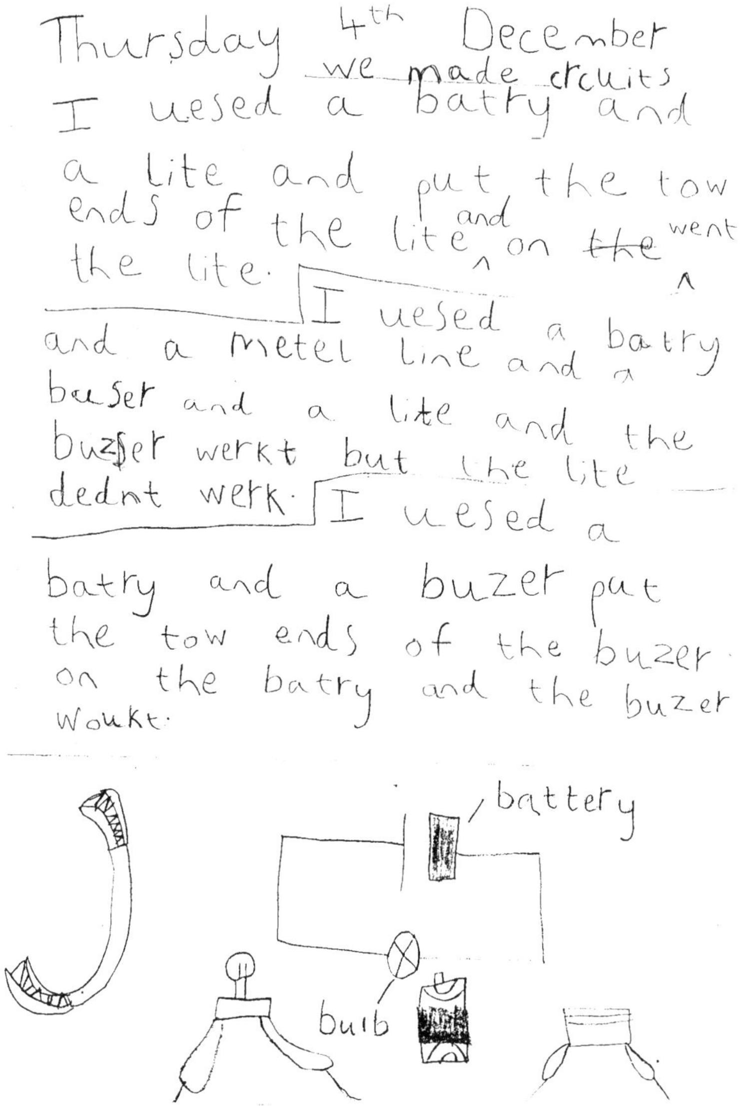

Thursday 4th December
we made circuits
I uesed a batry and
a lite and put the tow
ends of the lite and on the went
the lite.
and a metel line and a batry
buser and a lite and the
buzzer werkt but the lite
dednt werk. I uesed a
batry and a buzer put
the tow ends of the buzer
on the batry and the buzer
woukt.

battery

bulb

Figure 8.2

of writing expected, it is not surprising that Martin has written a recount. Many teachers will recognise this as a transitional stage. Martin has described three different activities and has indicated this by separating the writing into three sections. His spelling is largely based upon phonic analysis of words, e.g. 'lite', 'werkt', though he shows some awareness of conventional letter strings, e.g. 'ends', 'line'. (See Gentry's 'phonetic stage' in Chapter 7.) He demarcates sentences with capital letters and full stops. His handwriting shows generally correct letter formation and clear ascenders and descenders.

From the evidence in this writing, the teacher can obtain a clear idea of what she needs to teach to move the child forward. For instance, he might benefit from working with a writing frame, perhaps with the use of temporal connectives (e.g. 'First…', 'Next…', 'Then…'). Teaching the correct spellings of words he needed to use (e.g. 'light', 'buzzer', 'battery') and the correct terminology for 'wire', 'crocodile clip', would also help.

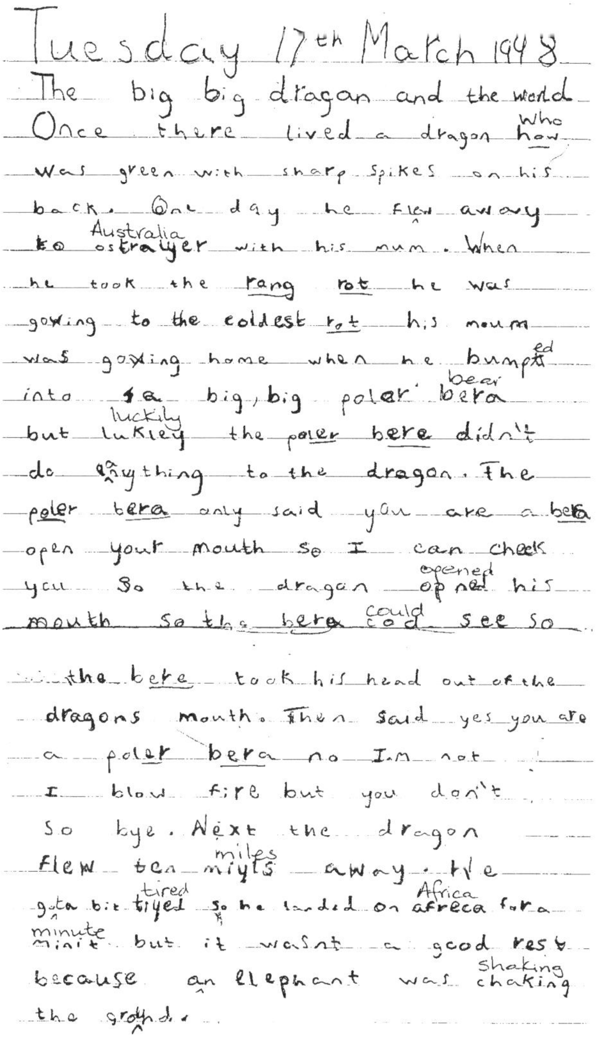
Tuesday 17th March 1998
The big big dragan and the world
Once there lived a dragon how (Who)
was green with sharp spikes on his
back. One day he flew away
to ostrayler (Australia) with his mum. When
he took the rang rot he was
goxing to the coldest rot his moum
was goxing home when he bumpt (bumped)
into a big, big poler bera (bear)
but lukiey (luckily) the poler bere didn't
do anything to the dragon. The
poler bera only said you are a bera
open your mouth so I can check
you So the dragon opned (opened) his
mouth so the bera cod (could) see so
the bere took his head out of the
dragons mouth. Then said yes you are
a poler bera no I.m not
I blow fire but you don't
so bye. Next the dragon
flew ten miyls (miles) away. He
got a bit tiyed (tired) so he landed on afreca (Africa) for a
minit (minute) but it wasnt a good rest
because an elephant was chaking (shaking)
the ground.

Figure 8.3

The story in Figure 8.3, written three months later, is incomplete, but shows some features of a narrative with a sequence of events in the 'adventures of…' manner, on an ambitious canvas (the world!). There is not, however, a series of events moving towards a conclusion, which is fairly typical of stories when the child has not thought through ideas first and thus rambles fairly aimlessly from one event to another (see

Chapter 6). His teacher had praised Martin's use of 'describing words' (though she has not given him an example of what she means), and he has the confidence to experiment with new vocabulary (e.g. 'route' spelt as 'rot').

Since the previous sample, his spelling has progressed. There are now many high-frequency words spelt correctly; some of the incorrectly spelt words show evidence of graphic awareness of conventional letter strings (e.g. 'poler') while others show spelling at the transitional stage (e.g. 'bera' for 'bear' and 'how' for 'who') with correct letters in the wrong order. He is using segmenting as a strategy for tackling unknown words in some instances (e.g. 'ostralyer' for 'Australia', 'miyls' for 'miles' and 'tiyed' for 'tired'). He still spells the inflectional '-ed' ending with a 't' ('bumpt') as he did in his first sample – 'werkt' for 'worked'. Sentences are sometimes demarcated with a full stop, but these are not always followed by a capital letter; there is no attempt to use inverted commas to mark direct speech. He uses the apostrophe correctly in the contraction 'didn't' but not in 'wasnt'; he does not use the possessive apostrophe in 'dragons'.

Martin needs guidance to develop his control of narrative form, so a way forward might include: encouragement to plan stories, so that he has a sense of where he is proceeding; talking with him about the structure of stories and clear demonstrations of these structures (see Chapter 6). After praising his correct spelling, the teacher should help him to learn those words that he has misspelt but which are near to correct forms, using the 'Look, cover, write, check' routine. You will notice on Martin's writing that the teacher helped him to learn the unchanging suffix '-ed', used in words such as 'bumped' (see Chapter 7). He should be invited to edit his own writing: he could, for instance, be encouraged to underline or circle for himself those words whose spelling he feels he might need to check. As we have emphasised in other places, he will need to know how to find those words from the classroom resources. You will see that there are other errors in Martin's writing (e.g. absence of inverted commas) but you need to be aware that he will not be able to take this all on board at the same time.

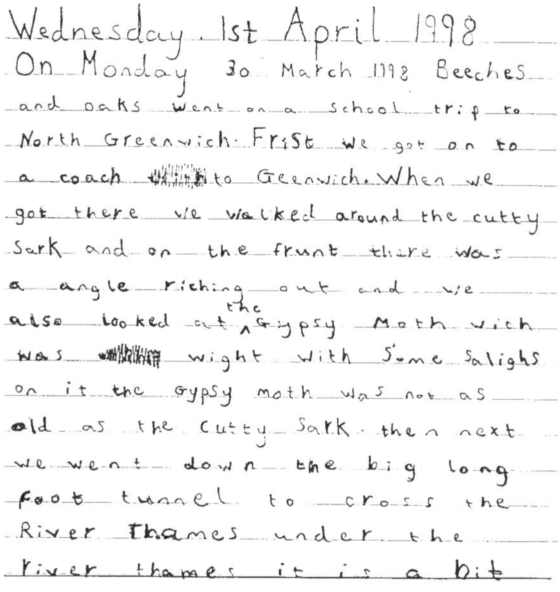
Wednesday 1st April 1998
On Monday 30 March 1998 Beeches
and oaks went on a school trip to
North Greenwich. Frist we got on to
a coach to Greenwich. When we
got there we walked around the cutty
Sark and on the frunt there was
a angle riching out and we
also looked at the Gypsy Moth wich
was wight with Some Salighs
on it the gypsy moth was not as
old as the Cutty Sark. then next
we went down the big long
foot tunnel to cross the
River Thames under the
river thames it is a bit

Figure 8.4a

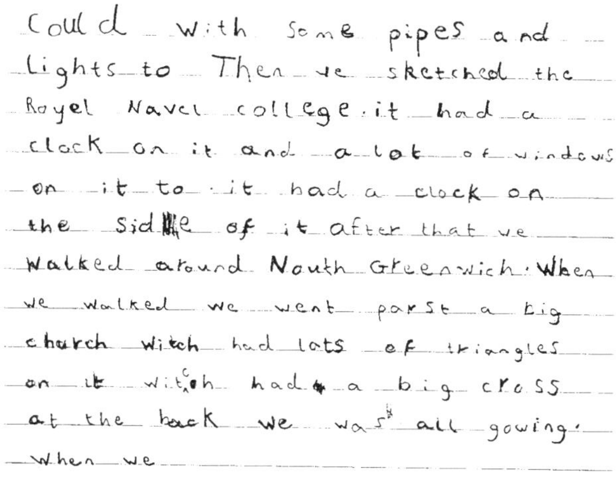

Could with some pipes and
lights to Then ve sketched the
Royel Navel college. it had a
clock on it and a lot of vindows
on it to it had a clock on
the sid le of it after that ve
walked around Nouth Greenwich. When
ve walked we went parst a big
church witch had lots of triangles
on it witch had a big cross
at the back we was all gowing.
When we

Figure 8.4b

The third example, Figures 8.4a-b, was written two weeks later. It is included because it shows progress in Martin's recount writing. It is chronologically organised and the sentences are linked with appropriate connectives – 'first', 'then', 'when', and 'next'. He writes in discernible sentences although they are not all correctly punctuated (see Chapter 7). One indicator of his spelling progress is the way he has taken on his teacher's help with the '-ed' ending, making no errors with 'walked', 'looked' and 'sketched'.

These three samples of writing show progress over time in several areas: control of genre, spelling strategies and handwriting.

Sampling in Key Stage 2

The samples of writing in Figures 8.5–8.9 cover a period of six months and a range of different kinds of writing in different curriculum areas. The writer, Jatinder, is a boy in Year 4. He was born in England – his mother is a monolingual English speaker and his father speaks both English and Panjabi. Jatinder is a fluent speaker, reader and writer of English and, although a speaker of Panjabi, he is not literate in it. The pieces comprise a book review, some scientific writing, a letter of invitation, a story and a diary. If we view these samples as a collection made by the class teacher over time, we can see that they reflect a range of purposes and forms. In every case the teacher had given clear guidance about what was expected in the particular form along with success criteria and, in some cases, had provided a planner for guidance. Some of these samples are presented as marked by the teacher, so that her responses to the writing can be seen. In this class, books are used so that there is a blank page alongside the child's writing where the teacher can write comments, suggestions and sometimes corrections and where the child can actually re-draft sections of the writing. Thus, when appropriate, the writer is given guidance about re-drafting content as well as indications of where spellings need to be checked (see section below on marking for further discussion on this).

If we look across these samples we can gather a good deal of information about Jatinder's writing.

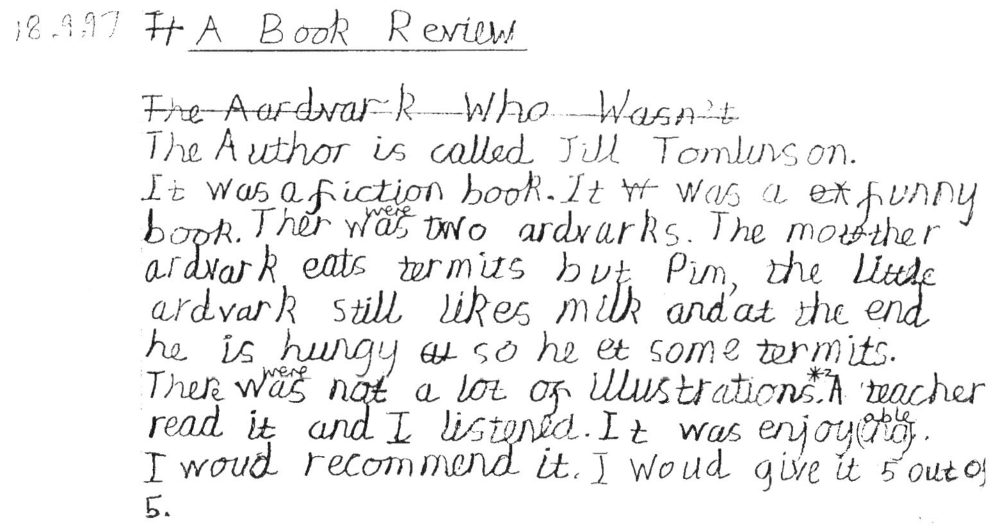

18.9.97 # <u>A Book Review</u>

~~The Aardvark Who Wasn't~~
The Author is called Jill Tomlinson.
It was a fiction book. It *H* was a ex~~f~~ funny
book. Ther w̃a̋s̃ two ardvarks. The mo*th*er
ardvark eats termits but Pim, the little
ardvark still likes milk and at the end
he is hungy *at* so he et some termits.
Ther w̃a̋s̃ not a lot of illustrations.*²A teacher
read it and I listened. It was enjoy(ing)able.
I would recommend it. I would give it 5 out of
5.

Figure 8.5

Figure 8.5, a book review of a title selected by the writer, is succinct, includes relevant
information about the book, a brief résumé and a personal evaluation.

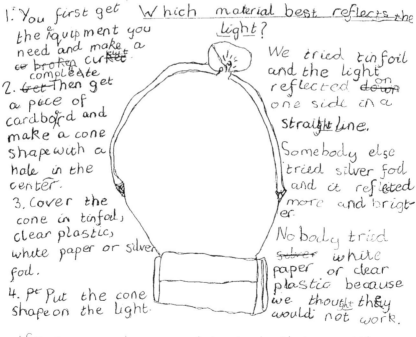

Figure 8.6

Figure 8.6 is about an experiment to find out which material best reflects light. It starts with a step-by-step (procedural genre) account of how the children went about the experiment and then records the findings. Jatinder has clearly separated the procedure (on the left) from the findings (on the right). Vocabulary is used accurately throughout but the voice of the writer, which is appropriately impersonal in the clearly expressed instructions, takes on an understandably personal tone when describing the results. Note the shifts in voice (from 'you' to 'we' to 'somebody' as he moves between the different types of writing.

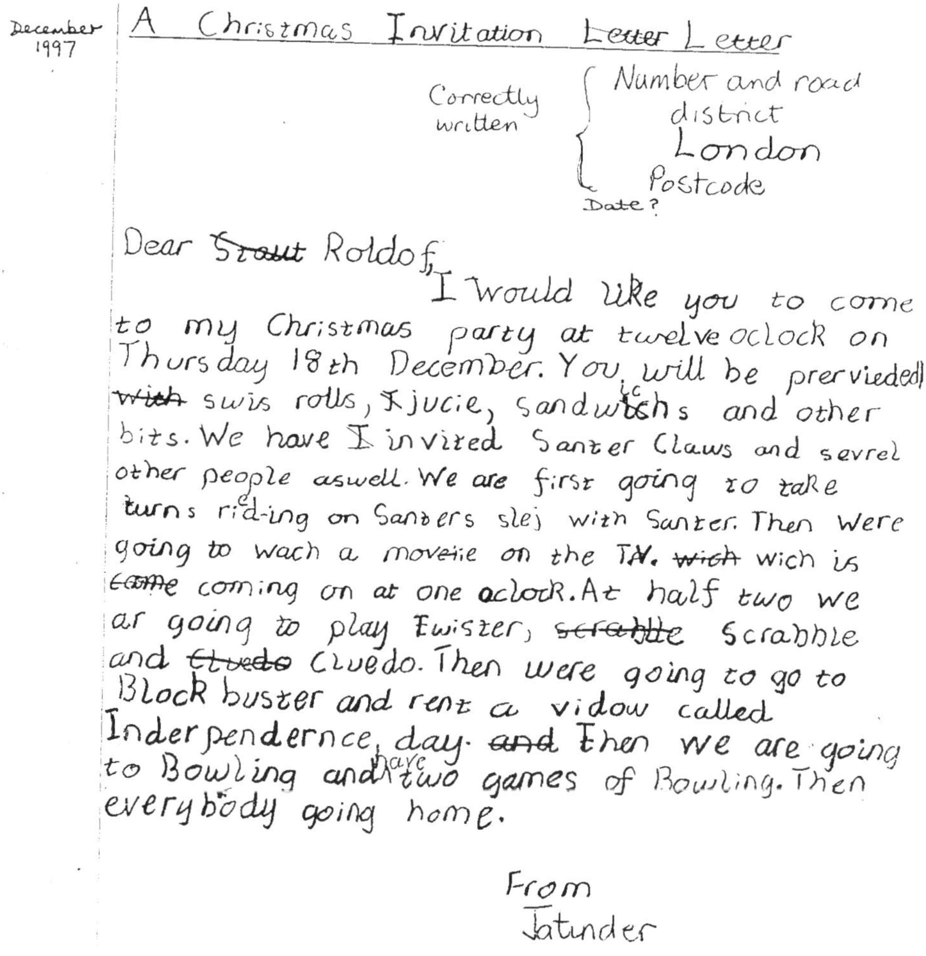

A Christmas Invitation Letter Letter

December 1997

Correctly written
{ Number and road
  district
  London
  Postcode
Date?

Dear ~~Srout~~ Roldof,
        I would like you to come to my Christmas party at twelve oclock on Thursday 18th December. You will be prervieded ~~with~~ swis rolls, Ijucie, sandwiths and other bits. We have ~~I~~ invited Santer Claws and sevrel other people aswell. We are first going to take turns rid-ing on Sanbers slej with Santer. Then were going to wach a movelie on the TV. ~~wich~~ wich is ~~come~~ coming on at one oclock. At half two we ar going to play Twister, ~~scrable~~ Scrabble and ~~cluedo~~ Cluedo. Then were going to go to Block buster and rent a vidow called Inderpendernce day. ~~and~~ then we are going to Bowling and have two games of Bowling. Then everybody going home.

From
Jatinder

Figure 8.7

In Figure 8.7, the address, which has been erased, was correctly laid out. This letter of invitation shows good knowledge of the letter format and tone. Writing in role to a fictitious character with an invitation to an imaginary party has provided the writer with a purposeful context and shows his command over a chronologically organised piece of writing.

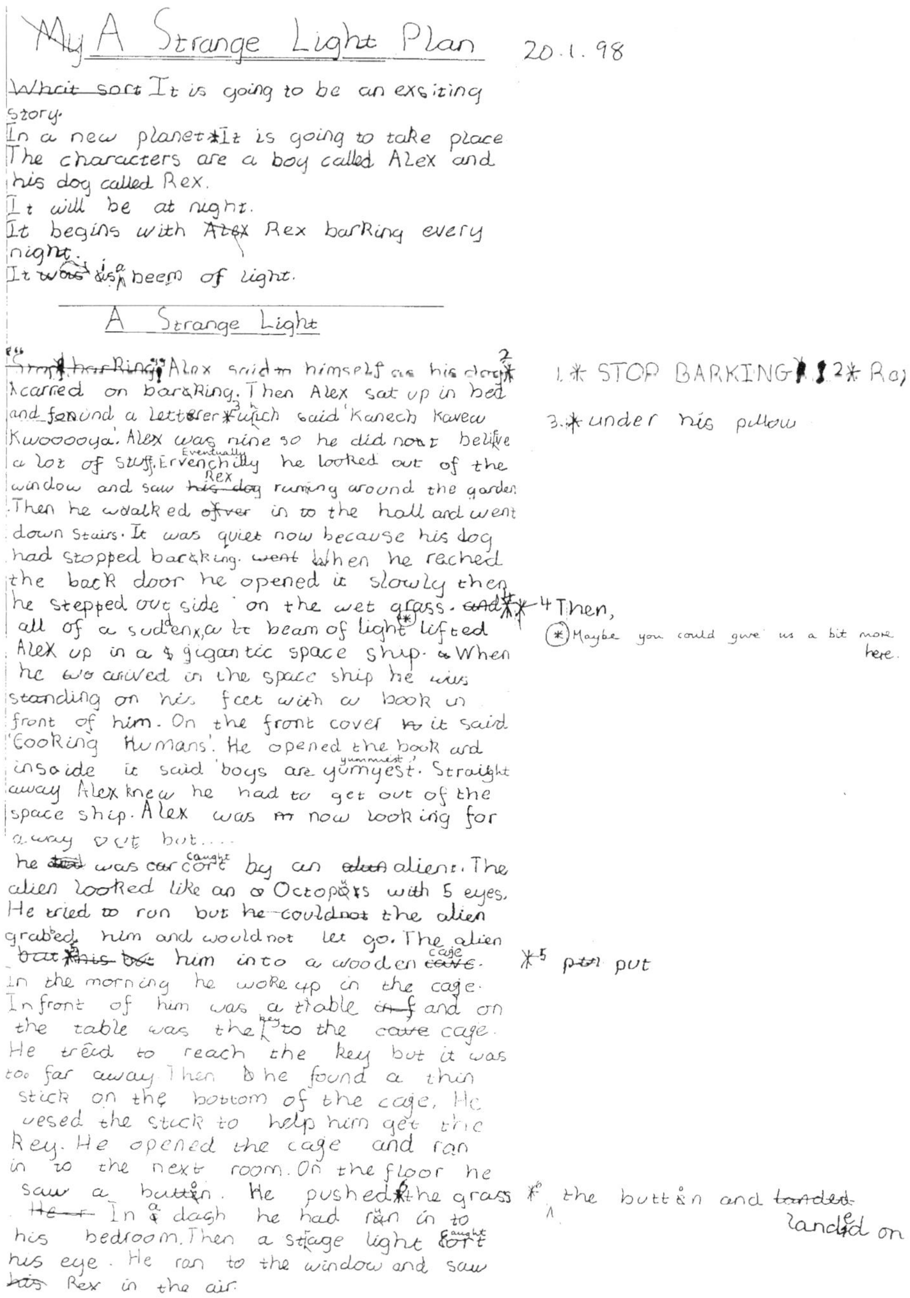

My A Strange Light Plan   20.1.98

~~What sort~~ It is going to be an exciting
story.
In a new planet ✱It is going to take place
The characters are a boy called Alex and
his dog called Rex.
It will be at night.
It begins with ~~Alex~~ Rex barking every
night.
It was ✱a beem of light.

A Strange Light

"~~Stop bar king~~" Alex said ~~to~~ himself as his dog ²
~~carred~~ on barking. Then Alex sat up in bed
and ~~found~~ a letter ~~which~~ said 'Kanech Kaveu
Kwooooya'. Alex was nine so he did not believe
a lot of stuff. ~~Eventually~~ he looked out of the
window and saw ~~his dog~~ Rex running around the garden.
Then he walked over in to the hall and went
down stairs. It was quiet now because his dog
had stopped barking. ~~went~~ When he reched
the back door he opened it slowly then
he stepped out side on the wet grass. ~~and~~ ✱⁴Then,
all of a suden ₐ a beam of light lifted
Alex up in a gigantic space ship. ~~a~~ When
he arrived in the space ship he was
standing on his feet with a book in
front of him. On the front cover ~~to~~ it said
'Cooking Humans'. He opened the book and
inside it said 'boys are yummyest'. Straight
away Alex knew he had to get out of the
space ship. Alex was ~~m~~ now looking for
a way out but....
he ~~got~~ was ~~cor~~ caught by an ~~alien~~ alien. The
alien looked like an ~~o~~ Octopus with 5 eyes.
He tried to run but he ~~couldnot~~ the alien
grabed him and would not let go. The alien
~~but this but~~ him into a wooden ~~cave~~ cage ✱⁵put
in the morning he woke up in the cage.
In front of him was a table ~~off~~ and on
the table was the ~~key~~ to the ~~cave~~ cage.
He tried to reach the key but it was
too far away. Then ~~b~~ he found a thin
stick on the bottom of the cage. He
vesed the stick to help him get the
key. He opened the cage and ran
in to the next room. On the floor he
saw a butten. He pushed ~~the grass~~ ✱⁶ the butten and ~~landed~~
~~He~~ In a dash he had ran in to landed on
his bedroom. Then a stage light ~~lort~~ caught
his eye. He ran to the window and saw
~~his~~ Rex in the air.

1. ✱ STOP BARKING ✱ ✱2✱ Rex

3. ✱ under his pillow

✱ Maybe you could give us a bit more
here.

✱⁵ ~~pen~~ put

Figure 8.8

In Figure 8.8, the story plan at the top allows Jatinder to decide on the setting, characters and opening line. He begins dramatically with speech without any preamble or scene setting. The content of this story derives from characteristic interests of boys of this age. The structure of the story is that of a true narrative, with a series of events, leading to a resolution (his escape), and with a most effective ending in the capture of the dog! He sustains the third person narrative throughout. There is some characterisation of the hero, Alex, in his cynicism about the letter. There is also some descriptive detail – 'wet grass', 'gigantic spaceship', 'wooden cage', 'thin stick', and 'in a dash'.

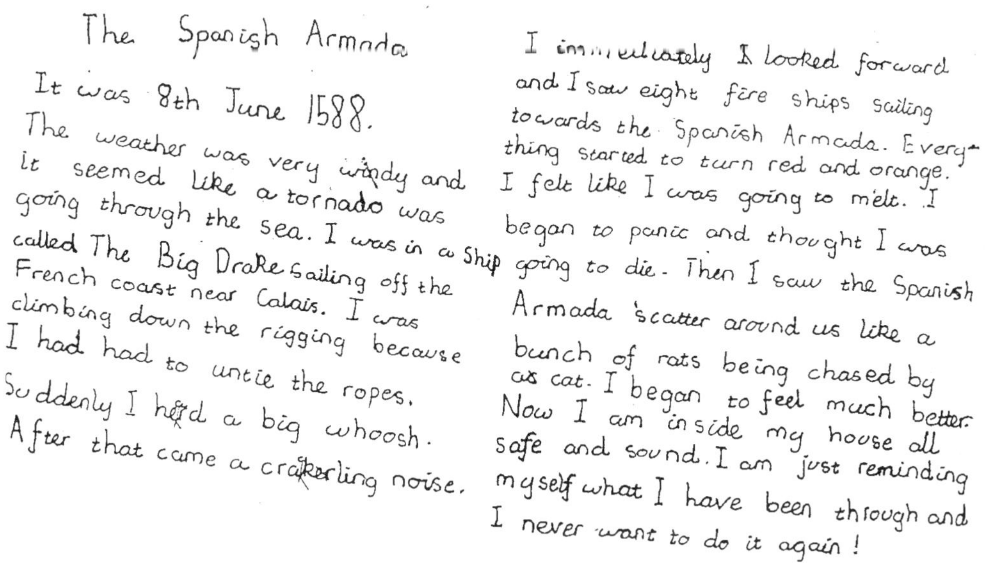

The Spanish Armada

It was 8th June 1588.
The weather was very windy and it seemed like a tornado was going through the sea. I was in a Ship called The Big Drake Sailing off the French coast near Calais. I was climbing down the rigging because I had had to untie the ropes.
Suddenly I herd a big whoosh.
After that came a crakerling noise.

I immiediately I looked forward and I saw eight fire ships sailing towards the Spanish Armada. Everything started to turn red and orange. I felt like I was going to melt. I began to panic and thought I was going to die. Then I saw the Spanish Armada 'scatter around us like a bunch of rats being chased by as cat. I began to feel much better. Now I am inside my house all safe and sound. I am just reminding myself what I have been through and I never want to do it again!

Figure 8.9

The diary entry in Figure 8.9 arose from the study of the Tudors in history. After finding out about the destruction of the Spanish Armada, the children were asked to write an account of the event in diary format. This required them to adopt the first person narrative voice. The final version was published as a diary for display. Jatinder successfully sustains the narrative voice and conveys real feeling (the heat of the fire and his fear and then relief). The teacher also kept the first draft of this piece of writing in which she had responded enthusiastically to his use of similes. It is important that your collection of samples includes drafts as these can reveal the whole of the writing process and not just the final, polished version.

With these samples in front of her the teacher is in a strong position to review Jatinder's progress. As you will have seen from the comments above, this is a confident, independent writer who is able to adjust his writing to different purposes and for different genres. His teacher has already provided models and guidance for these different genres, and, on the basis of this evidence, she is able to note areas where he needs more experience. She will be able to plan a range of opportunities to meet his needs, perhaps encouraging writing for a wider range of audiences beyond the classroom.

In all except the earliest sample, where he writes the spoken London dialect form ('there was two...', 'there was not many'), he uses standard written English. He shows increasing control over complex sentence structure ('I am just reminding myself what I have been through...' in 8.9), figurative language ('I saw the Spanish Armada scatter around us like a bunch of rats being chased by a cat' in 8.9), the passive voice ('he was caught by an alien' in 8.8), dialogue ('"Stop barking!" Alex said...' in 8.8) and use of reversed word order for dramatic effect ('...on the floor he saw a button...' in 8.8).

There is consistent evidence of Jatinder's control of the transcriptional features of writing. His spelling is generally accurate in frequently used words, both monosyllabic and polysyllabic, and he is not afraid to make attempts to spell unfamiliar words. His efforts are consistently sensible phonic attempts (e.g. 'prervieded', 'inderpendernce', 'ervenchilly', 'cort'). He uses punctuation confidently, including the exclamation mark, and is beginning to use inverted commas for speech. He also makes use of inverted commas for quotations ('He opened the book and inside it said "Boys are yummiest"' in 8.8). Only the story contains any use of paragraphing. His handwriting is legible and letters are well formed on the whole; they are joined some of the time, though he often prints when he is writing quickly. Some explicit teaching about the conventions of punctuation, about visual spelling patterns (e.g. for words with 'e' which might sound like 'er' in the child's particular speech patterns, such as 'eventually', 'even', 'parents') might be needed. He might also be given time to practise joined handwriting in order to develop a secure cursive script which will promote speed even in first drafts (see Chapter 7).

Writing conferences

With samples such as these, the child and parents, as well as any teacher, are able to review progress. The child can highlight those aspects of writing with which he is pleased and where he feels he has made progress, as well as reflect upon, and perhaps set himself targets for, areas he needs to work on. The child and his teacher can usefully think about how he feels he might best be helped and a record of such a discussion, sometimes called a writing conference, can be made so that the child can look back and see where he has developed. When you first undertake a writing conference with a child, it is useful to have an *aide-mémoire* of topics for discussion. Here are some prompts that you could use with a very young child. You would be unlikely to use them all, so select as you see fit.

- What do you think writing is?
- Can you show me some around the room?
- Can you write?
- Do you like writing?
- What do people write about?
- Do people write to you?
- What do people write at home for?
- Why do grown-ups write?
- Tell me about this bit of writing.
- What do you need to do to be able to write?

These prompts would be suitable for children in Key Stage 1 and 2:

- What makes a writer?

- Why do we need to write?
- Do you like writing?
- What do you find easy about writing; and what's hard?
- Do you write at home? What kinds of writing do you do?
- What kinds of writing do other people at home do?
- How would you teach a younger child to write?
- Do spelling and punctuation matter?
- What makes a good writer?
- Think of your favourite author and tell me what makes him/her such a good writer.
- Do we need to be able to do good handwriting? Can't the computer do it for us?
- Tell me about this bit of writing.
- Can you draw a writer/tell me what a writer looks like?

'Marking' work

As the discussion of the writing samples shows, the nature of the teacher's response and feedback to pupils is at the heart of effective assessment for learning. However, children are expected to write in every area of the curriculum, so teachers have a great deal of reading and assessing to do. Sometimes the writing will be a way of assessing a child's knowledge of another subject or a way of checking the child's recall of the details of an observation or a visit. In many cases, whatever the subject, the teacher may be tempted to 'mark' errors in spelling, punctuation or grammar and may make a general comment about the content or the quality of the work. Traditionally, the 'proper marking' of written work is one of the ways in which those who do not see what goes on in the classroom (e.g. parents) feel they can judge a teacher's effectiveness. It is the outward and visible sign that the teacher is doing her job well. In addition, children expect that teachers will read their work regularly and give them feedback; whether this is a positive or negative experience for them is another matter.

We need to reflect on what we mean by marking; in the past, it was all too often a proofreading exercise, with the teacher correcting errors of various kinds. Given the amount of time devoted to marking, we need to consider whether this is the most productive way of helping children to improve their writing skills. Not many children take our corrections so seriously that they never make errors again; furthermore, curriculum constraints often inhibit opportunities for reflection on errors in ensuing sessions. Qualitative judgements such as 'good' or even 'excellent' rarely give pupils an indication of what was considered in making the judgement.

When a teacher looks at a piece of writing by a child, it is easy to spot surface mistakes; however competent the writer, there will generally be some spelling and punctuation errors which appear to be in need of correction. Paying attention to these features can often prevent the teacher-reader from seeing beyond them to the content or message which was the purpose of the writing. You may need to think in terms of 'feedback' and 'response' to writing rather than 'marking' and 'correction', and to consider the ways in which this might be achieved.

One starting point is to ensure that young writers themselves understand the criteria by which writing will be assessed. Sharing the learning objectives and drawing up a list of success criteria with the children ensures that they are clear about what they are learning and the purpose of the writing. It also ensures that your feedback is appropriately focused. For example, when teaching pupils how to shape a piece of instructional writing, you might identify the following as success criteria:

- I can organise the ideas in a sequence
- I can use imperative verbs
- I can use time connectives

With these clearly established, both you and the pupils are able to reflect usefully on how far the learning intention has been achieved. Many teachers use a quick and easy device such as 'thumbs-up' ('I've got it'), 'thumb across' ('not sure') and 'thumbs-down' ('haven't got it yet') at the end of a session to ascertain the pupils' perceptions of their understanding. (You may also see teachers using traffic lights or smiley faces for the same purpose.)

The need to separate the compositional from the transcriptional aspects of writing has been identified throughout this book, but nowhere is this more important than in the process of assessment. Where the prime focus of the teaching has been on an aspect of transcription (e.g. the inflectional '-ed' ending), then this will be the focus of your response and the children's self-evaluation. But where the focus is primarily on composition, as in the example above, you will need to think carefully about how you will address transcriptional errors. This is not to suggest that the mechanics of writing are unimportant; indeed, precisely because the surface features are so rapidly judged, it is vital that teachers help children to get them right. As we saw in Chapter 7, errors should be regarded positively as evidence of learning and efforts to master the conventions, rather than as failure. We need to make considered and informed decisions about which errors to mark and how often. For example, after attending to the composition, some teachers ask pupils to identify two or three spelling errors that they want to work on. Other teachers identify typical patterns and trends in the pupils' spellings and address these specifically in discrete slots at the beginning of lessons as well as seeking out examples during work with shared texts. See the section on 'Independence and risk-taking' in Chapter 7 for other suggestions that support pupils' spelling development.

It is important that there is an agreed school policy on marking and correction, which children know and understand. In the absence of an existing policy, you will want to devise your own set of marking symbols which would be explained to the children and displayed in the classroom. These would need to make a distinction between the marking of transcriptional errors and ways of indicating re-drafting suggestions. Once established, these could be used by the teacher for her marking but also by the children in peer assessments against success criteria, in editing their own work, and in responding to each other's work. Some schools use success criteria 'ladders', which are used by both pupils and teachers to mark against given criteria.

The *PNS* (DfES, 2004a) offers the following steps for effective marking against the learning objective. Look back at Figure 8.8 ('A Strange Light Plan') as you read this. The objective for Jatinder's story was to 'use description to create an exciting adventure story'.

(1) Showing success

Using a highlighter pen, the teacher identifies three high spots in the child's writing which show understanding of the learning objective. In Jatinder's adventure story the teacher might highlight these sentences:

On the front cover it said 'Cooking humans'. He opened the book and inside it said boys are yumyest.

(2) Indicating improvement
This is where the teacher indicates (using an asterisk or some other symbol) where an improvement could be made.

(3) Giving an improvement suggestion
Now the teacher makes a specific suggestion about this improvement choosing from three types of prompt: reminder, scaffolded and example. In Jatinder's story, the teacher might asterisk this:

The alien put him into a wooden cage. In the morning he woke up in the cage.

- Reminder prompt: reminding the child of the learning objective, e.g. 'Can you add something here to make it more exciting?' Note that this type of prompt is most appropriate for more able children.
- Scaffolded prompt: offers specific, structured support, e.g. 'How were you feeling when you were left in the cage on your own all night?'
- Example prompt: provides actual words or phrases the child could use, e.g. 'Choose one of these sentences to put in after 'wooden cage':

  'Click!' went a key in the lock. He was a prisoner.
  He was all alone and very frightened.

  Note that both scaffolded and example prompts have the potential to offer significant support to less confident and motivated pupils.

(4) Making the improvement
It is, of course, crucial that the children are then given time to amend their work using the prompt!

(DfES, 2004a)

You may also hear of teachers marking using the 'Three stars and a wish' phrase. The principle is the same: three stars denote elements of the writing that meet the success criteria and the 'wish' is the improvement needed.

TARGET SETTING

Teachers – and children and indeed policy-makers who are concerned about raising standards – want to improve children's writing. To this end, negotiating and setting targets which children can aim at, seems quite logical. Talking with children about targets that they can achieve means that we can focus on 'process goals' rather than 'product goals' (see Chapter 2); the research of Black and Wiliam (1998) indicates that process goals give much better results.

For the classroom teacher the main focus needs to be on identifying learning targets 'which can be used with classes, groups or individual pupils and which focus on what children know and can do, their progress and areas for further improvement'

(QCA, 1999a: 5). In some local authorities, writing targets have been devised in the form of 'I can…' statements drawn from the National Curriculum Level descriptions. Most recently, the *PNS Support for Writing* materials (DCSF, 2008c) provide personalised targets derived from the *NC* sub-levels (Level descriptions broken down into (a), (b) and (c)) for pupils linked to the *PNS* strands and year groups. Pupils can self-evaluate (using, for example, the traffic light system described above) to identify an area for development and then be helped to select an appropriate target which will provide a marking focus.

Teachers need a system that is manageable. Some find it useful to divide targets into those for composition and those for presentation, sometimes using different coloured post-it notes so that the children can actually have the reminders in front of them as they write. Other teachers use target card flaps in the front of pupils' books; group targets can be used for guided writing (the sub-levels mentioned above are useful for differentiating).

But we need to sound a word of warning here. We have already established the importance of clear success criteria (that reflect the learning intention) at the heart of effective assessment for learning. Where targets coincide with these, all is well and good. But where they do not, they may be adding an additional layer which will either overwhelm or confuse the children. You need to exercise professional judgement in the context of your own school's policy.

ASSESSMENT OF LEARNING

Teachers' own continuous assessments for learning are intended to inform future planning for work which will enable children to make progress. The teacher is concerned primarily to tailor tasks to the observed strengths and needs of children and to enable the children to monitor their own progress. At the end of each key stage there is a statutory requirement for teachers to assess each child's completed progress, using the *NC* Levels. In addition, many schools use the optional QCA end-of-year tests to ascertain levels. This assessment of learning (aol) checks what each child can do at this point and records the *NC* level at which the child is working. For assessment of learning the teacher records a level of achievement for each child, using both information from her regular assessments and the level of attainment demonstrated through *NC* tasks and tests. These assessments are needed for teachers' reporting to parents but also for the school's monitoring of their own standards through Ofsted.

The Early Years Foundation Stage Profile

The *Early Years Foundation Stage Profile* (DCSF, 2008b) replaced baseline assessments and is a way of summing up each child's development and learning needs at the end of the EYFS. It aims to provide a consistent way of assessing young children's progress across different settings and to provide a profile of achievement by the end of the stage. There are 13 assessment scales taken from the stepping stones and Early Learning Goals and the guidance states that:

> Judgements against these scales should be derived from observation of consistent and independent behaviour. They should be predominantly based on observations of children's self-initiated activities.

It is expected that all adults who interact with the child should contribute to the process and that account will be taken of information provided by parents.

(QCA, 2007: 10)

These assessments must be passed to the local authority and to the school the child will attend at Key Stage 1; they must also be reported to parents.

Using the Level descriptions and Assessment Focuses

The *NC* provides statements describing the expectations for children at different stages. These are formally applied at the end of Key Stages 1 and 2.

Look back at the samples of work for Martin (Figures 8.2–8.4). As he is approaching the end of Year 2, and therefore Key Stage 1, it is appropriate to look at the *NC* Level descriptions and to decide which description best fits his current achievement. These samples of writing (formative assessments), together with information gathered by his teacher during the year, will provide evidence for this summative assessment. The *NC* description for Level 2 reads:

> Pupils' writing communicates meaning in both narrative and non-narrative forms, using appropriate and interesting vocabulary, and showing some awareness of the reader. Ideas are developed in a sequence of sentences, sometimes demarcated by capital letters and full stops. Simple, monosyllabic words are usually spelt correctly, and where there are inaccuracies the alternative is phonetically plausible. In handwriting letters are accurately formed and consistent in size.

The description for Level 3 reads:

> Pupils' writing is often organised, imaginative and clear. The main features of different forms of writing are used appropriately, beginning to be adapted to different readers. Sequences of sentences extend ideas logically and words are chosen for variety and interest. The basic grammatical structure of sentences is usually correct. Spelling is usually accurate, including that of common, polysyllabic words. Punctuation to mark sentences – full stops, capital letters and question marks – is accurately used. Handwriting is joined and legible.

Looking at these two alongside each other, it is clear that Martin has securely met all the criteria at Level 2 so consideration must also be given to Level 3. He is well on the way to meeting many of these criteria, certainly those which relate to the structure and content of the writing. But he does not yet meet the transcriptional criteria. We must, therefore, conclude that Level 2 is the best fit.

However, you will notice that these descriptions are very broad and it can be challenging trying to find the 'best fit' description for a child's achievement.

Further support in making these judgements is offered by the Assessement Focuses (AFs) for writing. These sit

> between the National Curriculum programmes of study and the level descriptions. They provide a more detailed assessment framework against which teachers can judge the outcomes of their teaching and their pupils' learning. They are tools for assessment, **not learning objectives**. Evidence for the AFs comes from all parts of the curriculum.

(DfES, 2006f)

There are eight AFs for writing:

(1) Write imaginative, interesting and thoughtful texts
(2) Produce texts which are relevant to task, reader and purpose
(3) Organise and present whole texts effectively, sequencing and structuring information, ideas and events
(4) Construct paragraphs and use cohesion within and between paragraphs
(5) Vary sentences for clarity, purpose and effect
(6) Write with technical accuracy of syntax and punctuation in phrases, clauses and sentences
(7) Select appropriate and effective vocabulary
(8) Use correct spelling

(http://www.qca.org.uk/qca_5631.aspx)

You will find guidance for using these, including useful 'questions to consider' and 'contexts for assessment' in the guidance offered by NAA's publication *Building a Picture of what Children can Do . . .*(2004).

Jatinder is in Year 4 and therefore not at the end of a key stage, so the use of Level descriptions to make summative statements about his writing is not statutory. At Key Stage 2, however, materials published by QCA (2008a) – *Assessing Pupils' Progress (APP)* – provide a structure for assessing writing (and reading) in order to track progress, inform planning and make considered judgements using the Level descriptions. The materials are based on the AFs for writing and comprise assessment guideline grid sheets along with standards files which include examples of pupils' writing at different levels. The idea is that teachers use these for just six pupils in the class (drawing from a range of ability) and then use these levels as a benchmark for the rest of the class. You will appreciate that the sampling discussed earlier in this chapter provides both the kind of formative steps required by assessment for learning as well as the evidence needed for assessment of learning as seen above.

It is important to add a word of caution here as the need to meet targets and perform well in league tables can lead to a Level-driven culture in school. One child told his teacher that 'using good punctuation makes me a Level 5 writer and not a Level 4 one any more'. Whilst such self-evaluation might be seen as useful, it is important that the drive to meet criteria does not override the pleasures and purposes of writing with which young writers should engage.

Moderation

Another set of descriptions has been provided by the Centre for Literacy in Primary Education in the shape of writing scales (Barrs, 1996). These scales map fine distinctions in children's writing achievements and may help you in amplifying the Level descriptions in the *NC*. Those teachers taking part in the piloting of the scales reported how useful they found the group moderation sessions:

> As well as providing a basis for quality assurance in assessment, moderation has other benefits. It encourages teachers to justify their judgements and to be more explicit about their approach to assessment . . . Moderation focuses attention on the evidence for teachers' assessments, and helps to demonstrate the kinds of evidence that can be most informative in

arriving at agreed judgements. In this way it can influence work on record-keeping in schools.

(Barrs et al., 1996)

Whatever way schools decide to record evidence, they will need to organise moderation sessions to ensure that all the staff are applying national standards consistently (see QCA, 2008b). The NAA (2004) see moderation as integral to national assessment arrangements and it is at the heart of making effective use of the *APP* materials. As well as meetings organised between staff, there will be moderation sessions with teachers from other schools, often organised by the LEA moderator.

National Curriculum Assessments

Although there have been slight variations in the content of the end of key stage *NC* assessments (commonly known as SATs) over the years since they were first introduced, the general form they take now seems to be fairly well established. For the *NC* assessments at Key Stage 1, the child's performance in several tasks and tests contribute to the teacher's assessment of the level of attainment using the *NC* Level descriptions. At the end of Key Stage 2, *NC* assessments are taken and, along with the teacher's assessment, results determine the level awarded. These national tests provide information which is used to monitor standards and to compare schools' achievements.

Key Stage 1

National Curriculum assessments at the end of Key Stage 1 are now made by teachers just as we made for Martin above. Assessments will be based on the child's performance throughout the key stage, though each child must be tested using a *NC* task/test at the end of Year 2. The writing tests must be administered to all children judged to be working at Level 1 or above. They are marked by teachers who choose a test from previous years. There is flexibility about which years' tests can be administered.

> Teachers may choose to administer the 2005 tests to some children in the class and 2007 tests to others. However, teachers must ensure that for the writing task, the longer and shorter task and spelling test are from the same year.
>
> (QCA, 2007: 21)

If the teacher's assessment differs from the task and test results, then it is the teacher's judgements that are reported. There is no obligation to report the task or test results (QCA, 2007).

As mentioned above, an important recent development in assessment arrangements is the requirement for teachers to be involved in moderation of assessments.

Key Stage 2

The content of the KS2 assessments changes from year to year, but the basic format and the aspects of writing being tested have remained, with very little variation, over the years. These formal tests must be taken by children throughout the country on the same dates in May and an examination timetable is set in advance. Schools must not open the packs of test papers until the day of the test. There is no doubt that children will need some preparation for these tests, especially if they have been used to working collaboratively and discussing ongoing writing with others. Ideally, there should be no need to change normal working practices in the classroom.

The long and short writing tests

Since 2003, writing at KS2 has been assessed through two tests: one is long (45 minutes) and includes time for planning and one is short (20 minutes). A spelling test is also included in the short test. In 2008, the short writing test was to write about 'Memories of the School Year' for a book being prepared by their class. In the 2008 long test, the children had to write a biography of Pip Davenport, an imaginary, famous funfair inventor from the past, making use of basic information provided on the test paper. There is no separate test for handwriting; it is assessed through the two tasks.

There is no invitation or opportunity to re-draft, though there might be time for editing. The fact that the test requires 'one-off' pieces of writing does not mean that all of the children's classroom writing should be produced in this way. The routines of planning and drafting will certainly help children in the test situation, though, in the weeks before the assessment, children should also have had some practice in planning and writing to time. Since 2002, Teachers have been given some guidance on the ways in which they can prepare children for these tests; the intention is to move away from the heavy focus on completing past papers and training for the test which has happened in some schools. Teachers are reminded that, 'if Year 6 pupils have experienced a varied, exciting and challenging curriculum throughout the year, they are likely to have developed the independent application of their skills needed to approach the test with confidence' (QCA, 2002).

These tests are marked by external markers but teachers are provided, in the sample materials, with a detailed breakdown, in marked examples, of how the AFs (see above) will be applied. Note, however, that these marking packs are only sent to the schools after the tests have taken place.

The spelling test

This is a separate test which takes ten minutes to administer. The teacher reads the passage (in 2008, about the silk trade) and the children write the words into the gaps in their version of the text, in the Spelling booklet. The teacher reads out the text before the children begin to write. These tests are also marked externally.

Instructions for these tests include a note reminding teachers that pupils with EAL are not permitted to use bilingual dictionaries and that translations should not be given in any of the English test materials. Many pupils who are at an early stage in developing fluency in English may, therefore, find the test activities rather stressful and you should be aware of the effect of the tests on the confidence of such children.

MANAGING RECORDS OF ASSESSMENT

What does all of this look like in practice? How can teachers keep in control of the data they collect, use it to inform their targets and, ultimately, the assessment of learning? Many LEAs and individual schools have developed frameworks for annotating samples of children's writing, for noting observations of children at work and for recording discussions with children. One of the most helpful is that provided by the *Primary Language Record* (Barrs *et al.*, 1988) or the *Primary Learning Record* (Hester *et al.*, 1993), developed by the Centre for Language in Primary Education (CLPE – now called the Centre for Literacy in Primary Education). Many subsequent record-keeping systems draw from the principles of the *Primary Language Record*.

Another record which has been developed by Croydon LEA, *Writing Development: a Framework* (Graham, 1995), focuses on common development patterns and provides a checklist of statements about children working within each *NC* Level, from 1 to 5. This framework makes a clear distinction between compositional and transcriptional features of writing and teachers highlight statements as they are observed in examples of a child's writing. The compilers point out that the unhighlighted statements provide guidance for teachers about the experiences and teaching which will need to be incorporated into future planning.

The NAA publication *Building a Picture of what Children can Do* makes suggestions about both contexts for assessment and ways of recording assessments. It is not expected that teachers will

> continually focus on individual assessment. Group task focus is a more realistic way to gain knowledge about children's skills and understanding and systematic coverage can be assured by focussing on a different group of children each week.
>
> (2004: 5).

This publication also suggests that teachers annotate plans, both to inform further planning and to 'note instances of individual achievement beyond or below that of the group' (p. 5).

Records of children's progress need to be careful and systematic and kept in ways which make them accessible to everyone involved with the child. They need to inform future planning as well as your judgements for National Curriculum assessments. Schools will have different policies and record-keeping frameworks. Whatever form these take, you need to ensure that your records allow for observation and sampling of children's work, to record achievement and strengths as well as areas for development in all modes of language. They should enable you to record information from discussions with parents, discussions with children themselves and comment from teaching assistants and teachers working with children who have English as an additional language.

This is how one infants school manage their records. For each child there is a folded A3 'Writing Record' card that is passed from class to class. It provides the vehicle for storing evidence from the regular sampling of writing that the teachers are expected to do. Samples are collected once a term and brief notes (under 'Date', 'Title and comments', and 'Further action') kept along with the samples. On the back of the card are 27 writing statements. These progress from (1): 'The child can hold a pencil and make marks on the page' through to (27): 'Using grammatically complex sentences, extending meaning'. This system is used to set targets that map on to *NC* levels (see below) on a complementary 'Writing Target Setting Sheet'. Here, the 27 statements are recorded again, this time with a column which matches the statement to the appropriate *NC* level and has three further columns for each term of the child's time in the school. Using the sample evidence the child's current level is established and a target is set. A third column for that term is there for the teacher to record what level was actually reached.

CONCLUDING POINTS

It is the whole writing experience which is the source of the detailed information needed to monitor each child's development and to plan appropriate teaching. Some of the writing experiences can be incorporated into traditional 'literacy' activities, but remember that you will need to make provision for more extended writing and for writing in the non-fiction genres associated with other curriculum areas. The renewed *PNS* framework allows for extended periods of time to be spent covering units of work in narrative, non-fiction and poetry. These expanded time-frames allow for more detailed analysis of text types as well as time for planning, drafting, editing and publishing.

If you look back at the writing samples from Jatinder you will see that some of these arise from science and history and that the characteristics of the different genres needed to be taught in the context of those subjects. The writing element of the English curriculum crosses curriculum boundaries and you will need to be aware of this when you monitor and assess children's writing output. If you have collected samples of writing and have annotated them throughout the year, not only will you be able to focus your planning more precisely, but you will also have all the information you need to make summative assessments of the children's progress at the end of the year.

Further reading

Clarke, S. (2001) *Unlocking Formative Assessment*. London: Hodder Education.

Clarke, S. (2008) *Formative Assessment in Action: Weaving the Elements Together*. London: Hodder Education.

NAA (2004) *Building a Picture of what Children can Do*. London: NAA.

QCA (2008a) *Assessing Pupils' Progress*. www.standards.dfes.gov.uk/primaryframework/assessment/app (accessed 12 September 2008).

Chapter 9

Meeting Individual Needs

Judith Graham

> We clearly need a body of research that addresses the writing problems faced by individual learners in today's classrooms. There is scant research focused on the children who struggle in writing classrooms across the grades; on linguistically diverse writers; on children, who despite all efforts, do not grasp sound-symbol relations; on children who are uninterested in writing; and on special needs children who are mainstreamed into writing classrooms.
>
> (Dahl and Farnan, 1998: 35–6)

In this chapter, we think about children as individuals who often demonstrate very different achievements in writing, not only in what they choose to write about but also in the levels of attainment that they reach. In most classes, among the children whose progress is sure and steady, there will be some children who write willingly enough but with many errors, some who tend to write about the same topic again and again, some who write at length but with no commitment and some who claim that they hate writing and do the bare minimum or refuse to write at all. In the first set of examples that follow, all these behaviours will be discussed and suggestions for help offered. Then, children who are gifted in writing are considered, as, undoubtedly, teachers want to do their best for these children even though their needs seem less urgent. Writing samples from the 'linguistically diverse' writers of whom Dahl and Farnan speak (see above quotation) and from individual boys and girls are then discussed. The chapter continues with a look at the grammatical errors which children make, and finishes with a summary of the formal arrangements which concern those children in school who are finding all aspects of literacy, including writing, difficult.

CHILDREN WHO WRITE WILLINGLY ENOUGH BUT WITH MANY ERRORS

Eight-year-old Bethany wrote this piece voluntarily and without help. I present it here with transcription aspects tidied up. I suggest you do not look at the original just yet.

> Once upon a time, there was a little boy. He was just at the edge of the cliff. He fell. I ran to the phone box and phoned the ambulance. The ambulance came as quick as possible. They took him to the hospital as fast as the ambulance went. He broke his head and he died.
>
> His mum and dad came to the hospital. They were very upset. They was crying all year because he was only four years old. His brothers and sisters were very upset as well. All of the family came to the funeral. All grandmas and all the grandpas came. They all sang to him.
>
> The next day was his birthday. They all made a cake. It was a chocolate one. And then they put some balloons up. They put lots of seats on the table. All the brothers and sisters sat down. And his mum and dad sat down. And they prayed to him. They had a birthday party.
>
> After that, they went out. They went to the cinema and had a good time and when they came back they thought about brother.

At this point you will probably feel that Bethany has done quite well to sustain a piece of writing of this length and that, on the whole, she has shaped the piece well and remained on topic, albeit swinging rather giddily between death and life. You will be impressed by her hold on family behaviour at crisis times and also by her characters' resilience. You may be wondering to what extent it reflects both fantasy and real elements in her life. On a second reading, you may note some confusion with genres: after a 'once upon a time' opening, we do not expect a disaster account and a first person narrator. You may also think that a child who demonstrates competence with two subordinate clauses, adverbial clauses of reason and of time, could be expected to write with even more complex sentences. But there is much to commend in this piece and to discuss with its author.

In Figure 9.1 you will see that Bethany's work has been presented with a lot of 'surface noise'. So much, in fact, that, in a busy classroom, there would not be time to 'translate' the piece as I have done in order to reveal its characteristics. You can see at a glance that Bethany has transcription problems of every kind. Spelling is phonically logical in some words ('wus a ponr' – once upon a; 'hosbtol' – hospital; 'sisds' – sisters; 'aftdr' – after) but not in others ('hudt' – head; 'ckee' – cake; 'fock' – thought). Her handwriting makes her spelling appear even more alarming: her representation of words such as 'party' and 'after', which appear to be spelled 'pute' and 'uftdr', are probably spelled 'pate' and 'aftdr'; but because she does not close her lower case letter 'a', the words have an apparent arbitrariness about them. Several other letters are wrongly or tentatively formed and re-formed so that we have to work hard to select the correct letter from a graphic arrangement that suggests many. Full stops are mostly in place but they are not followed by capital letters. Capitals, however, appear wrongly in 'MuM' and 'DaD' and 'Ran'. The piece is not paragraphed.

What is a busy teacher to do? In the long run, the most efficient and the most helpful action you can take is to devote time to this one piece and do a full analysis of it. You will then have so much information that you can work on with your pupil that the time will seem a small price to pay for the quality and efficacy of the help which you will then be in a position to offer. You will not, of course, be able or want to work on more than one or two noted items at any one time; there is ample evidence that children such as Bethany can become quickly discouraged or resistant if you point out too many errors. You will also want to decide an order of priority based on what Bethany can understand and what will make the greatest impact on the writing. Half a term spent working with her on the following should mean that the next piece you sit down to analyse has far fewer transcription errors. Some of Bethany's errors will be shared by others in the class and can be addressed during dedicated literacy sessions.

Presentation

- Encourage crossing out of a word and rewriting rather than the modifying and over-writing we see throughout this piece.
- Move her into cursive script (signs are there already) and encourage her to keep her pen on the page to form letters correctly.
- Word process to give her work a professional appearance. Word banks and spellcheck facilities should interest and support her.

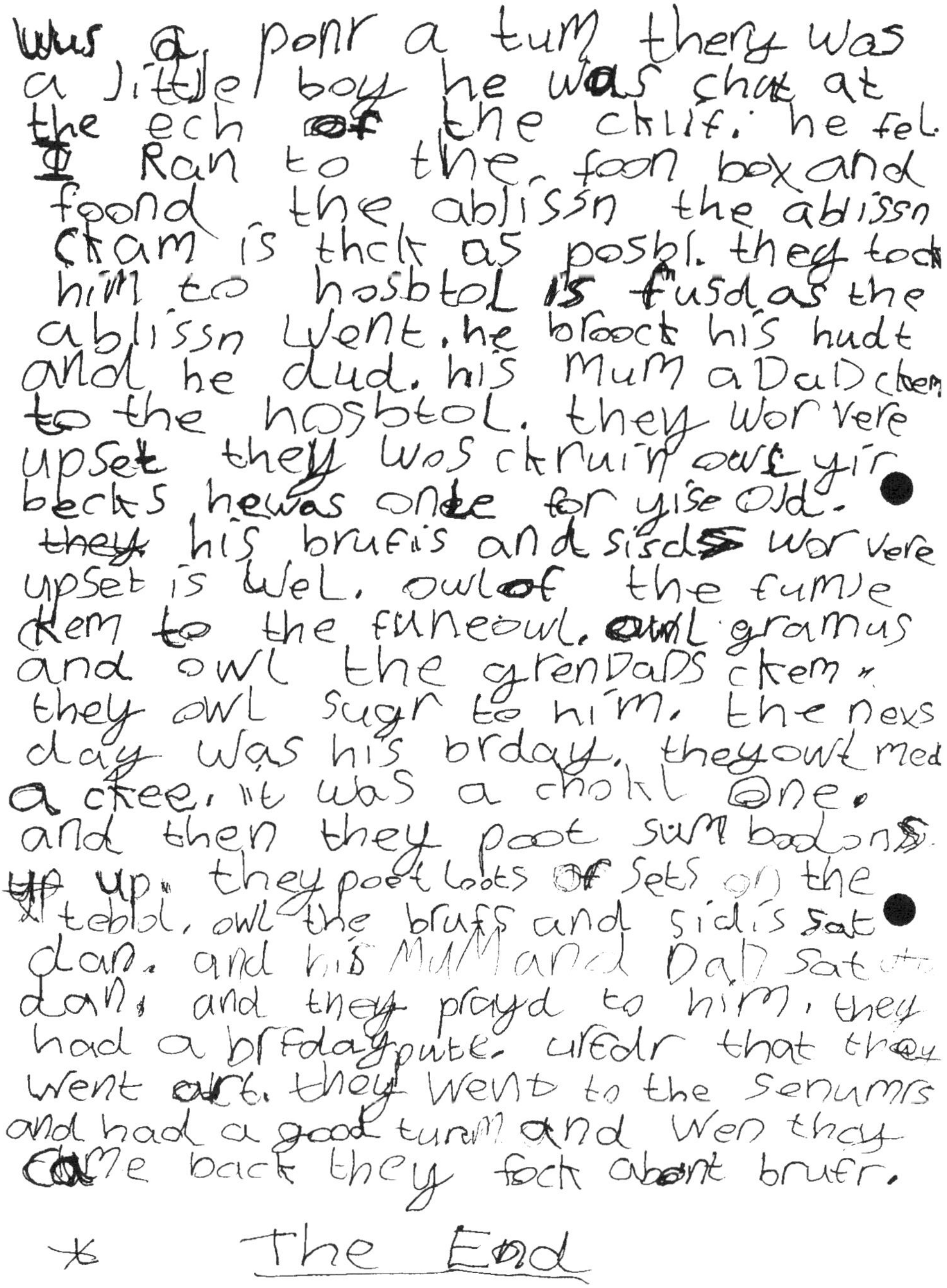

wus a ponr a tum thery was
a little boy he was chuc at
the ech of the chlif. he fel.
I Ran to the foon box and
foond the ablissn the ablissn
cram is thck as posbl. they tock
him to hosbtol is fusd as the
ablissn Went. he brooct his hudt
and he dud. his mum a DaD chem
to the hosbtol. they wor vere
upset they wos chruin owt yir
becks hewas onte for yise old.
they his brufis and sisds wor vere
upset is Wel. owl of the fumie
chem to the funeowl. owl gramus
and owl the grenDaDs chem
they owl sugr to him. the nexs
day was his brday. they owl med
a cfee. it was a chohl one.
and then they poot sum badons.
up up. they poot lobts of sets on the
tebbl. owl the bruff and sidis sat
dan. and his MuM and DaD sat
dan. and they prayd to him. they
had a brfday pute. ufedr that they
went oart. they went to the senumrs
and had a good tur and wen they
came back they fock abont brufr.

The End

Figure 9.1

Spelling

- Starting with words like 'was' (which she spells both correctly and incorrectly in this piece), get certain words into her sight vocabulary. Show her how well that works for her with other tricky words like 'the' which she always spells correctly.

- Get her to see that 'y' represents the sound at the end of many words ('only', 'very') where she is using an 'e'.
- Help her with the 'ck' digraph, at least at the start of words, where it is never found. Her spellings of 'cliff', 'came', 'crying', 'because', 'took' and 'broke' are all affected by an over-generalised use of 'ck'.
- Teach her that the inflectional suffix '-ed' is unchanging so it is very easy to get right in words like 'phoned' and 'prayed'. Similarly, knowing that the inflectional '-s' is for plurals will help her to avoid mistakes like 'yise' for 'years' (see Chapter 7).
- See if she can detect syllables and, if she can, teach her that every syllable has at least one vowel. She will then have more chance of getting 'brothers', 'sisters' and 'family' right.
- Help her to segment words orally so that she can hear their component phonemes. This may be useful in conjunction with seeing the words in print also – notice that her spelling of several words such as 'gramus' (grandmas) and 'funeowl' (funeral) probably indicates good aural ability but no visual fine-tuning.

Punctuation

- Show Bethany how good she is at putting in full stops and tell her you know that she can do it always. Teach her to follow full stops with capitals.

In addition to the above, you will have noticed that Bethany finds it very difficult to represent vowel sounds correctly: 'wor' – were; 'owl' – all; 'yir' – year; 'brufis' – brothers; 'fumle' – family. This is Bethany's biggest challenge. Achieve success in other areas first and then help her to detect regular patterns: 'others, smothers, mothers, brothers' (see Chapter 5). All the time, she will need to be reading and/or listening to you reading while she has her eyes on the text, so that her visual strategies develop to complement her aural discrimination.

Before we leave Bethany, it needs to be stressed that her willingness to write readily and at length is at risk unless your approach is sensitive. I have detailed the work that needs to be done on transcription aspects; I am not suggesting that there are no improvements to be made on the compositional side but, in relative terms, she is not doing too badly there, so keep her morale high while also making the odd suggestion – such as a bit more pre-planning and revision so that the storytelling opening goes and the 'I' in the story is clarified or excised. Publish her work so that she can see the correct forms of her words and so that she feels her work reaches a wider audience.

In Chapter 10, you will read about two children who have been receiving help for the specific learning difficulty dyslexia. Many teachers might well think that Bethany should be diagnosed similarly but at this point in her school life she was receiving help from home, from the teacher and from a classroom assistant, and she appeared to be making steady, if slow, progress.

CHILDREN WHO TEND TO WRITE ABOUT THE SAME TOPIC AGAIN AND AGAIN

Week 1 Some tanks can go into the water. They can still have the guns.
Week 2 The tank has two little guns and the little guns fire little bullets.
Week 3 Some tanks have little guns and big guns.
Week 4 The big tank is a 101 Fighter Fox.

(Kevin, aged 6)

There are plenty of explanations for children who tend to write on the same topic over and over again. They may have had success once and be living in hope that the experience will be repeated. They may be extremely interested in the topic and not realise that their rehearsal of content does not enchant everybody. They may feel that their position in the class as authority on a topic may be at risk if they move away from it. Importantly, they may be using the period of writing always about the same things to make progress in some of the transcription sides of writing. Above all, they may be nervous of branching out into new areas. Security in what they know may be important and you will want to respect this.

If you are sure that the writing is not showing any signs of growth for the child, in any area, then consider one or more of the following:

- Increase the amount of time which the child spends writing. We all tend to go round in circles if we do not write frequently enough.
- Get the child to read out work to the class more often in order to elicit peer reaction. The class comments may shift the child into providing more interesting detail and, eventually, into new areas.
- Publish the child's work so that an end-product marks visible achievement and, with luck, a sense of closure.
- Increase the child's exposure to a range of genres and provide new audiences. Kevin could be encouraged to make a picture book for younger children in which a disaster occurs to those guns under water.
- Support moves into new areas: with reading aloud, visits, TV programmes, the offer of taking dictation, writing frames, etc.
- Model (in shared writing sessions) how you move on to new topics when you think it is time.
- Congratulate him when he does branch out. (See further comments on this in 'Boys and Girls' below.)

Some time after Kevin wrote his early pieces about guns he was taken to HMS *Belfast* on the Thames. He dictated a long piece, including the following, to his teacher:

> Then we went over the bridge and we looked about. There was a 40 mm gun for shooting down aircraft and we put some money in and stood back. Then a voice said, 'This gun is for shooting down aircraft and in the background you will hear aircraft flying over you'. And then we turned two pedals and made the gun go up and down.

His interests have been respected; his classmates asked him lots of questions; his days of single lines are going to come to an end.

CHILDREN WHO WRITE AT LENGTH BUT WITH NO COMMITMENT

> Once upon a time there were some teddy bears. They went to school. They had the register and then they took out their books. One bear did not listen. He got sent to the corner and had to do sums all the time and then it was home time. When they got home they set off on a boat to go to France and had something to eat [etc.]
>
> (Lucy, aged 8)

Commitment, or lack of it, is difficult to demonstrate simply by presenting an end-product. The above child continued this piece for several more pages, adding incidents competently but in an unplanned and disaffected way. There are many such children who settle down immediately to write on given writing tasks and produce the required amount with little fuss and acceptable accuracy but do not seem to care about planning, revising, re-drafting, publishing or feedback. It seems as if they are privileging the length of the piece above content; this may be a reflection of teachers' messages about minimum length requirements regardless of genre.

Lucy does not, of course, keep us awake at night in the way that Bethany does. But there is much that we can do to improve her writing and increase engagement. Try some or all of the following:

- Increase the sense of audience. Children who write only for the teacher are in danger of losing a critical, reflective stance towards their writing. This writer is clearly imitating a young children's book; given the opportunity to read to a real audience of small children, she would probably have planned more carefully, added dialogue and ensured a sense of a significant problem and a final resolution and evaluation.
- Ask the child about the details that are so carefully avoided here. In talk, and when she realised that there was genuine interest in her ideas, this child said that it was because the bear had been so excited about France that he could not concentrate at school and that, because he had been fiddling with the teacher's things, he had had a smack. Many children just do not realise how such detail, far from holding up the story, gives the piece voice and particularity.
- Get writing partnerships going in the classroom (see Chapter 3). Other children will increase Lucy's ambition to improve her writing and getting closer to others' writing will make Lucy care about the community of writers to which she belongs.
- Encourage Lucy to write voluntarily rather than at prescribed times, so that she does not fall into the mechanical writing that she produces so easily on request. Inviting writing areas can be a great incentive (see Chapters 5 and 7).
- Find out what Lucy would really like to write about. Donald Graves' (1983) suggestions for notebooks for individual writing topics are useful.

CHILDREN WHO CLAIM THAT THEY HATE WRITING AND DO THE BARE MINIMUM OR NOTHING AT ALL

Once upon a time there was a dinosaur and

(Neil, aged 7)

Most scraps of writing like this end up in the wastepaper basket, thrown there after 30 minutes of a wasted lesson by an angry or despondent child or found by the teacher when she retrieves the tightly screwed up ball from under the desk. It is a situation familiar to most teachers and very worrying. Usually these children will add a word or two if you are sitting beside them but once you leave then they will dry up again. The reasons for this behaviour fall into two main categories: anxiety about getting it wrong and a shortage of ideas. The suggestions below deal with both these categories.

- Anxieties about getting it wrong are nearly always to do with transcription elements – letter formation, crossings-out, spelling errors, punctuation omissions. Occasionally they are about content; for instance, if the child is to write a non-fiction piece and you have expressly forbidden copying from information sources and the child does not know how to complete the task in any other way. If you can get the child dictating to you, not only has he the opportunity to witness innumerable lessons on how to form letters, punctuate, paragraph and spell but also more of his story is preserved, so that his morale is raised, and at some point he may be willing to take over the writing.

- Reassure the child that many excellent writers leave transcription aspects until after they have got their content down. Have an editing table in your classroom where the piece can go for tidying up by you or appropriate others.
- When the child is stuck on the spelling of a word, suggest that they 'have a go' in a notebook kept for that purpose. Find a source for the word in the classroom or write it for them (see Chapter 7). It is important that you do not give the impression that writing equals spelling, so keep this bit 'light'.
- Try to give more prior support before you expect writing. Make sure that the topic has been discussed, that a structure is identified and, on some occasions, supplied, that key words are written up to jog memories, that the audience for the piece is identified (see Chapter 4).
- Make it quite clear that this is not the final draft, but still ensure that materials with which the child is working are not too scruffy. Many a child will write more readily when they are given your special sharp pencil or a fine felt tip (see Chapter 7).
- If children lose heart, suggest that they look at other writers' work to see if they can find inspiration or solutions. Suggest that they go on to some different work and let them return to the piece another day. (Real writers do this.)
- Keep a record of the topics that are of interest to the child so that you can suggest an area when inspiration is short. Remind children of pieces that they have written which you have enjoyed.
- Provide small enticements to write; post-it pads and novelty notebooks may lure the most diffident of writers.
- Allow time away from writing to decorate or illustrate the piece. Time spent on, for instance, illuminating the first letter, is often used fruitfully to muse on how the text could develop.
- Use the computer both as an incentive and also as a reward for getting on with the work.
- Keep a file (with an index) of all writing done, however short, so that the child can see the progress being made.

You will see that there are common themes that keep occurring in these suggestions for children with writing difficulties or reluctance. In truth, what is good practice for all your class is good practice for these children too. Obviously there would be no need, for instance, to scribe for a fluent writer but that child, in her time, may have benefited enormously from such a practice. Regard your inexperienced writer as just that – inexperienced – and do not attribute errors to carelessness nor reluctance to laziness. It is mostly more complicated than that. One of the advantages of the old Literacy Hour – in the sense of a predictable classroom routine that will provide structure and regularity   is that it is the less secure children in your classroom who will appreciate the consistency and continuity. Try to provide as much writing time as possible for your children with difficulties, especially of extended pieces. You will also want to encourage writing at home as much as you can (see Chapter 3).

GIFTED AND TALENTED WRITERS

You will notice that able children are very quick to experiment with and put into their writing whatever models you have been sharing with them. Their private reading also influences their writing as does evidence of the written word that they see around them in a print-saturated environment. The conventions, tone, vocabulary and style of new genres seem to be effortlessly absorbed by them and no sooner have they mastered a form than they will begin to play with it, perhaps subverting its conventions to amusing effect. At a sentence level too, you may find that a taught session on, for instance, the use of subordinate clauses, will see gifted writers experimenting with how many subordinate clauses they can add to a main clause before the sentence becomes unwieldy. New vocabulary and especially new terminology delights them and will turn up immediately in their writing.

Some able children arrive in school writing accurately, fluently and enthusiastically. It is through the tasks you devise for your gifted writers that you will be able to cater for this deftness. Figure 9.2 is page 9 of a four-year-old's 'novel', written in a little spiral bound notebook, brought to school on the first day of term. The teacher saw many openings to extend this writing and offered the child the opportunity to write a little bit more about Hadrian's Wall as an entry for an encyclopaedia, to write about a day in the life of a Roman soldier on duty on Hadrian's Wall (she found and read W. H. Auden's poem to the child) or to draw a poster reminding rock climbers about safety. After discussion and deliberation, the child chose the last option, concentrating particularly on crash helmets, 'so that you don't bump your heads'. Noticing openings of this sort to extend range and depth of thinking is absolutely essential if gifted children (and all children) are not to stand still. It is hard to ensure that some of your work in dedicated literacy time stretches gifted writers, so it is in the guided writing (see Chapter 5) and opportunities for individual and extended writing that you will best be answering your pupils' needs.

Many written activities can be devised that suit the whole class, irrespective of ability. These tasks are of the open-ended type so that a gifted writer can write more, write with more depth and with more originality, but essentially on the same subject. Let us suppose a Year 5 class has been reading novels by 'a significant children's author', perhaps Dick King-Smith, and has begun with *Martin's Mice*, which is a story of a cat, Martin, who wishes not to eat mice but to keep them as pets. A written activity that asks children to rewrite an incident as a play scene might lead to opportunities for the gifted writer to write his or her scene with a detailed set of directions to a film director and/or camera crew. You may find the child turns the whole text into a play script, word processes it and insists that the class perform it!

Equally, you may devise a writing frame for most of the class to marshal their thoughts about the serious message of the novel: the rights of animals to be free and not kept as pets. Class discussion will precede this activity but the gifted writer will not need the writing frame and may turn in something that is balanced and logically

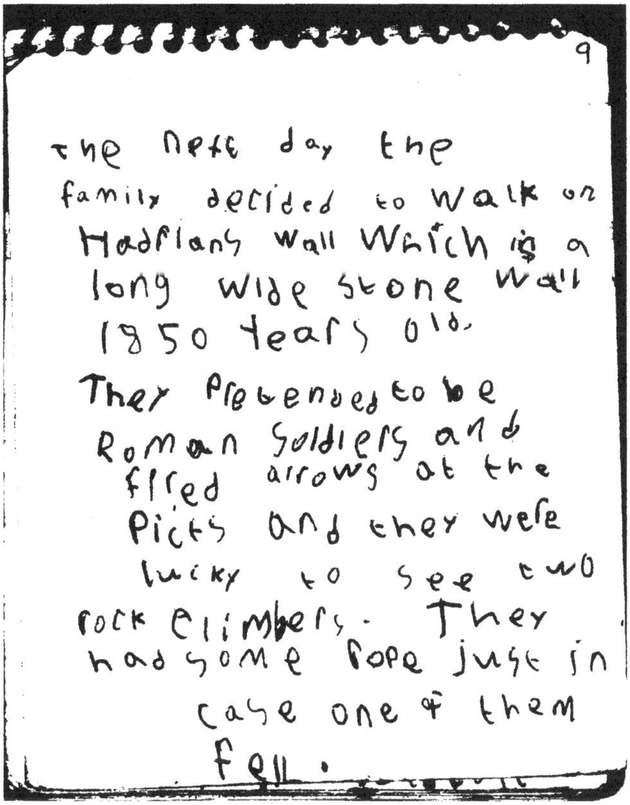

The next day the family decided to walk on Hadrians wall which is a long wide stone wall 1850 years old. They pretended to be Roman soldiers and fired arrows at the Picts and they were lucky to see two rock climbers. They had some rope just in case one of them fell.

Figure 9.2

structured, and could stand as an editorial in a newspaper. Few children in the class will go on to read Dick King-Smith's more challenging novels (*The Crowstarver* and *Godhanger*, for instance) but able children will, and can then be given tasks tailored to this wider reading. They can bring their reading of the author's novels together, perhaps in answer to a question such as, 'You have been asked to recommend a Dick King-Smith novel for a children's radio programme. Say why you would select one title rather than another.'

CHILDREN LEARNING TO WRITE IN ENGLISH AS AN ADDITIONAL LANGUAGE

Before we look at writing with children whose first language is not English, it is important to remind ourselves of what we know in three areas:

1   What do we know about how human beings learn language?
2   What do we know about how human beings learn a second or subsequent language?
3   What do teachers do to give children learning English access to good teaching?

What do we know about how human beings learn language?

We know that we learn language through being surrounded by people using the target language in meaningful circumstances. Because of the nature of children's early lives, some of the language they hear, especially that which is directed at them, is repeated, stressed and simplified. We know that children's language learning involves listening, thinking, playing and adjusting. We know that children experiment with sounds and use intonation 'tunes' to make themselves understood. We know that it is helpful if children are allowed to initiate topics of interest. We know that it is important that people respond to children's approximations and treat them as meaningful. We know that correction of the forms of the language is largely ineffectual in the early stages. Children will go on saying, 'I wented' and 'Mummy goed' and even 'I caughted it' for a long time despite well-meaning correction.

What do we know about how human beings learn a second or subsequent language?

Children learning English as an additional language need very similar conditions to those in which they learned their first language. They similarly need models; meaningful circumstances, some stressing, repetition and simplification, time to listen and no pressure to speak until ready; freedom to make mistakes; a chance to choose the topic; and a chance to play.

What do teachers do to give children learning English access to good teaching?

In the classroom, the teacher will have to respect the child's early silence and receive responses in non-verbal forms initially. The meaningful classroom that she has created for all children will serve those children learning English well. She will offer planned and structured group work where groups are, ideally, mixed race, gender, ability and language; she will recognise the power and learning potential in narrative, song, drama and storytelling; she will read from fiction and non-fiction texts to her class; she will organise computer time, visits, taped texts in the listening corner and numerous practical activities. She will want to pursue parental involvement and to ensure that the school adheres to its anti-racist policies. In addition, the teacher will check for anglo-centric content in her resources and activities, put up multilingual displays and bring texts in other languages into the classroom.

The teacher will need to make some moves more deliberately and be more focused in her language strategies when she is teaching children learning English, and thus she will encourage mother-tongue use, knowing as she does that progress there will be reflected in increased competence in English (see Chapter 2). She will use the bilingual TA to help her make fair assessments, of oral as well as written work, and she will team-teach with her where possible, especially in time devoted to literacy. She will ask for her help or advice in preparing big books and school-made cassettes in two or more languages. As far as writing is concerned, she will encourage children to write in all their languages, use older children to scribe for younger children in their first languages, taking dictation herself and invite parents to participate in writing activities with their children. She will have overlay keyboards and flexible computer software such as *Textease 2000* (a 'click and type' word processing package). Posters around the school and letters home will be in translated form as far as possible, not just to convey content but also to signal respect for the languages in the community. Software such as Clicker 4's *Wacky Sentences*, designed to support Gujerati children learning English, will further reinforce this respect for other languages.

Classroom examples

The following examples illustrate ways of working with children in the writing classroom in which it can be seen that the teachers and schools involved understand the importance of the areas discussed above.

Early Years Foundation Stage and Key Stage 1

A Year 1 class has been looking at scripts in various languages. All around the room are examples of Chinese, Bengali and Urdu, brought in by the teacher, the children and parents. After a visit to a Chinese restaurant in Soho (where some of the Chinese children were able to show off their reading of the menu), the Chinese script was very high profile for a while. Nil's writing, in Figure 9.3, is in both Bengali and Chinese.

The next piece, Figure 9.4, by Yesmin, is interesting as the gap between her competence in Bengali and English is apparent in the tentative copying of her name in the less familiar script used for English (scribed initially by the teacher). Direction and sequence of letters are a problem for her at this stage but her interest in different scripts ensured that she took notice as her teacher scribed for her and for the class.

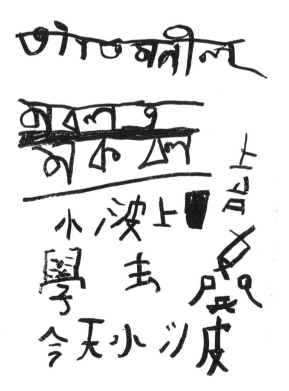

Figure 9.3

Figure 9.4

Shared writing produced a set of instructions and drawings for how to use chopsticks and then captions for a set of photographs of the visit to Soho Chinatown (later made into a spiral-bound class book). All the time, there was lots of emergent writing in several scripts to which the teacher responded positively. The piece by Mahbuba, Figure 9.5, was not 'translated' by the child, who was still at the silent stage, but the teacher pointed out features of various scripts, much to the child's pleasure.

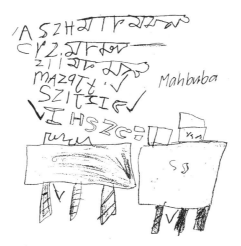

Figure 9.5

In this class, children chose which language they were going to write in and responded to the hospitality their teacher gave to their languages. The teacher dated, glossed and kept all work, even 'unfinished' pieces, and was able at the end of the children's first full year in school to share the progress made, both with them and with their parents. Anxieties, expressed by some parents that progress in English would suffer if first languages were encouraged, were mostly allayed in the light of the children's achievements.

Key Stage 2

In a Year 4 class, the teacher had been sharing traditional tales from several cultures with the class. *Bimwili and the Zimwi* (Aardema and Meddaugh) had been shared several times and a whole-class drama had developed (everybody became the drum, the seagull or the waves of the sea as required). Many of the children could retell the story in storytelling sessions and all the class could sing Bimwili's plaintive ditties. The class was bonded to this story forever, it seemed. Many children wrote alternative endings, extra scenes and interior monologues, but for the three children whose work is reproduced in Figure 9.6, the fluency they found came from a retelling. Not reproduced here is the fine picture they drew while they were planning the retelling.

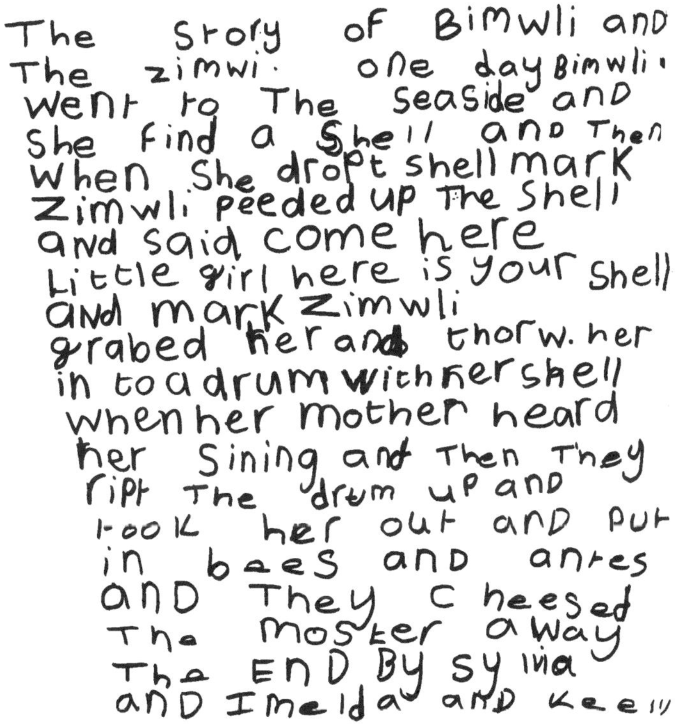
The Story of Bimwli and
The zimwi. one day Bimwli.
went to The seaside and
She find a Shell and Then
When She dropt shell mark
Zimwli peeded up The Shell
and said come here
Little girl here is your Shell
and mark Zimwli
grabed her and thorw. her
in to a drum with her shell
when her mother heard
her Sining and Then They
ript The drum up and
took her out and put
in bees and antes
and They cheesed
The moster away
The END By sylvia
and Imelda and Keeli

Figure 9.6

There are errors of course – the one the teacher chose to work on was the '-ed' suffix, which helped sort out 'dropt' and 'ript', where the children have not yet internalised the regular third person past tense and are representing what they can hear (Bethany

(Figure 9.1) has a similar problem). But remarkable is the control over the main shape of the story, the introduction of dialogue (albeit without punctuation) and a command over English sentence structure that is closing in on the standard within the class as a whole. Children experimenting with new constructions in writing – such as the sentence beginning 'When her mother' – tend to make errors which they cannot pick up with proofreading (Perera, 1984). They need increased familiarity with the constructions and careful teacher support in pointing them out.

Reading and writing connections

The work with traditional tales described above depends on the teacher being enthusiastic about reading aloud and building up the secondary world which children can then revisit any time in their heads. Re-readings allow deeper meanings to evolve and the texts assume greater and greater importance to children. In addition, with the all-important exposure to the unchanging text, children get some of that same repetition and intonation 'tune' that supported their entry into spoken language. It is very clear that children learning English can hold many of the structures and much of the vocabulary of English when the structures and words are charged with memorable and symbolic meaning. Many a child's writing discloses the rhythms, vocabulary and cadences of an original text, such as 'he begged and begged and begged but no...', or 'Now it was not long before...', or 'Suddenly a voice was heard', or 'Where there is water, there are fish and where there are fish, there are fishermen'. It reminds us how closely tied reading is to children's writing development. All children need to be read to as much as you can manage.

BOYS AND GIRLS

In a chapter on individual needs, the heading 'Boys and girls' may be rather surprising. It probably suggests a mass divided broadly into two roughly equal parts rather than the specialised few whom we have been considering up to this point under the headings of 'Children with difficulties', 'Gifted writers' or 'Children for whom English is an additional language'. But as groups, boys and girls left to their own devices tend to restrict their writing choices and boys, in particular, depend much on peer approval and what is considered fashionable. It is important to discuss the pertinent issues here, especially as there is ample evidence that a restricted range of writing and extreme brevity are key reasons for boys achieving considerably fewer Level 4s in their end of KS2 assessments (60 per cent of boys and 74 per cent of girls in 2008, although these figures are unreliable as in 2008 there were unprecedented problems in marking papers and reporting back to schools).

Social conditioning

Because subtle and not so subtle assumptions about sex roles are everywhere in society, including in our classrooms, and because these assumptions affect life experiences, we as teachers have a certain responsibility to try to counteract some of these limiting expectations. The differing social conditioning of boys and girls means that by the time children are in nursery school, a noticeable preference to play outside, to play with large construction toys and to draw and fantasise about large, often destructive, items is evident in the small boys. The girls will more commonly be drawn to activities at tables, be found in elaborate games of domestic play in play corners and be involved in talk with the adults around. In terms of their story reading and television watching and video game playing, noticeable general differences are observable, with girls and boys demonstrating clear gendered differences from an early age.

Classroom action

Teachers have tried to make changes in some of the following ways:

- by monitoring and guiding the activities that children choose in free time; parents and helpers can be useful allies to get the girls to play with Lego and to get the boys into the role play area;
- by discussing issues with children, e.g. their toys, colours of clothes for babies, advertisements, suitable presents for relations, etc.;
- by sharing books which foreground some of the issues, e.g. *Piggybook* (Browne), *Jump* (Magorian and Ormerod);
- by helping girls and boys to role play characters of the opposite sex;
- by checking that all children read fiction and non-fiction;
- by deciding what to do about certain traditional fairy stories and comics;
- by checking that both sexes are represented as central characters in the fiction shared;
- by checking illustrations of roles taken by male and female;
- by checking that authors are men and women;
- by inviting non-stereotypical visitors, e.g. female doctors and male nurses into the classroom for children to talk to. A male embroiderer invited into school worked a miracle for boys' needlework. Another class had a visitor (female) who had survived a Japanese earthquake (two days stuck in a lift) and, although her account was not overly heroic, her bravery left a marked impression, particularly on the boys of the class.

Writing and gender

Particularly in writing, teachers have often felt that gender differences are most marked. Boys and girls do very different things in their writing.

Early Years Foundation Stage and Key Stage 1

Under various action-packed pictures, these captions (transcription aspects are tidied up) appeared in the first school work produced by four-year-old Ben:

This is a dinosaur and a volcano erupted and some anti-aircraft guns and some people killed the dinosaur.

This is a sports car and an interceptor was in the sky.

This is a swimming pool and Aaron went off the diving board and it was the top board.

This is a golden eagle and it is on the mountains.

This is a dynamite and a aeroplane fired a long rope and a circle of bombs made the dynamite go off.

This is a lighthouse and a robber stole a ship and it was tied on a stick and the robber tried to cut the rope but he couldn't. This is a lunar module and it is taking off and two space men are climbing into the lunar module.

This is a submarine and a shark came along.

Here are four-year-old Claire's captions under her drawings:

I went to the seaside and it wasn't all in sand. It was in stones.

The princess is mending the giant's socks and she is sitting on a chair.

My brother Mark when he had a wobbly tooth it went down the plug hole.

We had a game of getting married and Natalie sprinkled (sbrigcwld!) the poppy petals on my head for confetti.

Gillian read me a story and then I went to sleep with my knees curled up.

Both sets of captions have imaginative and linguistic strengths but Claire's focus on family, friends, the personal and the domestic (even in the giant's home) is in marked contrast to Ben's inventory of all the most fantastical, violent, powerful and action-packed things he writes about.

Key Stage 2

Do matters change after the children have been in school for three or four years? It will probably not be difficult for you to guess which of the two recounts below was written by a girl and which by a boy. Each child was exactly the same age (7 years, 11 months).

We went to Seven Sisters Rocks to-day and we crossed the Suspension Bridge. We had to walk a long way and we saw an elm tree and it had Dutch elm disease. We climbed a steep rock. Then we got to the first one of the Seven Sisters rocks. We had a look down from the top of the rock and it was a brilliant view. We went to King Arthur's cave and it was full of rubbish. We had a snack. We had an apple and cucumber and raisins. Some people were rolling rocks down the drop. On the way back, we saw an ants nest and someone threw a stone on the nest and all the ants came out to repair it.

On Wednesday, Polly came to stay the night and we played with our little pets, the guinea pigs. We had Snowdrop which was an albino. It was all white with red beady eyes and Joseph, he had all sorts of colours just like a multi-coloured coat. And that's why we called him Joseph. Rachel tied her green bracelet into the cage and the baby guinea pigs jumped through. Polly liked Snowdrop best because it was an albino. Jessica, Polly's sister, was allergic to them so she could not hold them. Then we gave them a lesson to jump through the hoop. It was Snowdrop's turn first. He did it nicely. Then it was Joseph's turn. He did it a bit wrong. At the end of the lesson, we had our tea.

The first text confirms what is generally felt about boys' writing; that it roams further afield than that of girls, that it includes more action, and that it contains more evidence of interest in boyish behaviour. In this case, the boys who threw rocks over the edge and who stone the ants' nest receive no disapproval. (It is possible that the writer joined in with the activities.) It is probable that the audience the writer was hoping to interest in his piece was his own circle of boys who were on the outing, and peer approval is no small consideration as we have indicated earlier.

The second piece conforms to a general expectation of a piece from a girl of this age: it is home-focused and concerned with the intimate goings-on of life with family, friends and domestic animals. It is focused throughout on one topic and presents a story which is carefully shaped and cosy in its tone. The audience for this piece was ostensibly the girl's teacher; however, there is some indication that the extra information (how Joseph came by his name, where Jessica fits in) is considerately provided not only for her teacher but also, perhaps, for some wider, unknown audience.

A better future for boys and girls?

After one has read scores of pieces of writing which appear to confirm these general characteristics of the content and tone of girls' and boys' writing, one does doubt whether the efforts teachers make such as those outlined above can make much difference. Certainly, we need to investigate and research even more those classrooms where boys and girls are confounding our expectations. There is promising evidence, for instance, that the recent understandings of how to scaffold non-fiction writing with 'writing frames' is giving a boost to girls' writing in that area.

In looking through the notebooks of writing from several boys and girls (from which the above examples have been taken), I am struck by the fact that, although the trend in boys and girls is clearly gender-marked, in all the notebooks there were atypical examples of writing – far fewer in number but clearly there, nevertheless. Thus Ben drew a careful picture of his garden, captioned:

Daddy mended the fence and we had a picnic

and Claire had a dramatic picture, captioned:

A man and a boy are out in the frost with a dog and the dog fell in some ice and drowned.

At age 8, there was a comparable sprinkling of writing where one would be hard-pressed to guess whether the author was male or female. If teachers notice, commend, share and publish these unrepresentative pieces, children may begin to shift in their understanding of the range they can attempt. The impact of what children have read to them is also significant as is the gender of the reader. What is popular reading in the classroom is influential also. Eve Bearne (1998) knows of Year 6 boys who write romances while Judy Blume is the class cult reading, and girls who are laying out their non-fiction writing with large, exploded inserts and pull-out maps.

It is true also that boys are likely to read and write more and differently when they have male examples at school and at home. As most primary school teachers are female and as we cannot arrange for a male in every home, this becomes a tall order, but where schools have, for instance, invited male authors into school, writing's profile has been helpfully increased. Michael Rosen's school visits, where he shares his non-stereotypical poetry with children, have done their part in this long haul towards a widening of what girls and boys see themselves able to write.

It is perhaps important to end this section by reminding ourselves that there are schools where boys' achievements in National Curriculum assessments are just as high as those of girls. Research suggests that what these schools are doing right (for all pupils) is capturing the imagination with the choice of books read aloud, revisiting of texts through drama and role, and setting engaging writing tasks. These successful schools allow pupils considerable freedom to follow their own interests, and children write with a sense of purpose and audience. Teachers respond positively to compositional aspects so that pupils grow in their beliefs that they have worthwhile things to say. Above all, there is lots of talk – with partners and with the teacher – about all aspects of writing (Frater, 2000).

CHILDREN WHOSE WORK SHOWS GRAMMATICAL ERRORS

There have been several instances in the examples of writing that we have used throughout this book of children who import features of their spoken language into their writing. For all children, spoken language acquisition is ahead of written competence as they have obviously not had the same exposure to written language, which is nearly always in standard English. The most obvious errors in this respect are those of non-agreement of subject and verb; thus in Bethany's writing we find, 'the parents was crying' (Figure 9.1) and in Jatinder's writing, 'there was two ardvarks' (Figure 8.5). Other errors appear in writing in places where we would not notice them in speech. You see an example of this in, 'the shop keeper who owned the shop did not know that there was one everyone wanted the Christmas tree but it was too expensive' (Figure 7.10). In this section we look at key issues of grammar teaching.

What can be taught?

As we saw in Chapter 2 there has been considerable debate about how and what should be taught explicitly as far as grammar is concerned. We will not rehearse those arguments here but will remind you that the *PNS* provides a framework for contextualised grammar teaching. The difficulty will be to find ways round the abstractions involved in teaching some aspects. If you cannot explain a rule in straightforward language and in a way that children can take on, then it is probably wiser to put your time and effort into lots of examples of the rule in practice, so that children can generate their own understandings and definitions. It is also important to remember that many children have already acquired standard English and use it without error in their writing, so some in your class will bring a great deal of implicit understanding to the teaching you do.

The importance of reading to children and of children reading in the development of their acquisition of written standard English cannot be emphasised enough.

When to deal with grammatical errors that appear in individual writing

If children are well practised in reading their work aloud, either to themselves or to a writing partner, then they are more than likely to pick up some of their grammatical errors. When seven-year-old Tony read out his story and came to the sentence, 'That night the rabbit's mum comed to the lion's den ...', he said straightaway, 'That doesn't sound right', and changed 'comed' to 'came', the past tense of the irregular verb 'to come'. If a child's writing reaches the editing table with grammatical errors still present, individual help will need to be given by the teacher and final marking left in her hands so that no work reaches a wider public with non-standard slips in place. At this final stage the child will be far more interested in the lessons to be learned than if you interrupt the flow of composition at the start of the process. As this book has consistently maintained, it is most important that children know when it is most profitable to give their attention to the various different aspects of writing.

What do you need to know?

Many of the writers of this book were at school at a time when explicit grammar lessons did not happen. Because they are all curious about the language which they speak, write and teach, they have given themselves, and are still giving themselves, lessons about language. The fact that they recognise that there are linguistic niceties that they have yet to master does not mean that they are not 'good enough' users of their language. 'Negatives' and 'passives' do not give most of us many problems, but you might have to give yourself lessons to check on 'pronominal reference' and 'fronted constructions'! None of us should be complacent about his/her knowledge level and it is very important that we all remain curious and go on learning; curiosity about language as well as teacher subject knowledge have been strands throughout this book.

We should not be fearful of teaching children in all the ways that we have been describing even while we are still in the process of developing knowledge of terminology and more difficult linguistic concepts. You need to remember that the subject of this book is teaching about the whole of writing, not just grammar.

Struggling or gifted, writing in English as a first language or as an additional language, girl or boy, the children that this chapter focuses on will all flourish in your classroom when you give evidence of your interest in them and create an atmosphere in which mistakes are seen as moments for learning.

FORMAL ARRANGEMENTS FOR STRUGGLING WRITERS

There has been no shortage of initiatives aimed at alleviation of the serious problems that beset a minority of our pupils as far as literacy is concerned. You will see considerable overlap in the provision described in the three sections below and schools and local authorities may have introduced yet further programmes. There is universal recognition that problems should be identified and tackled early so that the familiar sense of defeat that we see in children who are still not reading and writing after the age of 7 or 8 can be avoided.

Special Educational Needs (SEN) Code of Practice

The *National Curriculum (NC)* is an inclusive curriculum, one to which all pupils, irrespective of ability and achievement, are entitled and in which they have the right to participate. Children's additional needs come in all shapes and sizes and this notion of inclusivity can be a challenging one for a new teacher. In 1981, the *Warnock Report* established the principle that some pupils should have a statement of 'special need'.

The 1993 Education Act tightened up arrangements and set out a Code of Practice (DFE, 1994), which stressed the need for early identification of difficulties, affirmed that children with SEN should be educated in the classrooms of mainstream schools and stated that their assessment should be school-based. It also established the notion of an Individual Education Plan (IEP) to be drawn up as part of the school-based assessment. Your greatest support and source of information in all these matters will be the school's Special Educational Needs Co-ordinator (SENCO). You will liaise with her over any worries you have about an individual's writing and, if it comes to it, you will construct an IEP with her guidance. All schools, early years settings and local authorities must, legally, identify, assess and provide for all children's special educational needs. The SEN Code of Practice (revised in 2001) asks for a continuum of provision – a graduated approach. In the first place, schools meet most children's learning needs through differentiation; teachers tailor their activities, spoken and written language to match individual pupils' different learning needs and styles. Those children who do not respond to differentiation and do not make adequate progress have to be given additional or different help. This school-based SEN provision is described in the Code as S*chool Action*. A similar system is set out for early education settings and described as *Early Years Action* and *Early Years Action Plus*. Teachers draw up an IEP which is developed in consultation with parents and involves the pupil as far as possible. The IEP should record strategies used to enable the child to progress, such as: the short-term targets set for or by the child; the teaching strategies and provision to be used and put in place; when the plan is to be reviewed; success and/or exit criteria; and outcomes (to be recorded when the IEP is reviewed).

If *School Action* has not helped the child to make adequate progress, *School Action Plus* is brought into play and the school asks for outside advice from the local authority's support services, or from health or social work professionals**.** If a child's needs cannot be met through *School Action Plus*, the local authority may consider the need for a statutory assessment and, perhaps, a Statement of Special Educational Need, which sets out the child's needs in detail and the special educational provision to be made for them. The statement must be reviewed at least annually. When you hear children described as statemented or 'with a statement', it is this statement that is meant.

The decisive factor for taking *School Action*, moving to *School Action Plus*, or considering whether a statutory assessment is necessary is whether the child is making adequate progress. The Code defines adequate progress and lists different kinds of progress, depending on the starting point and expectations for a particular child. Essentially, what is considered to be adequate progress for a particular child is a matter for the teacher's professional judgement.

The Code does not ignore the importance of working in partnership with parents and of the child's right to be involved in making decisions and exercising choice as far as his or her education is concerned. Liaison and consultation help progress.

The Primary National Strategy (PNS)

The *PNS* has embraced the three 'waves' of support for pupils identified by the *NLS*. The SEN Code of Practice (described above) with its 'graduated response' maps on to *PNS* waves.

In the first wave, all the children receive 'high quality teaching' in literacy work in the classroom. The teacher will make use of the routines and resources we mention in earlier chapters and will be ensuring that all the children are actively involved. She will work with individuals' learning styles and be encouraging independence and self-knowledge. A trained TA supports the teaching. The hope is that this *Quality First Teaching* will be effective for most of the class; assessment will identify those children who are struggling. Pupils may be at any point on the graduated response, as defined by the SEN Code of Practice.

The second wave of teaching is for those children who have been identified as struggling and for whom a special programme of support is needed. Daily sessions, usually from the TA and usually in small groups, will be set up for these struggling readers and writers. Sometimes a local authority will set up booster classes. The children are expected to catch up with their peers as a result of these interventions.

The third wave of teaching is for those children who have clear SEN needs. These needs may be related specifically to literacy or they may be more widely based. Specialist advice is sought at this point and both previous aims and styles of teaching may be changed. The intention is to reduce gaps in attainment and make it possible for the child to benefit from waves 1 or 2. The child ideally will receive individual support, which is often at the beginning of the afternoon, first thing in the morning or last thing in the afternoon, and in pre-school clubs. Ideally, writing arising from these sessions should be displayed in the classroom alongside other work. It is important that children do not miss the same thing every day and are present for classroom literacy work.

Government-funded literacy support programmes and materials

Three stages of support have been instituted by the government since 1999 that are typically implemented for children in wave 2. The *Early Literacy Support (ELS)* programme is designed to identify and support children who are clearly not making expected progress in their first term in Year 1. It usually takes place in term 2 of Year 1. The rationale for such early intervention is clear: support at this point prevents longer-term and more intractable difficulties later on. At the beginning of the spring term, in the child's first year at school, the teacher and the TA (who will have received special training) will start a programme of support.

For those children still needing help in KS2, the *Additional Literacy Support (ALS)* programme is appropriate. *ALS* is offered to those children who only reach a level 2c or 1 in their KS1 *NC* Assessments but who have currently no other support being offered. These materials are intended for use in classroom group work and rely on close collaboration between the teacher and the TA. The TA should run three guided reading and writing sessions each week, and the teacher one. The focus is on reading, writing and phonics.

The *Further Literacy Support (FLS)* programme is another set of intervention material offered to pupils in Year 5. It is designed to offer structured, additional support for those children who are still not making the expected progress in literacy. Based on *PNS* objectives, it offers teachers and TAs practical guidance and resources.

A QUICK CHECKLIST IF A CHILD SEEMS TO BE STRUGGLING

What procedures should you follow if you are concerned about the progress of an individual child? You may, for instance, be concerned that your child is exhibiting signs of dyslexia (Chapter 10). What follows is a checklist for you to use whatever your concerns:

● Look out for early warning signs.
  As well as difficulties specifically associated with writing, accompanying early warning signs may take the form of a range of difficulties such as: negative attitudes and poor self-esteem; difficulties in sequencing, remembering, co-ordinating; discrepancy between language skills and other abilities.
● Carry out appropriate diagnostic procedures.
  As well as your ongoing formative assessment, carry out an analysis of a piece of writing much as was we did for Bethany in the earlier part of this chapter.
● Implement an initial action plan.
  Use evidence from the above to plan some very specific teaching for the child with well-focused targets.
● Liaise with SENCO and parents.
  Discuss your findings with the SENCO and then with the child's parents and share your plan with them. The greater the partnership between you and the parents the better it will be for the child.
● If the child makes progress – good! Continue with carefully targeted steps.
  If the child does not make progress – keep liaising with the SENCO. You may decide that the child needs additional support as described above and that an IEP should be drawn up.

In the rest of this chapter we look at ways in which you can support the particular writing needs of the children in your class. We start with assessment, where you identify those needs, and then we look at ways of responding to them through out-of-class support and through your own in-class teaching strategies.

ASSESSMENT

As we have said above, when planning to meet the needs of children who are struggling with writing, you should start from your observations and assessments of the children. For a full discussion of assessment issues, you need to look back at Chapter 8. Here we want to make some general points as far as they relate to pupils who are finding writing difficult. First of all, you need to ensure that your records contain evidence of the child's achievements as well as his or her difficulties. Notes from parent and child conferences are a useful contribution to your overall view of the child. We have also talked about observing and recording the children's strategies as they write.

These records and observations will provide you with sufficient information for most children; however, for the children who are giving you concern, additional information is gained from periodically collecting an example of writing and closely analysing it. (This writing should not be written in test conditions; most children will underachieve in such circumstances.) It is at this point that you should be able to decide to what extent you can meet the child's needs in your classroom as these assessment tools will allow you to plan for tailored teaching that is responsive to the child's needs. If you think that you cannot, then you will need to discuss the child with other staff (e.g. the SENCO) in order to establish what additional support is available to you and whether an IEP is needed (see checklist above). Whatever the outcome of your discussions, pieces of writing and analyses provide you with sufficiently focused information to allow you to meet the *NC*'s principles for inclusion:

● the provision of suitable learning challenges;
● response to pupil's diverse needs;
● overcoming potential barriers to learning and assessment for individuals and groups.

(DfEE, 1999a, pp. 30–33)

At the heart of these principles lies your secure understanding of the writing process and of appropriate assessment procedures.

Everything that we have included in the chapters on resources and routines is relevant here. What is good practice for your class in general is good practice for your struggling writers. But, because they are struggling, because they lack experience, uppermost in your planning must be the question, 'How am I going to increase their opportunities to write and exposure to the written word?'

MEETING INDIVIDUAL NEEDS IN AND OUT OF THE CLASSROOM

Since the *Warnock Report* (DES, 1978), the withdrawal of children from class to receive extra individual support has become less common and in-class support is probably now the norm. There are advantages and disadvantages to both systems. It could be said that mature, competent writers write privately and that retirement to a small, quiet, comfortable room without distractions symbolises the act of writing. It is perhaps easier to build a relationship with one's tutor in the withdrawal arrangement and to feel that one's difficulties are being taken seriously. But someone who helps in the classroom can more readily ensure that work is not missed and that the child is not treated so obviously as special. The helper or extra teacher can keep more children under her eye and can more easily co-ordinate and discuss work with the regular class teacher.

Writing out of the classroom – Reading Recovery and Every Child a Writer

The main support arrangements that do withdraw children are *Reading Recovery* programmes. Despite its name, the programmes work on writing problems as much as reading difficulties. Because *Reading Recovery* is regarded as very effective and because its impact has been the subject of much research, we include some detail at this point. Brooks (2000) has evaluated 19 interventions including *Reading Recovery*.

Reading Recovery

Reading Recovery, developed by Marie Clay in New Zealand, was designed to prevent failure in young children (six-year-olds). Children thought to be at risk are withdrawn from class and given one-to-one teaching daily for about half an hour over 12 to 20 weeks. The hope is that such intensive and early teaching will eliminate some of the enormous costs later, not only in financial terms but also in terms of pupil stress and poor prospects of progress later on.

The characteristics of *Reading Recovery* are:

- intensive training of teachers (literacy methods, child development and children's books);
- high expectations conveyed to the child;
- a range of child-focused and meaning-based approaches;
- the linking of reading and writing;
- clear evidence given to the child of success.

A typical *Reading Recovery* session as described by Jean Hudson (in Harrison, 1992: 239–41) goes through the following seven stages:

1. rereading of two or more familiar books to practise reading skills and to develop reading fluency;
2. practice in letter identification using plastic letters on a magnetic board;
3. shared writing of a story to be read and reread;
4. rearranging a cut-up story to provide many opportunities to study individual words and their structures;
5. practice in analysing the sounds in words;
6. introduction and attempted reading of at least one new book;
7. individual variations depending on the child's needs, e.g. prediction, letter identification.

The clear benefits for children are:

- increased confidence that they will be able to read and write;
- an enthusiasm for books;
- a willingness to take risks and a corresponding reduction in the fear of failure;
- a wider range of strategies used;
- more independence;
- an early return to the normal work of the classroom.

The clear benefits for teachers and schools are:

- in-service training with clear, practical outcomes;
- raised standards of literacy as *Reading Recovery* children are no longer held back;
- better monitoring of all children;
- easier planning, as there is less differentiation to consider.

The *Reading Recovery* programme takes children out of the classroom in the early stages of reading but it offers principles for working with children, in KS1 and KS2, within the classroom, too. Indeed, the research evaluation of *Reading Recovery* (Burroughs-Lange, S. *et al.*, 2006) showed that a trained literacy expert in the school helped improve overall literacy throughout the school, not just for the children being withdrawn. Some children who 'qualified' for *Reading Recovery* help but for whom there was no space still improved far more than expected. Key features of *Reading Recovery* – the volume of reading, the choice of appropriate texts, creating personal texts, the explicit discussion of strategies for getting at words, and the focus on what the child already knows – are all key aspects of appropriate provision for the child who struggles with literacy.

There are programmes intended to provide in-class support for KS2 children (e.g. *Catch-Up*) and the DfES materials specifically for use with children in Years 3 and 4, the *ALS* and *FLS* materials described above, can be downloaded.

Every Child a Writer (ECAW)

In an extension to the successful *Every Child a Reader* (*ECAR*) programme, the government is piloting *ECAW*, initially in nine local authorities, a total of 135 schools and 2,500 children. The intention is that by 2011, 45,000 children will be covered, which is more than the projected number of children (30,000) scheduled to be covered by *ECAR*. This programme is a measure of the anxiety that is felt about the extent to which progress in writing lags behind that in reading (67% reached the expected level in writing compared with 86% in reading in 2008).

The children will be seven- and eight-year-olds, an older group than the six-year-olds selected for *ECAR*. As with *ECAR*, tuition will be one-to-one for the selected struggling writers. It remains to be seen whether the likely dominant focus on transcriptional aspects will ignore children's deeper needs to write about those aspects of their lives that are significant to them. This is no idle anxiety; the only example currently available for these sessions mentions the writing problem where a pupil might use 'and' and 'but' to start every sentence. Apart from this not being common writing behaviour in our experience, to put the stress on such items would be counter-productive, we feel. Purposes and audiences for writing will need to be uppermost in the teachers' minds – writing on the computer; writing about interests and hobbies; blogging; drama; encounters with literature; visits outside school; meeting/interviewing people; real tasks such as letter writing; composing instructions, etc. publishing work; and working on pieces of writing brought in from home – will need to be at the heart of the sessions. Throughout this book, we have emphasised how transcription aspects need to be in their rightful place; for struggling writers this is even more important.

PARENTAL INVOLVEMENT

We know, from various monitored projects, that most children whose parents read and write with their children make greater progress than those children whose parents are not involved. What has been less appreciated is that some children whose parents have received insufficient guidance and resources do not make progress and that those children are usually the very ones most in need of extra help. We suggest that if, as we hope, you are seeking to enlist parental involvement with your poor writers, it is important to talk regularly with the parents to ensure that you share the same views of what works for the child. Let parents tell you about the writing that goes on at home. With your encouragement, you'll jointly discover that more goes on than initially imagined. You should recognise that the older the child the harder it is to sustain parental contact over writing, but the more imperative it actually is to do so. Look out for materials for parents and carers that are translated into community languages. Even if you are not involved in one-to-one tuition, as in the *ECAW* programme, try to send home writing that the child has done in school and try to invite home writing back into the classroom.

CONCLUSIONS

It may appear that our view of the poor writer contains a protective element. In your experience, the poor writer may be a tricky, disruptive boy (most of the children with literacy difficulties are boys) who rejects all your efforts and whose attention span is of seconds not minutes. But our feeling is that all children want to write. Angry, rejecting behaviour when it comes to writing is a symptom of the grave realisation that fills the child of his incompetence in an area that society considers so essential and that he can see brings so much pleasure, knowledge and satisfaction to those around him. The anger is compounded by the evidence that it is so easy for some of his classmates. Most children with difficulties have missed vital early literacy experiences, have been confused by information that lets them down and have been allowed to slip through countless nets, ranging from inadequate resources to badly managed classrooms. We have stressed that collusion with defeatism or unconditional acceptance of the writer's low opinion of himself is not helpful, but a situation where we *blame* the victim is unforgivable. There is a great deal that can be done to help the poor writer, especially if it is done early enough. We are confident that if you can use some of the advice given here, then your sullen/terrified/indifferent/aggressive child will start to experience success and you will know the rewards of helping him to become a writer.

At the beginning of your career, trying to move a reluctant writer to commit pen to paper, or trying to decipher written scrawl, may seem almost impossible, but we hope you can draw inspiration from this book so that your increasing knowledge and repertoire of approaches, activities and strategies will enable you to respond creatively to your pupils' struggles and to read their writing with a fresh eye. The message of this chapter and of the book as a whole is that as a teacher of writing you need to be fully informed about writing processes and practice. You will then be free to enjoy your teaching and to respond constructively to all your pupils' varying and multiple needs.

Further reading and websites

Bunting, R. (2002) 'How to write really badly: supporting children with writing difficulties', in Williams, M. *Unlocking Writing*. London: David Fulton Publishers.

Burroughs-Lange, S. *et al.* (2006) *Evaluation of Reading Recovery in London Schools: Every Child a Reader 2005–2006*. London: Institute of Education, University of London.

Eyre, D. (2001) *Able Children in Ordinary Schools*. London: David Fulton Publishers.

Frater, G (2004) 'Improving Dean's writing: or, What shall we tell the children?' *Literacy*, 32(2), 78–82.

See also:

Catch Up. www.catchup.org.uk/pages/home.shtm (accessed 22 December 2008).

Cline, T. and Shamsi, T. (2000) *Language Needs or Special Needs? The Assessment of Learning Difficulties in Literacy among Children Learning English as an Additional Language: A literature review* [RR 184]. London: DfES. www.dfes.gov.uk/research/data/uploadfiles/RR184.doc (accessed 22 December 2008).

DfES materials: *Early Literacy Support* (2001); *Additional Literacy Support* (1999); *Further Literacy Support* (2002).

Everybody Writes. This website is dedicated to celebrating writing across the school and provides accounts of projects which have enthused and motivated pupils. http:/www.everybodywrites.or.uk

Every Child a Reader: The Results of the First Year. Published by *Every Child a Reader.* It contains case histories of individual children who have benefited from the *Reading Recovery* scheme. Copies of the report are available from www.everychildareader.org

Gifted and Talented. *Young Gifted and Talented.* http://ygt.dcsf.gov.uk/ (accessed 22 December 2008).

Milton Keynes EMASS (2004) *Guidance on the Assessment of EAL Pupils who may have Special Educational Needs.* Milton Keynes: Milton Keynes Council. www.mkweb.co.uk/emass/documents/website_EAL_SEN_Artwork.pdf (accessed 22 December 2008).

NALDIC *Principles of Good Practice.* www.naldic.org.uk/ITTSEAL2/teaching/Pedagogy.cfm (accessed 22 December 2008).

National Association for Gifted Children. http://old.nagc.org/index.html (accessed 22 December 2008).

Chapter 10

Specific Learning Difficulties in Writing

Cathy Svensson

'He joins in discussions enthusiastically but his written work is weak.'
'He still struggles with spelling, even with the words he comes across every single day.'
'I just can't quite put my finger on what the problem is.'
'I thought he was able until I saw his writing.'

A SPECIFIC LEARNING DIFFICULTY

Dyslexia is associated particularly with reading and spelling problems. It is described as a 'specific' learning difficulty as it represents a problem in one or more basic psychological processes. Closer scrutiny of the word highlights its meaning. It originates from the Greek word 'dyslexia': 'dys' meaning 'difficulty' or 'malfunction' and 'lexia', taken from the root word 'lexis' meaning words. Use of this term implies that dyslexia is not merely a reading difficulty but encompasses a wide range of language-based problems, accounting for a delay in aspects of both spoken and written language.

Although dyslexia is frequently described as a specific learning difficulty, it is nevertheless one of a number of such difficulties which include, for example, dyspraxia – derived from the word 'dys' meaning 'difficulty' and 'praxia' meaning the ability to carry out motor movement – and dyscalculia, which relates to problems in calculating number. Dyslexia, however, is the most common of these specific learning difficulties, reportedly affecting 3 to 10 per cent of the population across gender, age, socio-economic and international boundaries (Snowling and Stac, 2006). Based on these figures, it is reasonable to assume that in a medium-sized primary school of 300 children, 12 to 30 children may have literacy-related difficulties associated with dyslexia (Pavey, 2007).

DEFINING DYSLEXIA

There are many different definitions of dyslexia. Although the definitions are subtly different, they provide some insight into the condition. The British Psychological Society provides one of the most frequently cited definitions of dyslexia:

> Dyslexia is evident when accurate and fluent word reading and/or spelling develops very incompletely or with great difficulty. This focuses on literacy learning at the 'word level' and implies that the problem is severe and persistent despite appropriate learning opportunities.
>
> (British Psychological Society, 1999: 20)

While this definition captures the associated problems in reading and spelling at word level, it nevertheless falls short in providing an explanation for these difficulties; neither does it reflect the ongoing controversy between researchers, some of whom question whether dyslexia exists at all (Mansell, 2005).

A more recent definition by the International Dyslexia Association (IDA) goes further in identifying phonological processing as the source of the difficulty. Again, this definition draws our attention to associated problems in reading and spelling and highlights the disparity between the child's spelling and decoding when compared to cognitive abilities:

> [Dyslexia] is characterised by poor spelling and decoding abilities. These difficulties typically result from a deficit in the phonological component of language that is often unexpected in relation to other cognitive abilities and the provision of effective classroom instruction.
>
> (International Dyslexia Association, 2000)

The three key points to note here are:

- Reference to phonological processing is important, as it highlights the potential processing difficulties in phonological aspects a pupil with dyslexia may experience when faced with the demands of retrieving, remembering and making sense of information.
- The use of the word 'unexpected' reminds us that this difficulty does not have an impact on all aspects of learning. The difficulty is specific and associated with the sound system of language.
- The reference to the persistence of dyslexia, despite effective classroom instruction, highlights the deep-seated nature of dyslexia and makes us question what effective classroom practice is.

The point to make early on in this chapter is that while there is general agreement that the processes which underpin literacy are somehow compromised or 'differently wired' in dyslexia, whether there is an exact location of these difficulties remains the subject of ongoing debate. To complicate the discussion further, current understandings of dyslexia are influenced by alternative perspectives on the condition. Historically, dyslexia has been influenced by scientific theory which aimed to provide a biological, cognitive and behavioural explanation for the child's difficulties. In contrast, social scientists are concerned with the social construction of dyslexia as a disability. From their perspective, the blame rests with society for shaping expectations and the environment thereby creating a condition which we now label 'dyslexia'.

THE INCLUSION CONTEXT

This social viewpoint of disability has gained in importance over recent years and is central to this discussion. The viewpoint is reflected in *The Index for Inclusion* (Booth and Ainscow, 2002) and *Removing Barriers to Achievement* (DfEE, 2001). It is also reflected more widely in government's current policy agenda for inclusion. *The Special Educational Needs and Disability Act* (DfEE, 2000b) put individual needs at the heart of inclusion. The Act places the onus on schools to embrace and respond to all pupils' needs, to consider how the school can overcome 'barriers to learning' and make appropriate provision for diverse needs within a mainstream setting.

The SEN Code of Practice (DfE, 1994; DfEE, 2000b) puts special educational needs at the top of every school agenda. It is underpinned by the fundamental principles of inclusion. It categorises four areas of special educational need:

- Communication and Interaction;
- Cognition and Learning;
- Behaviour, Emotional and Social Development;
- Sensory and Physical.

It recognises the language-based nature of dyslexia and includes it in the category of Communication and Interaction needs. It rightly reminds us that individual needs may span more that one category. It states that all children with special educational needs should:

- have their needs met;
- normally be provided for in the mainstream classroom;
- have their views taken into account;
- have full access to a broad and balanced curriculum.

In this chapter we discuss two primary case-study pupils, one a pupil in a Year 1 class and one in a Year 6 class.

ASSESSING THE WRITTEN EVIDENCE

Immature spelling, handwriting and poorly organised composition underpinned by phonological processing difficulties are the writing problems most commonly associated with dyslexia (Reid, 2007). However, it is important to remember that such pupils often show strength in aspects of visual and spatial skills and creativity. It would, however, be simplistic to assume that any two children with dyslexia will present with the same profile of strengths and difficulties, and indeed the same applies to all children. Nevertheless, for all children, good formative and summative assessment should be the basis for effective provision. A sample piece of free writing is usually a good starting point for assessment, as the case study of our pupil, Con, below, demonstrates.

A CASE STUDY OF CON

Figure 10.1 is a Year 1 writing sample. Without a context for this writing it may look like early developmental writing of a four- or five-year-old in a Reception class. When we discover that the author, Constance (Con) is aged 6, in a Year 1 class, is a native English speaker, is considered of above-average ability in a high-achieving school, our perception of the writing changes. The writer is retelling her news. She has a story to tell but it is without a context and limited to a retelling of one main event. She tells us that she 'bent down to pick up her book'. We do not know that this is a most precious book that had been lost for a long time, given to her by her grandmother for her third birthday. She was so pleased to find her book again that she wrote this 'part' event as her news.

What Con knows about writing

When analysing writing it is always important to consider first of all what the child knows and can do. Con's writing shows that she knows:

Figure 10.1

- writing represents meaning;
- writing follows left to right sequential order;
- sounds are represented by letter shapes;
- spoken words are represented by separate units of letters;
- initial sounds are represented by particular letter shapes.

But

- her developmental delay is demonstrated by the immaturity of her writing;
- she has a story to tell but limits it to the bare minimum – it lacks context or awareness of audience;
- she has some knowledge of letter sound mapping; she limits this to first letter sounds in words except in writing the word 'bend' as 'bet'; she shows some early 'fuzzy' representation of other sounds in this word;
- she does not attempt to spell the high-frequency words 'to' and 'my';
- she omits to write the first word 'I' of her sentence;
- her handwriting is immature for a child in her second year of schooling. She is learning to write in a cursive script but close inspection of her writing reveals incorrect letter formation (see the 'g' and 'd' particularly) which may further inhibit her motivation to write.

Figure 10.2 is a sample of Con's work one year later.

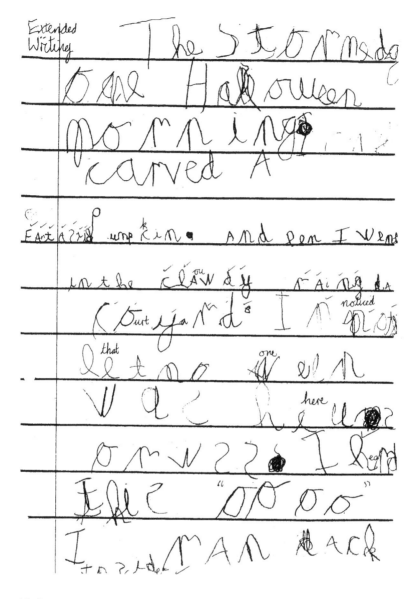

Figure 10.2

This extended piece of writing is a Hallowe'en story titled 'One Stormy Day'. It followed a series of work related to Hallowe'en ghost stories. It was completed with support: the title was copied by the child and key words of 'Hallowe'en', 'morning', 'pumpkin' and 'carved' were all supplied. What is evident is the improvement in Con's ability to tell a story which is facilitated by her improved confidence in spelling.

Figure 10.1 reflects scant knowledge of letter sound mapping of initial sounds only. Figure 10.2 shows a growing knowledge of letter sound mapping to the extent that the pupil notes the most significant sounds in a word, e.g. 'courtyard' is represented as 'coyrd', 'heard' is represented as 'hrd'. Some high-frequency words are written accurately and no longer represented by an initial sound only ('in', 'the', 'went', 'ran'). Note how Con can maintain more controlled handwriting and spelling at the start of her story. The demands of integrating the skills of handwriting, telling a story and spelling are particularly onerous and reflected in the later loosely controlled handwriting, erratic spacing between words and consistent reversal of 's'. Ongoing difficulties with applying graphic and phonic knowledge to encode words for spelling are reflected in the spelling attempts ('once' spelt as 'orwss' and 'one' as 'ween'). Such difficulties are a common feature of dyslexia.

Con's history

Closer scrutiny of Con's history reveals varied language and organisation difficulties highlighted by the demands made by the writing task. All are closely identified with dyslexia. These following characteristic features of the condition have been well documented by a number of researchers. Children may exhibit few, some, many or all of these difficulties in the following areas and in varying degrees:

- in language acquisition (Vellutino *et al.*, 2004; Lundberg and Hoien, 2001);
- in pronunciation and jumbling words (Blacock, 1982; Miles, 1983);
- in naming everyday objects and in word finding (Miles, 1974; Snowling and Stac, 2006; Sheffield, 1991);
- in recognising rhyme and alliteration, counting syllables and recognising and counting phonemes in words (Bradley and Bryant, 1983; Liberman and Shankweiler, 1985; Treiman, 1985; Goswami, 1991; Snowling, 1995);
- in auditory memory for words and letters (Gathercole, 2006);
- in visual discrimination and organisation (Fawcett and Nicholson, 1992 and 2001; Stein, 2001).

Although her problems were mild, Con exhibited some early signs of a phonological processing difficulty associated with dyslexia.

Language acquisition

Con was late to talk. Her mum noticed this when she compared her to her peers but felt that the fact that she was a very contented baby could account for it. She was almost 3 before she spoke in simple sentences. This is a skill most children begin to achieve around the age of two.

Oral problems in pronunciation and jumbling words

When Con did start to speak it was difficult to understand her because of mild articulation problems. Following a referral from the local GP she had speech therapy when she was 3. The interesting thing was that her difficulties were subtle and barely noted by her family. It was only on school entry that her parents again suspected she had a subtle speech delay when compared to her peers. For example, she said 'puter' for 'computer'; she could not say 'c' accurately, instead she said 't', pronouncing 'car' as 'tar'. Words starting with a cluster were simplified when spoken for example, 'climb' was pronounced as 'time'. On many occasions she referred to 'Father Christmas' as 'Farmer Christmas' and never seemed to notice her error.

Problems in naming everyday objects and in word finding

Con's difficulty in naming was first noted when she had a new baby sister. It took her some weeks to remember her sister's name, which was surprising as she was obviously so proud of her. The same sort of difficulty was evident in her memory for labels of even very familiar things: animals, characters in favourite stories, etc.

Recognition of the syllable, rhyme and the phoneme

On school entry, she was sociable and chatty but her poor phonological awareness was noted. In Reception, when playing 'I spy', Con could not detect the first phoneme in the word 'sun', suggesting that it might be 'b'. At the end of the Reception class, the teacher noted a welcome breakthrough: Con was beginning to hear initial and significant sounds in words and to recognise rhyme. She could count syllables in words: three syllables for 'croc-o-dile' and two for her full name. She was now at the stage of phonological awareness that many children reach by school entry.

Poor memory for words

Con took a long time to learn the usual nursery rhymes. She took time to learn new vocabulary associated with school such as 'welfare ladies' and 'secretary'. She found it hard to follow two-part classroom instructions, being only able to hold on to one simple instruction at a time. If sent on a classroom errand, she often forgot what to say or do. After she had heard a story she could not easily retell it.

Writing problems

Con was keen to represent meaning with mark-making and drawing, but in her case this developmental stage lasted an unusually long time. In stories she always had good ideas about what she wanted to write but she had problems sequencing her ideas into order, deciding what was the relevant part of the story, and where to start. In Reception, Con was a keen writer but took a long time to establish where to start writing on the page. She would happily start writing at the top right-hand corner of the page and work downwards, sometimes for long stretches of time, without realising her mistake. The same sort of difficulty was noted in her letter formation. It was very common for her to reverse letters and even words.

She took a long time to progress from writing 'on' as 'no', for example. She was confused by 'b' and 'd' and 'p' and 'q' and, like many children, found it difficult to tell them apart. Her difficulties meant she could not apply letter-sound knowledge effectively to her spelling.

By the end of Reception, Con could name five letters and write two from memory. She could write her name, and deviated versions of her name with many reversed letters featuring largely in her writing.

In Year 1 Con learned the other 21 letters of the alphabet. She could write 19 from memory and could map these on to the written letters. She was developing an additional strategy to 'make meaning' in writing, and to 'take meaning' from reading. Despite her above-average ability, by Year 2, her writing was similar to the writing of a Year 1 child.

Involving the parents

Parents were surprised when Con's earliest school assessments showed that her progress in reading was slow. Their response was that she loved books, reading and being read to, so therefore this did not seem possible. The class teacher explained to Con's parents that her love of books, her positive home support and her attitude to reading were all strengths that would help override her early literacy difficulties. She also explained to them the frequent negative impact of delayed speech acquisition and subtle speech problems, particularly on spelling and, therefore, on writing.

She suggested that she continue to monitor Con's progress carefully, and that together they set up an Individual Education Plan (IEP) (Table 10.1) which would:

- identify a specific short-term target to support her language and writing;
- highlight particular teaching approaches and strategies that would help her achieve these targets;
- involve the classroom assistant in her support programme;
- set a target date to review the success of her programme.

School Action

The class teacher collected a range of written evidence in order to build a comprehensive profile of Con's writing across the curriculum. Writing samples included diary writing, extended story writing and cross-curricular samples. She referred to previous end-of-year reading and spelling assessments and reviewed Con's current spelling support arrangements. In discussion with the SENCO, Con was placed on the 'School Action' SEN register, which meant that her needs were such that the school could adequately support her without involving outside agencies. It was agreed that additional school-based support would include group support three times weekly, to ensure access to the curriculum during the literacy sessions, and, in addition, individual support once weekly.

With the advice of the SENCO, the class teacher stressed the importance of using a wide range of teaching strategies rather than 'more of the same', which were obviously not working so well.

She explained some of her teaching strategies:

- the importance of making the writing process explicit as a model for Con to relate to;
- the need to engage as many sensory approaches as possible in the writing process;
- the impact of making language experiences 'live' as a stimulus for thought, language learning and writing;
- the need to maintain the excellent habit of reading and sharing varied texts with Con to provide suitable models of writing for her;
- the importance of separating out the skills of handwriting, composition and spelling, to avoid overload and maintain Con's sense of achievement and self-esteem.

Individual Education Plan

Name: Con		Start date:	January 2003
		Stage:	School Action
		Year:	2
		Review date:	April 2003

Main areas of concern

Con has been diagnosed dyslexic:
she has delayed literacy skills,
poor memory for words and weak listening skills.
Con's weaknesses are most evident in her writing.

Programme monitored weekly by class teacher and the
Learning Support Assistant (LSA) and half termly by the SENCO

Objectives	Success criteria	Support strategies	Classroom strategies
Underpinning language target: To be able to name the days of the week in sequence.	Days of the week known. Appropriate labelling of 'today' and 'tomorrow' noted in conversation.	Days of week memory games: 'On Monday I bought a…' Practise using related vocabulary daily: 'tomorrow will be, the day before', etc. Create and draw a simple timetable of activities for each day.	Classroom display of days and activities associated with each day. Discussion on 'today's day'. Display books that include days of the week, e.g. *The Very Hungry Caterpillar.*
Handwriting target: To be able to write 'Constance' in cursive script. To write 's' appropriately.	'Constance' and the letter 's' are written in neat cursive script. Success observed over time.	Write in glitter glue. Trace, finger trace over writing. Experiment with different writing implements. Extend handwriting practice to include daily bead threading and dot-to-dot activities.	Set up a class office. Provide a wide range of writing implements and accessories. Encourage self monitoring and peer review of writing.
Spelling target: To be able to spell 8 common words: *here, and, that, was, got, play, come* and *have.*	Con can spell 30 Year 1 and 2 common words (22 common words already known).	Concentrate on two words weekly. Use multisensory strategies. Make the words using wooden letters. Talk about the word. Say the word. Write the word really slowly in 10 seconds. How many times can you write the word in 30 seconds? 'Think and talk' about learning with Con and the method that works best for her. Foster a 'little and often' approach (5 minutes daily practice).	Stick word list on to desk. Use 'look, say, spell, cover, write, check' strategy as routine classroom practice. Encourage and model investigative and multisensory approaches to spelling.

Parent/carers have agreed: to support Con's Home/School Reading nightly. They recognise how sharing texts can improve Con's language/ reading and provide her with models of text to support her story writing. Class teacher to advise parents on recommended texts and approaches to reading.

Support arrangements: Con will have 3 x weekly group support in the Literacy Hour and 1:1 support for 30 minutes with a Learning Support Assistant (LSA). Group support in the Literacy Hour will ensure full curriculum access; individual support will target Con's specific needs.

Table 10.1

MEET SEBASTIAN IN YEAR 6

Sebastian (Seb) is aged 10. He is a Year 6 pupil. As with Con, his poor performance in writing is affected by very subtle language-related difficulties, noted, particularly at this stage, in his problems grappling with new French vocabulary and in learning times tables by rote. The interesting thing is that Seb has particular strengths associated with his difficulties, too. Though his handwriting is weak, his drawing, particularly of 3-D shapes, is very good. He has advanced ICT skills and is also an able mathematician.

Seb has struggled with the physical act of handwriting and making sense of spelling throughout his schooling. At the end of Year 2 he achieved Level 1 in the English National Curriculum assessments. He achieved Level 2 in Science and Maths as both these topics made fewer demands on writing and spelling proficiency, and therefore suited Seb. Currently, he works with the above-average ability group in maths, the average ability group in science and the below-average group for all writing and spelling-related activities. Despite producing very untidy, almost illegible, maths work, he can grapple with very complicated mathematical concepts confidently. His written English is inhibited greatly by his poor spelling. Because of this, he limits what he writes, which means his writing experience is minimal. This exacerbates his difficulties and, therefore, both transcription and composition skills show developmental delay.

Though his self-esteem is 'fragile', he is well supported by sensitive class grouping. He has opportunity to work with the lower ability group to receive 'nuts and bolts' support, and in the above-average group in those tasks that challenge his problem-solving and reasoning skills. Seb is on the 'School Action Plus' register as his needs are being reviewed by the local education authority.

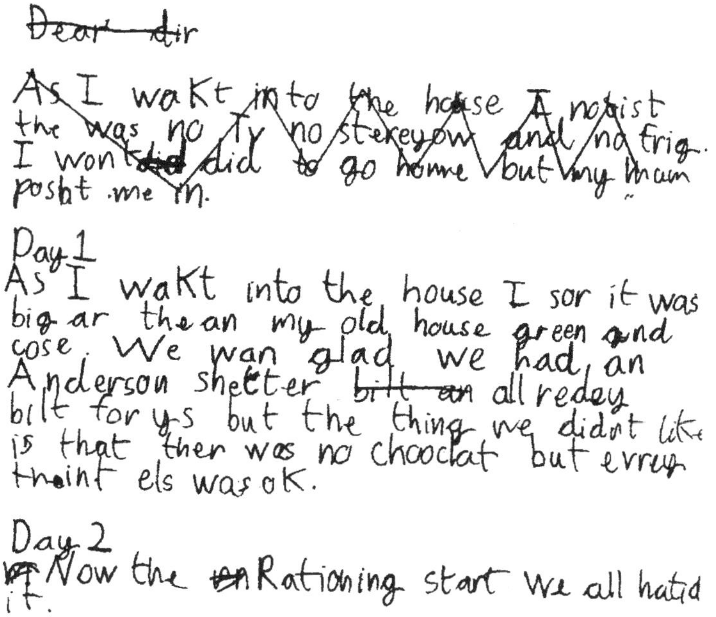
Dear dir
As I wakt into the house I nosist the was no Ty no stereyow and no frig.
I wont did to go home but my mam posht me in.
Day 1
As I wakt into the house I sor it was bigar thean my old house green and cose. We wan glad we had an Anderson shelter bilt an all redey bilt for us but the thing we didnt like is that ther was no chooclat but evrey thaint els was ok.
Day 2
Now the Rationing start We all hatid it.

Figure 10.3

In this writing activity (Figure 10.3) Seb was intellectually challenged by the topic of World War 2. The teacher used many rich and stimulating visual aids, pictures, video evidence and artefacts to support her teaching. These approaches were reinforced in a small support group before the writing activity took place. The objective for all the children for this lesson was 'to develop the skills of biographical and autobiographical writing in role'.

Seb gives an account of how he might have felt about the new home he was sent to in order to escape the war. The group support, offered by the learning support assistant (LSA), gave him and others in the group an additional opportunity to handle, review and discuss World War 2 artefacts and evidence, and gave him access to the writing task. He had a chance to practise using the language associated with this topic, and to think, reason and hypothesise about wartime conditions. Key words were highlighted and read, and their spelling discussed before writing.

We can see that Seb knows about writing first person diary accounts of his experience and is able to sustain the narrative voice. He has understanding of key concepts associated with the war such as Anderson shelters and rationing, but the writing lacks descriptive detail.

On the transcriptional side, he uses a sentence break appropriately and follows it with a capital letter. Spelling is mostly alphabetic (see Frith's model in Chapter 7). He spells words as they sound to him; for example 'bigger' is spelt 'bigar', 'cosy' as 'cose', 'already' as 'allredey', 'built' as 'bilt', 'else' as 'els' and 'every' as 'evrey'.

Many high-frequency words are correctly spelt, e.g. 'into', 'the', 'house', 'it', 'was', 'and', 'we', 'had', 'an' and 'for'. However, there are incorrect spellings for other high-frequency words such as, 'us' as 'ys', and 'sor' for 'saw'. Seb can certainly read these words accurately but cannot yet spell them when he is faced with the demands of planning and remembering what to write, how to spell and how to form his letters while controlling the movement of his pencil. It is clear that neither his memory for the visual sequence of letters in the word nor how the phonemes are represented by certain graphemes is securely established for him. His delay in establishing these skills impacts greatly on the quality and diversity of his writing experience.

His underdeveloped fine motor skills are reflected in his slow, non-fluent handwriting.

Inclusive classroom strategies

The three elements of inclusion (Figure 10.4) highlight the difficulty for the class teacher – to provide support for Seb while challenging him intellectually. She needs to consider her writing objective and whether it can be appropriately adapted or supported to suit his needs, matched to his learning style and made accessible in order to provide an inclusive learning environment.

The class teacher is fully aware of the need to incorporate a range of classroom strategies that will provide Seb with access to the writing curriculum. She uses a wide range of the 'dyslexia-friendly' approaches in the classroom which aim to incorporate high-level 'doing and thinking' rather than low-level 'copying and colouring'.

She incorporates the following dyslexia-friendly strategies to support his writing.

The Three Elements of Inclusion

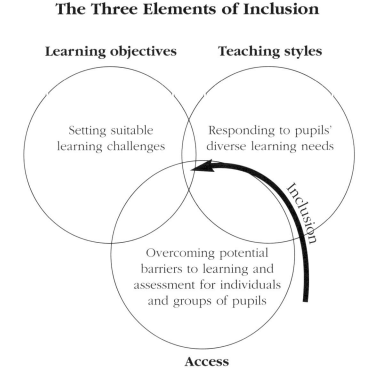

Figure 10.4

Teaching to strengths

- providing activities to extend reasoning, hypothesising and debating;
- using his skill in drawing to complement his writing;
- using strong visual support strategies and suitably uncluttered worksheets to engage Seb, thereby ensuring easy access to text.

Minimising the demand for a written response to each task by:

- using writing frames;
- providing cloze procedure activities;
- choosing from true or false statements to show knowledge of a topic;
- assigning a scribe to each group for oral activities;
- making use of voice recognition, predictive text programs and tape recording to record a response;
- using drama, hot seating and pair-share strategies to explore concepts and responses;
- introducing concept mapping, KWL grids, study skills and mind mapping to support pre-writing organisation.

Pre-empting Seb's needs

- backing up writing activities with access to visual and practical aids: lists of topic words, days of the week, alphabet strip, spellchecker or dictionary, and appropriate stationery (highlighter pens, markers, sticky notes);
- using innovative grouping arrangements so Seb works within appropriate class groups to match the requirements of the task and his needs;
- breaking writing tasks down into component skills to allow each separate skill to be supported.

Making classroom routines transparent and consistent

- providing a stimulating, well-organised and appropriately resourced classroom.

Specific targets for Seb

Specific SMART (**s**pecific, **m**anageable, **a**chievable, **r**elevant and **t**ime bound) targets are identified on Seb's IEP. The prime objective of these targets is to improve his spelling and phonemic awareness through teaching strategies that he can then apply to other words for learning.

Two different and complementary approaches are needed to support Seb's spelling, one method to support irregular spelling of common everyday words, the other to support learning words in word families.

- The common words 'saw,' 'were', 'us' and 'there' need active teaching in order to commit them to memory. The common words account for the vast majority of words Seb will need to use in his everyday writing. It makes sense, therefore, to target these words for spelling. They are frequently irregular so a 'sounding out' strategy alone does not work effectively; instead a multisensory approach is needed which will engage as many sensory channels as possible in the learning task. Spelling activities which involve seeing, hearing, feeling or doing (smelling and tasting are less practicable) will help ensure the best learning conditions. For example, strategies of 'look, say, spell, cover, write, check', and word building with wooden letters should be included as teaching strategies.

The second strategy to use is an investigative approach to spelling, which can be applied when the word to be learnt conforms to a spelling pattern.

- One area of difficulty (noted in the suffix spelling '-ed') can most helpfully be taught through collecting examples of using the '-ed' suffix to represent the past tense. In this way he would learn to generalise the rule.
- Rules and uses for 'y' at the end of a word (as in 'cosy' and 'every'); whether 'y' always makes an 'e' sound in this end position could also be investigated. Later the phonemes that the letter 'y' represents could be explored; for example, when does it it make a 'y' sound, an 'e' sound or an 'i' sound?

Specific IEP spelling targets include:

- to secure spelling (this half-term) of 18 key common words based on the Year 1 and 2 Literacy Hour words;

- to be able to use the suffixes '–ed' and '–er';
- to improve phonemic awareness;
- to know how the long 'e' sound at the end of a word is spelt.

The way forward

Seb needs both wide-ranging and specific support at different levels. He benefits from the stimulation of inclusive practices in a dyslexia-friendly classroom. Here, ideally, he can have his ideas challenged and extended. He has access to the 'big classroom picture' and the stimulation for writing that this provides. Group support for writing reinforces and supports the skills and processes he could not otherwise access independently. Here a wide range of differentiated writing activities and strategies can be explored and supported in a secure group setting. Individual support is ideal for his particular needs. Here specific difficulties can be picked apart and dealt with, while the essential opportunity for 'overlearning' writing routines and procedures can also be supported. In these ways the teacher is effectively integrating whole-class, guided group and individual support to provide the best learning opportunities for Seb.

Further reading

Buzan, T. (2003) *Mind Maps for Kids: An Introduction*. London: HarperCollins.

Hull Learning Services (2004) *Supporting Children with Dyslexia*. London: David Fulton Publishers.

Lewis, A. and Norwich, B. (eds) (2005) *Special Teaching for Special Children*. Oxford: Open University Press.

Reid, G. (2004) *Dyslexia: A Practitioner's Handbook*. Chichester: Wiley.

Reid, G. and Green, S. (2007) *100 Ideas for supporting Pupils with Dyslexia*. London: Continuum.

Reid, G. and Green. S. (2007) *The Teaching Assistant's Guide to Dyslexia*. London: Continuum.

Useful websites

Audio books
   www.simplyaudiobooks.ca
   www.school.booksontape.com
   www.listeningbooks.org.uk
British Dyslexia Organisation:
   www.bda-dyslexia.org.uk
Dyslexia Institute:
   www.dyslexia.inst.org.uk
   www.dyslexia-teacher.com
   www.creativelearningcentre.com
Software
   www.onchsoft.com
   www.SEMERIC.com
   www.wordshark.co.uk

References

Adams, M. J. (1990) *Beginning to Read: Thinking and Learning about Print*. Cambridge, MA: MIT Press.

Aldrich, R. (1982) *An Introduction to the History of Education*. London: Hodder & Stoughton.

Alexander, R. (2008) *Towards Dialogic Teaching: Rethinking Classroom Talk*. York: Dialogos.

Anderson, M. (2003) 'Reading violence in boys' writing'. *Language Arts*, 80 (3), 223–30.

Andrews, R. (2008) *The Case for a National Writing Project*. Reading: CfBT.

Baker, C. (1996) *The Foundations of Bilingualism*. Clevedon: Multilingual Matters.

Bannatyne, A. and Cotterell, G. (1966) 'Spelling for the dyslexic child'. *ICAA Word Blind Bulletin*. Winter.

Barnes, D. (1992) 'The role of talk in learning', in Norman, K. (ed.) *Thinking Voices: The Work of the National Writing Project*. Sevenoaks: Hodder & Stoughton.

Barrs, M. (1987) 'Learning to write'. *Language Matters* (2) and (3), 1.

Barrs, M. (1991) *Language Matters: Thinking about writing, No. 1*. London: CLPE.

Barrs, M. (1994) 'Genre theory: What's it all about?', in Stierer, B. and Maybin, J. (eds) *Language, Literacy and Learning in Educational Practice*. Clevedon: Multilingual Matters/Open University.

Barrs, M. (1996) 'The new primary language record writing scale'. *Language Matters*, 3. London: CLPE.

Barrs, M. and Cork, V. (2001) *The Reader in the Writer*. London: CLPE.

Barrs, M., Ellis, S., Hester, H. and Thomas, A. (1988) *The Primary Language Record: Handbook for Teachers*. London: CLPE.

Barrs, M., Ellis, S., Hester, H. and Thomas, A. (1990) *Patterns of Learning*. London: CLPE.

Barrs, M. and Thomas, A. (eds) (1991) *The Reading Book*. London: CLPE.

Barrs, M. and Pidgeon, S. (eds) (2002) *Boys and Writing*. London: CLPE.

Barton, D. and Hamilton, M. (1998) *Local Literacies*. London: Routledge.

Bearne, E. (1998) *Progress in Writing*. London: Routledge.

Bissex, G. (1980) *GNYS AT WRK: A Child Learns to Write and Read*. Cambridge, MA: Harvard University Press.

Black, P. and Wiliam, D. (1998) *Inside the Black Box*. London: King's College School of Education.

Blacock, J. (1982) 'Persistent auditory language deficits in adults with learning disabilities'. *Journal of Learning Disabilities*, 15 (10), 604–9.

Booth, T. and Ainscow, M. (2002) *Index for Inclusion* (revised edn). Bristol: Centre for Studies on Inclusive Education.

Bradley, L. and Bryant, P. (1983) 'Categorising sounds and learning to read: a causal connection'. *Nature*, 301, 419–21.

British Psychological Society (1999) *Dyslexia, Literacy and Psychological Assessment: Report by a Working Party of the Division of Education of the British Psychological Society*. Leicester: British Psychological Society.

Britton, J. (1982) 'Outline for a case study', in Pradl, G. (ed.) *Prospect and Retrospect: Selected Essays for James Britton*. London: Heinemann.

Brooks, G. (2000) *The Influence of Pre-school Experience on Early Literacy Attainment*. www.literacytrust.org.uk/research/brooks.html (accessed 22 December 2008).

Brownjohn, S. (1994) *To Rhyme or Not to Rhyme: Teaching Children to Write Poetry*. London: Hodder and Stoughton.

Bryant, P. and Bradley, L. (1985) *Children's Reading Problems*. Oxford: Blackwell.

Burroughs-Lange, S. (2006) *Evaluation of Reading Recovery in London Schools: Every Child A Reader 2005–2006*. London: Institute of Education, University of London.

Calkins, L. McCormick (1983) *Lessons from a Child: On the Teaching and Learning of Writing*. Exeter, NH: Heinemann.

Cameron, L. and Besser, S. (2004) *Writing in English as an Additional Language at Key Stage 2* and *Could They Do Better? The writing of advanced bilingual learners at KS2: HMI survey of good practice*. London: Ofsted.

Cashdan, A. and Grugeon, E. (eds) (1972) *Language in Education*. London: Routledge.

Cummins, J. (2003) BICS and CALP, http://www.iteachilearn.com/cummins/ (accessed 3rd June 2009)

Chomsky, C. (1971) 'Write now, read later'. *Childhood Education*, 47, 296–9.

CILT (2006) *Positively Plurilingual: The Contribution of Community Languages to UK Education and Society*. London: The National Centre for Languages.

Clark, C., Torsi, A. and Strong, J. (2005) *Young People and Reading*. London: National Literacy Trust.

Clark, C., Osborne, S. and Akerman, R. (2008) *Young People's Self-perceptions as Readers: An Investigation including Family, Peer and School Influences*. London: National Literacy Trust.

Clark, M. (1976) *Young Fluent Readers*. London: Heinemann.

Clark, U. (1996) *An Introduction to Stylistics*. Cheltenham: Stanley Thornes.

Clay, M. (1975) *What Did I Write?* London: Heinemann.

Clegg, A. (ed.) (1964) *The Excitement of Writing*. London: Chatto.

Cotton, P. (1992) 'Let's all join up'. *Child Education*, April.

Cox, B. (1991) *Cox on Cox*. Sevenoaks: Hodder & Stoughton.

Cremin, T., Bearne, E., Mottram, M. and Goodwin, P. (2008) 'Primary teachers as readers. *English in Education*, 42 (1), 8–23.

Crystal, D. (1995) *The Cambridge Encyclopaedia of the English Language*. Cambridge: Cambridge University Press.

Crystal, D. (2008) '2b or not 2b?'. *The Guardian*, Saturday, 5 July.

Curtis, P. (2008) 'Early years writing lessons "do no good"'. *The Guardian*, 14 July.

Dahl, K. and Farnan, N. (1998) *Children's Writing: Perspectives from Research*. Newark, Delaware: International Reading Association.

Daley, C. (2002) *Literature Search on Improving Boys' Writing*. London: Ofsted.

DCSF (2007a) *National Curriculum Assessments at Key Stage 2 in England*. London: DCSF.

DCSF (2007b) *Primary National Strategy: Improving Writing with a Focus on Guided Writing*. London: DCSF.

DCSF (2007c) *Statistics of Education: EAL Pupils in Primary and Secondary Schools: 1997–2008*. www.naldic.org.uk/docs/resources/KeyDocs.cfm (accessed 8 November 2008).

DCSF (2008a) *The Early Years Foundation Stage*. London: DCSF.

DCSF (2008b) *The Early Years Foundation Stage Profile*. London: DCSF.

DCSF (2008c) *Support for Writing* http://nationalstrategies.standards.dcsf.gov.uk/node/102759 (accessed 9 November 2008).

DeBaryshe, B., Buell, M. and Binder, J. (1996) 'What a parent brings to the table: young children writing with and without parental assistance. *Journal of Literacy Research*, March. http://findarticles.com/p/articles/mi_qa3785/is_/ai_n8751135?tag= artBody;col1 (accessed 14 October 2008).

DES (1967) *Children and their Primary Schools (The Plowden Report)*. London: HMSO.

DES (1975) *A Language for Life (The Bullock Report)*. London: HMSO.

DES (1978) *Primary Education in England*. London: HMSO.

DES (1982) *Education 5–9: An Illustrative Survey of 80 First Schools in England*. London: HMSO.

DES (1988) *English for Ages 5–11*. London: HMSO.

DFE (1994) *Code of Practice on the Identification and Assessment of Special Educational Needs. London: DFE.*

DfEE (1998) *The National Literacy Strategy*. London: DfEE.

DfEE (1999a) *The National Curriculum English*. London: DfEE.

DfEE (1999b) *Spelling Bank*. London: DfEE.

DfEE (2000a) *Curriculum Guidance for the Foundation Stage*. London: DfEE.

DfEE (2000b) *Grammar for Writing*. London: DfEE.

DfEE (2001) *Developing Early Writing*. London: DfEE.

DfES (2002) *Birth to Three Matters*. London: DfES.

DfES (2004) *Planning and Assessment for Learning: Assessment for Learning, Part 2*. www.standards.dfes.gov.uk/primary/publications/learning_and_teaching/1041163/ (accessed 29 November 2008).

DfES (2006a) Primary National Strategy. *Primary Framework for Literacy and Mathematics*. London: DfES.

DfES (2006b) *Progression in Narrative*. London: DfES. www.standards.dfes.gov.uk/primaryframework/downloads/PDF/Prognarrative.pdf (accessed 21 September 2008).

DfES (2006c) *Progression in Poetry*. www.standards.dcsf.gov.uk/primaryframework/downloads/PDF/Prog_poetry.pdf (accessed 21 September 2008).

DfES (2006d) *Literacy across the Curriculum*. London: DfES. www.standards.dfes.gov.uk/primaryframework/downloads/PDF/Literacy_across_curriculum.pdf (accessed 21 September 2008).

DfES (2006e) *The Independent Review of the Teaching of Early Reading (The Rose Review)*. London: DfES.

DfES (2006f) *Assessing Pupil Progress* http://nationalstrategies.standards.dcsf.gov.uk/node/102759 (accessed 9 November 2008).

DfES (2007) *Letters and Sounds*. London: DfES.

Dixon, J. (1967) *Growth through English*. Oxford: Oxford University Press for NATE.

DoE (1996) *The 1996 Education Act*. London: DoE.

Dombey, H. and Moustafa, M. (1998) *Whole to Part Phonics: How Children Learn to Read and Spell*. London: CLPE.

Ellis, S. and Safford, K. (eds) (2005) *Animating Literacy: Inspiring Children's Learning through Teacher and Artist Partnerships*. London: CLPE/Creative Partnerships.

Fawcett, A. J. and Nicholson, R. (1992) 'Automatisation deficits in balance for dyslexic children'. *Perceptual and Motor Skills*, 75, 507–29.

Fawcett, A. J. and Nicholson, R. (2001) 'Dyslexia and the role of the cerebellum', in Fawcett, A. J. (ed.) *Dyslexia: Theory and Good Practice*. London: Whurr Publishers.

Ferreiro, E. and Teberosky, A. (1979) *Literacy before Schooling*. London: Heinemann.

Fitzsimmons, P., Harris, P., McKenzie, B. and Turbill, J. (2003) *Writing in the Primary School Years*. Ontario, Canada: Thomson Social Science Press.

Foggin, J. (1992) *Real Writing*. Sevenoaks: Hodder & Stoughton.

Ford, B. (1963) *Young Writers, Young Readers*. London: Hutchinson.

Fox, C. (1993) *At the Very Edge of the Forest: The Influence of Literature on Storytelling by Children*. London: Cassell.

Frater, G. (2000) *Securing Boys' Literacy: A Survey of Effective Practice in Primary Schools*. London: Basic Skills Agency.

Frith, U. (1985) 'Developmental dyslexia', in Patterson, K.E. *et al.* (eds) *Surface Dyslexia*. Mahwah, NJ: Lawrence Erlbaum.

Gathercole, S. E. (2006). 'Nonword repetition and word learning: the nature of the relationship'. *Applied Psycholinguistics*, 27, 513–43.

Gentry, R (1982) 'An analysis of developmental spelling in GNYS AT WRK'. *The Reading Teacher*, 36 (2), 192–200.

Goodman, Y. (1984) 'The development of initial literacy', in Goelman, H., Oberg, A. and Smith, F. (eds) *Awakening to Literacy*. London: Heinemann.

Goswami, U. (1991) 'Recent work on reading and spelling development', in Snowling, M. J. and Thompson, M. (eds) *Dyslexia: Integrating Theory and Practice*. London: Whurr Publishers.

Goswami, U. and Bryant, P. (1992) *Phonological Skills and Learning to Read*. Mahwah, NJ: Lawrence Erlbaum.

Goswami, U. (1995) 'Rhyme in children's early reading', in Beard, R. (ed.) *Rhyme, Reading and Writing*. London: Hodder & Stoughton.

Graham, L. (1995) *Writing Development: A Framework*. Croydon: Schools Advisory Service. London Borough of Croydon.

Graham, J. and Kelly, A. (eds) (2008) *Reading Under Control: Teaching Reading in the Primary School*. (3rd edn). Abingdon: Routledge.

Grainger, T., Gooch, K. and Lambirth, A. (2003) 'Playing the game called writing: children's views and voices'. *English in Education*, 37 (2), 4–13.

Grainger, T., Gooch, K. and Lambirth, A. (2005) *Creativity and Writing: Developing*

Voice and Verve in the Classrom. London: Routledge.

Graves, D. (1981) 'Renters and owners: Donald Graves on writing'. *English Magazine*, 8, Autumn.

Graves, D. (1983) *Writing: Teachers and Children at Work*. Portsmouth, NH: Heinemann.

Gregory, E., Mace, J., Rashid, N. and Williams, A. (1996) *Family Literacy History and Children's Learning Strategies at School*. End-of-award report, ESRC Project R000-22-1186. London: Goldsmiths College.

Hackman, S. and Trickett, L. (1996) *Spelling 9–13*. London: Hodder & Stoughton.

Hall, N. (1998) 'Early years write from the start'. *Literacy Today*, 6 www.literacytrust.org.uk/Pubs/Hall.html (accessed 19 October 2008).

Hall, N. and Robinson, A. (eds) (1996) *Learning about Punctuation*. Clevedon: Multilingual Matters.

Hannon, P. and Bird, V. (2004) 'Theory, practice, research and policy', in Wasik, B. H. (ed.) *Handbook of Family Literacy*. Mahwah, NJ: Lawrence Erlbaum Associates.

Harding, D. (1937) 'The role of the onlooker', reprinted in Cashdan and Grugeon (op. cit.).

Harrison, C. (1992) *The Reading for Real Handbook*. London: Routledge.

Heath, S.B. (1983) *Ways with Words: Language, Life and Work in Communities and Classrooms*. Cambridge: Cambridge University Press.

Hester, H. with Ellis, S. and Barrs, M. (1993) *Guide to the Primary Learning Record*. London: CLPE.

Hoey, M. (1983) *On the Surface of Discourse*. London: Unwin Hyman.

Holbrook, D. (1964) *English for the Rejected*. Cambridge: Cambridge University Press.

Holbrook, D. (1964) *Children's Writing: A Sampler for Student Teachers*. Cambridge: Cambridge University Press.

Holdaway, D. (1979) *The Foundations of Literacy*. Sydney: Ashton Scholatic.

Holland, P. (2003) *We don't Play with Guns here: War, Weapons and Superhero Play in the Early Years*. Milton Keynes: Open University Press.

ILEA (1985) *The Volcano: Learning through Drama*. London: Inner London Education Authority.

International Dyslexia Association (2002) www.dyslexia-ca.org/ dyslexiadefinition.html (accessed 26 October 2008).

Jarman, C. (1979) *The Development of Handwriting Skills*. Oxford: Blackwell.

Jarman, C. (1982) *Jarman Handwriting Scheme*. Hemel Hempstead: Simon and Schuster

Kelly, A. and Safford, K. (2009) 'Does teaching complex sentences have to be complicated?' *Literacy*. In press.

Kenner, C. (1999) 'Children's understandings of text in a multilingual nursery'. *Language and Education*, 13 (1), 1–16.

King, M. (2005) 'Sense Stories: can a multi-sensory arts project inspire the uninspired writer?' in Ellis, S. and Safford, K. (eds) *Animating Literacy: Inspiring Children's Learning through Teacher and Artist Partnerships*. London: CLPE/Creative Partnerships.

Kress, G. (1982) *Learning to Write*. London: Routledge and Kegan Paul.

Lane, S. and Kemp, M. (1967) *An Approach to Creative Writing*. London: Blackie.

Langdon, M. (1961) *Let the Children Write*. Harlow: Longman.

Langer, S. (1951) *Philosophy in a New Key* (2nd edn). Cambridge, MA: Harvard University Press.

Laycock, L. (1996) 'Narrative and writing: young children's dictated stories'. *Early Childhood Development and Care*, 116, 53–63.

Lewis, M. and Wray, D. (1995) *Developing Children's Non-fiction Writing*. Leamington Spa: Scholastic.

Liberman, I. and Shankweiller, D. (1985) 'Phonology and problems of learning to read and write'. *Remedial and Special Education*, 6, 8–17.

Lundberg, I. and Hoien, T. (2001) 'Dyslexia and phonology', in Fawcett, A. (ed.) *Dyslexia: Theory and Good Practice*. London: Whurr Publishers.

McKay, D. (ed.) (1970) *Breakthrough to Literacy*. Harlow: Longman.

McWilliam, N. (1998) *What's in a word? Vocabulary Development in Multilingual Classrooms*. Stoke-on-Trent: Trentham Books.

Mansell, W. (2005) 'Dyslexia storm brews'. *Times Educational Supplement*, 2 Sept. London: TSL Education Ltd.

Marsh, J. and Millard, E. (2000) *Literacy and Popular Culture: Using Children's Culture in the Classroom*. London: Paul Chapman Publishing.

Marshall, S. (1963) *An Experiment in Education*. Cambridge: Cambridge University Press.

Marshall, S. (1974) *Creative Writing*. Basingstoke: Macmillan.

Martens, P. and Goodman, Y. (1996) 'Invented punctuation', in Hall, N. and Robinson, A. (eds), op.cit.

Martin, J. R., Rothery, J. and Christie, F. (1987) 'Social processes in education: a reply to Sawyer and Watson (and others)', in Reid, I. (ed.) *The Place of Genre in Learning: Current Debates*. Deakin: Deakin University.

Maybury, B. (1967) *Creative Writing for Juniors*. London: Batsford.

Maynard, S., Mackay, S., Smyth, F. and Reynolds, K. (2007) *Young People's Reading in 2005: The Second Study of Young People's Reading Habits*. Loughborough and Roehampton: USU and NCRCL.

Medwell, J. and Wray, D. (2007) 'Handwriting: What do we know and what do we need to know?' *Literacy*, 41 (1), 10–15.

Meek. M. (2001) 'Introduction', in Barrs, M. and Cork, V. *The Reader in the Writer*. London: CLPE.

Michael, I. (1987) *The Teaching of English*. Cambridge: Cambridge University Press.

Miles, T.R. (1974) *Understanding Dyslexia*. Sevenoaks: Hodder & Stoughton.

Miles, T.R. (1983) *The Bangor Dyslexia Test*. Wisbech: Learning Development Aids.

Millard, E. (2001) 'Boys, girls and writing'. *Literacy Today*, 26 www.literacytrust.org.uk/pubs/millard.html (accessed 14 October 2008).

Minns, H. (1990) *Read it to Me Now!* London: Virago.

Moffett, J. (1968) *Teaching the Universe of Discourse*. Boston, MA: Houghton Mifflin.

NAA (2004) *Building a Picture of what Children can Do*. London: NAA.

NALDIC Pupil Portraits. www.naldic.org.uk/ITTSEAL2/teaching/EALpupilportraits.cfm (accessed 8 November 2008).

National Writing Project (1989) *Responding to and Assessing Writing*. Walton-on-Thames: Nelson.

Ofcom (2006) *Media Literacy Audit: Report on Media Literacy Amongst Children*. London: Office of Communications.

Ofsted (1993) 'The implementation of the curricular requirements of the Education Reform Act: English key stages 1, 2, 3, 4. Fourth year, 1992–3: A report of Her Majesty's Chief Inspector of Schools.' London: HMSO.

Ofsted (2002) *The National Literacy Strategy: The First Four Years 1998–2002.* London: Ofsted Publications Centre.

Ofsted (2003) *Yes He Can: Schools where Boys Write Well.* London: Ofsted.

Ofsted (2004) *Reading for Purpose and Pleasure: An Evaluation of the Teaching of Reading in Primary Schools.* London: Ofsted.

Orange, A. (2005) 'Cric-Crac!' The Effect of Oral Storytelling on Children's Writing in Year 2 in Ellis, S. and Safford, K. (eds) *Animating Literacy: Inspiring Children's Learning through Teacher and Artist Partnerships.* London: CLPE/Creative Partnerships.

O'Sullivan, O. and Thomas, A. (2000) *Understanding Spelling.* London: CLPE.

Pavey, B. (2007) *The Dyslexia Friendly Primary School.* Paul Chapman: London.

Payton, S. (1994) *Developing Awareness of Print.* Birmingham: University of Birmingham.

Perera, K. (1984) *Children's Writing and Reading: Analysing Classroom Language.* Oxford: Blackwell.

Perera, K. (1989) 'Grammatical differentiation between speech and writing in children aged 8 to 12', in Carter, R. (ed.) *Knowledge about Language and the Curriculum.* London: Hodder and Stoughton.

Peters, M. (1985) *Spelling: Caught or Taught? A New Look* (2nd edn). London: Routledge and Kegan Paul.

Pirrie, J. (1987) *On Common Ground.* London: Hodder & Stoughton.

Pratley, R. (1988) *Spelling it Out.* London: BBC Books.

QCA (1998) *Can Do Better: Raising Boys' Achievement in English.* London: QCA.

QCA (1999a) *Target Setting and Assessment in the National Literacy Strategy.* London: QCA.

QCA (1999b) *Year 4 English and Mathematics Tests: Teacher's Guide.* London: QCA.

QCA (2001) *Standards at Key Stage 2. English, Maths and Science.* London: QCA.

QCA (2002) *Changes to Assessment 2003: Guidance for Teachers of Key Stages 1 and 2.* London: QCA.

QCA (2007) Tests and Exams Support http://www.naa.org.uk/naa_19637.aspx (accessed 17 April 2008).

QCA (2008a) *Assessing Pupils' Progress.* www.standards.dfes.gov.uk/primaryframework/assessment/app (accessed 12 September 2008).

QCA (2008b) *Assessing Pupils' Progress: Guidance for Planning In-school Standardisation and Moderation* www.standards.dfes.gov.uk/primaryframework/downloads/pdf/Guidance%20for%20planning%20and%20supporting%20inschool%20standardisation%20and%20moderation.pdf (accessed 12 September 2008).

Reid, G. (2007) *The Teaching Assistant's Guide to Dyslexia.* London: Continuum.

Richmond, J. (1990) 'What writers need', in *Making Changes: Resources for Curriculum Development.* London: HMSO.

Rosen, M. (1989) *Did I Hear You Write?* London: Andre Deutsch.

Safford, K. and F. Collins (2006) *EAL and English: Subjects and Language across the Curriculum* www.naldic.org.uk/ITTSEAL2/teaching/English.cfm (accessed 8 November 2008).

Safford, K., Collins, F., Kelly, A. and Montgomery, D. (2007) 'Language and Sport: exploring the field'. *Primary English Magazine*, 12 (3), 11–14.

Safford, K., O'Sullivan, O. and Barrs, M. (2004) *Boys on the Margin: Promoting Boys' Literacy Learning at Key Stage 2*. London: CLPE.

Sassoon, R. (1983) *The Practical Guide to Children's Handwriting*. London: Thames & Hudson.

Sassoon, R. (1990) *Handwriting: The Way to Teach It*. Cheltenham: Stanley Thornes.

Scardamalia, M. and Bereiter, C. (1985) 'Development of dialectical processes in composition', in Olson, D. (ed.) *Literacy, Language and Learning*. Cambridge: Cambridge University Press.

Shayer, D. (1972) *The Teaching of English in Schools*. London: Routledge and Kegan Paul.

Sheffield, B.S. (1991) 'The structured flexibility of Orton-Gillingham'. *Annals of Dyslexia*, 41.

Smith, F. (1982) *Writing and the Writer*. London: Heinemann.

Smith, F. (1984) 'The creative achievement of literacy', in Goelman, H., Oberg, A. and Smith, F. (eds) *Awakening to Literacy*. London: Heinemann.

Smith, P. and Inglis, A. (1984) *New Nelson Handwriting*. Walton-on-Thames: Nelson.

Snowling, M. J. (1995) 'Phonological processing and developmental dyslexia'. *Journal of Research in Reading*, 18 (2), 132–8.

Snowling, M. and Stac, J. (2006) *Dyslexia, Speech and Language*. London: Whurr.

Somekh, B. (2003) *Children Exploring a 'Fun' Web-site: Sites of Learning and Roles of Being*. Sydney: Proceedings of the International Federation for Information Processing; Working group open conference on young children and learning technologies, 34, 89–93 http://crpit.com/confpapers/CRPITV34Somekh.pdf (accessed 28 November 2008).

Stein, J. (2001) 'The magnocellular theory of dyslexia'. *Dyslexia: an International Journal of Research and Practice*, 7 (1), 12–36.

Street, B. (1995) 'Cross-cultural perspectives on literacy', in Maybin, J. (ed.) *Language and Literacy in Social Practice*. Clevedon: Multilingual Matters/Open University.

Teale, W. and Sulzby, E. (1986) *Emergent Literacy: Writing and Reading*. Norwood, NJ: Ablex.

Temple, C., Nathan, R. and Burris, N. (1982) *The Beginnings of Writing*. Boston, MA: Allyn & Bacon.

Torbe, M. (1995) *Teaching and Learning Spelling* (3rd edn). London: Ward Lock.

Treiman, R. (1985) 'Onsets and rimes are units of spoken syllables: evidence from children'. *Journal of Experimental Child Psychology*, 39 (1), 169–81.

Treiman, R. (1993) *Beginning to Spell*. Oxford: Oxford University Press.

Tunnicliffe, S. (1984) *Poetry Experience*. London: Methuen.

Vellutino, F. R., Fletcher, J. M., Snowling, M. J. and Scanlon, D. M. (2004) 'Specific reading disability (dyslexia): what we have learned in the past four decades?' *Journal of Child Psychology and Psychiatry*, 45 (1), 2– 40.

Vygotsky, L. (1962) *Thought and Language*. Cambridge, MA: MIT Press.

Vygotsky, L. (1978) *Mind in Society*. Cambridge, MA: Harvard University Press.

Wajnryb, R. (1990) *Grammar Dictation*. Oxford: Oxford University Press.

Wells, G. (1987) *The Meaning Makers*. London: Hodder & Stoughton.

Wells, G. (1999) *Dialogic Inquiry: Towards a Socio-cultural Practice and Theory of Education*. Cambridge: Cambridge University Press.

Whitehead, F. (1978) 'What's the use, indeed?' *Use of English*, 29 (2), 15–22.

Wilkinson, A. (1980) *The Quality of Writing*. Milton Keynes: Open University.

Wray, D. and Lewis, M. (1997) *Extending Literacy: Children's Reading and Writing Non-fiction*. London: Routledge.

Children's books

Aardema, V. and Meddaugh, S. (1988) *Bimwili and the Zimwi*. London: Macmillan.

Ahlberg, A. and Wright, J. (1980) *Mrs Plug the Plumber*. Harmondsworth: Puffin Books.

Ahlberg, A. (1987) *The Clothes Horse*. London: Viking.

Aiken, J. (1996) *Cold Shoulder Road*. London: Red Fox Books.

Barber, A. and Bayley, N. (1990) *The Mousehole Cat*. London: Walker Books.

Berry, J. and Brierley, L. (1994) *Celebration Song*. Harmondsworth: Puffin Books.

Brighton, C. (1985) *The Picture*. London: Faber Children's Books.

Browne, A. (1986) *Piggybook*. London: Julia MacRae.

Burningham, J. (2001) *Mr Gumpy's Outing*. London: Red Fox.

Carroll, L. (1872) *Through the Looking Glass*. London: Macmillan.

De Brunhoff, J. (1934) *The Story of Babar, the Little Elephant*. London: Methuen.

Deary, T. (1996) *Wicked Words*. Leamington Spa: Scholastic.

Fine, A. (1989) *Bill's New Frock*. London: Methuen.

Hastings, S. and Wijngaard, J. (1985) *Sir Gawain and the Loathly Lady*. London: Walker Books.

Hawkins, C. and J. (1984) *Mig the Pig*. Harmondsworth: Penguin Books.

King-Smith, D. (1997) *Godhanger*. London: Corgi.

King-Smith, D. (1999) *Martin's Mice*. London: Puffin.

King-Smith, D. (1999) *The Crowstarver*. London: Corgi.

Lewis, C. S. (1950) *The Lion, the Witch and the Wardrobe*. London: Geoffrey Bles.

Magorian, M. and Ormerod, J. (1992) *Jump*. London: Walker Books.

Moore, I. (1990) *Six Dinner Sid*. Hove: Macdonald Young Books.

Morpurgo, M. (1995) *The Wreck of the Zanzibar*. London: Heinemann.

Murphy, J. (1982) *On the Way Home*. London: Macmillan.

Naughton, B. (1970) 'Spit Nolan', in *The Goalkeeper's Revenge and other Stories*. Harmondsworth: Penguin.

Patten, B. (ed.) (1998) *The Puffin Book of Utterly Brilliant Poetry*. Harmondsworth: Puffin.

Pienkowski, J. (1984) *Christmas*. London: Walker Books.

Pullman, P. (2000) *The Amber Spyglass*. London: Scholastic.

Rosen, M. (1989) *The Bakerloo Flea*. London: Heinemann.

Rosen, M. (1995) *Walking the Bridge of Your Nose*. London: Kingfisher.

Rowling, J.K. (1997) *Harry Potter and the Philospher's Stone*. London: Bloomsbury.

Sachar, L. (2001) *There's a Boy in the Girls' Bathroom*. London: Bloomsbury Publishing.

Scieszka, J. and Smith, L. (1989) *The True Story of the Three Little Pigs*. London: Viking.

Story Chest (1980) *The Monsters' Party*. *The Hungry Giant*. Walton-on-Thames: Nelson.

Thomas, R. (1987) *The Runaways*. London: Hutchinson.

Westall, R. (1992) *Gulf.* London: Methuen.

White, E.B. (1952) *Charlotte's Web.* New York: HarperCollins.

Wilson, J. (2000) *The Illustrated Mum.* London: Corgi.

ICT resources

Crick Software (for Clicker products) www.writeaway.org.uk

Don Johnston Special Needs www.donjohnston.com

EasyBooks Deluxe: http://store.sunburst.com

Fisher-Marriott: www.fishermarriott.com

OUP www.oup.com/oxed/primary/literacy/ort/electronic

Photoshop www.adobe.com/uk/products/photoshop

Sherston: www.sherston.com/ e.g. *The Punctuation Show:* http://shop.sherston.com/
   ipw/guide.aspx?prodid=28

Textease www.teem.org.uk/2104

Author index

Adams, M. J. 10
Ainscow, M. 229
Akerman, R. 20
Aldrich, R. 170
Alexander, R. 71, 99
Allen, D. 6
Anderson, M. 24
Andrews, R. 9, 130
Armstrong, M. 67, 115
Baker, C. 12
Bannatyne, A. 135
Barnes, D. 70, 71
Barrs, M. 15, 16, 23, 100, 102, 103, 115, 126, 147, 196, 199
Barton, D. 11
Bearne, E. 19, 40, 217
Bereiter, C. 9
Besser, S. 38
Binder, J. 20
Bird, V. 11
Bissex, G. 5, 97, 140, 141
Black, P. 193
Blacock, J. 233
Bond, J. 98
Booth, T. 229
Bradley, L. 137, 233
Bragg, M. 135
Browning, R. 1
Brownjohn, S. 115, 118
Britton, J. 3, 4, 6, 78
Bruner, J. 72
Bryant, P. 137, 233
Buell, M. 20
Bullock, A. 3, 9, 78, 170
Bunting, R. 226
Burris, N. 140, 144
Burroughs-Lange, S. 224, 226
Bus, A. 41

Bussis, A. 147, 148
Buzan, T. 241
Calkins, L. 84, 90, 91
Cashdan, A. 3
Chomsky, C. 5
Christie, F. 14
Clark, C. 20
Clark, M. 4
Clark, U. 160
Clarke, S. 200
Clay, M. 4–5, 10, 78, 140, 223
Clegg, A. 2, 138
Cline, T. 227
Collins, F. xi, 36
Corbett, P. 115, 157
Cork, V. 15, 102, 126
Cotterell, G. 135
Cotton, P. 172
Cox, B. 158, 165
Cremin, T. 19
Crimmins-Crocker, J. 157
Cripps, C. 173
Crystal, D. 30, 132, 134, 135, 160, 167, 176
Cummins, J. 52
Dahl, K. 201
Daley, C. 23
Deary, T. 155
DeBaryshe, B. 20
Dixon, J. 4
Dombey, H. 148
Ellis, S. 199
Eyre, D. 226
Farnan, N. 201
Fawcett, A. J. 233
Ferreiro, A. 140
Fitzsimmons, P. 18, 20
Fletcher, J. M. 233
Foggin, J. 177

Ford, B. 2
Frater G. 23, 218, 226
Frith, U. 141, 142, 145, 146, 238
Gathercole, S. E. 233
Gentry, R. 141, 142, 143, 146, 147, 182
Gooch, K. 67
Goodman, Y. 140, 158, 164
Goodwin, P. 115, 130
Goswami, U. 137, 233
Graham, J. xii
Graham, L. 199
Grainger, T. 17, 19, 67, 115
Graves, D. 8–9, 72, 87, 90, 206
Green, S. 241
Gregory, E. 36
Grugeon, E. 3
Hackman, S. 153, 154
Hall, N. 33, 99, 160, 161, 164
Hamilton, M. 11
Hannon, P. 11
Harding, D. 3
Harris, P. 18, 20
Harrison, C. 224
Heath, S.B. 11, 97
Herbert, G. 117
Hester, H. 199
Hoey, M. 106
Hoien, T. 233
Holbrook, D. 2, 3
Holdaway, D. 71, 162
Holland, P. 23
Hudson, J. 224
Huxford, L. 157
Inglis, A. 174
Jarman, C. 167, 172, 174, 176
Johnson, P. 96, 99
Kelly, A. xii, 26, 32
Kenner, C. 36
Kemp, M. 2
King, J. 169
King, M. 35
Kress, G. 13, 162
Lambirth, A. 67
Lane, S. 2
Langer, S. 2, 3
Langdon, M. 2
Laycock, L. xii, 92, 154
Lewis, A. 241
Lewis, M. 15, 103, 115, 122, 123, 125
Liberman, I. 233
Lockwood, M. 119
Lowe, G. 130
Lundberg, I. 233

Mace, J. 36
Mackay, S. 20
Mansell, W. 228
Marsh, J. 23
Marshall, S. x, 2, 6
Martens, P. 158, 164
Martin, J. R. 14
Matthews, J. 45, 67
Maybury, B. 2
Maynard, S. 20
McGough, R. 154
McGuinn, N. 130
McKay, D. 5
McKenzie, B. 18, 20
Meek, M. 130
Medwell, J. 171, 178
Michael, I. xi
Miles, T. R. 233
Millard, E. 22, 23
Minns, H 97
Moffett, J. 3, 6
Montgomery, D. 26, 178
Morgan, M. 119
Mottram, M. 19
Moustafa, M. 148
Nathan, R. 140, 144
Neuman, S. 41
Nicholson, R. 233
Norwich, B. 241
Orange, A. 21
Osborne, S. 20
O'Sullivan, O. 23, 31, 32, 86, 141
Palmer, S. 130
Patten, B. 154
Pavey, B. 228
Payton, S. 78
Perera, K. 13, 103, 214
Peters, M. 138, 140
Piaget, J. 140
Pidgeon, S. 23
Pienkowski, J. 175
Pirrie, J. 118
Plowden, B. 14
Pratley, R. 153
Pullman, P. 168
Ramsden, M. 157
Rashid, N. 36
Read, C. 5
Reid, G. 230, 241
Reynolds, K. 20
Richardson, M. 172
Robinson, A. 99, 130, 160, 161, 164
Rosen, M. 118, 158, 168, 217

Rothery, J. 14
Rowling, J. K. 168, 169
Safford, K. xi, 11, 23, 26, 30, 31, 32, 36, 86
Sassoon, R. 170, 174, 175, 176, 177
Scanlon, D. M. 233
Scardamalia, M. 9
Sedgwick, F. 115
Shamsi, T. 227
Shankweiler, D. 233
Shayer, D. 1
Sheffield, B. S. 233
Smith, F. 8, 20, 87, 100
Smith, P. 174
Snowling, M. 228, 233
Somekh, B 29
Stac, J. 233
Street, B. 11
Strong, J. 20
Sulzby, E. 19
Svensson, C. xii
Taylor, J. 178
Teale, W. 10
Teberosky, A. 11
Temple, C. 140, 144
Thomas, A. 141, 147
Thomas, H. 115

Thompson, R. 157
Timmons, B. 169
Torbe, M. 135
Torgerson, C. 130
Torsi, A. 20
Treiman, R. 136, 233
Trickett, L. 153, 154
Truss, L. 169
Tunnicliffe, S. 118
Turbill, J. 18, 20
Velutino, F. R. 233
Vincent, J. 41
Vygotsky, L. 5, 9, 12, 48, 71, 72, 78, 123
Wajnryb, R. 92
Warnock, M. 219, 223
Washtell, A. xi
Wells, G. 10, 43, 71, 97
Whitehead, F. 4
Wijngaard, J. 175
Wiliam, D. 193
Williams, A. 36
Wilde, O. 66
Wilkinson, A. 6
Wilson, R. 99
Wolstonecroft, H. 40
Wray, D. 15, 103, 122, 123, 125, 171, 178

Subject index

For subjects such as Primary National Strategy, composition and transcription which occur throughout the book, we have given the page reference for significant entries and then used the Latin term passim (everywhere).

able pupils (*see* gifted and talented)
acronym 135, 154, 155, 166
adjacent consonants 153, 155
alliteration 155, 233
alphabet 49, 78, 132, 151, 175
ALS 221, 225
analytic phase 142, 146
animated film 61, 63
apostrophe 160, 163, 168, 184
ascenders 176, 178, 182
assessment 6, 8, 27, 72, 79, 222, 225
   Early Learning Goals 17
   focuses 195–6
   for learning 179–194
   moderation 196–197
   National Curriculum 78, 179, 197–198
   of learning 194–198
   of pupils' progress 196
   peer 76
   success criteria 69, 191–192, 194
audience 2, 3, 4, 9, 54, 60, 101–103, 123, 165, 172, 204, 205, 206, 207, 217, 218, 225
authorial voice 59

bilingualism 12, 36–39
blend/blending 17, 146, 153, 156
blogging 32–33, 225
book-making 96–97
boys 226
   and writing 23–29, 82, 104
   underachievement 28
British Psychological Society 228

calligraphy 81, 176
Catch Up 225, 226
characterisation 112–113
chatroom 32
chronological structure 52, 60, 66, 103–104
clause 13, 160, 202, 208
Clicker 5 95
code of practice 219, 220, 221

collaboration 71
collocation 38
composition 7–10, 100–130 and *passim*
compound word 134, 154, 156
computer 56, 61, 210, 225
conferencing 9, 77, 90
confidence 79, 84–85
'conscience alley' 71
consonant 137
consonant cluster 153, 156
copying 1, 7, 14, 79, 93–94, 238
culture
   activity 9
   background 11
   heritage model 4
   popular 26, 102

decoding 17
demonstration (*see* modelling)
denouement 53, 61
derivational affix 134, 156
descenders 176, 178, 182
developmental (*see* writing)
developmental delay 237
dialogue/dialogic 54, 71
dictate, dictation 46, 48, 50, 61, 80, 82, 91–93, 210
dictionaries 154
differentiation 220
difficulties (*see* problems)
digital
   expertise 39
   nonstandard forms 30
   television 29
   texts 34
   worlds 19,29
digraph 153, 156
directionality 79, 93
display 46, 81
draft/drafting 3, 74, 75, 83, 84, 86–89, 206
drama 69, 70, 102, 127

drawing 47, 50, 52, 54, 56, 70, 212, 216, 234
dyslexia 204, 222, 228–241

EAL 11–12, 36–39, 43, 50, 51, 61, 97, 209
early writing (*see* writing)
Early Years Action 220
Early Years Action Plus 220
Early Years Foundation Stage 17, 18, 68 and *passim*
Early Years Foundation Stage Profile 194
ECAR 225, 226
editing 70, 84, 87, 219
ellipsis 168
FLS 221
email 19, 29, 30–32, 33
emergent (*see* writing)
encoding 17
environmental print 150, 163, 166, 175
errors & misconceptions 55, 74, 84, 201–204, 214, 218, 219
etymology 132, 138, 154–5, 156
Everybody Writes 225, 226

family 19, 20, 21
    literacy 11
figures of speech 61
first order symbolism 12
FLS 221, 225
form (*see* writing)
formal (statutory) arrangements 219, 221
formality (*see* writing)

gender 19, 22
genre (text type) 14–15, 16, 103, 122–126, 202, 205, 206, 208
    discussion 14
    explanation 14
    instructional 46, 124
    persuasion 14, 43, 56, 128
    procedural 14, 187
    recount 14, 15, 60, 89, 181, 184, 216
    report 14
gifted and talented 63, 73, 201, 208, 214, 219
girls 22, 215, 217
'graduated response' 220
grammar 16, 38, 218–219
grapheme 136, 156
graphic awareness/strategies 74, 137, 138, 147, 153
graphologist 176

handwriting 48, 49, 50, 54, 55, 56, 59, 63, 79, 93, 140, 170–178, 202
    cursive 172–173, 176, 178, 190
    copperplate 1, 172
    diagonal join 178
    entry stroke 178
    exit stroke 178
    horizontal join 178
    left-handed 174, 177
    ligature 178
    orthography 156
'have-a-go' 207
homograph 152, 156
homophone 59, 63, 136, 152, 156
hot-seating 71, 127
hyperlink 34

ICT 35, 94–96
IEP 220, 235, 236, 240
inclusion 229, 238, 239
inflectional suffix 134, 137, 138, 156, 204, 213
interactive whiteboard 72, 74, 75, 88, 94
International Dyslexia Association 229

journals 4, 8, 26, 27, 28

KWL grid 125

language 19
    first 37, 52
    home 37
    problems 228, 233
    spoken 57
    study 210
    -rich curriculum 17
layout 125–126
learning
    objectives 69, 239
    styles 147–8
letters 48
    formation 79, 177
    lower case 48, 79, 176, 178, 181
    upper case 79, 178, 181, 202, 204
Letters and Sounds 148, 149, 150, 151
literacy
    hour 68, 207
    lists 45, 46
    texts 16
loan word 135, 154, 156
logographic phase 141, 145
'look-cover-write-check' 152, 184

marking 191–193, 214, 219
mark-making 42, 45, 46, 49, 66, 234
metalanguage 72
Microsoft Publisher 95
mobile phones 29
mode
    expressive 3
    poetic 3
    transactional 3
modelling/demonstration 70, 75, 84, 125, 205, 208, 210

mini-lessons 84
models of literacy
    autonomous 11
    ideological 11
morpheme 134, 137, 156
morphology 132–134, 156
motor skills 43, 46, 52, 171, 176, 177
multi-lingualism 36, 37
multimedia 19, 29, 33
    texts 70
multi-modal
    contexts 29–35
    text 43, 52, 54, 61
Multiverse 40

NALDIC 40, 226
names 46, 48, 50, 74, 82, 93, 140, 144, 181
narrative 14, 15, 61, 69, 103–104, 106–118,
    183, 184
    first person 50, 59, 114, 126, 202, 238
narrator 52, 53, 65
National Curriculum *passim*
National Curriculum levels 194, 195–196
National Literacy Strategy 16 and *passim*
neologism 135, 155, 156
non-fiction 120–126
note-taking 74, 125

observation and sampling 180–190
one-to-one correspondence 146, 181
one-to-one tuition 91, 225
onset and rime 137, 138, 141, 152, 153, 157
Ofsted 14 and *passim*
orthographic phase 141
ownership (*see* writing)

paragraph 202, 207
parents 45, 97–99, 225, 234
partners (*see* writing)
Photostop 35
phoneme 132, 136, 138, 153, 157, 181, 214
phonemic awareness and knowledge 10, 49,
    137, 157
phonics 16, 46, 49, 149
phonetic spelling 141, 146
phonic/phonemic strategies 137, 146, 147
phonological
    awareness 16, 46, 157
    processing 229, 233
picture making, pictures 48, 51, 61, 64
planning 28, 68–70, 71, 204, 206, 222, 223, 224
play 68, 214, 215, 216
poetry 43, 54, 56, 115–119
polysyllabic words 57, 59, 147, 154, 190
PowerPoint 29, 33, 98–99
pre-
    alphabet 78

communicative spelling 141, 143
composition 70
phonemic spelling 141
writing 82
writing activities 8
prefix 57, 132, 134, 137, 138, 150, 153–154,
    157
presentation 70, 71, 202
Primary National Strategy (PNS) 16, 17 and
    passim
prior knowledge 5
    presentation 9
    polysyllabic words 45
problems
    language based 233, 234, 237
    learning 73
    reading 228
    sequencing 234
    spelling 228, 234
    writing 234
process (*see* writing)
product 7, 206
proof-reading 84, 91
publishing 96, 118, 204, 205, 206, 225
punctuation 13, 16, 54, 55, 63, 157–169
    colon 159, 168
    comma 59, 159, 168
    exclamation mark 159, 163, 165, 167, 168
    full stop 159, 161, 169, 202, 204
    hyphen 169
    parenthesis 82
    question mark 159, 163, 165, 167, 169
    semi-colon 169, 220, 222, 225
    speech marks 169
purpose 9, 54, 74, 101–103, 123, 126, 207,
    218, 225
Quality First Teaching 221
quality text (*see* text)

reading
    and writing 126, 130, 214, 219, 221, 224
    aloud 65, 102, 105–106
    shared 69
Reading Recovery 223–224
representation 9, 81
resources (*see* writing)
response partner 56, 57, 77
rhyme and rhythm 46, 55, 234
rime and onset 137, 138
role-play 49, 70, 74, 82, 218
root word 132, 153–154, 157
Rose Review xii, 16

SATs (*see* assessments, *NC*)
scanning 75
School Action 220, 235
School Action Plus 220, 237

scribing 43, 46, 48, 60, 66, 70, 73
second order symbolism (*see* symbolism)
segmenting 17, 136, 146, 153, 184
self-esteem 84, 95, 98, 235, 237
self-help strategies 84–85
semi-phonetic spelling 141, 146
SEN 219, 220, 221, 229
shared reading 152, 166, 167
sight words/vocabulary 136, 137, 146, 152
SMART 240
Special Educational Needs (SEN) 39
specific learning difficulties 204, 228
spell-checker 95
spelling 131–157
   development 140–147
   invented 5, 140
   investigative 240
   rules 135
   test 198
   transitional 141, 147, 184
spoken and written language 12–14, 50, 72, 160–161
standard English 13, 218
storyboard 61, 63, 85
story 46, 66
   plots 106, 111–112
   structure 106, 111
   telling and retelling 69, 107
   -writing 14, 111
suffix 132, 138, 150, 153–154, 157, 184, 204, 213
symbolism 12, 48
   first and second order 12
synthetic phonics 16, 149

talk 68, 70, 71, 73, 114–115, 206, 215, 218, 225
targets 236, 240
target setting 84, 193–194, 199–200
Teacher Training Resource Bank (TTRB) 40
terminology 72, 208, 219
text
   digital 34
   messaging 19, 29, 30, 33
   multimedia 70
   spoken 50
   Textese 32
   visual 70
'three stars and a wish' 193
traditional tales 85–86, 103, 109
transcription 131–178 and *passim*

vocabulary 6, 54, 61, 106
vowel 204

Warnock Report 219, 223
'waves' 220–221
word banks 202
word-processing 87–88, 211
writing
   area (resource) 47, 49, 82
   autobiographical 43, 238
   beginning (see emergent below)
   bilingual 36–39
   collaborative 28, 71, 85–86
   community 19, 20, 46, 52
   conferences 190–1
   contexts 49, 74, 82, 101–103
   creative writing 2, 138
   cross-curricular writing 2, 120–121
   developmental 10, 139–40
   early 47, 78, 82
   emergent 4, 10, 78, 139–40, 212
   extended 111, 208
   frame 122, 123, 183, 205, 217
   gender 22–29
   guided 67, 75–78, 165
   histories xii
   home 20–22, 46, 225
   implements, tools 46, 47
   independent 8, 49, 67, 70, 76, 77, 79, 84, 85
   in role 46, 82, 126–130
   multilingual 36–39
   multimodal 63
   ownership 11
   partners 8, 90–91, 206, 218, 220, 222
   pretend 78
   process 7–8, 18, 48, 70, 138–139
   purposes 49
   re-drafting 56
   samples 222
   shared 67, 70, 71–75, 82, 152, 165, 166, 167, 205, 212, 224
   supported 70, 73
   teachers' own 9
   unaided 78, 79, 83–84, 142
   visual approaches 28
   workshop approach 8, 79, 87, 90

zone of proximal development 5, 72